LEFT IN THE WEST

Literature, Culture, and Progressive Politics in the American West

edited by Gioia Woods

UNIVERSITY OF NEVADA PRESS *Reno & Las Vegas*

University of Nevada Press | Reno, Nevada 89557 USA
www.unpress.nevada.edu

Cover design by Jinni Fontana

LIBRARY OF CONGRESS CATALOGING-IN-PUBLICATION DATA

Names: Woods, Gioia, 1968– editor.
Title: Left in the West : literature, culture, and progressive politics in the American West / Gioia Woods, editor.
Description: First edition. | Reno : University of Nevada Press, [2018] | Includes bibliographical references and index.
Identifiers: LCCN 2018011992 (print) | LCCN 2018015771 (e-book)
ISBN 978-1-943859-92-4 (pbk. : alk. paper) | ISBN 978-1-943859-94-8 (e-book)
Subjects: LCSH: Politics and literature—West (U.S.)—History. | Right and left (Political science) in literature.
Classification: LCC PS271 .L44 2018 (print)| LCC PS271 (e-book) |
DDC 810.9/3278—dc23
LC record available at https://lccn.loc.gov/2018011992

The paper used in this book meets the requirements of American National Standard for Information Sciences—Permanence of Paper for Printed Library Materials, ANSI/NISO Z39.48-1992 (R2002).

FIRST PRINTING

Manufactured in the United States of America

Contents

Illustrations

Introduction

Literature, Culture, and the Left in the American West

GIOIA WOODS

Popular Front Production

In the July 1935 issue of the journal *Poetry: A Magazine of Verse*, poet and art critic Harold Rosenberg published a report on the historic first meeting of the American Writers' Congress. A New York leftist, Rosenberg described in great detail the scene at New York City's Mecca Temple from April 26 to the 28th. Tickets could be had for as little as thirty-five cents, Rosenberg explained, and more than four thousand people, a "great audience of readers of books and magazines, composed of intellectuals, students, business men, and workers," gathered in recognition of the "unbreakable connection existing between the course and fate of culture and the art of writing" (224). Sessions on drama, fiction, and poetry dominated the conference, and questions over the "proper" role and form of literature in the revolutionary struggle engendered lively debate. Popular verse, or esoteric form? Poetry on the page, or in the street? Workers theater? Revolutionary symbolism? Artistic quality? Propaganda? Questions of political alliance also arose: leftist? socialist? communist? Poets and critics were joined onstage by union representatives and journalists. Delegates from Latin America, Japan, and Europe came together with American writers to call for social change. The crowd was so cosmopolitan, so inclusive of social class, so seemingly representative of the revolutionary struggle, that it led Rosenberg to see the event as a herald of universal desire: "the ideas and arguments might have been exchanged anywhere," he optimistically declared (226).

But in truth, the writers were not fully representative of the general population or even of the American Left, which included Communist Party members, fellow travelers, socialists, social democrats, and other progressives. Of the 216 politically engaged writers in attendance, 36 were women and 21 were African American. Only 64 of the attendees were from states other than New York (George and Selzer 47). And of those 64, very few were from states west of the Mississippi, and even fewer currently lived and made their careers in the American West.[1] The lack of representation of writers from the American West seems to suggest that a Left culture had not emerged there. But this is far from the case. Before World War II, the Left in the American West exerted a powerful influence in labor, literature, mass culture and entertainment, and news media. Moreover, the Left in the West was less ideologically divided than the East Coast Left.

The 1934 San Francisco General Strike, which writer Tillie Olsen remembered as a "battlefield," gave rise to the popular front in the West. This mass social movement of radical insurgency had its base in the longshoremen's union in California and eventually included workers from several sectors, including automotive, agriculture, canneries, and fisheries. This working class was multiethnic and multiracial; it had been created largely by displaced indigenous peoples and the migration of millions from western Europe, eastern Europe, Mexico, Japan, China, and the southern United States. There were periods of alliance between ethnic laborers and unions, and ugly periods of race riots and hate strikes, but the Left in the West organized a multiethnic working-class culture whose popular front gave rise to a multiethnic, experimental, and avant-garde network of writers and artists that did not diminish at the end of the "Red Decade."

The popular front's influence went well beyond the 1930s, Michael Denning argues, because it nurtured a generation of plebian writers and artists who introduced lasting narratives informed by class consciousness, anti-fascism, and civil liberties. This generation of writers and artists changed the way people imagined the world. The literary Left in the West was part of a cultural apparatus that included "workers theaters, camera clubs, film and photo leagues, composers collectives, Red dance troupes and revolutionary choruses" (Denning xv). The legacy of the popular front in the American West has potency into the twentieth and twenty-first centuries. It's embodied in the proliferation of art and literature in support of the American Indian Movement and the Dakota Access Pipeline protests, the farmworkers' civil rights movements and the Dreamers and DACA activism, and Black Power and #BlackLivesMatter projects.

If we imagine that first American Writers' Congress as a map representing the concentration of Left cultural activity in the first half of the twentieth century, the American West would appear to be barely populated. But Left cultural and literary activity, as *Left in the West* demonstrates, was thriving in large and small communities from Denver to San Francisco, Los Angeles to Seattle, from Tonopah, Nevada, to Carmel, California. The literary Left in the West shared many concerns with the East Coast Left, including labor, class, anti-fascism, and anti-imperialism. But because of Manifest Destiny and the distinct history of settler colonialism in western territories, western leftists developed concerns unique to the region, elevating issues of industrialization and environmental degradation, Native American sovereignty, and immigrant communities' access to power. And as this collection of essays makes clear, western leftists were (and are) deploying a broad range of literary genres to address these unique concerns.

Left in the West begins to correct the record by considering what Michael Denning calls a "broad and tenuous left-wing alliance of fractions of the subaltern classes" (6) as they are represented by authors, artists, and the products they produced within and against the physical and ideological spaces of the American West. Like Denning, my thinking for this editorial project is informed by Raymond Williams's concept of "alignment."[2] I characterize the "literary Left" by the presence and practice of cultural workers (writers, artists) who *consciously* align themselves, or are aligned *by others*, with a Left social agenda and the (literary or aesthetic) ways in which they do so. In this way, the reader is empowered to ask certain questions beyond the nature of the author's "commitment" to a Left agenda; we can investigate the deep context, the social and cultural milieu that shape and transform the author and the text. The literary Left is a diverse body that, in many ways, recognizes (or is recognized for) a specific set of social relations in which they, their texts, and their audiences operate. These social relations are largely dominated by a sense of class consciousness, anti-fascism and anti-imperialism, and various civil liberties and civil rights campaigns.

After World War II, there was an important shift among the literary popular front away from Marxism and party-line narratives and toward existentialism, social activism, and the politics of self-awareness as seen notably in the publishing roster of City Lights bookstore and press and other West Coast independent presses. The author may have died in 1967, but the creative act itself remained a potent sense of power for the leftist writer and the leftist audience. The essays collected here explore individual consciousness, the creative act, and a variety of institutional contexts in which these acts are performed. Together they create a complex and diverse portrait of how the "Left" is produced, defined, and deployed in politically engaged literature, art, and activism.

Alan Wald, in his important study *Exiles from a Future Time: The Forging of the Mid-Twentieth-Century American Left* (2002), reminds us that searching for "the writer's singular being and consciousness is not to become a biographer but to restore the self-activity of Left cultural workers as well as to supply some of the neglected mediations in the creative act—especially the mentality of the artist and the force field of...institutions" (xvi). Wald explains that "the Literary Left can only be fathomed as a social arena within which contests occurred among a diversity of qualifying factors," including "genders, ethnicities, and class backgrounds" (71–72). One factor that united the social arena across differences in the 1930s were those writers, artists, and culture brokers who were sympathetic to the urgency of Communist-inspired social change; Communism was recognized by many as a creative agent (and a sanctioned narrative) of social transformation, and the non-Communist Left was willing to work with Communists in their campaigns for labor rights and anti-fascism. Together they composed what Raymond Williams called a "structure of feeling," the culture of a particular time and place. In Hollywood, there were highly visible Communist and fellow-traveler writers and intellectuals, including, by midcentury, the Hollywood Ten.[3] Hollywood was not the only site of Left cultural activity, however. Throughout the West, in small towns and fast-growing urban centers, there were active collections of labor organizers, journalists, musicians, photographers, actors, philosophers, and activists who used art in a way that bore witness to labor, class, poverty, migration, environmental preservation, conservation and degradation, Native sovereignty, and the performance of nonnormative identities.

There is no doubt that Left-inspired cultural activity proliferated in the American West. But what are the dangers associated with a focus on regional political activity? In *Regionalists on the Left: Radical Voices from the American West*, editor Michael C. Steiner acknowledges how expressions of western regional identity have often been conflated with nostalgia, populism, and a retreat from the excesses of industrial modernism (5–7). Steiner counters the "nostalgic primitivism" with plentiful examples of a western regionalism that was, in the 1930s and 1940s, indicative of working-class foment and critical of environmental degradation. These writers, however, were often the targets of critics who saw land-based regionalism as sentimental, silly, and sometimes dangerously fascistic (8–9, 11). Steiner's organizing assumption is that a "progressive, even leftist regionalism [is] possible"; he and the contributors to his collection demonstrate this by "unearthing a tradition of left-wing regionalism in the West that defied reactionary stereotypes" (11). Many of the contributors in *Regionalists on the Left* examine the ways love and fealty to western lands became a source of protest and a place from which to mount critiques of capitalist greed and vast inequity. What these early and midcentury regionalists point to is the critical reevaluation of western regionalism in which "the grubby reality of western conquest, environmental exploitation, and racial conflict" reveals a region where cultures "collide and interact" (14). *Left in the West* not only assumes that the West is a "locus of cultural pluralism"

(Steiner 14) but that it is this very pluralism that gives Left activity in the region its force and character.

Left Beginnings

Left political activity in the United States can be traced back to the American arrival of German Marxists after 1848, social democrats after 1870, and anarchists after 1880. Each favored a particular path to revolution, whether defined by political action or trade unionism. The Socialist Party of America (SPA) was formed in 1901 and had some notable political success: by the beginning of 1912, there were 1,039 Socialist officeholders, including 56 mayors, 305 aldermen and councilmen, 22 police officials, and a handful of state legislators. Milwaukee, Berkeley, Butte, Schenectady, and Flint were run by Socialists. The SPA actively promoted socialist causes in a number of publications, including five English-language daily newspapers, eight foreign-language daily newspapers, nearly three hundred weeklies, and several monthly magazines (Draper 41–42). Clearly, writing about socialist ideals was reaching a wide, multilingual audience.

In 1905 the Industrial Workers of the World (IWW) was formed in Chicago. Convention minutes were printed and bound, as were volumes of poetry and songbooks exalting the working class. The Wobblies gathered socialists, anarchists, and trade unionists to the common cause of liberating the working class, and they had success in the western United States organizing workers in agriculture, lumber, and construction. The Communist Party of the United States was formed in 1919, and it, too, supported a vibrant tradition of Left literature and journalism. By the 1930s, hundreds of working writers identified as either Communists or fellow travelers. These writers, as Alan Wald points out, came from "different classes, ethnic groups, regions, traditions, and generations...and genders." They were united across difference "in an overriding identity as partisans in the international proletariat" (16).

The ideology of proletarian internationalism was readily apparent among areas of first- and second-generation Jewish settlement in New York City. By the time World War I began, one-third of Jews from

Russia and eastern Europe had emigrated to the United States. Due to pervasive repression in Russia and elsewhere, 70 percent of those emigrants had made their livelihoods as merchants and artisans; they were cobblers, barbers, tinsmiths, and tailors. Two-thirds who emigrated between 1908 and 1912 self-identified as "skilled workers" (Takaki 263, 267). Upwards of five hundred thousand Jewish emigrants settled in New York City's Lower East Side, and many thousands found work in the thriving garment industry. Workers joined unions, became politicized, and through organized labor "created a broadly based radical Jewish consciousness" (Takaki 279). The Communist Party of the United States of America, the Trade Union Educational League, and the American Federation of Labor all had their national headquarters in New York City.

Many Jewish writers and intellectuals found the promise of Communism liberating. Jewish consciousness helped forge avant-garde and popular front consciousness: "male writers, overwhelmingly white, and at least half of them Jewish," Wald explains, "set the tone on the leading bodies of the official, New-York based publications of the Communist Left" (254). For a long time, literary and cultural critics dismissed popular front and other working-class literature as contrary to avant-gardism. In the American West, however, the cultures of the popular front and the avant-garde deployed similar experiments with language, form, content, and audience. Considering the commonalities in their overlapping methods and purpose establishes rich connections readers may otherwise miss.

New York City also happened to be the nation's center of literary production. The "Big Six" trade publishers in the United States had their headquarters there, and several thriving left-of-center magazines, including *The Daily Worker*, *Partisan Review*, and *New Masses*, were produced there. This helps explain the concentration of Left cultural activity in the eastern United States. Of the western-born writers present at the first American Writers' Congress, most had left the West to move to New York City. Poet Genevieve Taggard, for example, was born in Washington State, grew up as the daughter of missionary parents in Hawaii, and graduated from the University of California,

Berkeley, before relocating in the East in 1920. Also a graduate of UC Berkeley, Josephine Herbst moved to New York City, became a journalist, and wrote proletarian fiction. Robert Cantwell graduated from the University of Washington and worked in a lumber mill in his home state before moving to New York in 1929. His best-known novel, *Land of Plenty* (1934), was published by Farrar. The *Washington Historical Quarterly* review of *Land of Plenty* downplays the western factory as a "vivid background" while foregrounding the quotidian, psychological suffering endured by all disenfranchised laborers, a common narrative strategy of the proletarian novel:

> Against the vivid background of a strike in a Washington lumber mill, Robert Cantwell projects his story of the everyday life of a group of factory workers. The accurate delineation of character by psychological method and the creation of a very definite atmosphere of distrust and uncertainty make this modern novel...a pertinent contribution to present day literature. (309)

Like Taggard and Herbst, Cantwell lived and wrote for the remainder of his life in the East, even though he is often remembered as a western writer. This regional association has to do partly with *Land of Plenty*, which was republished in 1972, and partly with *The Hidden Northwest* (1972), historical nonfiction about the pioneering Anglo-American men who shaped the natural and cultural landscape of the Pacific Northwest.[4]

Cantwell and his western fellows were introducing a western-style proletarian literature: like its eastern counterpart it was pro-labor, pro-working class, anti-fascist, and anti-imperialist, but it largely reflected a different set of concerns over ethnic identity, rurality and natural resources, and the economic pains of boom-and-bust. Much of that literature in the East and West was supported by local John Reed Clubs. In the "Draft Manifesto of John Reed Clubs," published in 1932 in *New Masses*, the editors (including Mike Gold, perhaps the most famous and forceful promoter of the literary Left) urged readers to reject "art for art's sake" and speak truth to capitalist power by developing rhetorical positions against "the influence of middle-class ideas in the work of revolutionary writers and artists" (3). It was members of New York's John Reed Club (JRC) who first developed the idea for the Writers' Congress.

The founding of the John Reed Club in 1929 was an important moment for the literary Left in the United States. The JRC's motto was "art is a class weapon"; it was committed to bringing revolutionary art and literature to workers and to empowering them to produce such works themselves. In order to accomplish this, the JRC sponsored exhibitions, dances, classes, and little, left magazines (George and Selzer 51). Founded by the editorial board of *New Masses*, club chapters soon popped up outside New York City in Boston, Cleveland, Chicago, and Detroit. John Reed Clubs eventually made their way west, to cities such as Seattle, Portland, San Francisco, and Hollywood. In 1932, a conservative estimate put the number of clubs across the United States at thirteen; by 1934, there were thirty chapters of the JRC in the United States, with more than twelve hundred members ("Draft Manifesto of John Reed Clubs" and Homberger 233).

Many of those chapters produced little magazines, the most famous of which was New York City's *Partisan Review*. Both Chicago and Los Angeles boasted thriving JRC magazines, while smaller communities concentrated on direct action, like the Carmel, California, chapter, which formed to protect migrant workers' rights (Homberger 233–34).

In January of 1935, just months before Rosenberg wrote his report for *Poetry* magazine, the National Committee of the John Reed Clubs issued a call for an organization that would unite writers and encourage them in the "participation in the struggle against war, the preservation of civil liberties, and the destruction of fascist tendencies everywhere" (Halas 143). Thus, the American Writers' Congress was born, and the literary Left gathered to "develop the possibilities for wider distribution of revolutionary books and the improvement of the revolutionary press, as well as the relations between revolutionary writers and bourgeois publishers and editors" ("Call for an American Writers' Congress"). By supporting the distribution of revolutionary literature, the American Writers' Congress gave rise to numerous revolutionary publishing efforts. In the American South, Midwest, and

West, writers and artists joined the cause to produce literature by and for the proletarian masses. On the West Coast, from Seattle to Los Angeles, little Left magazines, supported by the JRC and later by the American Writers' Congress, provided a venue for the literary Left in the American West. But possibly no vehicle was as effective at promoting the cause of revolutionary art in the West than the paperback book.

After its second meeting in 1937, the American Writers' Congress helped popularize a campaign for the wide distribution of paperback books. The Left had officially aligned itself with the paperback revolution: after 1935, books began to be produced on a massive scale and at a low price, giving a new, eager readership access to literature in an age when higher education was largely reserved for the social elite (Sen 444).[5] The paperback democratized knowledge, returning the book "to its true vocation, which is to be not a monument, but a vehicle" (Mercer 616). The paperback was not without its critics, but whether praised as an object of mass education, or decried as an object of mass barbarism, it certainly "blurred the line between high and low culture, between an intellectual elite and 'the masses'" (Mercer 623).[6] The paperback transformed the relationship between reader and text, and nowhere was this more potently realized than in the West Coast home of the new literary Left, San Francisco's City Lights bookstore and press, the nation's first all-paperback bookstore. But even before midcentury when City Lights and other independent presses in the American West began supporting the publication of Left and avant-garde literature, vibrant Left literary production was under way.

The Left in the American West

It's tempting to construct a neat narrative in which the journey of the literary Left begins in New York City and travels West. This fanciful story would align with other colonial narratives of westward expansion, but like those, it obfuscates regional complexities, including the details of violence and imperialism. Western literary and cultural criticism has benefited in recent years from critical trends that seek to uncouple the East-West binary and see the West instead as a complex zone of contact within a transnational context. Western cultural critic Susan Kollin, for example, calls for a reexamination of the region and its iconography in order to make room for the fluid, dynamic, national, and transnational "postwest" that challenges a fixed, predetermined understanding of an impermeable bordered region (Kollin xi). A postwestern approach to theorizing the literary Left in the West is especially useful for understanding the international, migratory, and constantly shifting Left ideology and the movement of laboring bodies; as critics we can, as Kollin recommends, "travel critically in many directions, between past and present and between regions and nations" (xvii). Contributors to *Left in the West* are able to identify a Left literature in the American West that developed in concert with international and national concerns around labor and the liberation of the proletariat, and in response to unique local factors influenced by western migration, ethnic identity, environmental degradation, and tribal sovereignty.

Much of the cultural work performed by western American literature is useful in critiquing the concept of "region" itself, helping us move beyond borders and boundaries and into an understanding of how the West is a space characterized by dynamic interactions among multiple subjects. After the 1934 San Francisco General Strike, proletarian literature proliferated in magazines and newspapers such as the *Pacific Weekly* and *People's World*, but long before the Red Decade, life-writing and autobiographical fiction in the West took up a specific Left agenda. In her 1884 memoir *Life Among the Piutes: Their Wrongs and Claims*, Sarah Winnemucca (Paiute), for example, advocated for her tribe's land claims in Nevada, for access to education, and for political enfranchisement. Oscar Micheaux's 1913 autobiographical novel, *The Conquest: The Story of a Negro Homesteader*, featured as its central character the only African American pioneer homesteading in South Dakota. Edith Maude Eaton, daughter of a British father and Chinese mother, worked as a journalist and published several short stories about the difficulties Chinese Americans faced in her adopted hometown of Seattle before 1910.

Left literary production in the American West uncovered the ways ethnic and regional histories collided to disrupt received notions of regional norms and national political platforms that prescribed Left cultural activity. The establishment of a black press in the West, for instance, points to the development of robust, Left-leaning political discussions among fast-growing communities marginalized by race and class. According to the 1910 U.S. Census, the literacy rate among African Americans in the West had reached nearly 90 percent, twice the rate of literacy among African Americans in the South. Black-owned newspapers at the turn of the century documented the way African American communities in the American West established collective identities; many of these "race papers" addressed civil rights issues, called for increased political engagement, and lobbied for black representation in local and state governments (Berardi and Segady 106). In 1905, for example, the *Colorado Statesmen* reported that black workers were irate over treatment by local trade unions and pledged to "support the unions when the unions act without discrimination" (qtd. in Berardi and Segady 101). Likewise, the *Denver Statesman*, "the leading race journal of the West," ran a weekly petition urging readers to become united to "ameliorate our hard condition industrially and politically" by moving "to incorporate the Negroes of this state into local leagues with representatives in a state body" (qtd. in Berardi and Segady 101).

The literary Left in the West also responded to the cultural and economic legacy of colonization. Among colonization's deleterious effects, many ethnic populations were prohibited from becoming citizens, and when they could, they were restricted from exercising their political rights.

Colonization of Native American lands and ongoing Indian wars in the nineteenth century forced thousands of Native inhabitants onto reservations, where their status as sovereign citizens was not fully ensured. Supporting a colonial strategy in North America and beyond, Admiral Alfred Thayer Mahan urged Congress to understand that no people had a "natural right" to land; the right to control and own territory depended on what he called "political fitness," and to him and many others, Native peoples were not in possession of such fitness (Takaki 211). The Dawes Allotment Act, passed by Congress in 1887, intended to turn Native Americans into "farmers and wage earners" by allotting 160 acres to discrete family units. The author of the act, Senator Henry Dawes, believed the tribal system had to be destroyed in order to "civilize" thousands of western tribal people (Takaki 221). Allotment, which neither improved working conditions for Native people nor connected them to agricultural wealth, was halted in 1934 and replaced by the Indian Reorganization Act, sometimes called the "Indian New Deal." Although Native Americans had been granted full U.S. citizenship in 1924, those living on reservations were prohibited from self-governance. The New Deal dismantled that prohibition, and, at least on paper, Native Americans gained some degree of political autonomy.

Other westerners of color similarly struggled for citizenship rights. Chinese laborers began arriving in the mid-nineteenth century, many of them fleeing the ravages of the British Opium Wars and the Taiping Rebellion. By 1870, sixty-three thousand Chinese were in the United States, the vast majority of them in California and other western states. Thousands worked in mining industries and on the transcontinental railroad. In protest of low wages and exploitative conditions, Chinese miners developed a tradition of striking, but were more often than not denied better conditions, trapped in the mountains, and starved until they came back to work (Takaki 181–82). Chinese laborers lacked political power: if they held a strike, bosses would threaten to import other workers of color to replace them. Chinese laborers did not have the protections of citizenship because of a 1790 federal law that reserved citizenship for "whites" (Takaki 181–82); the 1882 Chinese Exclusion Act restricted all Chinese immigration to the United States. It was not until 1944 that Chinese could become naturalized citizens.

With the Treaty of Guadalupe Hidalgo in 1848, the United States acquired Mexican territories that would become the states of California, New Mexico, Arizona, Nevada, and parts of Colorado and Utah. Thousands of Mexicans found themselves in the United States, were promised citizenship rights, but "found that democracy was essentially for Anglos only" (Takaki 165). Beginning in the 1880s, thousands of Mexican sharecroppers and peasants immigrated to the United States as agricultural workers. Unlike Chinese immigrants, they could be classified as "white" and thus be eligible for naturalization and citizenship, but local laws and customs often led to second-class citizenship. It is no wonder that a robust Left agenda, characterized by issues around migration, ethnic identity, and labor, became central to the political Left in the American West.

The industrial development of western lands, too, was (and remains) central to the concerns of the political Left in the West; a vigorous tradition of environmental literature, informed by conservation and preservation movements, and later, by deep ecology and "green Marxism," developed. In the nineteenth century, agriculture and the extractive industries drew a diverse labor force from all over the Pacific Rim, especially from Mexico, China, and Japan. Joined by immigrants from Germany, Scandinavia, and Ireland, by dispossessed Native Americans, and by African Americans scarcely two generations removed from slavery, the workforce in the West and Midwest was ethnically, racially, and linguistically diverse. Although industry bosses often pitted ethnic groups against each other to avoid strikes and labor shortages, often these groups came together across ethnic and racial differences in class solidarity.[7] Collectively denied citizenship, fair wages, and decent working conditions, laborers in the West found common cause in trade unions, even as western industries endured cycles of boom-and-bust.

The first two decades of the twentieth century saw western industries prosper. By the 1920s, however, agriculture, lumber, and mining suffered from overproduction and near collapse. The hub of labor activity before 1920 was San Francisco, and the movement tended to be broadly inclusive, politically active, and ideologically associated with the Left. Some particularly strong craft unions, such as the International Longshoremen's Association, advocated for better wages and labor conditions but shied away from political reform. Other unionizing efforts for workers in industries such as lumber, mining, and agriculture struggled because their workers were geographically isolated, did not communicate in English or were illiterate, and were sometimes divided into ethnically hostile camps (Malone and Etulain 50). These workers were drawn to industry-wide organizations that favored both economic and political change and that widely adopted a platform of nonintervention in World War I. Radical unionism spread throughout the region in the years leading up to the war, and western socialists joined the national peace movement. Many socialist workers opposed entry into the war because they saw it as a "capitalist war and a poor man's fight" (75). The IWW initiated a massive strike of lumber workers in 1917, and other anti-war militants formed societies to actively resist or sabotage the war effort. The war itself became central to a leftist's self-identification, especially as industrial production suffered.

After World War I, however, progressive political activists came under attack. Anti-war crusaders were charged with sedition, and race riots broke out from Seattle to Tulsa. "All across the West," historian Richard Etulain explains, "radical organizations fell back under the tide of conservative reaction" (Malone and Etulain 78). In the 1920s, the American West saw the growth of nativist sentiments, Ku Klux Klan activity, and a revival of "old time religion" and "political fundamentalism" (81). Despite this move to the right—or maybe in resistance to it—San Francisco maintained its liberal character, eventually becoming home to a vibrant literary Left. This explains in part why so much Left literature and cultural production tended to be centered in California. Nativist populism and stunning racial profiling are seeing a resurgence in the American West since the election of the forty-fifth president, Donald Trump. Thanks in part to a proliferation of communication technologies, the twenty-first century, even more so than in the twentieth, sees a diffuse, widely produced, and broadly circulated literary Left. More popular and critical attention is being given to increasing environmental degradation, long a hallmark of Left concern in the West.

Debates over land use became central to the western political and literary imagination after World War I. Responses to the dispossession of tribal lands in the name of Anglo imperialism, the rapid urbanization that relied on rerouting and damming scarce water supplies, overproduction in and exhaustion of agricultural areas, and the cultural clashes over the ethical deployment of environmental resources became embedded in the Left agenda in the American West after 1920.

Land preservation as a moral good for the nation's long-term health was an argument used by western reformers as diverse as John Muir, Aldo Leopold, and John Wesley Powell. It wasn't long before conservationists, communities, and capitalists were engaged in arguments over "proper use." Thus the literal and metaphorical West—that is, the physical landscape west of the 100th meridian and the ideological space associated with an American "new Eden"—became a political battleground on which the fight for resource extraction and community sovereignty continues, as the 2016–17 struggle over the Dakota Access Pipeline attests.

New Left in the West

Decades before the Standing Rock Sioux were joined by thousands of supporters in North Dakota to protect Indigenous water rights and protest the construction of the Dakota Access Pipeline, young people around the world in the 1950s and 1960s organized to protest corporate capitalism, bureaucratic communism, and imperialism. These international movements had in common a focus on direct action. Less attentive to the popular front's socialist agenda and the industrial working class, the New Left advocated for civil rights, peace, and broad social reform. In the United States, the successful bus boycotts in 1955 and 1956 led by Martin Luther King Jr. modeled nonviolent protest as a way to address social ills and improve society. The Student Nonviolent Coordinating Committee (SNCC) and the Students for a Democratic Society (SDS) focused on direct action as a method of effecting social change. Whether in Greensboro, North Carolina (SNCC), or Ann Arbor, Michigan (SDS), young people came together to criticize racial discrimination, systemic poverty, and the failure of world powers to achieve a lasting peace after World War II. Civil disobedience was called for as a way to promote participatory democracy. In 1964 on the campus of the University of California, Berkeley, the Free Speech Movement (FSM) sought to unmask corporate liberalism, an ideology that peace militant and standard-bearer for the New Left Staughton Lynd explains "solicits the oppressed to accept their oppression willingly because oppression describes itself as freedom" (Lynd 70). The charismatic leader of the FSM, Mario Savio, was the son of Italian immigrants and heir to a particular radical tradition among Italian Americans. In numerous public events, Savio described the way the California Board of Regents attempted to control public speech, thereby denying citizens opportunities for participatory democracy, the social antidote to corporate liberalism. In defiance of the control represented by corporate liberalism, a vibrant, avant-garde literary scene erupted in the Bay Area, giving voice to participatory and radical democracies.

Before and after World War II, writers seeking material reward went to New York City, the center of U.S. book publishing, or to Los Angeles, ground zero for the film industry. But in 1927, poet and translator Kenneth Rexroth settled in San Francisco. He saw unique possibilities there. Its inhabitants were not overly influenced by a Puritan ethic that, he believed, resulted in the stultifying character of American society. During the decades of aggressive westward expansion, San Francisco was settled by "gamblers, prostitutes, rascals, and fortune seekers who came across the Isthmus and around the Horn. They had their faults, but they were not influenced by Cotton Mather" (Sinclair 181). Rexroth settled in the Bay Area as a young man partly in response to the utopian possibilities he saw there. Like that of many in the New Left, Rexroth's political position was complicated by his growing resistance to Stalinism; writers and artists were seeking new ways of expressing their support for leftist ideology outside of Stalin's brutal regime. The American West itself offered the promise of social renewal and transformation. "There is no question but that San Francisco... is radically different from what is going on elsewhere," Rexroth recalled. "There are hand presses, poetry readings, young writers everywhere—but nowhere else is there a whole younger generation culture pattern characterized by total rejection of the official high-brow culture where... magazines like the *Kenyon*, *Hudson* and *Partisan Review* are looked on as 'The Enemy'" (Rexroth 507).

San Francisco had political advantages as well, summed up by Rexroth's socialist vision of "the city [as] a teeming international metropolis of laborers and artists, linked arm in arm against the background of the Sierras" (Davidson 7). In addition to the fertile ideological groundwork laid by the Left-leaning little magazine in the Bay Area, there was the simultaneous growth of well-attended poetry gatherings at San Francisco State College, in various galleries, and in private homes. In his essay "Disengagement: The Art of the Beat Generation," Rexroth argued that the groundswell of writers and readers of the counter-poetries "means that poetry has become an actual social force—something which has always sounded hitherto like a Utopian dream" (507).

A decade before the FSM occupied Sproul Hall on the campus of UC Berkeley, Rexroth met Lawrence Ferlinghetti at one of his literary soirees. Ferlinghetti had emigrated to San Francisco in 1952 to paint and translate poetry. Ferlinghetti shared Rexroth's politics and found other like-minded writers and thinkers in San Francisco. For Ferlinghetti, it was as if "the continent had tilted up, with the whole population sliding to the west" (Morgan and Peters xi). It seemed like the perfect place to realize his own utopian dream. In Paris, where Ferlinghetti attended the Sorbonne on the G.I. Bill, he had become enamored with the literary culture: lining the River Seine were *bouquinists*, open-air stalls selling all manner of books. Small bookshops, whose proprietors were also publishers, were among Ferlinghetti's favorite haunts.

In 1953 Ferlinghetti co-founded City Lights bookstore, and the following year launched its press. It was the work of surrealist and experimental writers, he maintained, that could perform the work of the New Left. This literature consciously disrupted formal conventions and called into question the dominant politics and cultural norms of midcentury America. At City Lights, Ferlinghetti cultivated this literary vision, and his bookshop and press became a beacon for New Left activity. City Lights published and sold literature that raised awareness about gay liberation, social reform, and global peace. As a staunch defender of free speech, Ferlinghetti himself became a central figure in the development of the new literary Left.

Proletarian and Ethnic Literatures

As social reforms in cities and schools took hold in the American West, literature by ethnic writers emerged. Beginning in the 1970s, literature by Latinx, Native American, Asian American, and African American writers challenged a homogeneous experience of traditionally leftist concerns. This body of literature questioned cultural sovereignty and foregrounded the way racial and cultural politics intersected with categories of class and power relations. This literature continues to define literary production in and about the West, and continues to revise twentieth-century understandings of leftist cultural activity.

As Tim Libretti explains in his article "Is There a Working Class in U.S. Literature? Race, Ethnicity, and the Proletarian Tradition," the proletarian literature of the 1930s was not a "fleeting aberration of a singular moment of intense political, social, and cultural ferment in U.S. history" (22). But critics became habituated to deriding "labor literature" as a shallow, inelegant form penned by "writers in uniform" and lacking true literary merit. In the West, proletarian literature has often gone unrecognized by scholars because of the way labor motifs interweave together with categories of race and ethnicity. While U.S. ethnic literatures are now the object of reading, teaching, and scholarship, the literature of work, labor, and class is still underrepresented. Libretti argues that the category of "proletarian literature" should be refined so that it includes a better analytical framework for how race, gender, and nation complicate notions of class. If scholars adopt a broad framework for working-class literature, post–Red Decade novels like Rudolfo Anaya's *Heart of Aztlan* (a strike novel set in New Mexico), Leslie Marmon Silko's *Ceremony* (a novel about class differences in war, on and off the reservation), and Maxine Hong Kingston's *China Men* (a collection of stories about sugarcane workers, railroad workers, and small business owners) become part of an evolving tradition of proletarian literature. It's important, Libretti reminds us, that these novels are read as examples of ethnic identity formation. However, by privileging ethnicity, readers may lose sight of how these novels also powerfully engage issues of class, labor, and work. The solution, of course, is not to elevate one reading strategy over another, choosing, say, class over race or ethnicity, but to engage the way class experiences intersect with race, ethnicity, and gender. And, as I argue here, the way this body of literature engages the complexities and nuances of the American West only enriches our reading and study. For example, taking into account the segregation experienced by western laborers, and the way they were often pitted against one another to prevent labor solidarity, points to the manner in which laboring bodies were already and always constituted as racialized (or gendered) bodies. Consider the powerful one-act plays that El Teatro Campesino (Farmworkers' Theater) and its founder and artistic director Luis Valdez staged beginning in 1965 on the Delano grape strike picket lines. The *actos* dramatized conflicts between workers and owners, educated audiences about the plight of Chicano/a farmworkers and the need for a union, and demonstrated the intersections among gender, ethnicity, and class. El Teatro Campesino earned an Obie Award in 1969 for "demonstrating the politics of survival."

Western American literature that is class-conscious challenges a homogeneous experience of Left identity. In the 1920s, Mike Gold, the charismatic writer, editor, and activist, said the purpose of proletarian literature was to "build up a picture of what the working class in this country looked like" (qtd. in Libretti 26).

Into the Twenty-First Century

The literary Left continues to evolve in the twenty-first-century West. Karen Tei Yamashita's 1997 *Tropic of Orange* features a multiethnic cast in Los Angeles and Mexico dealing with geopolitical borders, the legacies of colonialism, and the shifting markers of identity. Michael Chabon's novel *Telegraph Avenue* (2012) examines the multiple layers of class, ethnicity, and displacement in Oakland, California; Viet Thanh Nguyen's novel *The Sympathizer* (2015), winner of the 2016 Pulitzer Prize for fiction, critiques the Vietnam War and its legacy as experienced by relocated Vietnamese in Los Angeles. These novels directly address the intersection of class, work, and ethnicity within and against the distinct physical and ideological framework of the American West. And again, as the literary Left in the American West addresses the contemporary rise of white nationalism, gun violence, travel bans, border walls, the shrinking of public lands, gender inequity, transgender violence and discrimination, escalation of the threat of nuclear war, and rampant anti-intellectualism, cultural workers respond with literature, music, and visual art, which continue to refine and revise the meaning of what it means to be Left in the West.

The Essays

By examining the relationship between western American literature, the literary Left, and the political forces that shape and are shaped by them, we come to a new understanding of the region, its place among global and political ideologies, and its unique people, places, and concerns. Literature responds to and embodies political and social forces. It also critiques and changes political forces. The essays collected here consider the multiple pressures that exist between literary production and political milieu. Several of the contributors to this collection examine the way political coalitions—from environmentalism, to labor, to civil rights—shaped cultural activity in the American West. Other contributors probe the way literature intervenes in significant ways in the political, particularly in the practice and performance of a "Left" political identity, one that is characterized by dissent, departure, and disruption. These essays perform this cultural work by revealing contradictions, describing cultural constraints, interrogating historical moments, and debunking literary assumptions.

Part 1, "Left Movements: Institutions and Ideologies," examines ways normative ideas about private and public life take shape, become institutionalized, and are resisted to produce alternative meanings, signs, and symbols. In the opening essay, "'Activism Brings Out the Best in All of Us': Toward a History of Peace and Justice Movements in Utah from the 1960s to the Present," John S. McCormick dives into a rich, largely untapped archive of interviews with peace and justice activists in Utah to construct a surprising narrative of consistent, creative activism in that red state. Activists in Utah, McCormick explains, sustained a variety of movements and organizations, from anti-militarist to environmental. The personal narratives included here are moving, funny, and insightful; together these stories suggest answers to questions at the heart of Left activism: What conditions inspire left-of-center, radical values? What sustains activism, especially in a conservative political climate? What tactics are effective and in what arenas? This opening essay truly represents a beginning. By transmitting the stories people tell about their political engagement and activism, McCormick calls attention to the centrality of the creative act of the Left cultural worker. By bringing this significant archive into the light of cultural and literary criticism, McCormick initiates inquiry that scholars of the American West would be wise to continue.

What follows is an essay about environmental value and the resistance to market-driven ideology. Daniel Rinn, in his essay "Deep Ecology in Humboldt County: Bill Devall and a Philosophy for Action," considers the work and life of philosopher and deep ecologist Bill Devall. In response to logging practices in Humboldt County, Devall developed a praxis of environmental activism that was profoundly informed by deep ecology. Devall's ideology, Rinn explains, emerged at the confluence of New Left politics, radical environmentalism, and personal affection for the American West.

In "'An International, Dissident, Insurgent Ferment': Lawrence Ferlinghetti and the Left Coast," Gioia Woods tells the story of two interrelated figures who shaped the counterculture of the American West: Lawrence Ferlinghetti and San Francisco's iconic City Lights bookstore. As bookshop, publishing house, host of the West Coast paperback revolution, sponsor of the Beat movement, home of the Pocket Poets Series, torchbearer for free speech movements, and early promoter of global comparative literature, City Lights has continuously been in the avant-garde of literary experimentation and cultural revolution. It is a site shaped by the historical encounters between conformity and resistance, those dichotomous tensions that characterized Cold War culture. Here Woods argues that the bookshop is a space deeply informed by a set of utopian ideologies that prepares the framework for resistance, transgression, and social change.

Social change is the clear motive behind Woody Guthrie's ballads. In "The Traditional Roots of Woody Guthrie's *Dust Bowl Ballads*,"

William Clements carefully unpacks the historical tradition that informs Woody Guthrie's ballads. In doing so, he situates those ballads as important social documents that shed light on a time and place in twentieth-century America. Clements also deconstructs the performance of Guthrie's Left identity. He became a distinct western hero of the Left, Clements explains, by personifying "the grass-roots leftist who had developed his sensitivity to the needs of the 'common man' through his own experiences...rather than by reading and studying armchair treatises prepared by the intellectual elite who dominated the leftist political scene back East." Guthrie's experiences in California, Clements argues, were crucial to the development of his commitment to leftist and social issues. Like Bob Dylan, who was awarded the Nobel Prize for Literature in 2016, Woody Guthrie deployed the great American song tradition to create a new poetry.

Finally, there is a significant tradition of western American life-writing that critiques structures of power while reimagining identities outside the political and institutional structures that limit them. In his essay "Luis J. Rodriguez's *Always Running*: Between Chicano Nationalism and the Left," José Navarro develops a critical framework he calls "barrio-biographics" through which critiques of the nation-state, predatory violence, and racial capitalism can be read in autobiographies like Rodriguez's 1993 *Always Running: La Vida Loca, Gang Days in L.A.* In an astute reading, Navarro examines how the legacy of American imperialism gives rise to the conditions that spawn modern gangs. Navarro reads Rodriguez's celebrated gang memoir as a narrative of coming to political consciousness within the contexts of colonialism, trauma, and white supremacy.

Part 2, "Left Readings: Rewriting Region and Radicalism," gathers essays about writers, artists, or texts that advocated for complete political or social reform. Sometimes this reform took shape as a challenge to the real and imagined borders of the American West.

Ward Moore, who published his first novel of speculative fiction, *Greener Than You Think*, in 1947, can be understood as one of those radical voices. Moore's leftist critique, contributor Robert Yusef Rabiee explains, is situated "in the very specific dilemmas of the American

West—of land use, irresponsible suburbanization, the cult of the image, and the rhapsodic imagination of endless expansion that characterizes social life in the west in general and Los Angeles in particular." In "Eschaton of Abundance: Ward Moore's *Greener Than You Think* as Transcendentalist Satire," Rabiee untangles an intriguing knot of themes that inform Moore's unique novel: postwar optimism, suburbanization, indifference to western ecologies, and transcendentalism. These themes come together as necessary components of an "eschaton of abundance," a perpetual state of crises spurred by unplanned development. Rabiee's energetic reading of Moore's novel is a thoroughgoing and deeply contextualized treatment that rescues *Greener Than You Think* from obscurity and places it within a tradition of postwar novels that critique consumer culture and its devastating environmental and cultural effects.

Unlike Moore, who worked in the genre of speculative fiction, celebrated writer Mari Sandoz wrote with gritty realism about issues of class, poverty, and genocide in the American West. Sandoz, contributor Bette Weidman explains, was moved by personal experience to a leftist critique of American society. In "Mari Sandoz: A Writer's Politics," Weidman carefully reads Sandoz's fiction and biographical writing to argue for a "writer's politics," a personal radicalism not inspired by party affiliation but by her own relationship with the West. Throughout her prolific career, Sandoz explored the ways colonialism perpetrated multiple injustices and offered insightful critiques of capitalist profiteering. Sandoz questioned the dominant understanding of western regional prosperity by exposing how its borders are shaped by family trauma, labor strife, environmental degradation, and gender inequality. For Sandoz, Weidman explains, the personal was deeply political.

Radical anti-capitalist and pioneering bioregionalist Peter Berg advocated "breaking the master's tools." Berg, a "key environmentalist you have probably never heard of," is the subject of William Lombardi's essay "'Poisons Up to the Waist in a Junkyard of Breaking Machines': Peter Berg, Bioregional Ethics, and the Trouble with the Master's Tools." Reinhabitation, suggests Lombardi, is Berg's solution to recentering region and resisting colonization. In this essay, Lombardi recuperates Berg's life and work, claiming him as a "significant figure in the U.S. West counterculture."

Critique of the machine is a productive line of inquiry in radical fiction. John Schwetman provides an incisive reading of John Steinbeck's novel *Grapes of Wrath*, one that extends the usual consideration of the iconic work as "proletarian fiction." In "Contact Points: The Roadside Diner's Machinery of Work in John Steinbeck's *The Grapes of Wrath*," Schwetman persuasively argues that the novel introduces and sustains a critique of the technologies of production and mediation and in so doing challenges the notion of an ideal western agrarian paradise. From the bulldozer, to the tractor, to the "shiny metal gadgets of Al's diner," Steinbeck's mechanized forces herald the disruption of community and represent an encroaching industrial order. Through this Marxist critique, Schwetman mounts a fresh discussion of individual and collective identity, labor, travel, and commodification.

The career of San Francisco Renaissance poet Jack Spicer is marked by a vigorous rewriting of the frontier myth. He rewrote region, contributor Alex Trimble Young maintains, by imagining the frontier as a site of queer desire. In his essay "'The Queen of the Mad Frontier': Settler Colonialism and Jack Spicer's Queer Politics," Young revisits the legacy of Spicer. Here Young reads Spicer's work as a conflation of western regional identity, queer sexuality, and radical political commitment. Reading through the lens of settler colonialism, which in part seeks to expose and dismantle false narratives and structures of settler belonging, Young successfully teases out how a sort of frontier popular sovereignty was central to the poet's literary politics. Young relies on a rich record of letters, interviews, and political ephemera to describe how Spicer's poetics point us to a new reading of radical literary production in relation to the power structures it seeks to transform.

Part 3 of *Left in the West*, "Left in Transit: Success and Limitations," considers the benefits to and challenges of transition and migration, especially relative to individual and collective identities. In "New Bohemias, California Style: The Intimate and Global Networks of Photographic Modernism," Audrey Goodman examines group identity in response to the growth of the international political Left. The emergence of bohemian artist networks in the 1930s in California and Mexico, Goodman argues, signaled a modernist aesthetic that privileged materiality, landscape, and the body. Goodman explores how specific public and private spaces became landmarks of bohemian culture, and how both social and aesthetic arrangements practiced by bohemian photographers led to a new visual language that was a "collective protest." In her analysis of the work of Edward Weston and Tina Modotti in particular, Goodman reveals the way the practice of Left identity was crucial to the aesthetics of western bohemian communities.

Contributor Lisa Udel analyzes the representation of tribal identity in transit through space and time in her essay "'Backward in Time and Forward in Dream of Unknown Memory': Deborah Miranda's Unsettling Colonial Genealogies." Miranda's (Esselen/Chumash) *Bad Indians: A Tribal Memoir* entangles personal and tribal genealogies with national genealogies of settler colonialism, violence, and resistance. Through Udel's close reading of this evocative, multilayered memoir, the nuances of historical, psychological, and communal materials are revealed as they intertwine to construct an affirmation of contemporary indigeneity. Deploying the settler colonial history that attempted to replace Indigenous communities with invasive settler societies, Udel successfully argues that Miranda "uses the memoir to trace personal, tribal, and national lineage, noting the ruptures and bridging the gaps, recording 'the good, bad, and ugly,' however painful." Miranda's work thus recalls the violence and disruption wrought by settler colonialism and provides a record of resistance and longevity.

Emily Lutenski continues the theme of women, life-writing, and the literary Left in her essay "Leaving the West for the Left: Louise Thompson Patterson, the New Negro Movement, and Black Women's Activism." Here Lutenski uncovers significant unpublished work by Thompson, a Harlem Renaissance figure who lived much of her activist life in the American West. Using biographical and historical modes of inquiry, Lutenski describes how Thompson's long life, letters, and unpublished memoirs suggest that her leftist, feminist, pro-black activism emerged within the complicated and sometimes contradictory intersection of the New Negro movement, black internationalism, and a western geography that was at best ambivalent and at worst violently resistant to the construction of radical black political solidarity. Despite this, Thompson continued to seek out and create black female spheres of influence in the American West.

The collection closes with a richly contextualized reading of a western American classic that reveals the limitations of a narrow Left political engagement. In "Charlotte Perkins Gilman's *Herland*, Race, and the California Suffrage and Women's Club Movements, 1896–1911," Darcie Rives-East shows how Gilman's relationship to women's clubs heightened her opposition to opportunities for racial justice and eventually contributed to the erasure of women of color in her iconic novel. Along the way, Rives-East describes a particular construction of Californian Progressive Era womanhood and feminine citizenship that was white, upper class, and informed by particular assumptions regarding labor and access to power.

THE VIBRANT TRADITION of the literary Left in the American West is instructive to us now as we confront the resurgence of hate, division, and bigotry. As alt-right groups, neofascists, new nativists, and white supremacists attempt to claim power by insisting hate speech and harassment are "opinions" protected by free speech, creative work by the ethnic, queer, environmental, proletarian, and existentialist cultural worker carves a space from which to launch dissent and resist authoritarianism. Although the dramatic shift in public politics signaled by the 2016 presidential election is still unfolding, it seems clear that a new, twenty-first century popular front is on the rise.

Notes

1. A notable exception was the preeminent novelist, poet, and critic Malcolm Cowley. Although born in Pennsylvania and widely known as the expatriate representative of the Lost Generation in Paris and literary advisor to Viking Press, Cowley had an

enormous impact as the Stegner Fellowship teacher at Stanford University in 1960. Among his students were Ken Kesey and Larry McMurtry.

2. See Michael Denning's *The Cultural Front: The Laboring of American Culture in the Twentieth Century* (1996, 2011) and Raymond Williams's *Resources of Hope* for discussions of commitment and alignment.
3. The Hollywood Ten was a group of ten witnesses who refused to cooperate with the House Un-American Activities Committee. They cited the First Amendment (freedom of speech, right of assembly, freedom of association), but were each found in contempt of Congress, fined $1,000, and sentenced to one year in federal prison. All ten writers were fired by studio executives, thus beginning the period of the Hollywood blacklist. Those writers included Alvah Bessie, Herbert J. Biberman, Lester Cole, Edward Dmytryk, Ring Lardner Jr., John Howard Lawson, Albert Maltz, Samuel Ornitz, Robert Adrian Scott, and Dalton Trumbo. Trumbo, born and raised in Grand Junction, Colorado, was the only native westerner of the group.
4. For an excellent critical biography of Robert Cantwell's life and work, see T. V. Reed's *Robert Cantwell and the Literary Left: A Northwest Writer Reworks American Fiction* (2014). Reed examines the development of Cantwell's political consciousness, describes his career within the context of the Red Decade and beyond, and argues for a full recovery of Cantwell and his profound influence on U.S. literature. In order to do so, Reed disentangles the long-held critical assumption that "political commitment and literary quality are mutually exclusive" (3).
5. The workers education movement attempted to counter the notion that education should be available only to the upper classes. It established programs with the help of unions and universities to make education widely available to workers. A. J. Muste described the two differing philosophies undergirding the movement. The first is "to extend to workers the same cultural advantages and opportunities as other classes in society have enjoyed"; the second is to recognize the workers' unique context, psychology, and social role, thus to design an educational experience that equips them to "solve their problems, raise their status, and discharge their function in our social order" (Muste 738).
6. Michael Denning draws attention to the "hidden labor" involved in the paperback book: the labor of becoming literate. Motion pictures, sound recording, and broadcasting technologies were developed and made communication easier to decode (Denning 40).
7. Cane-field plantations were notorious for the ethnic divide-and-conquer strategy. In Hawaii, Filipinos, Puerto Ricans, Chinese, Japanese, Portuguese, and Korean workers eventually came together as the Hawaii Laborers' Association to demonstrate their class. The Japanese-Mexican Labor Association (JMLA) was formed in Los Angeles in 1903, and even though members faced racial discrimination when they tried to join with the local chapter of the American Federation of Labor, the JMLA became a "powerful force for organizing farm laborers" (Takaki 174).

Bibliography

Berardi, Gayle K., and Thomas W. Segady. "The Development of African-American Newspapers in the American West: A Sociohistorical Perspective." *The Journal of Negro History*, vol. 75, no. 3/4, Summer–Autumn, 1990, pp. 96–111.
"Call for an American Writers' Congress." *New Masses*, vol. 14, no. 4, January 1935, p. 20.
Davidson, Michael. *The San Francisco Renaissance: Poetics and Community at Mid-Century*. Cambridge, GBR, Cambridge University Press, 1991.
Denning, Michael. *The Cultural Front: The Laboring of American Culture in the Twentieth Century*. Verso, 2010.
"Draft Manifesto of John Reed Clubs." *New Masses*, vol. 7, no. 12, June 1932, p. 4.
Draper, Theodore. *The Roots of American Communism*. Viking, 1957.
George, Ann, and Jack Selzer. "What Happened at the First American Writers' Congress? Kenneth Burke's 'Revolutionary Symbolism in America.'" *Rhetoric Society Quarterly*, vol. 33, no. 2, Spring 2003, pp. 47–66.
Halas, Duncan. *The Comintern*. Bookmarks, 1985.
Homberger, Eric. "Proletarian Literature and the John Reed Clubs 1929–1935." *Journal of American Studies*, vol. 13, no. 2 Aug. 1979, pp. 221–44.
Kollin, Susan. *Postwestern Cultures: Literature, Theory, Space*. U of Nebraska P, 2007.
Libretti, Tim. "Is There a Working Class in U.S. Literature? Race, Ethnicity, and the Proletarian Literary Tradition." *The Radical Teacher*, vol. 46, 1995, pp. 22–26.
Lynd, Staughton. "The New Left." *The Annals of the American Academy of Political and Social Science*, vol. 382, March 1969, pp. 64–72.
Malone, Michael P., and Richard Etulain. *The American West: A Twentieth-Century History*. U of Nebraska P, 1989.
Mercer, Ben. "The Paperback Revolution: Mass-Circulation Books and the Cultural Origins of 1968 in Western Europe." *Journal of the History of Ideas*, vol. 72, no. 4, Oct. 2011, pp. 613–36.
Morgan, Bill, and Nancy J. Peters, editors. *Howl on Trial: The Battle for Free Expression*. City Lights Press, 2006.
Muste, A. J. "Workers Education in the United States." *Religious Education*, vol. 24, no. 8, 1929, pp. 738–45.
Reed, T. V. *Robert Cantwell and the Literary Left: A Northwest Writer Reworks American Fiction*. U of Washington P, 2015.
Review of *Land of Plenty*, by Robert Cantwell. *Washington Historical Quarterly*, vol. 25, no. 4, 1934, p. 309.
Rexroth, Kenneth. "Disengagement: The Art of the Beat Generation." *Beat Down to Your Soul: What Was the Beat Generation?*, edited by Ann Charters, Penguin, 2001, pp. 493–508.
Rosenberg, Harold. "The American Writers' Congress." *Poetry: A Magazine of Verse*, vol. 46, no. 4, July 1935, pp. 222–27.

Sen, Mandira. "The Paperback Revolution." *India International Centre Quarterly*, vol. 10, no. 4, Dec. 1983, pp. 443–65.

Sinclair, Mick. *San Francisco: A Cultural and Literary History*. Interlink Books, 2004.

Steiner, Michael C. *Regionalists on the Left: Radical Voices from the American West*. U of Oklahoma P, 2013.

Takaki, Ronald. *A Different Mirror: A History of Multicultural America*. 1993. Back Bay Books, 2008.

Wald, Alan. *Exiles from a Future Time: The Forging of the Mid-Twentieth-Century Literary Left*. U of North Carolina P, 2002.

I

LEFT MOVEMENTS

Institutions and Ideologies

1

"Activism Brings Out the Best in All of Us"

Toward a History of Peace and Justice Movements in Utah from the 1960s to the Present

JOHN S. MCCORMICK

Utah has a long history of peace and justice activism. This surprises many people, but it should not, because the existence of a hegemonic political and social order does not predict whether or not opposition to that hegemony will exist. It does not necessarily prevent opposition to prevailing beliefs, values, and practices. We can begin to discover the nature and motivations of opposition when it does emerge in such a social order by listening to the voices of activists as they work to find points of entry into the dominant discourse, to challenge, interrupt, and disrupt it, to push back, to think and act outside the boundaries of the "permissible."

This essay is an overview of peace and justice movements in Utah from the political left, in particular the radical left, during the last half of the twentieth century and the early years of the twenty-first. It is based in large part on the more than 125 oral history interviews with peace and justice activists now on deposit at Utah Valley University's George Sutherland Archives that are a substantial part of its Oral History of Utah Peace Activists Project. Though the interviews took place between 2006 and 2009, historians and others have not made much use of them, and they remain largely untapped. They are by no means exhaustive; they do not include many peace and justice activists. Even so, they allow us to say more about peace and justice movements in Utah than was previously possible. At the same time, they are such a rich resource that this essay is only a sketch of what could easily be a much longer account of both individual activists and the organizations of which they were a part. The interviews raise, and offer insight into, a range of questions—among them: What brought people whose social milieu was shaped by a conservative political climate and a dominant religion to radical belief and activity? What has it meant to be an activist, in particular a radical activist, in a conservative state where the influence of the Mormon church cannot be ignored and where what Rocky Anderson has called a "culture of obedience" exists (Anderson 19)? What sustained their commitment? At what costs? What does it take to be effective under such circumstances? What relationship did Utah radicals and radical groups see between peace and justice? Between anti-militarism and, for example, environmentalism? How did they confront the challenge of living in a way consistent with their values? What led Deanna Taylor, for example, to co-found a Utah chapter of the international group Radical Cheerleaders, and C. T. Butler and Keith McHenry to found Food Not Bombs, whose intention was both to provide free meals to the hungry and to call into question an economic system based on profit and militarism and the political system that supported it? What brought Utah Phillips to singing and storytelling and Alex Caldiero to poetry and performance as forms of radical action, and Archie Archuleta, Dayne Goodwin, and Diana Lee Hirschi to lifelong radical commitment? What led to the formation of Word Warriors, whose goal was "Confronting Oppression with Expression"? And to the founding of publications like the *Desert Sun: Utah's Peace News; buzzkill: salt lake's occasional anarchist rag;* the *Utah Free Press: A Socialist Monthly;* and the *Mormon Worker*, a "socialist, anti-war newspaper from a Mormon perspective, loosely modeled on the *Catholic Worker*" (Van Wagenen 3). What led to the founding of Mormons for Equality and Social Justice (MESJ), a national organization with several dozen chapters throughout the United States that addresses a range of issues, including gender and racial equality, militarism, and environmental justice? How did the answers radicals gave to such questions influence the ways they thought about their activism and the impact they might have? In other words, the interviews allow us to examine what might be called "the making of a radical," and in some instances, the "unmaking," in general and in Utah specifically.

In this regard, what is clear from the interviews is the emphasis Utah radicals placed on creating and sustaining a community of people engaged with others in a common enterprise in Utah and across the country and the world. Acting with like-minded people created powerful bonds, a feeling of belonging, a realization that a person was not alone. Such a feeling of connection to others and to a cause gave them a sense of their combined strength, helping them to sustain their vision, nerve, and the confidence that they might make a difference, helping to combat loneliness, isolation, discouragement, and a sense of impotence.

As part of this, as a way of sustaining a sense of possibility and a culture of opposition, many Utah radicals stressed the importance of a variety of approaches and range of activities, the importance of activists speaking, marching, rallying, distributing literature, organizing concerts and festivals, holding poetry readings and art exhibits. That is, they emphasized the importance of what Barbara Ehrenreich has called "festivity." Such activities, she argues, both empower those who participate in them and threaten ruling parties who seek to maintain their dominant position (Ehrenreich 94).

The challenges radical movements on the Left have posed to the status quo in the United States have been stronger at some times than at others, but they have always existed. This has been true in Utah as well (McCormick and Sillito; Berman). Beginning with the arrival of Mormons in 1847, and continuing to the present, Utah has a longstanding tradition of individuals and groups calling into question the fundamental principles on which American society has been organized; calling for thoroughgoing changes; seeking to get to the root of problems, rather than dealing with symptoms; and challenging existing assumptions about what is good and what is moral.

The Mormon church was one of dozens of utopian communities, both secular and religious, founded in the United States in the early and middle years of the nineteenth century, and Mormons saw their immigration to Utah beginning in 1847 as an opportunity to escape the country's deeply rooted inequalities and begin anew. Subsequent groups of Utah radicals included the Liberal Party of the 1870s and 1880s; the Knights of Labor in the 1880s; the Populist Party in the 1890s; anarchists, Wobblies, and Socialists in the late nineteenth and early twentieth centuries; Communists in the 1930s; old and new leftists in the 1960s; and numerous groups since then, among them the Wasatch Coalition for Peace and Justice; Vietnam Veterans Against the War; Military Families Speak Out; and the Brown Berets.

Specific features of this radical tradition include the election to public office of at least 115 members of the Socialist Party of America in more than a dozen Utah cities and towns between 1901 and 1923; mass marches and demonstrations of the unemployed through the streets of downtown Salt Lake City and other Utah cities during the 1930s that Communist Party members and sympathizers had organized; and the "One-Man Revolution" in the 1960s of Christian anarchist and pacifist Ammon Hennacy. The 1980s and 1990s saw the founding of the Committee in Solidarity with the People of El Salvador (CISPES); the Central America Solidarity Coalition (CASC); a Utah local of Democratic Socialists of America (DSA); the Great Peace March for Nuclear Disarmament in 1986; and the near election in 1991 of a member of the Socialist Workers Party, Nancy Boyasko, to the Salt Lake City Council. Her goal in running was to "be a voice for the struggles and rights of working people in this city. And a link to struggles of working people around the world" ("Vote Socialist Workers"). Among the features of Utah's radical history in the first decade and a half of the twenty-first century was a rally in August 2005 to "End the Unjust War in Iraq"; the first annual Imagine Peace Fest in 2006; a Liar's Convention in downtown Salt Lake City in March 2007 to protest the Bush administration's continuing prosecution of its war in Iraq and to remember those who had died as a result of the war; a Salt Lake City Main Street Plaza Kiss-In in 2009; the 2009 founding of the Revolutionary Students Union, with chapters at the University of Utah, Utah Valley University, and Salt Lake Community College; the annual observance, beginning on April 1, 2010, of Fossil Fools Day, sponsored by the group Peaceful Uprising; and an art show in 2017 at the Mestizo Institute of Culture and Arts in Salt Lake City entitled "Hands Up, Don't Shoot," which explored "themes of police brutality and violence against underrepresented groups" (Staker).

The 1960s in the United States, the period from the mid-1950s to the early 1970s, was a significant focus of the Oral History of Utah Peace Activists Project interviews. It was a volatile and passionate time when virtually every aspect of American life was challenged and called into question. Utah was very much a part of the ferment. A number of peace and justice groups founded earlier continued to be active, including chapters of the Women's International League for Peace and Freedom (WILPF); the Fellowship for Reconciliation (FOR); the War Resisters League (WRL); Women Strike for Peace; the National Association for the Advancement of Colored People (NAACP); the Socialist Workers Party (SWP); and the Industrial Workers of the World (IWW). In addition, beginning in the 1960s, and continuing to the present, more than one hundred peace and justice groups have been founded.[1] Not all of them were radical groups, though many were, but they all had radical elements and radical potential. Some were short-lived; others lasted longer; some have continued to the present; and new ones continue to be established. Many were chapters of national organizations; others were local. Some were part of religious groups, while others were secular. Their members and supporters included a range of people in terms of race, ethnicity, class, gender, age, sexual orientation, and religious affiliation. They included those whose involvement was short-term and those whose commitment was lifelong. They linked peace with other concerns, including, increasingly, environmental issues. They organized countless marches, rallies, demonstrations, sit-ins, teach-ins, picket lines, vigils, and encampments. They undertook long-term letter-writing campaigns, engaged in civil disobedience and direct action, and were arrested. They took part in guerrilla street theater. They organized an "alternative commencement" at Brigham Young University in spring 2007 to protest its decision to invite Vice President Dick Cheney to speak and award him an honorary degree. They occupied Salt Lake

City as part of the nationwide Occupy movement. They worked to stop the Carter and Reagan administration's plan to construct a nearly 100,000-acre MX missile base in Utah and Nevada. They sponsored an annual Tooele County "Toxic Weekend" encampment—"A Raging Shindig Against Air, Water, and Ground Pollution"; sent delegations of Utah women who traveled to the Soviet Union in the late 1980s for a series of meetings with Russian women to promote peace; and supported Iraq War veteran and military journalist Marshall Thompson's walk the length of Utah in 2006 to protest the war. They mounted an "Eyes Wide Open" traveling exhibit that consisted of a pair of combat boots for every American soldier and Iraqi civilian killed in the Iraq War. They staged protests against a proposed coal-burning power plant near Capitol Reef National Park and a proposed nuclear waste site near Canyonlands National Park, which included a "U-235 relay race." U-235 is the atomic weight of uranium, Bruce Plenk, one of the participants, explained, but 235 miles was also roughly the distance from the proposed nuclear waste site to Salt Lake City, and opponents of the site participated in a relay race to the state's capital city, passing a baton with petitions opposing the site rolled up inside it (Plenk 15–16).

Over a period of years Utah peace activists working to ban nuclear testing joined with activists from Nevada and other states in organizing regular protests and a long-term "peace camp" at the 1,360-acre Nevada Nuclear Test Site (NTS) sixty-five miles northwest of Las Vegas. Between its establishment in 1951 and 1992, the site was the primary location for testing U.S. nuclear devices. During those years 1,021 nuclear detonations occurred there. One hundred of them were "atmospheric," or aboveground, explosions that created the characteristic mushroom clouds that became synonymous with the explosion of nuclear bombs. Beginning in the late 1950s, and in particular during the 1980s and early 1990s, the NTS was the site of regular protests and acts of civil disobedience, including on the anniversaries of the bombing of Hiroshima and Nagasaki. From 1986 through 1994, 536 anti-nuclear protests were held. They involved more than thirty-seven thousand participants and led to nearly sixteen thousand arrests. Most of the demonstrations were sponsored by either the

American Peace Test (APT) or the Nevada Desert Experience (NDE). The biggest protest took place in March 1988. Held over a ten-day period, nearly three thousand people were arrested, including more than twelve hundred in a single day.

Deb Levine participated in many protests at the NTS. "We were there," she said, "because we really believed that this was wrong, that building nuclear weapons was wrong, and that…if you don't test them, then you're not going to use them" (Levine 5). Dee Rowland took part in a number of protests and was arrested three times. "I couldn't be true to myself if I did not speak out against this," she said. What particularly drew her to the protests was that they were not just aimed at stopping a particular war but were part of a "comprehensive type of peace movement" (Rowland 8). When arrested and tried for trespassing, protesters at the NTS often employed what Bruce Plenk, a lawyer in one of the cases, called the "necessity defense," arguing that "in order to stop this nuclear testing…yes, we trespassed but it should be excused because of the significance of preventing nuclear war, violating international treaties, and violating the rights of the Western Shoshone people" on whose land the test site was located (Plenk 7). That argument was not successful in defending protesters at the NTS, but it was at the January 1990 trial of protesters at the gates of Hercules, Inc., a Utah company that built engines for Trident missiles. When three protestors were arrested and tried for trespassing, the jury agreed with their lawyer, Ron Yengich's, "choice of evils" defense that what Hercules was doing was a "crime against humanity" that required them to break governmental laws in the name of a higher law (Yengich 7).

Several dozen groups working for peace and justice in the 1960s began as "anti-war," or "peace," or "peacemaking" bodies protesting the Vietnam War. Even though a majority of Utahns always supported the war, and Utah sent to Vietnam the fifth highest percentage in the nation of males eligible for the draft, a significant anti-war movement emerged in the state. The anti-war movement in the United States involved a range of political positions and philosophies, but radicals were a significant part of it, and it is fair to say that radicalism in Utah was revitalized in part through opposition to the Vietnam War. Activists argued for the necessity of not only stopping a particular war, but eliminating an economic and political system that made war inevitable. As Hans Ehrbar put it: "in order to solve the issues of peace, justice, environmental issues, etc., we must become a different kind of society" (Ehrbar 10).

Utah's first anti–Vietnam War protest march took place in downtown Salt Lake City in fall 1964. Paul Wharton was one of about ten participants. "We were jeered, we were heckled, mustard, ketchup, you name it thrown at us, epithets of all kinds and descriptions," he recalled. "But after the first one you get used to it" (Wharton 4). A march the next spring, on April 18, 1965, attracted about forty participants. Four and a half years later, on October 15, 1969, as many as seven thousand demonstrators joined in a full day of protest, beginning with a "teach-in" at the University of Utah and continuing with a march to the Federal Building in downtown Salt Lake City where speakers read the names of Utahns killed in Vietnam and called for an immediate withdrawal of U.S. forces from the war. The last major demonstration was on May 15, 1971, when several thousand protestors gathered at the State Capitol building for a rally and then marched to Pioneer Park, where six hundred more people joined them for another rally. Leading the march was a group of active-duty military personnel carrying a banner that read, "GIS AGAINST THE WAR." Following them were members of Vietnam Veterans Against the War wearing worn fatigues with their combat service medals attached. Founded in 1967, the VVAW expanded rapidly nationally, and in Utah as well, as soldiers returned home. It was a key group in anti-war efforts in Utah, as it was nationwide, and it has remained an important anti-war presence ever since.

The demonstration had been sponsored by the Wasatch Peace Action Coalition. One of its founders was Dayne Goodwin. From its earliest days, he was central to the growing anti–Vietnam War movement in Utah in the 1960s, and he has remained a full-time peace activist ever since. Bangs Tapscott, the first president of the Utah chapter of the Peace and Freedom Party, described him as "one of the most focused and single-minded radicals I've ever met" (Tapscott 10). Josh Gold called him "Salt Lake City's finest Peace and Justice activist," a person "fundamentally dedicated to stopping war and the social, political, and economic madness it requires" (Gold 496n). Any number of people credit Goodwin for their own activism and commitment. "Dayne Goodwin is my mentor and teacher," said Linda Parsons, who has been active in a number of groups, including the Wasatch Coalition for Peace and Justice, the Center for Economic Justice, Jobs with Justice, and the Green Party. "I'd hate to see Salt Lake City without him. He's just the core of what is organized anti-war and anti-globalization in this city" (Parsons 9). According to Isaac Giron, a founding member of the Brown Berets, Goodwin said to him before an anti–Iraq War rally in March 2004, "'You should go up there and speak. There aren't that many young Latino anti-war activists out there. Why don't you jump up there and say something?' So I did. And I've been speaking in almost every rally since" (Giron 3).

Goodwin's influence over nearly fifty years has been enormous. So has Robert "Archie" Archuleta's, and for an even longer period of time. Almost from the moment of his arrival in Utah in 1953, he has been involved in one way or another in virtually every peace and justice movement—organizing, marching, picketing, speaking, writing. "We were able to organize peace movements," he said, "able to organize anti-discrimination movements, pro civil rights, pro civil liberties." He was a founder of the Utah Coalition of La Raza; the Utah Migrant Council; the GI Forum; the Utah Peace Action Coalition; and the Utah Peace and Freedom Party, and an organizer of every anti–Vietnam War protest, and of virtually every protest of every war the United States has been involved in after that, including the invasion of Grenada, the Gulf War, and the Iraq War. "Almost anything that had to do with peace, I was there, I tried to be there," he said (Archuleta 15). Archuleta opposed not just particular wars, but all wars, and, like Goodwin, the structural conditions of the economic and political system that made militarism inevitable.

In his commitment to working for peace and justice, and the perspective he brought to it, Archuleta cited a number of influences, among them his mother's resistance to the blatant racism he and his family, and Latinos in general, experienced when he was growing up in

Colorado and Idaho; his sensitivity at an early age to issues of both race and class and their complex interplay; and his experiences following his move to Salt Lake City with men and women who had dedicated "almost their whole lives to fighting for peace, and so it infected me, and it was a good infection" (Archuleta 16). His study of U.S. history, "like taking the territory, nearly half of Mexico, taking Puerto Rico, taking the Philippine Islands, Guam, and even Hawaii in a way, Panama," also influenced him, he said, "so that it began to dawn on me that really, unless things change we'll continue to have one war after another, and that it was my lot in life to oppose that" (Archuleta 13).

An important anti–Vietnam War group in Utah in the 1960s was an affiliate of the Peace and Freedom Party (PFP). Many of its founders and most active members were faculty at the University of Utah, but it included others as well, both liberals and radicals. Its overarching goal was to legitimize and organize the left wing in Utah, and in addition to opposing the Vietnam War, it addressed a range of issues, including civil rights, gender equity, and the rights of labor. It began with a sense of optimism. "We thought we could do anything," Earl Jones said (Jones 3). His increasingly radical perspective was rooted in his experience growing up in Ogden, Utah. "I grew up with a sense of class," he recalled. His family was working class, "but there were families in my elementary school that were multi-millionaires, and I always felt uneasy around them, unsure about the implications of that.... I was a paperboy, delivering papers to the wealthiest community in Ogden, so I knew their homes, and I collected the monthly [dues].... I had face-to-face contact with them." He also delivered papers in one of the poorer sections of town, and "it was a good kind of lesson about class culture" (Jones 7). In 2007, nearly forty years after the founding of the Utah Peace and Freedom Party, Jones's politics had not changed. He saw the wars in Iraq and Afghanistan as not just "current aberrations of a good government, but they are just the latest in 150 years of U.S. imperialism.... I don't see very many people who are willing yet to say that capitalism corrupts everything it touches. That is the enemy. Corporate America is the enemy, or Global Corporate. It's now global.

They don't belong to any one country anymore, they're all over. So global capitalism is the enemy" (Jones 10).

The Utah Peace and Freedom Party candidate for the U.S. Senate in 1968 was Bruce "Utah" Phillips. Though he and the party knew he had no chance to win, they saw his campaign as a way to bring their perspective to the broader community. He polled some three thousand votes while telling Utah voters that he was less interested in electoral than in "confrontational" politics (*Salt Lake Tribune*, 25 Aug. 1968). After the election he left Utah to pursue a career as a professional storyteller who used "folksong and other materials as a form of artistic support" for his storytelling (Stewart 225), and he often returned to Utah to perform, for example at the Joe Hill Memorial Concert on Labor Day, 1991, which marked the seventy-fifth anniversary of Joe Hill's execution. Like Hill, Phillips was a member of the radical labor union the Industrial Workers of the World (IWW). As a Wobbly he indicted capitalism as an unethical system that exploited workers, and many of his songs and stories focused on the "casualties of the profit system" and the "class war between rich and poor, between those who create wealth and those who merely own it." His point of view was reflected in his own compositions, such as "Room for the Poor," and in the Wobbly songs that he both performed and recorded, including "All Used Up" and "Dump the Bosses Off Your Back."

Much of what Phillips sought to do through his songs and stories was to convey a sense of the past that might help lay the foundation for the radical change the IWW envisioned, and he was impatient with those who dismissed the past as irrelevant. He was interested in telling stories—the kind often left out—of strikes, and labor leaders like Mother Jones, and tramps and ordinary workers. In his view, "the long memory is the most radical idea in the country. It is the loss of that long memory which deprives our people of that connective flow of thoughts and events that clarifies our vision, not of where we're going, but where we want to go" (Phillips and Sorrels). Anti-nuclear activist Mary Dickson made a similar point in talking about the potency of the "eraser" and the importance of combating efforts to erase particular events from people's memory (Dickson 16). By the 1990s Phillips had come to believe that the tactics activists had engaged in for so long—mass demonstrations, sit-ins, civil disobedience, vigils—were no longer effective. "That's why the peace movement isn't working," he said, "because everything we do is totally predictable. And it all has to change" (Phillips 8). It was a point more and more Utah radicals would raise—the extent to which traditional tactics might be replaced with ones more effective, including street theater.

Ammon Hennacy was a significant influence on Utah Phillips, leading him to conclude that "I needed to become a pacifist" (Phillips 6), as well as on other activists in Utah and throughout the United States. Part of the Old Left, Hennacy continued to believe that labor and workers would be the instrument for bringing about fundamental change. That put him at odds in some ways with the emergent New Left of the 1960s, while Phillips, in contrast, sought to bridge the gap between the two. Born in Ohio in 1893, Hennacy joined both the Socialist Party of America and the IWW as a young man; served two years in prison for his opposition to World War I; worked with Dorothy Day and her Catholic Worker movement in New York City throughout the 1920s and 1930s; and spent most of the 1940s and 1950s active in a variety of peace and social justice movements in the southwestern United States and writing for the *Catholic Worker* newspaper, while earning a living as a day laborer. He came to Utah in 1961 to spread the philosophy of Christian anarchism, and until his death nine years later was an influential member of Utah's radical community, conducting his "one-man revolution" of picketing, fasting, letter writing, education, and acts of civil disobedience on behalf of anarchism, pacifism, and opposition to capital punishment. He established the Joe Hill House, named for the IWW songwriter and organizer of the early twentieth century, and modeled on Dorothy Day's shelter for homeless men and women in New York City. Every year on the anniversary of the dropping of the atomic bomb on Hiroshima on August 6, 1945, he fasted and picketed in front of the Federal Building in Salt Lake City one day for each year since the United States had dropped the bomb. He picketed in front of the LDS Church Office Building to demand the Church's support for open housing; he called it to account for not opposing the Vietnam War; and he nailed lists of questions on the chancery next to the Cathedral of the Madeleine demanding that the Catholic Church explain why it did not speak out against the war. On January 5, 1970, at age seventy-six, he walked up the steep State Street hill in Salt Lake City to the Utah State Capitol building to picket on behalf of two convicted murderers who were scheduled for execution. On the fourth day he collapsed, struck by a heart attack, and died six days later.[2]

The Utah Peace and Freedom Party lasted for less than two years and then dissolved. There seem to have been two reasons. In the first place many of its members were worn out. "A lot of people had been literally eating and sleeping Peace and Freedom Party and doing their job on the side," Earl Jones said. "It was a lot of work, and it did detract from my own personal work. It was nice to get back to that. And after it was over…I just kind of went back to work with my painting and my own career and I haven't really been fully engaged or involved in anything since," though his political values and orientation have not changed (Jones 6). Secondly, internal divisions, historically a problem for the Left, worked to undue the PFP. "At some point some people within that group became much more radicalized and became followers of what was called then I believe the Progressive Labor Party," explained Bruce Landesman, the Peace and Freedom Party's last president.

> It was a Maoist inspired party.… There was a split between those of us who were more moderate and less ideological and wanted the organization to continue on fundamentally devoted to ending the war and promoting civil rights, and those who wanted to turn it into a Marxist organization and parade an ideology that the rest of us thought would have no popular appeal. This led… some of the more ideological people to quit and that led ultimately to the ending of the whole movement. (Landesman 5)

A flourishing counterculture, intertwined with peace and justice movements, emerged in Utah in the 1960s, as it did nationwide. Thus, a 1969 Grateful Dead concert at the University of Utah was a fund-raiser for Students for a Democratic Society (SDS), and the Cosmic Aeroplane bookstore and "head shop" in Salt Lake City housed a draft counseling center and hosted a range of radical speakers and events. Ken Sanders Rare Books has served much the same function since it opened in the late 1990s. "The twelve years that this store has been here, good god almighty, it would have been hard to book more anti-war events in this store than during the Bush Occupation years," Sanders said. "One of the most powerful things we ever did here was during the original four Bush years. We had Gino Sky and Ray Obermayer, two Idaho poets, come down here." Obermayer "took this whole wall of the store and put up these series of really ugly paintings that had three dimensional objects and giant spikes pounded into them.... He apologized for the ugliness of the art, but [said] because of the subject it had to be ugly.... He wrote this long narrative poem about his incarceration and his torture" during World War II. "This was right at the exact time that Abu Ghraib was coming out and the interrogation methods were identical, they waterboarded him then" (Sanders 23). At another anti-war rally at the bookstore, Utah poet Alex Caldiero, who intended that some of his poetry have an "overt political edge to it," recited out of a gas mask as an act of peacemaking (Caldiero 10). Caldiero's intent was to contribute to a new vocabulary and way of thinking, to what Debbie Johnson, of Military Families Speak Out, called a "change of consciousness" (Johnson 9). On another occasion, Sanders said, "We were fortunate enough to get Anne Waldman to do a reading here. She's an old beat poet that is one of the most striking anti-war poets we have.... She doesn't just get up and read a poem, she sings them, she performs them." For Sanders, as for Utah Phillips, such events were more consequential than rallies. "What the hell are we going to accomplish at a rally?" he asked (Phillips 24).

After a period of relative quiet following the end of the Vietnam War, groups on the left posing radical challenges to the status quo reemerged. Thus, in the early 1980s the Committee in Solidarity with the People of El Salvador (CISPES) and the Central America Solidarity Coalition (CASC) sought to build a movement opposing Reagan-Bush administration policies in Central America specifically and the fundamentals of U.S. foreign policy more generally, while supporters of Democratic Socialists of America (DSA) formed a coalition to put socialism back on the political agenda in Utah. The DSA was founded in 1982 as a result of a merger of the Democratic Socialist Organizing Committee, led by Michael Harrington, and the New American Movement, a coalition closely identified with the New Left of the 1960s. A Utah DSA chapter was formed in May 1983. Over the next several years it published a monthly newsletter; sponsored public forums; brought national DSA leaders to the state, including Harrington, as well as civil rights and labor leaders, among them Cesar Chavez; participated in national DSA conventions and commissions; and supported local efforts of CASC and CISPES, including co-sponsoring a fall 1984 march and rally protesting President Reagan's visit to Salt Lake City to speak at the national convention of the American Legion as part of his reelection campaign.

After several vibrant years, Utah's DSA chapter dissolved for the same reasons the Peace and Freedom Party had eighteen years earlier—burnout of many of its members and internal divisions. Even so, explicitly socialist groups have continued to be active in the state. Utah Socialists was organized in August 1980. It emphasized the necessity of democratic structure, process, and practice in a socialist movement and in a future socialist society; support for the liberation struggles of women, people of color, gays and lesbians, and the differently abled; and a global perspective. Since then several other socialist groups, including Youth 4 Socialist Action, Solidarity, and the Wasatch Socialist Party, have also been founded, and in 2016 a new Utah chapter of Democratic Socialists of America was organized.

As Utah approached the end of the twentieth century, another generation of Utah radicals sought ways to bring about fundamental change. Again, a few examples, among many, make the point. In 1994 a Salt Lake City branch of the international group Food Not Bombs (FNB) began serving free hot vegetarian meals to homeless people at various locations in the downtown area. The group also had branches in other Utah cities and towns, including Ogden, Provo, and Price. FNB's first local had been organized in Massachusetts in 1980. Its cofounders, C. T. Butler and Keith McHenry, were both raised in Logan, Utah. "The name Food Not Bombs," they said,

> states our most fundamental principle: society needs to promote life, not death. Our society condones, and even promotes, violence and domination.... Food Not Bombs has chosen to take a stand against violence and hunger; we are committed to nonviolent social change by giving out free vegetarian food, thus celebrating and nurturing life.... We want to replace the culture of death with a culture of "Plumbers Not Bombs," "Daycare Not Bombs," and "Health Care Not Bombs." (Butler and McHenry 71–72)

FNB's message was "simple and powerful," historian Howard Zinn wrote: "No consideration of money, no demand for profit, should stand in the way of any hungry or malnourished child or any adult in need. Here are people who will not be bamboozled by 'the laws of the market' that say only people who can afford to buy something can have it" (Zinn ix–x).

Other radical groups of the last dozen years or so have included People for Peace and Justice; the Committee for War Criminals Prosecution; Salt Lake Code Pink; Students for Freedom and Democracy; Cache Valley Peace Works; Dialogue for Peace; Revolutionary Students Union; and the Wasatch Coalition for Peace and Justice (WCPJ), an umbrella group of more than two dozen peace and justice organizations. Its mission statement clearly indicated its radical potential: it called for an end to U.S. military intervention in the Middle East and throughout the world; supported the Palestinian people's right to self-determination; advocated that "U.S. tax dollars be used for Public Needs—food, housing, health care, education, environmental protection and economic security for all—not for war"; supported constitutional and workers' rights for everyone living in the United States; affirmed the inherent value and equality of all people; and held that racist views of any group, including Arabs and Jews, were antithetical to movements for peace and justice ("About the Wasatch Coalition").

Among the groups of the WCPJ were the Brown Berets and a Utah chapter of the national organization Veterans for Peace. In addition to supporting the coalition's mission statement, they each addressed particular concerns falling under it. Founded in April 2006, the Brown Berets described itself as a working-class, community-based, direct action organization established in opposition to other Latino groups that it considered "way too polite to the system" (Giron 3). It promised to fight for "better living conditions for our people and all oppressed people all over the world" and, as a "reactivation" of the 1960s group of the same name, saw itself as "the next generation of revolutionaries in Utah." According to one of its founders, Isaac Giron, its membership was relatively young, ranging in age from eighteen to early thirties, and just about evenly divided between males and females. Giron described himself as a "Chicano militant…an activist, fighting and struggling for the people.… It's become my life, what I live for," and he operated from a deep sense of outrage. "I'm just sick of it," he said. "I'm sick of my people being what Oscar Zeta Acosta called the cockroach people because everyone steps on them. But regardless they keep coming back. That's how my people are, that's what our reality is.… The cultural poverty, the destruction of the culture of our indigenous ancestors, it all combined has just pissed me off." His activism, he said, was part of a long tradition of which he was deeply proud. His mother was the daughter of a guerrilla in El Salvador. "Now I truly feel like I'm the continuation of the struggle my grandfather fought. I'm the continuation of the struggle my uncle died for in El Salvador and my family in Guatemala, in Quiche, the Mayan people, what they fought for and what they continue to fight for" (Giron 7). Who was the enemy? "The Capitalists, that's how I see it," he said. "The people who are running the country, the people whose money and whose interest the soldiers are fighting for in Iraq. The people who came to the Americas looking for gold in order to bring the riches back to the Queen of Spain and the Roman Church. Those people, the greedy people, racists, the people that are our class enemies, the ones that exploit the poor.… Those are the enemies. They've always been the enemy" (Giron 7–8).

Because Utah was so conservative politically, Giron said, peace and justice activists in the state were "real strong and real tough and real dedicated in what they believe in.… It makes the people that are activists, dedicated activists. They go all the way for their struggle" (Giron 6). And he was optimistic that the activism of the Brown Berets would make a difference, if not immediately, then in the long run. "It just takes a lot of time.... The struggle is far from over. We've still got a long way to go in order to truly see what we're going to accomplish with our struggle" (Giron 6–7).

Veterans for Peace was "dedicated to building a culture of peace, exposing the true costs of war, and healing the wounds of war" ("Who We Are"). Following his arrival in Utah in 2004, Dr. Robert Littlehale, a physician who had been in the Army Medical Corps in Vietnam, became active in the Utah chapter. For him it was important not only "to bring the troops back from Iraq and treat them with dignity and respect once they got home" and recognize that "they would be damaged physically, spiritually, and emotionally and certainly with some form of PTSD," but also to oppose U.S. "militarism" and the "exporting of violence" throughout the world, which, in his view, was not an aberration, but a long-standing feature of the country's history (Littlehale 3). A priority for him, and other Utah members of Veterans for Peace, was what he called "counter-recruiting"—speaking to high school and college students about the misleading information military recruiters provided when they spoke to students (Littlehale 3–4).

Utah Veterans for Peace also emphasized the importance of networking with other peace and justice groups. "There is not enough unification or networking among the various peaceniks, as I call them," Littlehale said. "In Utah there is an uphill battle because...it is the belly of the beast. It is a place where traditional values are held and where there is a certain unanimity of opinion for the war with the notion that 'might makes right'" (Littlehale 5).

One strategy Utah Veterans for Peace employed in their work to educate people about the realities of war was guerrilla street theater. Larry Chadwick, a founder of Utah Veterans for Peace, and later president of the Utah chapter of Vietnam Veterans Against the War, described an occasion when the latter group held a "mock search and destroy mission" in Salt Lake City in the early 1970s. As part of it, he said, "we set up our night camping position, just like we would in Vietnam, on the

Governor's lawn." The goal was to call attention to the growing number of Vietnam veterans who opposed the war and to provide a sense of the realities of war to city residents who were far from a war zone. "We wanted to get people talking about the war," Chadwick said. "What I was convinced of, and I still am today, if people will talk about it, if people will debate, no matter how hot they debate it, they will come to some essence of truth" (Chadwick 4–5). Similar events took place across the United States. One of them, Operation Rapid American Withdrawal (RAW), was a four-day event over Labor Day weekend 1970 that included an eighty-six-mile march from Morristown, New Jersey, to Valley Forge State Park in Pennsylvania that culminated in a four-hour rally that more than fifteen hundred people attended. The march was designed to dramatize the kind of search-and-destroy missions U.S. soldiers conducted in Vietnam. As marchers passed through towns on their way to Valley Forge, they made group sweeps, took and interrogated prisoners, seized property, and cleared houses with the aid of previously planted actors portraying citizens. According to Al Hubbard, one of Operation RAW's organizers, "we plan to demonstrate how, when troops move into a town, they sometimes snatch people out of a crowd and search them to see if, for example, they're carrying proper ID cards, or because they're suspected of harboring Viet Cong" (Hunt 46–47).

Since the end of the Vietnam War, groups in Utah working for peace and justice have continued to embrace guerrilla street theater. For example, Pom Poms, Not Bomb Bombs, Utah's Radical Cheerleaders, founded in 2003, sought to provide an answer to the question of how to make a difference in a conservative state when traditional tactics such as marches and rallies seemed increasingly ineffective. Their response was guerrilla street theater—not to replace marches and rallies, but as an additional tactic. They performed at anti-war rallies, at Utah's annual Pride Day celebrations, at the State Capitol building on the opening days of the state legislature, and on other occasions on behalf of a range of issues, including peace, women's reproductive rights, and gay rights, devising cheers based on the particular issue they were addressing.

The cheerleaders dressed "funky," co-founder Deanna Taylor said. "A lot of what we wear is red t-shirts, with 'Free Speech Zone' on the front.... And black bottoms, like garbage bag skirts or just black pants or skirt" (Taylor 13). During a weekend in Washington, DC, in September 2006, when the group participated in Camp Democracy, they wore prisoner-like outfits of black-and-white stripes and large papier-mậché heads of President Bush, Vice President Dick Cheney, Secretary of Defense Donald Rumsfeld, and other members of the Bush administration, whom they called the "Bush Chain Gang," at speeches, rallies, vigils, and other occasions, and they handed out cards in restaurants and bars and on city sidewalks containing information about the "war crimes of the Bush administration." "It is so enlightening," Taylor said, "to see people's faces. They're shaking their heads in agreement and laughing with you. It's different than just going up to them, as me, a regular person, and handing them a piece of literature" (Taylor 16).

Taylor was also active in other groups, including People for Peace and Justice of Utah, of which she was a founding member; Justice, Economic Dignity, and Independence for Women (JEDI Women); Citizens Action Network; the Divine Strake Coalition; and the Green Party. She and her husband, Tom King, came to feel strongly that they "couldn't be arm chair activists anymore, that we had to do something.... I have children and I now have a grandson and one on the way," she said. "I feel like I can't sit by and be silent anymore.... I just think about the future and the example that I want to set for my kids. A lot of times they'll say to me, 'Mom don't tell me what you are doing, because I'm afraid you're going to get arrested.' And I have been arrested before. I haven't told them that. But I can't sit by idly.... I am an advocate of civil resistance as a last resort after you've tried everything else" (Taylor 9–12).

For Michael Minch, professor of philosophy and director of Peace and Justice Studies at Utah Valley University, doing peace and justice work in Utah was challenging because of "a bizarre, inexplicable attitude, disposition, suspicion that's pervasive in Utah...that is not welcoming to justice and peacemaking communities, and strategies and discourse, and is often hostile to it." In addition, he said, "we don't live in a very diverse culture here. And I think diversity is a part of what drives concern for peace and justice and strategies for peace and justice" (Minch 6). From this Minch drew two conclusions. The first was the importance of continuing to act because it was "the right thing to do, the truthful thing to do." That realization began, he said, when "I read the Bible and took it seriously in a way I hadn't before," and he came to a "robust and solid conclusion that Jesus disallows violence. And to be a follower of Jesus means one must renounce violence. It's ipso facto. It's non-negotiable. To take Jesus seriously means one has to...wage peace. That was in the late seventies. I've been a peace maker, to whatever degree I've been one, from that point onward," with the ultimate goal of not only addressing particular issues but working to create "justice and egalitarian economic and social systems" (Minch 2).

Minch acknowledged that for many activists religious beliefs were not the basis of their thought and action. His point, however, was the importance of an ethical commitment, whatever its source, as the basis of activism, and the necessity of living a life consistent with one's values. That was true as well for other Utah radicals. The question Chris Foster asked himself was, "What do I have an ethical obligation to do?" More specifically, "Am I willing to jeopardize my job and my career on behalf of my values?" and under certain circumstances, he concluded, the obligation to act outweighed everything else (Foster 19–20). For Rick Miller, "I can't be a peace activist unless I walk every step of the path all the time. I have to be a peaceful person myself" (Miller 9). That meant, for example, that he became a vegetarian because he did not want to be responsible for killing. Diana Lee Hirschi's long-term commitment to peacemaking eventually led her to become a "total pacifist" and a Quaker. "I went to my first Quaker meeting," she said, "and I thought, 'Oh, this is great! I love this!' And my daughter said on the way home, 'Well, Mom are we Quakers now?' and I said, 'Yup.'" Several years later she quit her full-time job to "work for nuclear disarmament." That meant joining the protests at the Nevada Nuclear Test Site and living for most of a year at the peace camp there. Hirschi was also one of the three people arrested for protesting at the gates of a company that made components for Trident missiles. "I've been arrested more times than

I ever thought to count," she said, and her long-term pacifist commitment was costly. "We don't have any money," she said. "I have no health insurance. I have no security whatsoever. This is an interesting test of all my beliefs" (Hirschi 6). Carla Hintz joined Military Families Speak Out because she saw the Iraq War as "unforgiveable and unconscionable" and not worth the life of one American soldier. She felt an ethical obligation to act on her beliefs, and her commitment was unrelenting. "I can't be sold," she said. "I can't be cajoled. I can't. My responsibility as a citizen goes far beyond the ballot box. If only it were so easy that we do our civic duty and punch a lever on election day and then leave the rest to fate. That's not how it works, especially when it comes to committing a nation to war" (Hintz 12). Linda Parsons likewise found herself "fully in an activist mode, I hope for the rest of my life" (Parsons 2). A socialist, deeply critical of the capitalist economic system, she was involved in particular with the Center for Economic Justice, Jobs with Justice, and the Wasatch Coalition for Peace and Justice. "Activism," she said, "brings out the best in all of us. It brings out the best in me. It gives my life purpose. I'm passionate about what I do and feel. I feel that to work towards social and economic justice is a very precious thing. I'm glad I can do it. I hope someday for a revolution. I hope I live to see a revolution" (Parsons 11). Hans Ehrbar emphasized the importance of doing peace and justice work in Utah and not minimizing its significance or wishing he was somewhere else in a more hospitable environment where he might be part of a larger group and feel that he was more effective. "You just have to be where you are and push the envelope there," he said. "That's how we can make change.... Life put me here. That's where I am and that's where I have to try to be effective and, as I said, everyone pushing the envelope in the place where you are, that's how you can get change because if lots of people do this you can rely on other people doing the same thing" (Ehrbar 13). Such work was rewarding, Ehrbar said, and he felt "privileged" to be able to do it. At the same time, in common with many other leftists, he struggled to remain optimistic. On the one hand he found himself saying, "I think we will be amazed how quick changes can come." On the other hand, "I'm kind of pessimistic about it. I think the chances that we can turn it around and have some good outcomes may be 20 percent. Eighty percent it's going to be barbarism." In his view the future would be either socialism or barbarism, and he feared it would be the latter (Ehrbar 15).

Minch's second point, and another common theme for Utah leftists, was that sustaining the commitment to do the ethically right thing and combating a sense of isolation, impotence, and discouragement required being part of a community. "The response of our society and the response of our culture and the response of people in general to peace is fear and hostility," he said. "And dismissiveness. But all peacemakers need to be a part of a peacemaking community, a peaceable community. Some particle of what Martin Luther King called 'The Beloved Community.' We need to have some connection to a community of peace to be peacemakers. It cannot work any other way, or else you will just give in to cynicism. You will wear down and wear out" (Minch 7). In the view of longtime activist Brenda Chung, it takes considerable courage and commitment to be a peace activist in Utah, "where you know you are by far the minority." But, she said, it was important to keep at it because there are a "fairly large group of people in Utah who actually are for peace, are anti-war, but they feel like they're the only one that feels that way. They feel isolated. They just don't feel there's any point, or any place for them to speak out." So, she said, regular events, like weekly peace vigils or rallies, provide evidence to people who feel that way that they are not alone, that others feel the way they do, and so "they join, or slowly they speak up a little bit, or slowly they feel a little more hopeful." In Utah, she thought, "It's both more difficult but also really more important to carry on with peace activism" (Chung 17).

During the period under consideration here, the mid-twentieth century to the early years of the twenty-first, radical Left movements for peace and justice, and those with radical potential, have been a constant presence in Utah, finding expression in a number of ways. Some were short-lived, while others were longer lasting. The important point, though, is that while particular expressions have come and gone, the underlying impulse, deeply rooted in earlier radical movements, and addressing a range of issues, has remained. This goes against the expectations of many people. It is still common to think of Utah as so conservative that such movements never existed or, to the extent they did, were of little consequence. This view, however, is both simplistic and ahistorical, essentially equating Utah's conservative present with its past and oversimplifying both. Utah has always been enormously complex, its history the story of many peoples, experiences, and voices. Part of that complexity—and evidence for it—is a continuing radical presence.

What I've said here is only a sketch of what could easily be a much longer discussion. It leaves out much and only begins to address the questions I asked at the beginning of the essay. An expanded discussion would look in greater depth at the groups and individuals I've discussed and would examine many more specific events and actions they undertook, and it would examine subjects I've almost entirely neglected, from the civil rights movement to the women's movement to the anti-apartheid movement, the LGBTQI rights movement, the Occupy movement, the Black Lives Matter movement, and the environmental movement—and more. Such an undertaking would provide a more complex sense of the past, one less narrow and exclusionary than that prevailing for so long. Accounts of radical activism are not just subplots in a larger epic that remains essentially unchanged. They not only complicate the story, but lead to a fundamentally different one, making all the more pressing questions such as, To whom does the past belong? Who has the right to recover their histories, and who does not? Who will be acknowledged and heard and who will not? Whose interests will be served and at whose expense?

Notes

1. They include Cache Valley Peace Works; Cache Citizens Opposed to the Nuclear Arms Race; Department of Peace; Code Pink; Democratic Socialists of America; Dialogue for Peace; Not in Our Name; Peace Activists United; Utahns Against Hunger; Utahns for a Nuclear Weapons Freeze; Utahns United Against the Nuclear Arms Race; Interfaith Peacemaking Resource Center; Utah Physicians for Social Responsibility; Utah Peace Test; Never Again; Peace and Freedom Party; Healthy Environment Alliance of Utah; Alternative Community; Students for a Democratic Society; Student Mobilization to End the War in Southeast Asia;

United Front Against the War; Utah Workers Alliance; Writing to Stop Nuclear Testing; Community Abuse Prevention Service Agency; Peace Brigade; Military Families Speak Out; Veterans for Peace; Vietnam Veterans Against the War; Utah Coalition to End the War; Utahns for a Just Peace in the Holy Land; Occupation NO! Peace and Justice for Palestine; Green Party; More Light Presbyterians; Mormons for Equality and Social Justice; MX Information Center; We the People for Peace and Justice; Utahns for Clean Air; Wasatch Coalition for Peace and Justice; National Conference of Communities and Justice; Utahns United; Utah Women Unite; Women Concerned About Nuclear War; Women's Forum; Utah Indivisible; Sustainability Salon; Central America Solidarity Coalition; Committee in Solidarity with the People of El Salvador; Divine Strake Coalition; Citizen's Education Project; Citizens Action Network; Citizens Call; Utah Clergy and Laity Concerned; Society of Survival; Downwinders; Peace Works; Peaceful Uprising: Defending a Livable Future Through Empowering Non-Violent Action; Brine Shrimp Alliance; American Indian Movement; Brown Berets; Revolutionary Students Union; Gay Liberation Front; Queer Nation; ACT UP; Parents, Families and Friends of Lesbians and Gays; Pride at Work; Utah Coalition of Gay, Lesbian, and Bi Union Activists and Supporters; Utah's Familia: Trans Queer Liberation Movement; Doctors and Nurses Against the War; Food Not Bombs; Pom Poms Not Bomb Bombs! Utah's Radical Cheerleaders; Culture Jammers; Crossroads Urban Center; Community Coalition Center of Utah; Utah Issues; Justice, Economic Dignity, and Independence for Women (JEDI Women); Disability Rights Action Committee; Utahns Against Hunger; G.I. Forum; El Centro Civico Mexicano; Spanish Speaking Organization for Community, Integrity, and Opportunity; Utah Coalition of La Raza; Joe Hill Club; Gandhi Alliance for Peace; Utah Peace Action Coalition; Northern Utah Peace Alliance; Utah Peace House; Peace and Justice Commission, Utah Catholic Diocese; U.S. Labor Against the War; Utah Jobs with Justice; Utah Socialists; Wasatch Socialist Party; Solidarity; Utah Veterans Against the War; Veterans Peace Coalition; Twisted Sisters; Youth 4 Socialist Action; Occupy Salt Lake; Peace Advocacy Coalition; Black Lives Matter; Word Warriors; and Peaceful Advocates for Native Dialogue and Organizing Support.

2. Hennacy published two books: a memoir, *The Book of Ammon* (n.p., 1965); and *The One-Man Revolution in America* (Ammon Hennacy Publications, 1970). For insightful discussions of Hennacy's life and thought, see Amy Maestas, "Ammon Hennacy: A One-Man Revolution," *The Event* [Salt Lake City], 14–28 Mar. 1996, pp. 8–12, and Patrick G. Coy, "The One-Person Revolution of Ammon Hennacy," *A Revolution of the Heart: Essays on the Catholic Worker*, edited by Patrick G. Coy, Temple UP, 1988, pp. 134–73.

Bibliography

"About the Wasatch Coalition for Peace and Justice," wasatchpeaceandjustice.org/aboutus.htm.

Anderson, Ross C. (Rocky). Transcript of interview with Kathryn French, 3 Oct. 2007, Sutherland Archives, Utah Valley University, Orem, Utah.
Archuleta, Robert "Archie." Transcript of interview with Kathryn French, 26 Jan. 2009, Sutherland Archives, Utah Valley University, Orem, Utah.
Berman, David R. *Radicalism in the Intermountain West, 1890–1920: Socialists, Populists, Miners, and Wobblies.* UP of Colorado, 2007.
Butler, C. T., and Keith McHenry. *Food Not Bombs.* Sharp Press, 2000.
Caldiero, Alex. Transcript of interview with Kathryn French, 5 Feb. 2008, Sutherland Archives, Utah Valley University, Orem, Utah.
Chadwick, Larry. Transcript of interview with Kathryn French, 1 Jul. 2006, Sutherland Archives, Utah Valley University, Orem, Utah.
Chung, Brenda. Transcript of interview with Kathryn French, 14 Apr. 2008, Sutherland Archives, Utah Valley University, Orem, Utah.
Dickson, Mary. Transcript of interview with Kathryn French, 13 Oct. 2007, Sutherland Archives, Utah Valley University, Orem, Utah.
Ehrbar, Hans. Transcript of interview with Kathryn French, 4 Apr. 2008, Sutherland Archives, Utah Valley University, Orem, Utah.
Ehrenreich, Barbara. *Dancing in the Streets: A History of Collective Joy.* Metropolitan Books, 2006.
Foster, Chris. Transcript of interview with JoEllen Perez, 20 May 2009, Sutherland Archives, Utah Valley University, Orem, Utah.
Giron, Isaac. Transcript of interview with Kathryn French, 7 Nov. 2006, Sutherland Archives, Utah Valley University, Orem, Utah.
Gold, Josh. "Learning About Peace and Justice Work." *Journal of the Utah Academy of Sciences, Arts, & Letters*, vol. 88, 2011, pp. 495–512.
Hintz, Carla. Transcript of interview with Kathryn French, 17 Sept. 2007, Sutherland Archives, Utah Valley University, Orem, Utah.
Hirschi, Diana Lee. Transcript of interview with Kathryn French, 13 Apr. 2007, Sutherland Archives, Utah Valley University, Orem, Utah.
Hunt, Andrew E. *The Turning: A History of Vietnam Veterans Against the War.* New York UP, 1999.
Johnson, Debbie. Transcript of interview with Kathryn French, 9 Feb. 2007, Sutherland Archives, Utah Valley University, Orem, Utah.
Jones, Earl. Transcript of interview with Kathryn French, 13 Apr. 2007, Sutherland Archives, Utah Valley University, Orem, Utah.
Landesman, Bruce. Transcript of interview with Kathryn French, 12 Sept. 2006, Sutherland Archives, Utah Valley University, Orem, Utah.
Levine, Deb. Transcript of interview with Kathryn French, 20 May 2008, Sutherland Archives, Utah Valley University, Orem, Utah.
Littlehale, Robert. Transcript of interview with Kathryn French, 18 May 2006, Sutherland Archives, Utah Valley University, Orem, Utah.

McCormick, John S., and John R. Sillito. *A History of Utah Radicalism: Startling, Socialistic, and Decidedly Revolutionary*. Utah State UP, 2011.

Miller, Rick. Transcript of interview with Kathryn French, 10 Jul. 2007, Sutherland Archives, Utah Valley University, Orem, Utah.

Minch, Michael. Transcript of interview with Kathryn French, 15 May 2006, Sutherland Archives, Utah Valley University, Orem, Utah.

Parsons, Linda. Transcript of interview with Kathryn French, 1 Apr. 2006, Sutherland Archives, Utah Valley University, Orem, Utah.

Phillips, Bruce "Utah." Transcript of interview with Kathryn French, 6 May 2006, Sutherland Archives, Utah Valley University, Orem, Utah.

Phillips, U. Utah, and Rosalie Sorrels. Liner notes to compact disc, *The Long Memory*, Round House Records, 1996.

Plenk, Bruce. Transcript of interview with Kathryn French, 23 Feb. 2008, Sutherland Archives, Utah Valley University, Orem, Utah.

Rowland, Dee. Transcript of interview with Kathryn French, 12 Sept. 2006, Sutherland Archives, Utah Valley University, Orem, Utah.

Sanders, Ken. Transcript of interview with Kathryn French, 2 Jun. 2009, Sutherland Archives, Utah Valley University, Orem, Utah.

Staker, Brian. "Don't Shoot, I'm an Artist!" *City Weekly* [Salt Lake City], 23 Feb. 2017, p. 18.

Stewart, Polly. "Urban Pioneers: The Folk-Music Revival in Utah, 1959–1966." *Utah Historical Quarterly*, vol. 74, Summer 2006, pp. 220–30.

Tapscott, Bangs. Transcript of interview with Kathryn French, 6 Oct. 2006, Sutherland Archives, Utah Valley University, Orem, Utah.

Taylor, Deanna. Transcript of interview with Kathryn French, 9 Nov. 2007, Sutherland Archives, Utah Valley University, Orem, Utah.

Van Wagenen, Will. Transcript of interview with Kindra Amott, 24 Nov. 2008, Sutherland Archives, Utah Valley University, Orem, Utah.

"Vote Socialist Workers Nancy Boyasko for City Council District 4." Campaign flyer, copy in possession of author.

Wharton, Paul. Transcript of interview with Kathryn French, 7 Feb. 2007, Sutherland Archives, Utah Valley University, Orem, Utah.

"Who We Are." *Veterans for Peace*, veteransforpeace.org/who-we-are/our-mission. Accessed 22 June 2018.

Yengich, Ron. Transcript of interview with Kathryn French, 14 Apr. 2008, Sutherland Archives, Utah Valley University, Orem, Utah.

Zinn, Howard. "Foreword." *Food Not Bombs*, by C. T. Butler and Keith McHenry, Sharp Press, 2000.

2

Deep Ecology in Humboldt County

Bill Devall and a Philosophy for Action

DANIEL RINN

Too often, philosophers are rendered impotent
by their inability to act
without analyzing everything to absurd detail.

—DAVE FOREMAN, 1983

In thinking, talking, and writing about environmental ethics,
environmental philosophers
already have their shoulders to the wheel.

—J. BAIRD CALLICOTT, 1999

There seems to be a gulf separating the work of environmental activists and philosophers. The abstruse writing of cloistered academics can appear ineffectual to a seasoned activist who is interested in direct action. As Dave Foreman, co-founder of Earth First!, once argued, an instinctual understanding of environmental rights is enough to spur activism (Foreman). Philosophers, of course, are hardly unaware of the concern expressed by figures such as Foreman. Indeed, Andrew Light has argued that environmental philosophy is too focused on questions concerning metaphysics, rendering the task of translating theory to practice difficult, if not impossible (Light). Although it is important to analyze and debate the status of humanity in the natural world, disagreements in the murky field of metaphysics should not overshadow the common ground environmentalists share. For other thinkers, however, underlying metaphysical commitments are at the heart of environmental problems. Environmental ethics cannot move forward until philosophers close the debate between ecocentrism and anthropocentrism. For this reason, J. Baird Callicott suggests philosophers are "helping to reconfigure the prevailing cultural worldview and thus helping to push general practice in the direction of environmental responsibility" (Callicott, "Beyond the Land Ethic" 43).

An old debate that has surfaced periodically in the history of the Left, the tension between theory and practice entered a unique context with the advent of the environmental movement. Environmental philosophy is impossible to separate from action in a particular context. We rarely develop neat metaphysical positions independent of how we interact with our surroundings. Theory and practice are deeply entangled with a sense of place, a phenomenon that is readily on display in the environmental writing of Bill Devall (1938–2009). Although he was a thoroughgoing deep ecologist, Devall's theoretical commitments were not anchored solely in the abstractions often associated with philosophy. He shared Callicott's ambition to "reconfigure the prevailing cultural worldview," but his work simultaneously reflected Foreman's radicalism as well as a commitment to understanding dissenting perspectives. As a result, the development of Devall's work was complex, reflecting the various ways in which ideas, environment, and historical context are embedded in a causal web with no single point of origin.

Devall's ecological writing rested at the confluence of New Left politics, an emerging environmental movement, and his rich experiences in the American West. Coming of age in the postwar United States certainly filtered his view of the world; he belonged to a larger countercultural moment that witnessed the expression of various forms of radicalism. As Devall's fondness for Humboldt County, California, illustrates in the extreme, however, larger currents are never unaffected by the relationships that bind a person to a specific place. Although he channeled the New Left and a number of environmental philosophers in his criticism of American consumption, it was his experience of the redwoods that imbued his writing with both sobriety and passion.

Devall seamlessly integrated his experiences and ideas into a body of work that operated on two distinct levels. His time on the North Coast pushed him to adopt both a metaphysical monism and a pragmatic methodology—a feature of his thinking that wedded theory and practice. Historically, deep ecology was predicated on a monistic ontology, a belief that humans are part of a larger natural whole. In his effort to carefully expand and interrogate his own environmental outlook, Devall was drawn to this family of ideas as he gravitated to the more radical wing of environmental thought. As a form of ecocentric thinking, deep ecology easily aligned with an environmental activism that sought immediate, sweeping changes in how humans interacted with the nonhuman world. Devall, however, also understood the limits of environmental philosophy. Having witnessed firsthand the debates between environmentalists and loggers in Humboldt, he was receptive to the concerns of those who feared the economic repercussions of new environmental regulations and the choice to lead a green lifestyle. He could easily cross the line dividing the reform and radical wings of the environmental movement and the Left more generally. His writing was thus marked by a commitment to understanding opposing views. Philosophy, history, and autobiography intermingled in his work as he aimed to appeal to theorists, practitioners, and those who remained critical of environmentalism.[1]

We're Not in Kansas Anymore: Becoming Native to Humboldt County

William Bert Devall was born in Kansas City in 1938 during the final years of the Great Depression and before World War II. During the war, his father worked long hours in a factory manufacturing boats for the military. His mother was a college-educated schoolteacher who, upon marriage, decided to leave her career and devote her time to homemaking. She managed the household and, during the war, planted a victory garden to supply fresh fruits and vegetables. His grandparents' farm also provided access to fresh meat, eggs, and produce. The economic growth generated by the war made an impression on young Devall's childhood. He would come of age in an era of rising consumer expectations and an incredible increase in living standards. An "Age of Exuberance," as he often called it, defined consumer behavior, as Americans sought larger houses and more appliances, cars, and wealth. The industrial economy reduced nature to mere resource as cities and suburbs came to define the geography of American experience.

These changes altered his life at home in sometimes subtle ways. Although frugal, his parents occasionally talked about buying a bigger house and a nicer car and taking more costly vacations. Their diet changed as they looked to the supermarket, rather than the family farm, for a wide variety of cheap, processed, and packaged food. New technology appeared regularly—lawn mowers, home appliances, and, perhaps most important, the television. TV programming began structuring daily activities, as he and his parents wanted to avoid missing their favorite shows. All of these changes effected a larger transformation in the American mind (Devall, "Living Richly"). Consumption deflected the impulse to think critically about society. For a growing number of young people, it appeared as though a pernicious complacency was stymieing creativity and obscuring deep-reaching forms of social injustice. A revolt against the establishment was afoot.

Sit-ins, teach-ins, demonstrations, and protests were all features of the political landscape in the post-WWII era. Pioneered by members of the civil rights movement, these types of direct action became a common trait of the New Left. Taking aim at disenfranchisement, nuclear proliferation, the Vietnam War, and the centralized power of the state and corporation, among other features of American culture, the prominent New Left organization Students for a Democratic Society (SDS) advocated a radical form of civic republicanism (Miller). Participatory politics ranged from deliberation to direct action and could take place in locations as diverse as the factory floor or the university. On the more radical side of the New Left, theorists such as Herbert Marcuse advocated revolution rather than democratic participation. Hinting at the complacency that young Devall found so disturbing, Marcuse argued that oppression was totalizing. In the logic of advanced industrial society, he suggested, humans and nature were both reduced to "instrumentalities" in a "web of domination" (168–69). Devall found himself on a similar trajectory of thought.

He believed the Age of Exuberance encouraged Americans to objectify nature. The natural world existed as an economic and aesthetic resource open to human exploitation. An anthropocentric outlook converted wilderness into lumber, mines, farms, and pastures. Devall lamented: "Our view of nature from the suburbs was increasingly truncated.... We literally lost touch with nature" (*Living Richly* 27). Chemicals from personal care products and appliances such as refrigerators and air conditioners damaged the environment. Chlorofluorocarbons (CFCs) wrought havoc on the atmosphere. Experts understood the risks new products presented to the health of the natural world, yet Americans were unwilling to part with the comfort and convenience of new technologies. Figures such as William Vogt, Rachel Carson, Stewart Udall, and Aldo Leopold offered warnings about an impending ecological crisis, but the momentum of the new consumption ethic was difficult to arrest. For Devall, Americans regarded ever-increasing production and consumption as paramount. "Humans," he wrote, "could not wait for the rhythm of nature. More and more Americans were in a hurry to get more production from nature" (*Living Richly* 39). Devall himself was not particularly inclined to question the underlying nature-culture binary that underwrote his childhood years. His work as a conservationist would not begin until he left Kansas.

After earning a BA in sociology from the University of Kansas in 1960, Devall departed the Midwest to pursue graduate training. He completed an MA in sociology at the University of Hawaii and finished his graduate work at the University of Oregon, where he earned a PhD in 1970. During his time in Oregon, he developed a nascent understanding of environmental problems. Books about suburbanization, pollution, and the rise in human population contributed to his "abstract and vague" awareness of the limits of American exuberance (Devall, *Simple in Means* 6). His timing could not have been better.

Devall's developing ecological awareness paralleled changes in the New Left. Following the formation of the Weather Underground, the movement imploded in the late 1960s just as environmentalism was coming into its own. The fissure between the moderate and radical wings of the Left encouraged many activists to explore other outlets for political expression. Coupled with events such as the 1965 blackout and garbage strikes in New York City, the Ohio River catching fire, and the Santa Barbara oil spill in 1969, a substantial portion of the New Left base moved in a decidedly environmental direction (Gottlieb 96). As a result, many refugees of the Left would apply their passion and organizing skills to environmental causes after a brief hiatus from politics and activism. The founding of organizations such as the Population Crisis Committee (1965), the Chesapeake Bay Foundation (1966), and the Freshwater Foundation (1968) soon followed (Sale 13). Books by Paul Ehrlich, Stewart Udall, Barry Commoner, and Rachel Carson challenged the assumptions of the age by inviting Americans to reconsider the ultimate cost of unbridled consumption (De Steiguer 202).

Environmentalists shared with New Left activists a suspicion of modern industrial culture. Broad, stinging critiques of race relations, corporate capitalism, and imperialism could easily apply to questions about environmental degradation. Both movements rejected the logic of domination at work in the way humans related to each other and the environment. The legacy of the Left would persist in the search for alternative modes of living, which gave rise to communes and a back-to-the-land impulse that dovetailed nicely with environmental values (Gottlieb 96). Groups such as the New Alchemy Institute and the Institute for Social Ecology established a firm connection between social and environmental justice. Murray Bookchin's formulation of social ecology expanded on New Left social criticism and motivated a new breed of activist. The fissure between radicals and moderates that drove many into the environmental movement also endured. Elements of both the radical and conservative wings of the Left's countercultural politics would find their way into Dave Foreman and Edward Abbey's monkeywrenching, Gaylord Nelson's teach-ins and organized protests, and the direct action of Greenpeace.

In a broad sense, environmental activists simply continued the New Left's assault on modern industrial culture, but they chose a new field of focus. More directly highlighting the problematic relationship between humanity and nature, they moved beyond the framework of political and social theory. Devall found himself right in the center of these developments. As his own hesitant ecological awakening suggests, however, incorporating the environment into a new social vision proved difficult. Despite his early encounters with environmentalism while in Oregon, he did not immediately understand its philosophical implications. It was not until moving to Humboldt County in 1968 that Devall's understanding of environmental degradation began to take definite form.

The redwood forests of Northern California absolutely enthralled the recently credentialed sociologist. The "awe and mystery of the primeval forest" evoked in Devall the feeling that he was the first person to ever experience their "silent splendor" (*Simple in Means* 6). Places like Tall Trees Grove, a remote stand of redwoods nestled alongside the clear waters of Redwood Creek, restored "a sense of mindfulness, of awareness of our interconnectedness with the forest as a wild place" (*Simple in Means* 7). Devall was not articulating "an elaborate philosophical argument" in these moments of awe (*Simple in Means* 7). He only had a "feeling that it was wrong to clear-cut such old trees" (*Simple in Means* 7). Before embarking on a systematic philosophical project, he pointed to the central role of experiential knowledge as a source of critical insight. Such experiences could lead to "physical pain, a kind of suffering" when he saw logging trucks loaded with old-growth logs (*Simple in Means* 7). Devall's felt connection to the redwoods only intensified as he settled into a life in Humboldt County. Securing a position in the Sociology Department at Humboldt State University in Arcata, he would make a permanent home on the North Coast.

Devall began a process described by the agrarian thinker Wes Jackson as "becoming native" to a place (Jackson 36). Indicative of a romantic naturalism in his work, he wrote about the terrain of his new home, he learned its history, and he developed a sophisticated understanding of its ecology and people. Redwood Creek Valley continued to attract the sociology professor. He often visited his friend Richard at the "Home Ranch," a beautiful tract of land near Horse Mountain. Devall reflected on the area's history, noting the wanton destruction of Yurok villages as settlers pressed into the valley pursuing gold in the 1860s. By the 1890s, some of the remaining Yurok population adopted European ranching practices. Richard was himself rooted in this history, and he tried to keep the traditions of his ancestors alive by avoiding technology and continuing practices such as basket weaving. Humboldt County's history was riddled with various forms of injustice. Richard had to apply for permits before collecting basket-weaving material on lands originally inhabited by the Yurok tribe. The Home Ranch, itself, could hardly escape the incursions of the outside world. Simpson Timber Company started logging nearby areas and began considerable aerial spraying of pesticides on the ridge just opposite the ranch. Logging in the fifties, sixties, eighties, and nineties destroyed multiple stands of mature Douglas fir, oak, and madrone (Devall, *Living Richly* 107–9). Devall tried to buy land in the area in an effort to preserve it, but was unable to secure a loan with his salary from HSU. Redwood Creek Valley and its environs clearly left an impression on him.

Devall deeply identified with Humboldt County itself. He regarded the area as a complex ecological system that he now belonged to. Writers such as David Rains Wallace had confirmed his ecological instincts (*Living Richly* 107). Wallace looked to the nearby Klamath Mountains and Siskiyou forest to understand the natural processes that bound nature and culture. Devall learned from Wallace that evolution existed "as a continuum still linked with its past," and the "place of the human in evolution is not unlike the dreamer's in the dream" (Wallace 15). Human consciousness was an emergent property of natural processes. Although the mind could guide some of these processes, humans could not stand outside of and "*control* evolution"; as natural beings we would always remain embedded in a reciprocal relationship with the world we hoped to shape (Wallace 133). Devall had found Wallace's naturalism particularly revealing as he stood in Redwood Creek Valley. He wrote: "The land is alive, animated, changing in its own ways in response to natural geological changes as well as changes wrought by humans...over the past hundred years" (*Living Richly* 111). Wallace's work reinforced the experiential insights Humboldt imparted to Devall when he arrived. In simultaneously contemplating place and ecology, he began developing a more complex philosophy. This project would introduce his early naturalism to the growing field of environmental ethics, which drew on work in philosophy, psychology, and other disciplines in the humanities and social sciences.

Becoming One with the Redwoods: American Environmental Philosophy and Monism

Devall would later be surprised by his ecological awakening and subsequent commitment to environmental philosophy. Reminiscent of other radical leftists, he believed the Age of Exuberance produced a hegemonic ideology, one that equated nature with lifeless matter and resource. As an observant sociologist, he understood the difficulty of challenging deeply engrained social norms and ways of thinking. The presence of a new environmental movement thus proved quite shocking. He remarked, "Nothing in my high school or college education prepared me for the fact that basic philosophical underpinnings of our attitudes toward society and toward nature would be severely challenged from 1960 onward" (*Living Richly* 23). He, of course, was not alone. Academic philosophers did not generate the values that motivated the environmental movement; in fact, environmental philosophy arrived later, providing an ex post facto theoretical basis for the activism of the sixties and seventies (Hay 246).

Environmentalism pushed the boundaries of philosophical debate. As the scholar Peter Hay argues, the new movement "opened up the most genuinely new field of ethical disputation that has been seen in many years. It constitutes nothing less than a challenge to the very basis of western value systems" (17). Environmental thinkers argued that an uncritically held anthropocentrism pervaded Western thought. In a seminal essay, the historian Lynn White Jr. suggested that Christian dogma "bears a huge burden of guilt" for environmental problems because it encouraged a belief in "man's transcendence of, and rightful master[y] over, nature" (White 1206). The Western tradition was badly in need of a new metaphysics and value system. While some thinkers such as John Passmore suggested Western metaphysics could be reconciled with an ecological worldview (Passmore

27), most followed White in believing philosophy was in need of a radical overhaul. The majority of early environmental philosophy was devoted to providing a nonanthropocentric foundation for a new ethics. As debates between philosophers would illustrate, however, the presence of a shared objective did not imply the existence of a shared metaphysics.

J. Baird Callicott and Peter Singer both supported a radical extension of moral considerability to the nonhuman world, but they used very different metaphysical systems to support their ideas. Influenced by Jeremy Bentham, Singer suggested that nonhuman sentient beings were entitled to moral consideration in a utilitarian pleasure/pain calculus (Hay 37). He found in Bentham a framework for challenging the narrow humanism at work in Western philosophy. For Callicott, this was hardly a radical departure from an anthropocentric logic. In looking to the presence of individual sentience, he argued, Singer was merely extending a reductive conception of humanism to include other advanced life-forms ("Animal Liberation" 38). Animal liberation was, ultimately, based on an atomistic metaphysics that regarded the individual as the focus of all ethical concerns. As a result, Callicott described the world of early environmental philosophy as a "triangular affair." To his reading, Singer's "humane moralism" shared the same flaws as a traditional "moral humanism," leaving philosophers only one serious candidate for a new environmental ethics. Captivated by the writing of Aldo Leopold, he championed an ethical holism that anchored rights in the "biotic community" rather than sentient individuals ("Animal Liberation" 44). For the more radical environmental philosopher, it seemed, the entire edifice of Western metaphysics and values had to be completely razed in order to develop a responsible ethics. By turning a critical eye toward the atomism in "shallow" environmental perspectives, the Norwegian philosopher Arne Naess pursued this very goal.

In 1972, Naess outlined the tenets of deep ecology in a lecture he gave in Bucharest. "The Shallow and the Deep, Long-Range Ecology Movement: A Summary" appeared in print a year later. In Naess's early iteration of his philosophy he posited the necessity of "biospherical egalitarianism" (95). Showing the influence of developments in physics and ecology, the concept suggested that organisms and matter alike existed only as points on a "biospherical net or field of intrinsic relations" (Naess 95). In this view, the "field" of relationships held an elevated ontological status in comparison to the entities it joined. In fact, the concept of an individual—from particle to person—loses meaning when considered in isolation from a web of relationships. If intrinsic relations superseded individual entities as the focal point in this metaphysics, it suggested the line separating life and (lifeless) matter was fundamentally arbitrary. Naess states, "The total-field model dissolves not only the man-in-environment concept, but every compact thing-in-milieu concept" (95). Living organisms existed as larger "knots" in the field of relations, indicating they differed in complexity, but not kind, from inorganic material. The total field image had profound implications for the notion of selfhood.

The Australian philosopher Warwick Fox developed Naess's metaphysics into a "transpersonal ecology." Beginning with Naess's assumption that humans (or any individual entity) are always embedded in a larger fabric of relations, Fox argued that the psychological drives behind resource exploitation and preservation were actually the same. Environmental destruction resulted from a "desiring-impulsive" self, which regarded the world in appetitive, childlike terms (Fox 60). Conservationists check this drive by suggesting nature is a limited resource that needs to be efficiently managed. Wise use will ensure a greater material payoff. Preservationists, too, suggest something similar when they argue wilderness has aesthetic or experiential value. Both exemplify the attributes of the "rationalizing-deciding self," which introduces a strategic instrumentalism into our relationship with the world (Fox 61). In order to escape this latent anthropocentrism, some philosophers have argued that nature has intrinsic value—rights independent of human concerns. For Fox, however, this latter argument was fatally flawed.

Although intrinsic value theory was conceived by a "normative-judgmental self," it still fell back on the atomism that informed the desiring-impulsive and rationalizing-deciding selves (Fox 61). Fox argues that the normative claims of intrinsic value still take the individual human as the most important referent in ethics. We might develop a more expansive understanding of rights and interests beyond the human world, but "these interests are still related to a self that is conceived in a narrow, atomistic, or particle-like sense" (Fox 68–69). Reminiscent of Marcuse, who looked to Freud to understand systemic flaws in modern rationality, Fox relied on the field of transpersonal psychology to complicate our understanding of self-identity. While Marcuse was radical for challenging false consciousness and one-dimensional thought, Fox pushed even further by calling into question the very existence of the individual. Humans can access an "experience of commonality" with other entities, he argued (Fox 81). In doing so, formal ethics becomes unnecessary, for "one will naturally (i.e., spontaneously) protect the natural (spontaneous) unfolding of this expansive self (the ecosphere, the cosmos) in all its aspects" (70).

Conscious of walking a thin line between atomistic individualism and organic or mystical conceptions of self, Fox was very careful to argue that a transpersonal self is "*relatively* autonomous" (82). His transpersonal self does not get lost in his conception of monism. Citing ecological science, physics, evolutionary biology, and chaos theory, he argued that humans and every other entity are features of a "single unfolding reality," but this does not mean "that all entities are fundamentally the same nor that they are absolutely autonomous" (82). A nature enthusiast could develop a sense of self that includes a tree, he suggested, but this does not mean that person is "literally…that tree over there" (82). By focusing on the ability of humans to extend a sense of self while maintaining individual agency in the world, deep ecology encouraged environmentalists to act on behalf of nature in ways that exceeded the limits of New Left political and social theory.

Fox and Naess both conceived of deep ecology as a broadly applicable method of asking questions. The philosophy was based on a complex metaphysics and value theory, but in emphasizing the need for human action they were also receptive to other ideas or beliefs that produced a similar environmental ethics. Fox argued that deep ecology was not about choosing the correct ecophilosophy; instead, it acknowledged the varied criteria we might rely on when framing a desire to protect the natural world. Our choice will be based on considerations such as "which is the more relevant to our experience, which is the more exciting or appealing to certain kinds of temperaments...which is the more likely to influence behavior, and so on" (Fox 93). Naess had made a similar point earlier, arguing that the application of his philosophical principles will "show many variations" and has to be sensitive to "regional differences" as activists champion the environmental cause (Naess 100). To this end, he would later drop references to biospherical egalitarianism because if taken too literally, it suggested humans could not even sustain vegan diets, which required the destruction of plant matter. He argued that action to satisfy "vital needs" was certainly permissible, even a necessity (Hay 45). Sorting out what constituted a vital need would be largely dependent on context and place, but the principles of deep ecology provided a framework for navigating that exact question. While living in California, Bill Devall would be drawn to the metaphysical and methodological commitments of Naess and Fox as he interrogated his own desire to protect the natural world.

Devall's initial experiences of walking among the redwoods in Humboldt County were always present in his work as an environmental writer. Seeing the destruction caused by logging in the area had led him to ask, "Is this all a forest means...a factory for growing trees? Will all ancient redwood forests be clear-cut in the name of making them more efficient factories for fiber?" (*Simple in Means* 7). He intuitively believed the answer was no, but he was able to muster only a vague defense for this claim. Redwoods were old, he thought, and lived in the area much longer than humans. These ancient trees, he reasoned, "should have their own space just as humans have their space" (*Simple in Means* 7). Although it was enough to prompt his local activism, his answer was not intellectually satisfying and only seemed to provoke more questions.

Devall grew "more interested in the reasons why a whole civilization would become dedicated to bringing vast areas under intensive management for narrow goals" (*Simple in Means* 7). Places like Tall

Trees Grove and the Home Ranch had shaken him out of a reality defined by consumption, efficiency, and a reductive scientific method. In his initial daze he began grasping at an underlying unity he felt while in primeval forests. Indeed, despite Fox's claims to the contrary, Devall lost himself in the redwoods—he became "literally that tree over there." Over the course of his career at HSU he would write various books and articles drawing on Naess and Fox that addressed the need to develop a radically new ethics. As he would later realize, "environmentalism is a response to our existential condition. In a culture dominated by humanism and technology, radical environmental sensibilities come from a sense of the peril" we feel when facing "the demands of our existence" ("Deep Ecology" 252). The Age of Exuberance, however, shielded from view the "intimate understanding of our modest place, as a species" in this world (*Living Richly* 88).

In the modern era, it would be difficult to maintain an environmental sensibility that stressed the humble position of humanity in nature. The fundamental problem of modernity, for Devall, was the persistent inclination "to define what is not me as 'the other'" (*Simple in Means* 40). As Naess had suggested, it made sense to draw lines around an individual or an environment for the purposes of communication. Unfortunately, the utility of this exercise was severely undermined when these categories acquired ontological weight. Devall continued: "When the other is a bioregion, a forest or a redwood tree, then it is a 'thing,' an object which can be manipulated by and for humans for narrow purposes" (*Simple in Means* 49). Referencing a number of thinkers such as Martin Heidegger, Jacques Ellul, Lewis Mumford, and Theodore Roszak, he argued that "within the dominant ideology of modernism we assume environmental problems have technological solutions" ("Ecological Consciousness" 178). Reform environmentalism was essentially co-opted by this logic. In a society increasingly dependent on a "secular priesthood of experts," reformers simply look to their own experts to leverage their appeals in regulatory agencies, courts, and in the realm of public opinion ("Ecological Consciousness" 179). The compounded effect of these developments was a never-ending "treadmill of problems" ("Ecological Consciousness" 180).

Having objectified the environment, we relied on technology to correct the environmental disasters we caused, but this only created new, unpredictable problems. Only a radical environmentalism could escape this absurd cycle.

In an effort to mitigate humanity's dire existential state, Devall adopted an ecocentric environmental philosophy. Following Naess, he argued that experiential knowledge and intellectual effort could enable "*self-realization*" and encourage individuals to practice a form of "broader identification" (*Living Richly* 67). He was drawn to the normative force of deep ecology, but he insisted that "ontology is the center of ecosophic concerns" (*Simple in Means* 44). Accordingly, he suggested the necessity of maintaining a sense of the "total-field image," that body of relations so important in Naess's metaphysics, as a means of nudging the development of an ecological consciousness. Only then would a broadly constituted self respect "natural biodiversity and evolution" as well as other "myriad self-realizing beings" ("Deep Ecology" 248–49). Although our experience of "individuated" entities suggested the world was an amalgam of independent parts, Devall argued that we could come "home to our broader self" (*Living Richly* 58–59). Influenced by Fox's Tree of Life metaphor, he pointed out that human individuation was not a complete illusion—every leaf on a tree is permitted some freedom of movement (*Living Richly* 59). Humans possessed agency in natural processes, as clear-cutting in the redwood forests plainly illustrated. Their destructive potential was, however, matched by a capacity for creative thought and emotion, making them a unique variation on the tree. Devall suggested hopefully: "By recovering our connection to the Tree of Life, we can possibly reconnect, in our recovery process, with the roots of life, with our sense of place in the biosphere, in the cosmos" (*Living Richly* 59).

Deep ecology certainly presented a radical alternative to the ideology of modernity, but it would take more than a new metaphysics to challenge anthropocentrism. Reconnecting to the Tree of Life had to be accomplished intuitively. For someone like Devall, who, in standing in the redwood forest, awoke to the possibility of an underlying unity in nature, this seemed a relatively easy leap to make. Indeed, he wrote, "the more we know of a specific place intimately—know its moods, seasons, changes, aspects, native creatures—the more we know our ecological selves" (*Simple in Means* 47). Perhaps belying the difficulty attending this step, ecological intuition was an important feature of deep ecology's intellectual landscape. For Naess, we could intuit the principles of biospherical egalitarianism (Naess 96). Devall suggested the same, writing that an "intuitive, experiential understanding of interconnectedness" could reveal the plain truth of the complex metaphysical claims that deep ecology posited (*Living Richly* 65). The murkiness of metaphysics could be dispelled in one easy moment. Devall was lucky, however. A chance intuition had been sparked by a particular place. His experience was incredibly rare. In fact, as he would admit, a sense of place and ecological intuition were almost impossible to achieve in an age of denial.

Borrowing ideas from the ecopsychology of Joanne Macy and Fox, Devall argued that the power of intuition was severely curtailed in the modern era. The pressures of daily life easily limited our field of concern. Pressure to pay bills, perform at work, or navigate myriad other problems left little time or energy for reflection. He stated, "People must totally despair of the central value of modernity, that is the value of economic growth.... They must despair that humans have any ability to 'solve' the environmental crisis" ("Twenty-Five Years" 31). Humans would not critically consider the endless pursuit of economic growth until confronted with the limits of the natural world. For some, intuition would have to wait. Channeling the environmental thinker Bill McKibben, Devall bluntly argued that we must experience the "death of nature" ("Twenty-Five Years" 31). Only after a period of despair and grief would society be open to "a renewed sense of wildness, broader self-identification, and a sense of joy in the realization that the human place in the cosmos is modest and small" ("Twenty-Five Years" 31). Collapse and crisis could generate ecological awareness on a larger scale than chance intuition or sense of place. In either case, however, recognition of the fieldlike nature of reality would inspire a commitment to radical environmentalism.

Despite its emphasis on monism, intuition, and self-realization, deep ecology was primarily a philosophy for action. Joining the philosopher George Sessions, Devall argued, "We cannot change consciousness by only listening to others, we must involve ourselves. We must take direct action" (Devall and Sessions, *Deep Ecology* 8–9). Self-preservation was synonymous with environmental concern in the framework of deep ecology. Expressing a principle articulated by Naess and Fox, Devall reasoned that a broadly realized self would immediately act to protect the "right [of other species] to follow their own evolutionary destinies without human intervention" ("Ecological Consciousness" 182). An ecological self acted to resist the incursions of the human world on naturally occurring processes. "Ecological resisting," as he would call it, entailed rejecting narrowly conceived technological solutions to environmental problems ("Ecological Consciousness" 183).

A form of nonviolent activism, resistance amounted to a "pattern of acting" that included "befriending" and advocating on behalf of ecosystems ("Ecological Consciousness" 185). Resisting departed from the reformist tradition, which sought to "mitigate some of the worst forms of air and water pollution" for the narrow purpose of protecting "human health and safety" ("Ecological Consciousness" 184). Progressive reform politics, more often than not, relied on policy and regulation to reconcile economic growth with moderate demands for environmental protection. Devall opted for more fundamental changes in lifestyle and politics. He was a proponent of reduced consumption, "voluntary simplicity," and grassroots activism (*Living Richly* 82, 122). In many ways, however, deep ecology left the particularities of activism open to interpretation. Devall continued Naess's tradition of providing general principles and ideas for practice rather than specific directions. He articulated a philosophy that encouraged the creative potential of its individual practitioners.

Saving the Redwoods: The Making of a Pragmatic Methodology

Devall definitely had an ideal environmentalist-type in mind when contemplating the implications of deep ecology's metaphysics. A completely realized ecological self had many of the qualities of Bigfoot, that legendary beast so prevalent in Pacific Northwest culture. Bigfoot inhabits the forest free of technology and is seemingly in complete step with ecological processes. "Perhaps," Devall wrote, "Sasquatch does exist—as an ideal" (*Living Richly* 39). Living in tune with the forest was admirable, but he also understood this as a motivating principle rather than an immediately tangible goal. He was a proponent of activism, but held this did not necessarily entail an uncompromising radical agenda that one might associate with the Weather Underground or the tactics of Earth First!–style ecotage. There were many roads to Bigfoot's ecotopia. It is true that Devall's own despair at the destruction of the redwoods had led him to a deep critique of modern values. He even hoped the principles of deep ecology might help usher in a paradigm shift in the modern world, but this was a distant goal as well. Considering the normative thrust of his philosophy, it is perhaps surprising that it left room for a pragmatic methodology. Devall's experience as an activist and observer in Humboldt County, however, made him sensitive to the concerns of those who did not share his views. After witnessing the shortcomings of political and legal processes of redress concerning the redwoods, he began to focus more directly on changing hearts and minds.

Devall arrived in Arcata during a pivotal year in the history of Humboldt's redwood forests. The movement to preserve remaining old-growth forest, which began in 1918 with the formation of the Save the Redwoods League, achieved a dubious victory in the passage of a 1968 bill to establish Redwood National Park (Schrepfer xiv). The bill was a compromise, reserving the Redwood Creek Valley for the purpose of wilderness recreation as well as clear-cutting. The legislation protected only a thin line of forest immediately surrounding the creek. Logging trucks soon traversed the ridges above, signaling the destruction wrought on the creek's tributaries. As soon as the bill was signed into law, the California Board of Forestry granted Arcata Redwood Company, Simpson Timber, and Georgia-Pacific permission to harvest trees throughout the area. Redwoods outside of the park along Skunk Cabbage Creek, which the Sierra Club had hoped to preserve, also fell to the ax shortly after the act was passed. The secretary of the interior was actually authorized to protect these areas if it could be shown they were crucial to preserving the aesthetic and ecological value of the park. Despite pressure from the Sierra Club and Friends of the Earth as well as the existence of formal studies indicating the destructive potential of logging around the park, the government refused to intervene (Schrepfer 186). Illustrating a pattern in the larger trajectory of the "timber wars," in the absence of public pressure at the national level, state and federal authorities refused to disrupt alliances between vested interests and government agencies in local politics. The California Board of Forestry would side with local businesses unless pressured to do otherwise.

The new professor of sociology closely watched the debate surrounding the passage and implementation of the bill. In these moments his tone reflected the sober analysis of a social scientist rather than the lyrical prose of a romantic. According to Devall, local and national administrators of the National Park Service "were concerned with their own careers and the bureaucratic viability of the Park Service as an organization over the possibilities for fulfilling the preservationist dream" ("Redwood National Park" 86). The Park Service was primarily focused on longevity, prioritizing the life of its organizational bureaucracy over its stated mission. Logging companies in Del Norte and Humboldt Counties presented fierce resistance to the park, going so far as producing clever bumper stickers that proclaimed "Don't Park My Job" ("Redwood National Park" 83). City councils, county boards, and proponents of the tourist industry also pressured the Park Service to consider the economic repercussions of park management. As a result of this pushback, the park itself was only 58,000 acres, considerably smaller than the proposed 90,000 acres ("Redwood National Park" 83). Despite the reduced size of the park, logging interests still posed a significant threat. Nearby clear-cutting encouraged preservationists to request that the Park Service exercise its discretionary power to create a buffer zone in the area. Three separate studies confirmed the ecological hazards of these logging operations. In the third study, Richard Curry, the associate director of the Park Service, stated that the timber industry "posed the greatest threat to the park" (Schrepfer 190). Yet no action was taken. For Devall, the political system had suffered a fundamental malfunction.

The Park Service and the Redwood National Park bill were co-opted by vested interests in northern California. Opponents of the park were able to monopolize the language of public interest by focusing on "the economic potential of sawed redwoods for corporate profit" ("Redwood National Park" 86). Local preservationists were at an immediate disadvantage: it was impossible to quantify aesthetic, spiritual, or ecological value in an analysis of "short-range market conditions" ("Redwood National Park" 86). On the administrative side, the National Park Service was new to the area and hoped to easily integrate with the community. Devall argued that the superintendent of the park was too "anxious to make friends for the Service" and, as a result, risked "capture" by private interests ("Redwood National Park" 83, 86). The whole episode revealed "the deeply conservative bias of the agency to perpetuate the status quo of power" and hinted at deeper problems in the American political process ("Redwood National Park" 88). The bill made no ecological sense and, to Devall's reading, it in no way reflected the mission of the National Park Service.

A nefarious realism had eroded the dream of preservationists. Their values were essentially discounted in a process that favored economic analysis and institutional inertia. Devall concluded that interest-group politics was not democratic. Public agencies are not neutral, nor is power evenly distributed among private groups. Liberal democratic ideals rang hollow. The belief in government as neutral arbiter among competing interests was an illusion, at least in Humboldt County.

Devall's concern about the co-option of the 1968 bill was not unfounded. Forestry policy in California had rested on a form of corporatism in which the timber industry was afforded a large degree of independence from government oversight. Regulatory boards tended to be dominated by industry representatives (Speece 14–15). Before World War II, the Save the Redwoods League had practiced what one historian calls "the genteel tradition of land acquisition" (Speece 100). Activists would raise money to buy and protect land with sensitive natural features. This method became untenable as timber harvests increased during the postwar economic boom. The Redwood National Park fight marked a departure from the genteel strategy in that it was a forced buyout—private property was essentially confiscated for the purposes of environmental protection (Speece 100). Although the 1968 bill was a significant challenge to timber companies, the corporatist regime remained largely intact. Confronted with the limits of political processes in his new home, Devall joined other North Coast activists in exploring alternative means of effecting change.

The movement to save the redwoods would evolve through the seventies and eighties. Environmentalism in Humboldt became more intense after a new generation of activists migrated to redwood country in the 1960s. Many of these migrants were veterans of the New Left and were thoroughly steeped in sixties counterculture. Robert Sutherland, a founding member of the Environmental Protection Information Center (EPIC), headed to the North Coast after a stint in Haight-Ashbury where he organized a commune and experimented with LSD (Speece 87). Much of EPIC's membership, too, had ties to social justice movements (Speece 89). New Left migration continued into the 1980s and beyond, bringing Darryl Cherney, Betty Ball, and Judi Bari, among others. The new generation of activists joined the North Coast environmental movement, and, repeating a pattern of development Devall himself experienced, they adapted their ideas and past experience to the unique cultural landscape of Humboldt County. Although it is true that activism did intensify over the course of the timber wars, especially as outsiders joined the fight to save the redwoods, North Coast activists generally remained sensitive to the dependence of locals on the timber economy. At times, the groups could even find common ground.

Activists and local workers shared an anti-corporate sentiment as well as a desire to restore local autonomy and control of natural resources in Humboldt County (Speece 88). In this view, logging became problematic only when nonlocal corporate interests sacrificed ecological health and long-term employment in pursuit of maximum profits. Clear-cutting a forest not only damaged the overall health of the ecosystem, it also reduced the potential for future harvests and, as a result, limited the job security of loggers. These moments of agreement between environmentalists and loggers illustrated, in part, the legacy of moderate forms of New Left strategy. Activists were responsive to local context and endorsed deliberation and forms of nonviolent direct action in an effort to reform, not destroy, the way of life in Humboldt. Resisting the urge to dismiss human interests in their ecological framework, Cherney and others also welcomed the philosophical insights provided by deep ecology, specifically the work of local HSU professor Bill Devall (Speece 145).

Despite his frustration with the 1968 bill, Devall remained committed to a pragmatic methodology. Timber companies and local leaders in Humboldt County had been operating within the confines of a flawed conceptual schema he hoped to challenge. Although protests and nonviolent resistance coupled with a deep critique of political processes could cut straight to the core of the problem, he recognized these were not always the best methods. Similar to Cherney, who never developed the extreme misanthropy of Dave Foreman's biocentrism, Devall never abandoned his desire to work with members of his new community (Speece 145). He admitted that "depending on the circumstances and situation," anthropocentric arguments can be "effective" (*Living Richly* 13–14). In fact, "for tactical purposes it is quite reasonable to use shallow, reformist arguments in certain political campaigns" (*Living Richly* 27). Hardly anthropocentric himself, he was willing to consider this perspective if it helped forward the cause of the environment in some capacity. At the same time, Devall was a proponent of radicalism, but, in truth, he believed the term could refer to more than social action and policy.

A radicalism, more than anything else, called for a "different postmodernity emphasizing a 'new' cosmology, bioregionalism, animism, and modesty on the part of humans" ("Twenty-Five Years" 24). Responsive to the charge of "environmental fascism" and criticism from theorists such as Val Plumwood, who argued that deep ecology simply replicated the egoism at the center of Western rationality, Devall's work often fell back on a form of pluralism (Plumwood).[2] He often cited various thinkers, even reproducing extended passages from their texts, in a deliberate effort to illustrate the numerous avenues available for arriving at a satisfactory environmental ethics. Deep ecology required a radical change in metaphysics, but one could arrive at this goal in a multitude of ways. He regarded the philosophy as an evolving framework capable of adapting to new contexts and incorporating new ideas. It provided a common ground for a number of divergent positions. "Some of these," he wrote, "could be based on Native American traditions, on Buddhist traditions, or on other cultural traditions and philosophical perspectives" ("Deep Ecology" 249). To some degree, deep ecology was simply a synonym for ecocentrism, which meant that ecofeminism, romanticism, pre-Socratic Greek philosophies, New Age theories, and other ideas could comfortably reside in a deep ecological framework.

Thinking about method would bring Devall back to the idea of place. He was resistant to dogma, even in his own philosophy, because it was not sensitive to local variation or changing context. If his metaphysics suggested mind and nature were not ontologically distinct, then it followed that knowledge of a particular environment was self-knowledge. As a result, he departed from a spectator theory of knowledge and articulated a "participatory epistemology" that regarded knowledge as place-dependent ("Ecological Consciousness" 181). The idea of a passive mind accruing knowledge of a detached world was a fiction. Knowing was an activity that required full immersion in an environment. Showing the influence of Wendell Berry, Devall remained cautious regarding expert or scientific knowledge because of its tendency to objectify the world and ignore the relationships that bound a community to its environment (Berry 115). Devall, however, was unwilling to challenge the totalizing and exploitative features of modernity with a counter-dogma. Instead, he wrote, "multicentric epistemology, pluralism, cultural diversity, and emotional commitment to local community are antidotes to the hegemony of national power controlled by political and corporate elites" ("The End" 171). He looked to "place" in an effort to resist a tyranny of the mind. A community could frame its commitment to place within a number of traditions, which is why he believed systems as different as Christianity, Buddhism, and pantheism could lead to deep ecology positions (*Simple in Means* 12).

Pragmatic methodology emphasized practice. If corrupt and inert political processes and bureaucracies remained as obstacles to environmental protection, then one could focus on a change in lifestyles. Devall admitted, however, "none of us has complete consistency between our philosophy and our practice. Our practice is dependent in many instances on our life situation, the community in which we live" (*Living Richly* 70). He advocated everything from downscaling, energy reduction, gardening, and conscious consumption to intentional communities, activism, and numerous other activities. He reiterated, however, "I am not a champion of a dogmatic approach.... I am not a fundamentalist who preaches the True Way" (*Living Richly* 10). Devall himself was unable to afford upgrading his home to meet new efficiency standards, nor was he particularly enthusiastic about sacrifice or "living as a hermit in a small room" (*Living Richly* 10). He returned to the idea of the ecological self on this point. He was less concerned with the specific contributions an individual made so long as they consciously cultivated a life grounded in community and place. "Practicing," he wrote, "is experimental and experiential" (*Simple in Means* 119). The ecologically conscious person is not perfect. He or she will experiment through practice, testing new modes and ideas in an effort to participate responsibly in a broader community.

Conclusion: Redwood Summer and Humboldt in an Age of Trump

Devall applied the principles of experimental practice and ecological cultivation throughout his life and work. He continued to watch the development of environmentalism and remained concerned about the fate of the redwoods. By 1978 Congress passed a second Redwood National Park act that expanded the park by forty-eight thousand acres. Aside from a few remaining groves of old growth, much of this new land had been heavily logged. Having harvested in the area and thus deflated its productive potential beforehand, the timber companies benefitted from the most costly government land purchase in

American history (Schrepfer 242). Conflict between preservationists and loggers in Humboldt County did not end with the expansion of the park. Isolated pockets of old growth remained unprotected. Relations deteriorated further when Maxxam Corporation, in a hostile takeover, assumed ownership of Pacific Lumber Company in 1985 (Speece 120).

A pattern of resistance soon developed as activists challenged the practice of liquidation logging ushered in by the new corporate overlord. Tree-spiking, road-blockading, tree-sitting, and other forms of direct action and protest were combined with legal action to prevent Maxxam from stripping the remaining forests. Controversy ensued when California Proposition 130 threatened to circumscribe harvesting practices in these remaining groves. By 1990, the logging industry was moving to harvest quickly in case the measure passed (Widick 225). Devall watched as activists organized Redwood Summer. Modeled after Freedom Summer of 1964, the movement was designed to protest the actions taken by timber companies and raise public awareness about environmental injustice.

Environmentalists faced a backlash, however. Reactionaries marched at the Saturday farmer's market in Arcata. They denounced organic food and carried signs stating "Take back America," "America, love it or leave it," "Earth First out of Humboldt County," and "No more lawsuits" (Dunlap and Mertig 60). Timber companies attempted a greenwashing media blitz, some even releasing large ads showing their full support of Earth Day (*Living Richly* 8). They also organized financing for a yellow-ribbon campaign that championed the right to work for loggers. Their rhetoric suggested activists were un-American ecoterrorists committed to destroying California's logging culture (Widick 227). The sentiment was not new. Anti-environmentalism clearly surfaced on a national scale in the Sagebrush Rebellion of the 1970s and 1980s; following the rise of the "silent majority," it was embedded in a larger conservative backlash against the New Left. Employing fairly standard conservative rhetorical strategies, anti-environmentalists embraced individual rights discourse and proposed a "People First!" agenda.

While facing these reactionary campaigns, however, the sociologist and Humboldt native did not second-guess his philosophy or his method. Devall noted how local landowners were fervently committed to an idea of "property rights" that held no regard for community, integrity, or the health of the land itself (*Simple in Means* 59). As with his earlier work, he returned to the importance of place and the ecological self. He was still hopeful these components of deep ecology would make an impact as he and Humboldt County entered a new millennium. In 2006 he reflected, "In spite of political setbacks from 1980 to the present, there is evidence that major principles of philosophy and place-based community espoused by the environmental movement have become embedded in American culture and society" ("The End" 164). Environmentalism was not ending, according to his assessment. If anything, the environmental movement was adapting to new economic, social, and political circumstances.

Devall died in Humboldt County at the age of seventy. He had lived there for thirty-eight years. He knew the North Coast "in many of its moods—darkness and rain of winter, great storms, floods, drought, hazy long hot days of summer." He always identified with the region. "[It] has become part of my 'body,'" he wrote (*Simple in Means* 59). His writing remained focused on bridging the chasm separating the difficult abstractions of metaphysics from the world of direct action and practice. The monism at the center of his metaphysics was hard to grasp, and even harder to imagine as a source of motivation for activists. He understood, however, "the intimate relationship between action, intuition, and reflection" (*Simple in Means* 6). He hoped a sense of place would allow one to intuit an ecological consciousness, but, as something of a pragmatist, he also believed a person could arrive at self-realization in any number of seemingly contradictory ways. For this reason, deep ecology will continue to evolve as new environmental problems surface.

Large-scale cannabis production operations have replaced the timber industry as a leading threat to Humboldt's ecosystem. Despite increasingly lenient cultivation laws, the Humboldt County sheriff estimates that 95 percent or more of recent production is for the black market (Sadiq). According to Scott Bauer, a scientist with the California Department of Fish and Wildlife, large-scale and unregulated cultivation is typically accompanied by illegal road grading and water diversion from streams, as well as other hydrologic damage caused by bulldozers (Sadiq). All of these activities pose direct threats to salmon and steelhead populations. There is a get-rich-quick mentality driving the expansion of marijuana cultivation as people flock to the county from all over the world to participate in the burgeoning underground market. As Bauer's concerns illustrate, it is unlikely that participants in this economic boom are remotely invested in the county. As current watershed restoration projects in the area face new threats, we should keep in mind Devall's analysis of the Age of Exuberance.

Get-rich-quick schemes are not new, but recent events suggest a short-sighted economic calculus is experiencing a fierce comeback. Devall once gestured toward Donald Trump's *The Art of the Deal* (1987) as symptomatic of a pathology in American culture. He pointed out that the book appealed to the desires of Americans to quickly make money. Expressing revulsion, he wrote, "The quick deal, even the shady deal with junk bonds and loans from financially unstable savings and loans associations, fueled the orgy for more" (*Living Richly* 38). Devall's critique of the Age of Exuberance clearly remains pertinent. The 2016 presidential election does not bode well for those worried about the environment or their community. The Trump administration is dismissive of minority rights, climate change, and all forms of environmental regulation, which are viewed as unnecessary obstacles to economic growth.

Witnessing unconstitutional immigration bans, new pipeline construction, and a wrongheaded rejection of the Paris climate agreement, it is hard to deny Devall's conclusions and the importance of his writing. The necessity of caring for a community as though it were an extension of your very being will always remain present. Progressives would do well to follow Devall's example. Not only does his concept of an expanded community provide a firm basis for environmental ethics, it also underscores the importance of reaching out to the opposition. As Trump's surprising victory illustrates, the radical aims of social and environmental justice will fall on deaf ears if the Left fails to understand and communicate with those outside its ranks.

Notes

1. Devall wrote widely, publishing with popular presses as well as in various academic journals. Collaborating with George Sessions, an American deep ecologist, he was largely responsible for the popularization of deep ecology. Much of his environmental writing was aimed at a general audience and blended rigorous philosophical discussion with accounts of his own ecological awakening, local history and myth, and thorough explications of environmental outlooks he thought resonated with his own. He crossed into a number of genres as a writer—sometimes invoking the romantic naturalism of John Muir and Henry David Thoreau. These moments were tempered by his training as a social scientist who was acquainted with the methods of philosophy, psychology, history, and other academic fields. Known for being more methodologically oriented than Warwick Fox and similar philosophers, he described deep ecology more generally as a framework for asking questions. See Hay 41.
2. Devall's activism embroiled him in debates outside of Humboldt County. Critics had charged that ecocentric philosophers elevated the whole over the part, the population or group over the individual, producing fanaticism and a totalitarian moral philosophy. The philosopher Tom Regan labeled monistic environmental philosophies a form of "environmental fascism" (Regan 362). Mounting criticism also appeared from ecofeminists such as Val Plumwood, who argued that deep ecology reinforced the problematic patterns of thought it was designed to transcend. Plumwood suggested the "transpersonal self" was conceived in the tradition of Western rationalism and therefore elevated "reason" over nature. By emphasizing the "universal" over the "particular," deep ecologists ignored the importance of partial self-identification. The self was embedded in kinship networks and any number of other relationships that funded emotional experience. Deep ecologists, Plumwood suggested, were too eager to find continuity in a universal self, which ignored the multiplicity of perspectives available in the world. Devall's writing was susceptible to these criticisms to a degree. He was a monist, which would draw the ire of anthropocentric thinkers as well as some ecofeminists, but he held a pluralistic conception of self. He pushed for a more expansive sense of self, but he recognized the problems associated with completely dissolving self-identification. His metaphysics would always be checked by his methodology. See Nash and Plumwood.

Bibliography

Berry, Wendell. *What Are People For? Essays.* North Point Press, 1990.

Callicott, J. Baird. "Animal Liberation: A Triangular Affair." *Environmental Ethics*, edited by Robert Elliot, Oxford UP, 1995, pp. 29–59.

———. *Beyond the Land Ethic: More Essays in Environmental Philosophy.* SUNY P, 1999.

De Steiguer, Joseph E. *The Origins of Modern Environmental Thought.* U of Arizona P, 2006.

Devall, Bill. "Deep Ecology and Radical Environmentalism." *Society and Natural Resources,* vol. 4, no. 3, 1991, pp. 247–58.

———. "Ecological Consciousness and Ecological Resisting: Guidelines for Comprehension and Research." *Humboldt Journal of Social Relations,* vol. 9, no. 2, 1982, pp. 177–96.

———. "The End of American Environmentalism?" *Nature and Culture,* vol. 1, no. 2, 2006, pp. 157–80.

———. *Living Richly in an Age of Limits.* Gibbs Smith, 1993.

———. "Redwood National Park: The Clearcutting of a Dream." *Humboldt Journal of Social Relations,* vol. 2, no. 1, 1974, pp. 82–91.

———. *Simple in Means, Rich in Ends: Practicing Deep Ecology.* 1st ed., Peregrine Smith, 1988.

———. "Twenty-Five Years Since Earthday: Reflections of a Sometime Social Activist." *Humboldt Journal of Social Relations,* vol. 21, no. 1, 1995, pp. 14–34.

Devall, Bill, and George Sessions. *Deep Ecology: Living as If Nature Mattered.* Gibbs Smith, 1985.

Dunlap, Riley E., and Angela G. Mertig. *American Environmentalism: The U.S. Environmental Movement, 1970–1990.* Taylor & Francis, 1992.

Foreman, Dave. "More on Earth First! and the Monkey Wrench Gang." *Environmental Ethics,* vol. 5, no. 1, 1983, pp. 95–96.

Fox, Warwick. "Transpersonal Ecology: Psychologizing Ecophilosophy." *Journal of Transpersonal Psychology,* 22, no. 1, 1990, pp. 59–96.

Gottlieb, Robert. *Forcing the Spring: The Transformation of the American Environmental Movement.* Island Press, 1993.

Hay, P. R. *Main Currents in Western Environmental Thought.* Indiana UP, 2002.

Hays, Samuel P., and Barbara D. Hays. *Beauty, Health, and Permanence: Environmental Politics in the United States, 1955–1985.* Cambridge, GBR, Cambridge University Press, 1987.

Jackson, Wes. *Nature as Measure: The Selected Essays of Wes Jackson.* Counterpoint, 2011.

Light, Andrew. "Compatibilism in Political Ecology." *Environmental Pragmatism,* edited by Andrew Light and Eric Katz, Routledge, 1996, pp. 161–84.

Marcuse, Herbert. *One Dimensional Man: Studies in the Ideology of Advanced Industrial Society.* Beacon Press, 1964.

Miller, Jim. *Democracy Is in the Streets: From Port Huron to the Siege of Chicago.* Harvard UP, 1994.

Naess, Arne. "The Shallow and the Deep, Long-Range Ecology Movement: A Summary." *Inquiry,* vol. 16, no. 1–4, 1973, pp. 95–100.

Nash, Roderick F. *The Rights of Nature : A History of Environmental Ethics.* U of Wisconsin P, 1989.

Passmore, John. *Man's Responsibility for Nature*. Gerald Duckworth, 1974.
Plumwood, Val. "Nature, Self, and Gender: Feminism, Environmental Philosophy, and the Critique of Rationalism." *Hypatia*, vol. 6, no. 1, 1991, pp. 3–27.
Regan, Tom. *The Case for Animal Rights*. U of California P, 1983.
Sadiq, Sheraz. "Budding Regulation in One of California's Marijuana Meccas." *PBS News Hour*, 29 Dec. 2016, pbs.org/newshour/bb/regulation-californias-marijuana-meccas/.
Sale, Kirkpatrick. *The Green Revolution: The American Environmental Movement, 1962–1992*. Hill & Wang, 1993.
Schrepfer, Susan R. *The Fight to Save the Redwoods: A History of Environmental Reform, 1917–1978*. U of Wisconsin P, 1983.
Speece, Darren F. *Defending Giants: The Redwood Wars and the Transformation of American Environmental Politics*. U of Washington P, 2017.
Wallace, David R. *Klamath Knot*. Sierra Club Books, 1983.
White, Lynn. "The Historical Roots of Our Ecological Crisis." *Science*, vol. 155, no. 3767, 1967, pp. 1203–7.
Widick, Richard. *Trouble in the Forest: California's Redwood Timber Wars*. U of Minnesota P, 2009.

3

"An International, Dissident, Insurgent Ferment"

Lawrence Ferlinghetti and the Left Coast

GIOIA WOODS

Right after New Year's Day in 1951 Lawrence Ferlinghetti boarded a train. He was leaving Baltimore and heading west, to San Francisco. He had never been to San Francisco, but what he heard from friends made him believe the city might suit him. The thirty-one-year-old Ferlinghetti had recently returned from Paris, where he had spent several G.I. Bill–funded years as a graduate student at the Sorbonne. He loved the Paris cafés, the museums, the cheap red wine, the publisher-owned kiosk-style bookshops, and the thriving art scenes. He had an academic interest in cities, too, evidenced by his dissertation, "The City as Symbol in Modern Poetry: In Search of a Metropolitan Tradition." He was unhappy with the idea of living in New York, which seemed to him "an uneasy metropolis, featuring the new all-plastic, nylon-reinforced television mentality" (qtd. in Silesky 43). On January 5, Ferlinghetti arrived in Oakland, and took the ferry across the bay. As he suspected it would, the city appealed to him immediately. It provided a sort of urban pastoral, an escape from the invidious effects of American consumer culture. The political mood, the artistic foment, and the Bay Area "little magazine" combined to make San Francisco the perfect place to launch a revolution in poetry and publishing.

Ferlinghetti's revolution changed the literary landscape of the American West. He became a pioneer of the avant-garde poetry that came to characterize the midcentury San Francisco Renaissance, a playful blend of proletarian concerns and formal experimentation. Ferlinghetti became a central poet and publisher in the literary development of the Beats, and owner of the first-ever all-paperback bookshop in the United States, City Lights. Critics have recognized him as a populist poet whose long and prolific career helped change the course of American literature and culture after World War II. By insisting on a wide-open poetry of engagement, Ferlinghetti succeeded in taking poetry out of the classroom and into the streets. As he wrote after being acquitted of obscenity charges in 1957, his mission as a poet and publisher was to challenge the "barren, polished poetry and well-mannered verse which had dominated many of the major poetry publications" during the 1940s (Ferlinghetti, "Horn on *Howl*" 43).

Ferlinghetti's life was characterized by the necessity for self-invention. He was born on March 24, 1919, to a multicultural and multilingual family. His father, Charles Ferling, had emigrated from northern Italy to New York's Yonkers area in the 1890s. Ferling was a well-educated man who spoke French, Italian, and English and worked in real estate and as an auctioneer. Clemence Mendes-Monsanto, Ferlinghetti's mother, was the child of equally well educated French and Sephardic (Portuguese-Spanish) Jewish immigrants. Seven months before Lawrence Ferlinghetti's birth, Charles Ferling died, and Clemence Ferlinghetti suffered an emotional collapse that resulted in her commitment to the state hospital in Poughkeepsie, New York. Lawrence's four older brothers were placed in a boarding home in Ossining, New York, but the infant Lawrence went to the care of his great-aunt Emily Mendes-Monsanto. In 1920, Emily packed up her new ward, left her husband, and moved to the Alsatian capital of Strasbourg, where she lived for the next four years. Emily returned to New York and her estranged husband, Ludwig, in 1924, and the French-speaking Ferlinghetti began to learn English as his second language. After a short stay in a New York orphanage, Ferlinghetti moved with his aunt to Bronxville, New York, where she had secured a job as the live-in French tutor to the wealthy Bisland family. She did not stay long, however. Only months after moving in, Emily left the Bisland family mansion.

The six-year-old Lawrence was taken in by Presley and Anna Bisland and raised as their own son (Woods 66).

In school, Ferlinghetti (who still called himself "Ferling" after his father) wrote poetry, kept a journal, and worked at the print shop. After reading Thomas Wolfe's *Look Homeward, Angel* (1929), Ferlinghetti determined to attend Wolfe's alma mater, the University of North Carolina. From 1937 to 1941 he studied English and journalism there, became the circulation manager of the college newspaper, *The Daily Tar Heel*, and worked on Wolfe's old *Carolina* magazine as a sports writer. After graduation he enlisted in the navy, participated in the landing at Normandy in June 1944, and arrived at Nagasaki six weeks after the atomic bomb was dropped. What he saw there made him an instant pacifist: "hands sticking out of the mud...broken teacups... hair sticking out of the road" (qtd. in Cherkovski 39).

Ferlinghetti's growing political anarchism was reinforced by the circles of artists and writers he found himself among in San Francisco. In October 1951 Ferlinghetti and his wife, Kirby, joined leading West Coast poet and pacifist Kenneth Rexroth at his home for one of his famed soirees. There Ferlinghetti met writers and artists who shared his politics and growing determination to challenge the aesthetic and political status quo. The guests at Rexroth's apartment, including poets Philip Lamantia and Robert Duncan, represented a resurgent, postwar avant-garde that rejected ideological conditioning and advocated a recuperation of the perceptions denied by the dominant culture. Rexroth's guests sought an alternative to the McCarthy-era enforcement of social norms and consumer culture. They created what historian Daniel Belgrad calls a "culture of spontaneity." Spontaneity, Belgrad explains, was an aesthetic challenge to Western rationalism and its ontology of objectivity. Western rationalism separated objective truths from subjective perception; the avant-garde mounted a postmodern romantic critique against that rationalism by favoring mind-body holism and perception. Those gathered at Rexroth's place believed that Western rationalism included the technological drive to master nature. Ferlinghetti had witnessed the fallout of Western rationalism in Nagasaki, and in San Francisco he developed a poetic aesthetics able to sustain a critique of the military-industrial complex.

San Francisco itself was an ongoing product of spontaneity, and thus the perfect location from which to engage in alternative politics and aesthetics. Although the city was western in its geography, it remained separate from the frontier narrative that shaped much of the West. In his *Autobiographical Novel*, Rexroth described San Francisco as a "wide-open town," similar in nature to the open-form aesthetics developed as part of the culture of spontaneity.

> It is the only city in the United States which was not settled overland by the westward-spreading puritan tradition, or by the Walter Scott fake-cavalier tradition of the South. It had been settled mostly, in spite of all the romances of the overland migration, by gamblers, prostitutes, rascals, and fortune seekers who came across the Isthmus and around the Horn. They had their faults, Rexroth believed, but they were not influenced by Cotton Mather. (366)

"Open form" or "wide-open" poetry found favor with the San Francisco Renaissance poets, including Ferlinghetti. Ferlinghetti shared with his friend Rexroth the belief that the avant-garde American poet must reject the idea that "a poem is an end in itself, an anonymous machine for providing aesthetic experience," and embrace the poem as a radical tool for urgent communication (Rexroth, "Disengagement" 506). After poet Pablo Neruda complimented Ferlinghetti by saying, "I love your wide-open poetry," Ferlinghetti began to use Neruda's phrase to describe his own style and topical content. "Wide open," Ferlinghetti explained in a 2009 interview, "also refers to the 'open form' typography of a poem on the page" (Benson). Both San Francisco and the wide-open poetry developed there were more inclusive than the formal prescriptions New Criticism allowed. It was a poetry of heteroglossia, a pluralistic form that invited alternative voices into conversation with one another. The formal and political nature of spontaneity captured Ferlinghetti. His first published collection of poetry, *Pictures of the*

Gone World, established his interest in intertextual play among objective and subjective realities:

> Dada would have loved a day like this
> with its light-bulb sun
> which shines so differently
> for different people
> but which still shines the same
> on everyone
> and on everything
>
> (*Pictures* no. 23)

Rexroth's belief in San Francisco as an alternative to the frontier narrative influenced Ferlinghetti's work. In the early 1950s, Ferlinghetti worked part-time covering the San Francisco art scene for *Art Digest*, and was particularly moved by a Morris Graves exhibit. Graves was an abstract expressionist from the Northwest and a regular at the Rexroth soirees. His bird paintings, influenced by his study of Japanese and Chinese art and calligraphy, became the subject for an early Ferlinghetti poem. It begins,

> The wounded wilderness of Morris Graves
> is not the same wild west
> the white man found
> It is a land that Buddha came upon
> from a different direction
>
> (*Coney Island* 25)

The poem embodies the aesthetic principles of spontaneity: it identifies the colonized west as wounded and suggests a revision to the narrative of the frontier. An interest in Buddhism and mysticism was a feature of the culture of spontaneity, because they offered to the westerner an alternative reality in which the dichotomy between objective and subjective was dissolved. The poem continues by describing Graves's West as "a wild white nest / in the true true mad north / of introspection."

Graves's bird paintings often depict birds amid the bright white lines of a nest. By conflating an alternative West, one not "found" by the "white man" but constructed (and reconstructed) from a variety of different sources much like a bird's nest, Ferlinghetti succeeds in imagining a postmodern West that is both heterotopic and heteroglossic. Graves's West, and by extension the West that Ferlinghetti began to imagine and then promote through his work as publisher, poet, and bookshop owner, is spontaneous, not authoritarian. The growth of the culture of spontaneity in the American West is a direct response to 1950s Cold War cultural hegemony. "Spontaneity," according to Belgrad, "posed intersubjectivity, in which 'reality' was understood to emerge from a conversational dynamic" (5). The perfect place to encourage the dialogic construction of culture, Ferlinghetti believed, was a bookshop.

City Lights

Like the poem, and the city, a bookstore can also be a vehicle for social reinvention. From its founding, City Lights provided a level of mediation between the individual artist and the normative pressures exerted by social forces by championing literary experimentation. In the 1950s, much literary experimentation in the Bay Area and beyond was purposed to disrupt Cold War nationalism, the Red Scare, heteronormativity, and political conformity.

City Lights bookstore might never have happened but for the chance meeting between Ferlinghetti and Peter Martin. Martin, a San Francisco State sociology instructor and publisher of the small avant-garde magazine *City Lights*, knew Ferlinghetti by sight, because he had published some of Ferlinghetti's Jacques Prévert translations in his magazine.[1] Ferlinghetti and Martin shared the conviction that Prévert's poems, with their combination of direct language, anarchist sentiment, and nonconformist content, would interest San Francisco readers; they captured the proletarian feeling for the importance of the quotidian experience, and pushed poetic form into the realm of experimentation.

Both Ferlinghetti and Martin were political radicals. Martin, the son of an assassinated Italian anarchist, was determined to make books affordable for the underclass, and Ferlinghetti, the poet, painter, and

World War II veteran, was determined to produce art as a vehicle for radical pacifism. On a June morning in 1953, with a handshake and a $1,000 investment, Ferlinghetti and Martin became co-owners of a utopian ideal: a "left-leaning, anti-authoritarian bookshop and publishing house," the first in the nation to sell only paperback books (Emblidge 31). Ferlinghetti identified the way commercial values and elitist assumptions were off-putting to the general reader. "When I first came to town in the early fifties," Ferlinghetti recalled, "there was no book store to walk into to browse, no place to talk to people, to just hang out. I remember going into downtown bookstores and immediately being approached by clerks who wanted to know exactly what I was looking for" (Sipper).

Through Martin's and Ferlinghetti's early efforts, City Lights became, by the mid-1950s, a site that exemplified their utopian goals. Existing social infrastructure could not provide the kind of intellectual center the pair saw as necessary, and they filled that need with City Lights. Ferlinghetti articulated the manner in which City Lights was a utopian project: "We were open seven days a week till midnight, and we literally could not shut the doors at closing time. We seemed to be responding to a deeply felt need" (Sipper). This is just the kind of activity that composes what sociologist Lucy Sargisson calls a "critical" or "transgressive" utopia: a space with "subversive and transformative potential," a space with a dual function, one from which social critique can be mounted and alternative political spaces can be created (Sargisson 3). City Lights quickly became a space "rooted in the unfulfilled needs and wants...of groups...in their unique historical context" (Sargisson 11). For over sixty years the bookshop has consistently deployed utopian rhetoric in order to create a safe space from which to practice radical political identity, social nonconformity, and experimental literature. "We're still part of that," City Lights book-buying coordinator Paul Yamazaki told me. "Through publishing and our foundation and our collaborative work, we want to develop readers from all classes for a society that can think critically, one that has deep literacy. Whether it's about the war, or housing, educational things, or class issues" (Yamazaki).

The historic meeting between Martin and Ferlinghetti took place in front of the Artigues Building, a triangular structure with four storefronts, designed in 1907 for the French investors who commissioned it. In 1953, the classical revival-style building had Chinatown at its back, North Beach at its front, and three occupants: an Italian bookseller, a flower shop, and Martin's studio. From the studio above the flower shop, Martin produced his magazine *City Lights*, which published San Francisco Renaissance poets like Robert Duncan, Philip Lamantia, and Jack Spicer.

The Artigues Building's flower shop folded in 1953, and Martin decided to open a small bookshop in the vacated space. He hoped the bookshop could help support his literary magazine. Martin's belief in his *City Lights* magazine was in keeping with national trends in experimental literature and New Left values. The "little magazine" had, by then, a long history of successfully challenging both highbrow and middlebrow values. It did so, as David Bennett explains, by defining "its art as an adversary of the dominant culture" (500).

For Martin, that experimentation had to translate into his deepest utopian goal: providing the underclass with cheap radical literature. If he was going to support his own little magazine by opening a bookstore in a vacated flower shop, he might as well use the space to sell the kind of literature that would foment class revolution. In doing so, Martin helped revolutionize readers' relationships to books and bookstores. "It was Peter Martin's brilliant idea to have the first all-paperbound bookstore in the country," Ferlinghetti recalled ("City Lights"). The paperback began to leave behind its dime-novel reputation, too. "Pete's idea was to start a pocket bookstore and pay the rent for the magazine, which was on the second floor," Ferlinghetti explained. "It was a genius idea because publishers had just started publishing quality paperbacks. Up till then there were only murder mysteries and science fiction, 25-cent, 35-cent pasted-together pocket books" (Benson).

Paperbacks had been around for nearly one hundred years, and had been at the center of the debates over what constituted proper literature for nearly as long. In 1860 brothers Irwin and Erastus Beadle launched "Beadle's Dime Novels," a series that also came to be known as "yellow backs" on account of their distinctive color. The dime novel market flourished, and numerous publishing houses released their own series, mostly covering historical fiction, war, and the American West. In 1877 Deadwood Dick, the original "man in black," the noble outlaw, was born, and the demand for stories about him and other serial heroes grew.

Despite being sold by the millions to the working class, Deadwood Dick and dime novels did not find favor in all segments of society. Yes, the dime novel made it financially possible for more people to become readers, but readers of what? Some believed the sensationalism, violence, lack of moral clarity, and identity confusion found between those yellow covers could lead to crime and social decay. Dime novels came under fire from the cultural elite, who prescribed literature as a social tonic that would instill Victorian values: "the working class should read stories of self-help that emphasized the work ethic and the highly esteemed bourgeois family" (Sullivan and Schurman 3). Literature should instruct citizens in the proper social order, but dime novels did not count as literature. Blood and thunder narratives featuring heroes who operated outside the law were *not* what the doctor ordered. Or were they? On closer scrutiny, late nineteenth-century dime novels *did* reinforce conventional values. Even though Buffalo Bill and Horatio Alger did not dress like the cultural elite who criticized them, they enacted virtues of patriotism, bravery, self-reliance, and nationalism. For better or worse, the dime novel canonized the subject and theme for popular literature. And the debate over what constituted "fit" subjects for literature continued into the twentieth century, right through the doors of 261 Columbus Ave.

The dime novel declined during the early decades of the twentieth century. Several publishers made attempts to produce more "literary" paperbound books, but with little market success. "Respectable" readers still associated this newer iteration with its former disreputable yellow-backed self. This all changed when Robert de Graff, an industry innovator with experience producing hardback reprints with softer price tags, launched the Pocket Books series. An advertisement in the *New York Times* heralded the birth of the paperback revolution in 1939:

> Never again need you dawdle idly in reception rooms, fret on train or bus rides, and sit vacantly staring at a restaurant table. The books you have always meant to read "when you had the time" will fill these waits with enjoyment. (qtd. in French 255)

As indicated by the advertisement, these books were meant to be a convenient way to occupy one's idle time: to prevent dawdling, fretting, and vacant staring. These "pocket books" were sold in drugstores, cigar shops, train stations, and newsstands throughout New York City. They differed from earlier paperbacks in important ways: the titles were reprints of popular hardback editions, were genuinely pocket sized at 4½ by 6½ inches, and boasted waterproof covers that gave them durability. The first printing consisted of ten diverse titles from *Wuthering Heights* to *Hamlet* to *Bambi*. Five thousand copies of each title went on sale on a June Monday; by Tuesday Grand Central Station had completely sold out of its share, and by July second editions of all titles went to press. Soon Pocket Books was joined in the market by Penguin and Red Arrow, and despite the outbreak of World War II, the paperback craze flourished (Appel 13–14).

But despite their now useful social function of keeping idle hands busy, the paperback still had trouble dumping its low reputation. In the same year Lawrence Ferlinghetti shook hands with Peter Martin to launch City Lights bookstore, the *Saturday Review* ran an editorial describing the paperback novel as "180 ... lurid, sensational, extremely unimportant pages bound in the bosom of its heroine" (Appel 13).

But once the modern pocket book made its way to the West Coast, it went from diversion to tool of revolution. City Lights imagined the cheaply produced and cheaply sold book as a way to put experimental literature, philosophy, and social critique into the hands and pockets of many readers, especially those readers not targeted by publishers of expensive hardbound books. The paperback was given a permanent home in City Lights. Unlike the transitional spaces where most paperbacks were sold—bus stops, train stations, and drugstores—City Lights invited loitering and dwelling and made room for reading and conversation. The bookshop gave the paperback the potential to be serious literature, literature that could effect social transformation, not simply recapitulate dominant values. Martin and Ferlinghetti were explicit about inducing in their patrons the desire to seek an alternative set of midcentury values. In its outdoor and indoor paperback kiosks, City Lights stocked paperbacks that confounded New Critical values of impersonality, highbrow aesthetic standards, and middlebrow media consumption. The bookshop sold alternative magazines and newspapers along with new and used paperbacks. Much of the material reflected Martin's and Ferlinghetti's radical politics, and the store soon became a gathering place for the San Francisco New Left, a new popular front made up of those writers and artists who were disillusioned with social norms and determined to use creative cultural production to generate something new.

The Little Magazine

By the time Peter Martin began publishing his arts and culture periodical *City Lights* in 1952, the little magazine had an identifiable ideological enemy embodied by *Time/Life* publisher Henry Luce's famous advice to "accept wholeheartedly our duty and our opportunity as the most powerful nation in the world and in consequence to exert upon the world the full impact of our influence, for such purposes as we see fit and by such means as we see fit" (Luce 63). It is this exceptionalism that the New Left little magazine positioned itself to resist. Media critic Marshall McLuhan's stunning 1949 description of a media-induced social neurosis informed the editorial missions of many little magazines. McLuhan accused the *Time/Life* corporation of encouraging Americans to become "emotionally charged spectators" instead of engaged, informed citizens (McLuhan 15). In order to inoculate against the chauvinism of Luce's American Century, McLuhan prescribed the "*untrancing* of millions of individuals by millions of individual acts of will" (15). The little magazine movement in the United States pursued these acts of will to help break the trance and resist the "American century." And like Greenwich Village forty years earlier, San Francisco proved fertile ground for radical activity.

Kenneth Rexroth and others had long insisted that San Francisco was the perfect place to grow the new literary Left. Rexroth had settled in the Bay Area as a young man partly in response to the utopian possibilities he saw there. San Francisco was traditionally a strong union town, and Rexroth saw a place where his radical politics could shape culture. "There is no question but that San Francisco...is radically different from what is going on elsewhere," Rexroth observed. "There are hand presses, poetry readings, young writers everywhere—but nowhere else is there a whole younger generation culture pattern characterized by total rejection of the official high-brow culture...where magazines like the *Kenyon*, *Hudson* and *Partisan Review*, are looked on as 'The Enemy'" ("Disengagement" 507).

The Bay Area magazine *Circle* was in the avant-garde of these concerns: it championed free speech, resisted conformity, and helped develop an insurgent aesthetic. It was published beginning in 1944 in Berkeley by George Leite, who was sometimes assisted by Bern Porter, an atomic bomb–era physicist turned experimental artist. Leite, like many of the writers he published in his magazine (including Kenneth Rexroth, Philip Lamantia, and William Everson), was a conscientious objector during World War II. Like his fellows, Leite was an anarcho-pacifist. He believed that any violence, especially that perpetrated by war, was a form of authoritarian control. The masses could not be subdued through force, state control, or propaganda; instead, if each individual was awakened, "untranced," people would enter freely into an enlightened social contract with one another. Unlike Old Left literature, notable for its propagandistic style, its realism, and its socialist conversion narratives, New Left literature tended to perform its cultural work by changing the reader's psyche through a combination of romantic mysticism and surrealism.

Perhaps its most important legacy was the way *Circle* advocated a repositioning of cultural centers from East to West, a "remapping" of literary and social space. Leite and Porter explain their position in this editorial statement from the inaugural volume of *Circle:*

> A circle can be measured beginning at any point: we decided to start our measure on the West Coast. There are many reasons

> for this choice: much excellent work is being done here without local representation. For example, six of the present contributors have been printed many times in the eastern literary magazines...; there is no reason why this work should be sent to the eastern seaboard, with the usual delay of many months before the material is either accepted or rejected. Also it seems to us that in many cases the material selected is inferior to the works rejected. This of course implies a difference in critical approach; **so be it**. We believe that to be of any value a work of art, whether poetry or prose, must be alive and virile; we are temperamentally unable to accept dullness. (Leite 1)

Leite, along with Rexroth, Martin, and Ferlinghetti, believed a surreal aesthetic was especially suited to awakening people to a world outside social constraint. Surrealism could untrance the spellbound masses. Within the surrealist framework, art did not change culture by producing propaganda in the service of the revolution; art changed culture by reawakening conscience. Writers whose work was published in *Circle*—including Rexroth, Lamantia, and Everson, along with Henry Miller, Kenneth Patchen, Anaïs Nin, E. E. Cummings, and Robert Duncan—largely "forsook the topical nature of realist art in favor of the more 'abstract' project of transforming...awareness" (Belgrad 21).

In order to establish a new critical school of thought in the West, *Circle* editors Leite and Porter believed uncompromisingly in freedom of expression. Again, from their first issue:

> It is one of our major hopes in this world-wide struggle for freedom that there will be included a possible freedom of literary expression, which so far has existed in the Constitution alone. The position of Henry Miller and his works in our society should be a cause of shame to every American. There is no need to go into his case here; we have all been made aware of the power of censorship in the last few months. (2)

Henry Miller, who had moved to Big Sur in 1940, was a frequent contributor to *Circle* magazine. For the next two decades, his *Tropic of*

Cancer and *Tropic of Capricorn* were censored in the United States. Miller's work became emblematic of the desire to entrance the American public.

Leite produced a total of ten issues of *Circle* until he went broke in 1948. Other little magazines continued with *Circle*'s example: the magazine *Berkeley*, published by Bern Porter; *The Illiterati*, published by the conscientious objector camp in Waldport, Oregon; *Ark*, published by Kenneth Rexroth's Anarchist Circle; and of course *City Lights*, published by Peter Martin.

From 1952 to 1955, *City Lights* published film and cultural criticism, poems, short fiction, and philosophical essays. The goal of heightening consciousness is made clear in Robert Duncan's "An Open Letter to CITY LIGHTS," published in the magazine's first issue in July 1952. The magazine's purpose, he wrote, should help us (citizens, artists) understand "what we are...to make the city conscious of itself.... Now what I like about the idea of CITY LIGHTS at this point is that it invites us all to turn from the manufacture of culture...back to the field of experience" (Duncan 1).

Duncan's essay in many ways signals a postwar shift in popular front literature away from Marxism and labor organizing and toward existentialism and direct action. By choosing Duncan's open letter to introduce his first issue, Peter Martin endows the magazine with a widely recognized bohemian, anti-authoritarian tone. In 1944, Duncan had achieved notoriety for his essay "The Homosexual in Society," published in the magazine *Politics*, in which he calls for a gay rights movement. Duncan's *City Lights* letter also established the existentialist nature of the magazine by insisting that the editorial focus remain "alive" with the experiences of the city (1). In the third issue of *City Lights*, the same issue that includes Ferlinghetti's Prévert translations, the editor Herbert Kaufman recalls Duncan's introductory injunction in the essay "A Note on Reading Poems." To read a poem, Kaufman explains, is to enter an existential situation in which we "catch momentarily the essence of an experience" and "extend our accountability" (Kaufman 38). "What happens afterward," Kaufman concludes, "depends upon the success" of the poem (38). "One shouldn't let intellectuals / play with matches," begins one of Ferlinghetti's Prévert translations (50); in another, children witness and are "wonderstruck" by the blooming of an "instantaneous water-lily";

> Never later in their memory
> Could this flower fade
> This sudden flower
> Made for them
> Instantly
> Before them
>
> (49)

Like its predecessor *Circle*, *City Lights* published work that embraced the avant-garde mission to "dissolve the aesthetic back into the social and political realms, in order to translate such values or experiences back into life praxis" (Bennett 483).

What Peter Martin and little magazine editors like him hoped would happen afterward was the "untrancing" of America. The little magazine supported experimental literature, nonconformist thought, and existentialist values. Beat literature would not have been possible without them. The political, philosophical, and artistic groundwork laid by these magazines shifted the nation's literary consciousness from East to West and made possible what Ferlinghetti called "antiwar, anarchist...antiauthoritarian, civil libertarian attitudes, coupled with a new experimentation in the arts" (Schwartz 374).

Martin sold his share of the bookstore to Ferlinghetti and left San Francisco in 1955, and Ferlinghetti continued to fine-tune his vision of the bookshop as an explicitly utopian space. Ferlinghetti established City Lights Publishers in 1955. The press and the inaugural series, the Pocket Poets Series, became the central publishing venue for Beat poets (Ginsberg, Corso, Ferlinghetti himself) and for the international avant-garde. By insisting on making the work of new, often radical poets available in cheap quality paperbacks at City Lights, Ferlinghetti brought to the public those artists whose work challenged political and intellectual restrictions. Ferlinghetti published poets whose political allegiances challenged both new conservative and Old Left values. Third in the Pocket Poet Series was anarcho-pacifist poet Kenneth Patchen's *Poems of Humor and Protest*, which took on the legacy of the world wars, the Korean War, and the domestic war against poor and criminalized youth. The bookstore became a central meeting place for pacifist conversations, and later, during the Vietnam War, a launching pad for anti-war protests and happenings. Fourth in the Pocket Poet series was Allen Ginsberg's *Howl*. After Ferlinghetti was found not guilty of publishing and selling obscene writings, the bookshop became central to free speech concerns and changed the standards for freedom of speech throughout the publishing world. At the height of the Cold War, Ferlinghetti published number sixteen in the Pocket Poet Series, *Red Cats*, which featured poetry from behind the Iron Curtain. Finnish poet Anselm Hollo translated the work of three Russian poets—Semyon Kirsanov, Andrei Voznesenky, and Yevgeni Yevtushenko—for an American audience, effectively globalizing Beat literature. Beat and San Francisco Renaissance literature is often rightly criticized for excluding and objectifying women writers, but before 1960, Ferlinghetti's press had published Marie Ponsot, Denise Levertov, and Diane DiPrima. In the anthology celebrating the fortieth anniversary of the Pocket Poets Series, Ferlinghetti, who edited the retrospective, called his press "a little cultural exchange program" that established a "world without walls" that brought together "poets separated by language or geography, coalescing in a truly supra-national poetic voice" (Ferlinghetti, *City Lights* i–ii).

Throughout the 1970s, City Lights Publishers grew, and Ferlinghetti continued to write, record, and perform his own poetry. His most significant poem of the 1970s, "Populist Manifesto," was first recorded at San Francisco radio station KPFA in 1975 and was published in the 1976 collection *Who Are We Now?* This long poem captures what biographer Larry Smith calls "the best of Ferlinghetti" (Smith 41). The orality, the political determination, the conviction that poetry matters—all these elements are present. Ferlinghetti opens the poem by publicly and energetically declaring his motive:

Poets, come out of your closets,
Open your windows, open your doors....
Come down, come down...
down from your foot hills and mountains,
out of your teepees and domes.
The trees are still falling
and we'll to the woods no more.

(*Who Are We Now?* 61)

Here Ferlinghetti urgently seeks "Whitman's wild children" (63) and excoriates them to "keen" and "rejoice" and "communicate with all sentient beings" (62). True to his decades-long populist vision, Ferlinghetti reminds his audience that poetry is the "common carrier / for the transportation of the public / to higher places" (64). Ferlinghetti published two more populist manifestos; in each, the poet argues for a "tradition that more closely binds the poet's art and life" (Smith 72).

In 1998, San Francisco mayor Willie Brown named Lawrence Ferlinghetti as the city's first poet laureate to honor the poet and publisher for his long and distinguished career. Ferlinghetti, an outspoken critic of the way government grants and gifts have the unpleasant side effect of curtailing a writer's free speech, received the public honor with the following quip: "In Plato's republic, poets were considered subversive, a danger to the republic.... I kind of relish that role. So I see my present role as a gadfly, to use as a soapbox to promote my various ideas and obsessions" (Janofsky 1998).

In his nineties, Ferlinghetti continued to use his pulpit as populist poet and public intellectual to reinvent America and the world. In early October 2012, he was awarded the Janus Pannonius International Poetry Prize from the Hungarian PEN Club. Although the prize came with 50,000 euros, Ferlinghetti declined it, citing his lifelong commitment to human rights and free speech. In a letter to the president of the PEN Club, Ferlinghetti explained that because the prize was partially funded by a Hungarian government whose policies "tend toward authoritarian rule and the consequent curtailing of freedom of expression and civil liberties, I find it impossible for me to accept the Prize in the United States" (Staff). Ferlinghetti recommended the prize money be used to support Hungarian authors whose writings "support total freedom of speech, civil rights, and social justice" (Staff).

Ferlinghetti is perhaps best known for his significant contributions as writer, editor, and publisher of the literary Beat movement. His contributions to the growth of the literary Left and the culture of spontaneity it developed, however, reach far beyond the Beats. For over sixty years he has been a consistent voice for the literary Left, championing literary activists who used art in a way that bore witness to labor, class, poverty, migration, environmental preservation, conservation, and degradation, Native sovereignty, the performance of nonnormative identities, and resistance to fascism, imperialism, and authoritarianism.

Notes

1. Prévert was an important influence on the development of Ferlinghetti's populist poetic imagination after he had discovered the French poet's verse scrawled on a paper tablecloth in a Saint-Brieuc café. Prévert's 1945 collection *Paroles* sold more than five hundred thousand copies in France. Ferlinghetti explained this almost unheard-of market success by arguing that his poetic hero resonated deeply with a disaffiliated generation: "Prévert," Ferlinghetti wrote, "spoke particularly to the French youth immediately after the War, especially to those who grew up during the Occupation and felt totally estranged from Church and State" (Prévert 4).

Bibliography

Appel, Benjamin. "The Paperback Revolution." *Saturday Review*, 28 Nov. 1953, pp. 13–14.

Belgrad, Daniel. *The Culture of Spontaneity: Improvisation and the Arts in Postwar America*. U of Chicago P, 1998.

Bennett, David. "Periodical Fragments and Organic Culture: Modernism, the Avant-Garde, and the Little Magazine." *Contemporary Literature*, vol. 30, no. 4, 1989, pp. 480–502.

Benson, Heidi. "Catching Up with Lawrence Ferlinghetti." *San Francisco Chronicle*, 19 Mar. 2009, sfgate.com/default/article/Catching-up-with-Lawrence-Ferlinghetti-3247418.php.

Cherkovski, Neeli. *Ferlinghetti: A Biography*. Doubleday, 1979.

"City Lights Bookstore Tour." *City Lights Booksellers & Publishers*, www.citylights.com/bookstore/?fa=books_tour. Accessed 23 July 2018.

Duncan, Robert. "An Open Letter to CITY LIGHTS." *City Lights*, vol. 1, July 1952, p. 1.

Emblidge, David M. "City Lights Bookstore: 'A Finger in the Dike.'" *Publishing Research Quarterly*, vol. 21, no. 4, 2005, pp. 30–39.

Ferlinghetti, Lawrence, editor. *City Lights Pocket Poets Anthology*. City Lights Books, 1991.

———. *Coney Island of the Mind*. New Directions, 1958.

———. "Horn on *Howl*." *On the Poetry of Allen Ginsberg*, edited by Lewis Hyde, U of Michigan P, 1984, pp. 42–53.

———. *Pictures of the Gone World*. City Lights Books, 1953.

———. *Who Are We Now?* New Directions, 1976.

French, Warren. "The First Year of the Paperback Revolution." *College English*, vol. 25, no. 4, Jan. 1964, pp. 255–60.

Janofsky, Michael. "A City's Most Famous Poet Gets It in Writing." *New York Times*, 12 Aug. 1998, nytimes.com/1998/08/12/us/a-city-s-most-famous-poet-gets-it-in-writing.html.

Kaufman, Herbert. "A Note on Reading Poems." *City Lights*, Spring 1953, pp. 37–38.

Leite, George. *Circle*. Berkeley, 1944.

Luce, Henry R. "The American Century." *Life Magazine*, 17 Feb. 1941, pp. 61–65.

McLuhan, Marshall. "The Psychopathology of *Time* and *Life*." *Neurotica*, vol. 5, Autumn 1949, pp. 5–16.

Prévert, Jack. *Paroles*. 1958. Translated by Lawrence Ferlinghetti, City Lights Books, 1990.

Rexroth, Kenneth. *An Autobiographical Novel*. Doubleday, 1966.

———. "Disengagement: The Art of the Beat Generation." *Beat Down to Your Soul*, edited by Ann Charters, Penguin, 2001, pp. 493–508.

Sargisson, Lucy. *Utopian Bodies and the Politics of Transgression*. Routledge, 2000.

Schwartz, Stephen. *From West to East: California and the Making of the American Mind*. Free Press, 1998.

Silesky, Barry, *Ferlinghetti: The Artist in His Time*. Warner, 1990.

Sipper, Ralph. "A Cultural Catalyst" (City Lights promotional sheet, 1979). Reprinted in *California Living: The Magazine of the San Francisco Sunday Examiner and Chronicle*, 19 Jan. 1975.

Smith, Larry. *Lawrence Ferlinghetti: Poet-at-Large*. Southern Illinois UP, 1983.

Staff, Harriet. "Lawrence Ferlinghetti Declines 50,000 Euro Prize from Hungarian PEN Club." *Poetry Foundation*, https://www.poetryfoundation.org/harriet/2012/10/lawrence-ferlinghetti-declines-50000-euro-prize-from-hungarian-pen-club. Accessed 23 July 2018.

Sullivan, Larry E., and Lydia Cushman Schurman, editors. *Pioneers, Passionate Ladies, and Private Eyes: Dime Novels, Series Books, and Paperbacks*. Haworth Press, 1996.

Woods, Gioia. "Lawrence Ferlinghetti." *Dictionary of Literary Biography: Twenty-First-Century American Poets*, vol. 374, Gale, 2014, pp. 64–77.

Yamazaki, Paul. Personal interview, 18 May 2010.

4

The Traditional Roots of Woody Guthrie's *Dust Bowl Ballads*

WILLIAM M. CLEMENTS

Though influenced by childhood experiences in Oklahoma and Texas and later affected by contact with progressive politics in New York City, songwriter Woodrow Wilson Guthrie's experience in California affirmed his commitment to leftist political and social causes. There he observed the plight of his fellow Okies as they tried to survive in what they had vainly hoped would be an Edenic setting. He also had his first formal contact with political activism through mentoring by local communists and socialists and through involvement in attempts to organize migrants from the Midwest. Guthrie produced his first socially conscious songs while in California, and he continued to draw on experiences of migrants to the state for subject matter throughout his career in songwriting and performing. He revisited the state several times after he had become part of the East Coast folk song scene, and he consistently affected a western persona. He projected what eastern leftists perceived as an "authentic" demeanor. Seemingly unlettered, grounded in the musical traditions of rural America, and accompanying himself on guitar (the trademark musical instrument of singing westerners in contemporary popular culture), Guthrie personified the grassroots leftist who had developed his sensitivity to the needs of the "common man" through his own experiences and firsthand observations rather than by reading and studying armchair treatises prepared by the intellectual elite who dominated the leftist political scene back East. His combination of folksy western persona with social consciousness resulted in a body of poetic work, much of it intended to be performed as songs, which has helped to define the intersection of folk and popular music with political and social idealism into the twenty-first century. His early collection of verse set to music, *Dust Bowl Ballads*, epitomizes ways in which he blended a folk song–based aesthetic, grounded in his identity as a westerner and treating the subject of westward migration, with political ideas codified by a western experience that might seem foreign to that aesthetic.

It took some hard traveling for Guthrie to make it to the RCA Victor recording studio on April 26, 1940. The trek had begun in 1912 in Okemah, Oklahoma, where Guthrie was born into a middle-class family whose fortunes would collapse due to economic changes, bad business planning by his father, his sister's death in a housefire, his father's incapacitation also from a housefire, and his mother's institutionalization owing to what would later be diagnosed as Huntington's disease. After enduring life on Okemah's streets, Guthrie headed west. In Pampa, Texas, he read about psychology and Eastern religions in the public library, began to develop an interest in music, especially that of the Carter Family and the new western swing that was emerging in the mid-1930s, became a professional sign painter, and married a local girl. But the West continued to entice him, particularly since he was straining under the hardships of living on the economic fringes of Pampa's oil boom and suffering through the unpleasantness of the dusty, dry climate. So on he went to California, where family members helped to get him established in a musical career. Guthrie fronted several radio programs, performing hillbilly tunes he'd learned from as early as his time in Okemah as well as increasingly songs of his own composition about the lives of his fellow migrants. He adopted progressive politics and followed actor and leftist Will Geer, bound for New York City to take the lead role in a stage production of *Tobacco Road*. Guthrie drove his family (now consisting of a wife and three children) back to Pampa and then, alone, caught a bus as far as Pittsburgh. He hitchhiked the rest of the way to New York during some of the year's coldest weather and arrived in the city in February 1940. There he met other musicians who had absorbed the hillbilly aesthetic and were also developing their own socially conscious music, which drew on that aesthetic. He also encountered Alan Lomax, researcher for the Library of Congress Archive of American Folk Song. Lomax found Guthrie entrancing not only for his broad repertoire of traditional music picked up in Oklahoma and Texas and from hillbilly records but for the songs he was writing. Lomax documented Guthrie's repertoire in a series of recordings done in Washington, DC, and was instrumental in arranging for Guthrie to record for Victor. At the April session Guthrie recorded eleven songs, all of his own composition. For the most part, these songs constituted the material that would be released within a few months as two albums called *Dust Bowl Ballads*.[1]

Along with "This Land Is Your Land," the songs that make up *Dust Bowl Ballads* have remained Guthrie's most enduring literary and musical creations. They reflect the grassroots progressivism that came to color all his work, but they also refract his past experiences with folk and popular music. They demonstrate in specific terms how Woody Guthrie forged a connection between forward-looking politics and a traditional musical and literary aesthetic.

The sources for Guthrie's political views—far to the left of his father, who was active in the Democratic Party—have occasioned much speculation (see, e.g., Kaufman). Exactly what those views were remains subject to some debate as well. Clearly, he became radicalized in California, where his observations of the living and working conditions of his fellow migrants convinced him of the inequalities of means and opportunities in American life during the 1930s. His exposure to formal progressive ideals, originally through journalist Ed Robbin, helped to alert Guthrie to individuals and organizations, particularly the Communist Party, that shared his vision of the unfulfilled American dream. But he seems to have brought to California an anti-establishment perspective that recognized the conflicting interests of the moneyed upper class and those who found themselves barely surviving from day to day. He identified with the latter, though he never worked in the fields as did many who had also migrated westward from the Midwest and South. Certainly he found Communism attractive, but for the most part Guthrie did not adhere to the party's teachings, which he may not have always fully understood. As one analyst of

Guthrie's political and social views has put it, he developed a "radical hybrid political ideology which incorporated elements of Christian socialism, social banditry, populism, Jeffersonianism, collectivism, 'commonism,' and the ideology of the Communist Party" (Briley 43).[2] His ideas emerged from a range of sources, "some of which came out of a rural progressivism...and others that he picked up in his travels throughout America" (Jackson 222). They were not always consistent except for their class-conscious support of those at the bottom of the social scale, which included people dispossessed of their economic heritage during the 1930s and who sought to ameliorate their situations by moving to California.

Guthrie realized early on that his most effective contribution in support of social and economic justice would be the songs he created. Though he had not yet embellished his guitar with the slogan, "This machine kills fascists," by the time he arrived in New York City he had performed in a range of venues where his original compositions were well received: Communist Party rallies, union events, the several radio programs that he fronted. Like many other songwriters who hoped to attract the attention of those affected by injustice, Guthrie recognized that his songs would be most appealing if cast in the familiar aesthetic of "hillbilly" music, the commercial offshoot of the musical folk heritage that he had begun learning in Okemah. In other words, Guthrie modeled his compositions on folk songs.

Though a "gifted re-creator of folk traditions" (Reuss 273), Guthrie did not originate the idea that folk songs could be effective vehicles for social commentary and protest. In the American tradition, his work had been predated by many others, perhaps most notably Joel Hillstrom, a Swedish immigrant who as "Joe Hill" wrote songs for the Industrial Workers of the World ("Wobblies") during the first two decades of the twentieth century. Contemporary with Guthrie, Mary Magdalene ("Aunt Molly") Jackson and her half-siblings Sarah Ogan and Jim Garland had used folk song as the foundation for their pro-union, anti-management songs about violent responses to attempts to organize coal miners in the southern Appalachians. Other notables who preceded Guthrie in writing "American folk songs of protest" (as

John Greenway denoted the material) included Florence Reece, also from the mine patches, and textile worker Ella May Wiggins. At the time he was writing the songs that would become "Dust Bowl ballads," Guthrie may not have known of all of these fellow songwriters, but he realized that basing socially conscious music on folk models had considerable potential. He appeared on the scene at a time when revived interest in those models had emerged among musicians who were seeking to spread their progressive ideas through music. Previously the Composers' Collective, a Communist Party organization, had encouraged creation of avant-garde material by formally trained musicians such as Aaron Copland, but by the mid-thirties they had realized that music based on folk and popular traditions had more potential for reaching the audiences whom they hoped to influence (Kaufman 36–37).

Richard Reuss, one of the earliest scholars to attend to Woody Guthrie's work, noted that this work followed a pattern already operating among midwestern migrants in California. Okies there "produced lore born of its traumatic life to supplement the older materials brought along in the trek west. Traditional forms of folksong and folk expression were retained, but lyric and prose content frequently were altered to reflect contemporary experience" (277). While they followed his community's creative and re-creative lead, Guthrie's songs for *Dust Bowl Ballads* are notable for their consistency of conscious purpose and of voice: that of a politically aware commentator reminiscent of fellow Oklahoman Will Rogers, though with a much more radical perspective that encouraged the same sort of social awareness that Guthrie's persona evinced.

Patterns of traditional song as well as particular pieces in the hillbilly repertoire had the advantage of familiarity. The audiences who made up Guthrie's primary intended audience had grown up in this musical heritage, and the commercial performers whom they favored were musicians who did not stray too far from it. In particular, Guthrie was attracted to the Carter Family, a trio from southwestern Virginia who had achieved commercial success through their performances of traditional material and of original compositions that resembled the music of the southern mountains. Guthrie knew that the Carter Family approach to music represented the familiar and the trusted. He also realized that his progressive ideology was not so familiar and might even be distrusted by some of his listeners. Conveying this ideology in musical vehicles that had already gained a following might encourage listeners to pay attention, not to dismiss it automatically as something alien to their concerns. Moreover, Guthrie often used melodies and structures of hymns and gospel songs, allying his seemingly radical message with core values in his community of listeners.

Meanwhile, he could use the sentiments conveyed in traditional music—for example, nostalgia for the "old southern home," a familiar theme in hillbilly music—in juxtaposition with the realities encountered by the migrants whose lives his songs described. Guthrie might substitute accounts of problems faced by working-class folk during the 1930s for idyllic descriptions of peaceful log cabins in the pines where people lived out their simple but fulfilling lives. Listeners familiar with the original songs on which he based his creations or with the general tenor of the musical tradition would be struck by the ironic juxtaposition of the romantic expectations of the tradition with the hard realities of Depression-era existence.

Though Guthrie was a consummate performer and seemed to relish being the center of attention, he also recognized that for his songs to have a real social impact they had to elicit audience participation. Not only would listeners be able to sing along if they were familiar with his models, but those models were structured in ways that encouraged group participation: repetitive patterns in which only a few words might change from stanza to stanza, frequently used refrains that a crowd could quickly learn, for example. At a union rally or similar venue, Guthrie might expect to have the whole crowd joining in as he worked his way through a song. Folk songs provided examples for how this might be accomplished. Moreover, the songs were often expandable. Except for ballads, which required the singer to work out a story line, many of the songs Guthrie wrote based on traditional models could go on almost interminably, or they could be abbreviated. In other words, particular performances could respond to the exigencies of specific situations.

While the songs written by Guthrie were not "folk songs" in the sense that they had passed through oral tradition, they reflected that tradition for very practical reasons. Moreover, Guthrie was himself steeped in this tradition, which included ballads, "'heart' and religious songs," cowboy songs, dance pieces, blues, jigs, and harmonica melodies (Reuss 276). Lomax's astonishment at the number of songs that he knew when he arrived in New York City in 1940 suggests Guthrie's command of folk and hillbilly music. At the time he recorded *Dust Bowl Ballads*, that music represented the extent of his musical knowledge. So even if he had no practical reasons for grounding his compositions in that music, he knew no other models that he could have employed so easily and effectively. As Reuss puts it, "the rural Southwest...gave him an instinctive knowledge of ballad structure, folksong style, and the folk idiom." His time as an itinerant in California had offered "crucial themes for his pen, drawn from first-hand observation," while his "innate sense of social concern" received focus from Communists and other West Coast radicals (282). Clearly, deterministic forces shaped the content and style of his compositions and performances, and the results, while radical in content, were conservative in style and approach, "deliberately composed within the framework of the American southern folk music tradition he was most familiar with" (Reuss 295).

For some time before 1940 RCA Victor had been encouraging Alan Lomax to record an album of folk songs. His experience working in the field with his father John during the 1930s, the set of publications he was beginning to produce, his continued association with the Library of Congress Archive of American Folk Song after his father's retirement, and his familiarity with traditional musicians especially in the South and with the movement to popularize folk music that was emerging in New York City confirmed Lomax's status as an expert culture broker. In fact, the recording company trusted him enough to accept his recommendation that they arrange the sessions with Guthrie that led to *Dust Bowl Ballads* when Lomax himself was unable to comply with Victor's request (Szwed 162–63). The company recognized that Guthrie's work had the potential for exploiting the same market as Steinbeck's *The Grapes of Wrath* (both novel and film) and may have stipulated that he write a song based on Steinbeck's work. While the other material that he recorded had most likely all been written in California or—in a couple of cases—during his years in the Texas Panhandle, the long ballad "Tom Joad" was written in New York City in April 1940. Guthrie was already a seasoned performer; his radio experience in California had given him a sense of ease in a production studio. On April 26, 1940, he recorded eleven songs, one of which—"Tom Joad"—was so long that it had to be recorded in two parts. Only one of the songs, "Talkin' Dust Bowl Blues," required a second take. On May 3 he recorded two more songs, bringing the total to thirteen songs on fourteen sides. In July, Victor released two albums, *Dust Bowl Ballads Vol. 1* (Victor Records P-27) and *Dust Bowl Ballads Vol. 2* (Victor Records P-28). Each consisted of three ten-inch 78 rpm disks. Since "Tom Joad" required both sides of one disk, a total of eleven songs appeared on the two albums. Two of the pieces recorded by Guthrie, "Pretty Boy Floyd" and "Dust Bowl Blues," were not released until 1964 when Victor reissued the two albums as a single long-playing record (RCA Victor LPV-502).[3]

In the short term, *Dust Bowl Ballads* could not be counted as an overwhelming success. The scant critical notice generally suggested that while somewhat interesting as social documents, Guthrie's songs offered little of musical significance. Sales were also limited and, for the most part, restricted to "college intellectuals and members of the political left" (Cray 182). The audience for whom Guthrie had intended the songs had little exposure to them, except in Pampa, where a druggist set up speakers on the sidewalk and broadcast the songs. Of course, subsequent interest in these songs, many of which have been covered by other musicians, has perceived them as more important—not only as social documents that shed light on a time and place in twentieth-century America but also as effective musical, literary, and political extensions of folk song.

Guthrie drew on the traditional material that he had been performing most of his life by directly parodying specific pieces, by adapting narratives to an established ballad aesthetic, by exploiting narrative formulas that had characterized Anglo-American folk song for centuries, by incorporating genre patterns from the blues and talking blues, and by setting many of his compositions to traditional melodies. While grounding his songs sufficiently in tradition to appeal to his intended audience, Guthrie used his models as vehicles for his progressive political and social views. In a column written for *The Daily Worker*, he characterized the songs as "liberal as the dickens and as progressive as the angels.... They came out of the hearts and mouths of the Okies" (qtd. in Klein 165)—a statement that speaks to both their radical message and their roots in tradition.

The most obvious parody among the *Dust Bowl Ballads* is Guthrie's recasting of the gospel song "The World Is Not My Home." Usually attributed to early twentieth-century gospel songwriter Alfred E. Brumley, the song is an upbeat statement of Christian otherworldliness. The speaker in the song's lyrics stresses that he or she is "just passing through" this life and unable "to feel at home in this world anymore." Instead, the speaker's true home is in heaven, and his or her "treasures are laid up somewhere beyond the blue." The song is not so much a rejection of the world of the flesh as it is a positive identification of what the speaker believes to be his or her real home. Notable for its lack of negativity, its sprightly rhymes, and its catchy melody, the song would have been well known to those grounded in the evangelical Protestantism that had come to dominate grassroots Christianity since the Civil War. It does not excoriate worldly concerns; it simply disregards them.

Though he subscribed to the fundamental tenets of Christianity and had, in fact, been baptized while living in Pampa, Guthrie joined many of his fellow progressives in his dissatisfaction with the religion's apparent lack of concern with social injustice. That attitude had found particular expression in Joe Hill's "The Preacher and the Slave." Set to the melody of "In the Sweet By-and-By," Hill's song, one of his best known and most likely familiar to Guthrie, mocked the "Starvation Army" and its promise of "pie in the sky" when a believer died instead of suggesting ways to improve earthly existence. Guthrie did not follow Hill's mocking lead in his parody of "The World Is Not My Home," but

"I Ain't Got No Home"[4] does suggest that real problems in this world need to be addressed. It affirms the claim that Guthrie "rejected any type of religious song that urged listeners to passively accept the wrongs in this world in the hope of receiving heavenly rewards" (Jackson 64). The four stanzas of his composition each end with "I ain't got no home in this world anymore" and catalog some of the issues that the speaker, "a wanderin' worker" who had formerly been a sharecropper, faces as he tries to survive: police who "make it hard wherever I may go"; fellow members of the underclass who are stranded on a "hot and dusty road that a million feet have trod"; an economic system in which the "gamblin' man is rich and the workin' man is poor." The speaker's own history includes having been driven from his home by a "rich man," the loss of his wife who "took down and died upon the cabin floor," and the surrender of his crops to "the banker's store." Dispossessed of his livelihood and of opportunities for happiness, he has nowhere to go but the way of the migrant. Heaven may await him at the end of his life, but for the time being he is more concerned about his earthly situation. Though many of Guthrie's songs are notable for their wit and sardonic humor, "I Ain't Got No Home" is not one of them. But it is particularly effective if one is familiar with the piece that Guthrie is parodying. The contrast, which many in his intended audience would recognize, between the cheerful otherworldliness of the gospel song and the cheerless portrayal of the displaced speaker in Guthrie's work does not critique conventional Christianity, as "The Preacher and the Slave" tended to do, but suggests by implication that religion should not simply ignore the hard lives of people in this world. Guthrie's biographer Joe Klein believes that Guthrie wrote the song in response to the gospel song's popularity in the migrant laborers' camps in California[5] and that it marked a turning point in his thinking about religion and social action—a rejection of the passive Eastern spirituality he had read about in the Pampa Public Library. At the least, it was "an attack on inaction" (120). It operates most meaningfully, though, for an audience familiar with its gospel music source.

While a parody of that source, Guthrie's song ironically exploits a recurrent theme in the hillbilly music performed by the Carter

Family and others: nostalgia for "the old southern home." Songs that develop this theme often feature a speaker, far from his or her ancestral home, who looks back longingly on a romanticized childhood and youth spent in a cabin tucked away in an Edenic setting in a verdant mountain hollow. The speaker looks forward to returning to the site of former pleasures either to visit or to live out the rest of his or her years. The Carter Family discography lists several "old southern home" pieces, including "My Home Among the Hills," "My Clinch Mountain Home," "My Little Home in Tennessee," and "My Old Virginia Home." The creator of the gospel song on which Guthrie based "I Ain't Got No Home" probably had this theme in mind but suggested that one's true home was not "a cabin in the pines" but heaven. It even stresses its point by suggesting the despair that would result if the hope for a heavenly home proved groundless: "If Heaven's not my home, then Lord, what will I do?" While Guthrie does not reject aspirations for heaven, his take on the gospel song speaker's sense of alienation from an earthly home was prosaically matter-of-fact: "Reason why you cant feel at home in this world any more is mostly because you aint got no home to feel at" (qtd. in Kaufman 25). Moreover, the song's focus on a homelessness that has resulted from an unjust social and economic system does not allow for the hope that heaven can substitute for worldly alienation (Shumway 131).

More generic as parody than responsive to a particular song, Guthrie's "Dust Pneumonia Blues,"[6] which refers to an actual medical condition that victims of the Dust Bowl potentially faced, represents his take on the blue yodels of Jimmie Rodgers, another recording artist from the hillbilly tradition who influenced Guthrie and was a favorite of the audience to whom he directed his musical attention.[7] Rodgers's thirteen blue yodels, recorded between 1927 and 1933, used the conventional three-line blues stanza but added an innovative yodel at the end of each stanza. While most of the blue yodels dealt with the familiar blues theme of tension in male-female relations, Rodgers usually included some sardonic humor. Moreover, Rodgers's own ultimately fatal lung problems, to which he occasionally referred in his lyrics, afforded a precedent for the topic of Guthrie's seven-stanza composition. The song strings together images of dust pneumonia, which the speaker has so bad that a physician tells him, "you ain't got long, not long." He admits that the song should have some yodeling in it, but "I can't yodel for the rattlin' in my lung." It ends with a stanza that exploits a tall tale motif familiar in drought-prone areas of the American West and Midwest:

> Down in Texas my gal fainted in the rain,
> Down in Texas my gal fainted in the rain.
> I throwed a bucket of dirt in her face just to bring her back again.

Not dependent on an audience's familiarity with a specific song, as is "I Ain't Got No Home," this parody would resonate with pointed sonority for listeners who knew Rodgers's blue yodels. Also more fatalistic, "Dust Pneumonia Blues" does not assign blame for the speaker's ailment to an unjust social system; the weather is the villain here. When the song is experienced within the context of the other *Dust Bowl Ballads*, though, the listener might suspect that dust pneumonia sufferers were more likely to be those who tried to earn a living in the harsh weather than bankers and other white-collar members of the upper classes.

Another way in which Guthrie based his songs on folk tradition involved his understanding of ballads, wherein, according to Reuss, his "profound comprehension of the folksong idiom is most evident" (285). He had been hearing narrative folk songs since his childhood in Okemah, and often those songs adhered to an aesthetic that foregrounded condensation of the narrated events, a montage technique of plot development that ballad scholars have called "leaping and lingering," reliance on stark contrasts especially in character presentation, narrative single-strandedness, and the use of commonplaces (Hodgart; Olrik). These characteristics undergird the stories that Guthrie recounts in several songs among the *Dust Bowl Ballads*, especially his account of a dust storm that swept through the Great Plains and Southwest, including Pampa, Texas, in 1935, and his retelling of Steinbeck's narrative in *The Grapes of Wrath*. In fact, Lomax believed that Guthrie had so mastered the ballad idiom that he was writing material "that will fool a folklore expert" (qtd. in Kaufman 40).

During his years in Pampa, Guthrie had plenty of opportunities to experience the dust storms that provided the focal image for *Dust Bowl Ballads.* The frequency and intensity of those storms had increased during the mid-1930s, a point that Guthrie noted and connected to economic hard times in the pamphlet he wrote to accompany the albums:

> Dust storms is not exactly a new thing—but up till five or six years ago they was mighty few and far between. This business of such awful and terrible dust storms, so black you cant see your hand before your eyes, or a light in your room, or a dollar in your pocket, or a meal on your table—that's what's new, that's what the old timers cant figger out. (*Pastures* 43)

The most dramatic of these storms occurred on April 14, 1935—known as "Black Sunday" or sometimes "Black Easter," even though the storm actually occurred on Palm Sunday—and impressed not only Guthrie but many of those in the Texas Panhandle and elsewhere who experienced it (Grider). Guthrie responded with a ballad, probably written soon after the event and used in *Dust Bowl Ballads.* Familiar with the disaster ballad, including songs that related weather-based catastrophes such as "The Cyclone of Rye Cove" (recorded by the Carter Family in 1929), Guthrie was working out of a tradition when he wrote "The Great Dust Storm (Dust Storm Disaster),"[8] although he probably had no particular song in mind as his model. The seven-stanza composition tells its story discursively, using a set of images that stress the widespread effects of the storm ("From Oklahoma City to the Arizona line, / Dakota and Nebraska to the lazy Rio Grande") and its virtual inundation of the countryside ("It covered up our fences, it covered up our barns, / It covered up our tractors in this wild and dusty storm"). These images, which generally take up a stanza each, create tableaus as Guthrie "leaps" from one to "linger" on another. Although it produced no dramatic scenes of devastation, fatalities, or injuries as did the tornadoes that figured in several American ballads, the dust storm created enough chaos that it encouraged people to pack up their belongings and head for a more salubrious climate. Guthrie's distinctive touch in "The Great Dust Storm" is his emphasis on the event's apocalyptic dimensions. The disaster ballads with which he was familiar generally drew morals about the vanity of material goods, life's transitory nature, and the need to be prepared to encounter God at any time. Though he did not develop the image in spiritual terms, Guthrie clearly perceived Black Sunday—and by extension perhaps the Dust Bowl in general—as marking the end of a way of life. He and his neighbors in Pampa, where he was living when the storm hit, "thought it was our judgment, we thought it was our doom." Those folk who had huddled in their "oil boom shacks" to escape the storm "thought the world had ended, and they thought it was their doom." Guthrie also believed their way of life in mid-America had come to a close and that their only hope lay in escaping to paradisaical California, which sadly would not live up to the migrants' expectations. In "The Great Dust Storm" Guthrie uses a single event to epitomize what had become a chronic phenomenon: a climate that had turned on its inhabitants, who were already suffering from the economic downturn that was a half a decade old when the storm hit. He has given an individualized humanity to the disaster, "stripping it down, animating it, giving it a human face" (Kaufman 19). Guthrie included another song, "Dusty Old Dust," which responded to Black Sunday in *Dust Bowl Ballads*. That song, thought to be one of the first he composed, also presents a set of somewhat isolated images, some of which are treated with sardonic humor. "The Great Dust Storm," like other songs in the disaster ballad tradition, has no comic relief.

Guthrie's most ambitious attempt to compose a song based on the ballad aesthetic with which he was familiar from oral tradition was his retelling of the plot of *The Grapes of Wrath* in seventeen stanzas, which required two sides of one of the 78 rpm disks that made up the record albums. Opinions differ on whether he had read Steinbeck's novel or was basing his narrative on John Ford's film. Guthrie, who affected an unlettered persona, tended to suggest the film as his source and claimed his ballad made Tom Joad's story available to those who could not afford the price of a theater ticket. He seems to have been creating a

Tom Joad "for the masses, even broader masses than those who bought the best-selling novel" (Simon and Deverell 183). However, he had met Steinbeck in California and was actually quite well read. So it is possible that he had read the novel.

"Tom Joad"[9] was apparently written at RCA Victor's request. Guthrie composed it sometime after his interviews with Alan Lomax in February 1940 and used as its tune that of the outlaw ballad "John Hardy," which he encountered, according to conventional opinion, while staying in the Lomax household.[10] The Guthrie legend has him writing through the night at Pete Seeger's apartment in New York City. Seeger awoke to find his living room littered with cast-off paper, Guthrie sound asleep on the floor, and the seventeen stanzas typed and ready to perform. Those stanzas show the ballad aesthetic at work perhaps in the way that it had operated for generations of broadside ballad composers who predated Guthrie.

Clearly Guthrie had to exercise the ballad-based aesthetic of condensation to get Steinbeck's narrative into seventeen stanzas. He does so by eliminating extraneous detail, by focusing his attention almost exclusively on a main character, by ignoring the complexities of that character, by defining conflicts in starkly realized contrasts, and by singling out a few incidents from the novel without developing transitions between them. The result is the story of Tom Joad as an emergent martyr for progressive ideals and as having taken the first step toward becoming the "social bandit" (Hobsbawm 13–29), whose formularized career Guthrie used in another of the *Dust Bowl Ballads*.

Like Steinbeck's novel, Guthrie's song begins with Tom Joad leaving Oklahoma's state penitentiary after serving part of his sentence for manslaughter. The first seven stanzas set up the situation: Joad's catching a ride with a trucker to get home, his falling in with Preacher Casey and finding that home abandoned, learning that the family has "been tractored out by the Cats" (that is, displaced by agribusiness interests that are having the old homestead leveled), and his finding his family and loading the car to head west. The narrative is elusive and allusive, each stanza capturing an image and, in the fashion of traditional balladry, moving to another image without developed transition.

The Joads' trek westward receives only minimal attention in Guthrie's version of the narrative; it is treated in one stanza that focuses on the deaths of Grandpa and Grandma Joad. The remaining ten stanzas treat the violence that Tom and Casey witness as local authorities brutalize migrants. Casey's response to that violence, landing him in jail and ultimately resulting in his death and Tom killing a deputy sheriff, set the scene for the ballad climax: Tom's vow to spread the gospel according to Casey (that "everybody might be just one big soul") and his vow to his mother to become a defender of the defenseless.

This is *The Grapes of Wrath* in minimalist terms. Many of Steinbeck's characters are mentioned only in passing, and some who figure fairly prominently in the novel disappear altogether. The ballad focuses single-strandedly on the development of one character: the titular Tom Joad. Others such as Muley, Grandma and Grandpa, Ma, and especially Casey appear because they affect Tom's story. Such subplots as the marital troubles of Tom's sister Rose of Sharon have no place in a plot shaped by the simplicity demanded by the ballad aesthetic. Contrasts emerge clearly, and Tom's decision to assume a socially responsible role develops out of those contrasts. The reader does not get the contexts provided by Steinbeck's interchapters, the rich descriptions of settings along Route 66, the exploitative policies of landowners and their lackeys in California law enforcement, or the horrors of life in migrant camps and boxcars. Such descriptions lie beyond the ballad aesthetic.[11] Guthrie has chosen to focus on those features of Tom Joad's story that stress his message—the song's "emotional core," to use a term from ballad scholarship (Coffin 246): the provocations in Oklahoma and California that drive Tom to his climactic decision at the end and the philosophy of universal brotherhood that fuels that decision. Even though he exercised his balladic license to condense, Guthrie's version of the Joad story and the Tom Joad character delivered a clear political message. That message, argue Simon and Deverell, was clearer "than those offered by either John Steinbeck or John Ford." They suggest that he "turns Tom Joad into a dogged union organizer with an uncompromising Popular Front agenda" (184). But because Tom's story ends with his decision to adopt that agenda, Guthrie does not implement one of the most important ballad formulas that has informed Anglo-American folk expression. That formula finds fuller expression in another piece that he recorded at the two *Dust Bowl Ballads* sessions.

Although Guthrie demonstrated his familiarity with ballad aesthetics in "The Great Dust Storm" and "Tom Joad," both of which tell their stories in ways that would be generally recognizable to listeners who had grown up hearing traditional narrative folk songs, he also more specifically invoked ballad tradition by exploiting particular formulaic approaches. This is most evident in *Dust Bowl Ballads* in his account of the career in social banditry of Charles "Pretty Boy" Floyd.[12] At least since the emergence of a body of expressive culture treating Robin Hood, ballads about whom found their way into Child's canonical nineteenth-century anthology of English and Scottish popular ballads, the career of the social bandit has been narrated in formulaic terms. Recently, Graham Seal has outlined a narrative framework that defines that formula ("Robin Hood" 74–75; see also Seal, *Outlaw*). Although Guthrie was probably not familiar with the Robin Hood ballads collected by Child, few of which have appeared in oral tradition on this side of the Atlantic, he might have come to know Robin Hood through other sources. He certainly had encountered what Seal calls the "Robin Hood principle" in songs about American outlaws, especially the well-known ballad dealing with Jesse James, who had flourished in the Midwest a couple of generations before Guthrie and whose folk song reputation was well known. One of Guthrie's best-known pieces, "Jesus Christ" (not one of the *Dust Bowl Ballads*), uses the tune from the most popular Jesse James ballad for its melody. Guthrie applied the Robin Hood principle to the career of an Oklahoma outlaw who had figured in headlines during the mid-thirties and whom John Steinbeck has his characters invoke as the ultimate rebel against Depression-era repression in *The Grapes of Wrath*. In fact, at the end of Steinbeck's novel, and Guthrie's song based on the novel, Tom Joad seems headed to become, like Guthrie's Floyd, a social bandit.[13]

Charles Floyd grew up in Sallisaw, Oklahoma, a hundred or so miles east of Okemah, a region with a history of lawlessness that included such luminaries as the James brothers, the Dalton gang, the Doolins,

Belle Starr, and Cherokee Bill (Klein 3). His youth was marked by petty crimes in defiance of local authorities. Those crimes came to more general attention when he took part in the robbery of the local post office. A St. Louis payroll robbery in which Floyd participated in 1925 led to a string of other crimes and a national reputation that he enjoyed until his death in 1934. Guthrie took this unpromising figure—a person whom ballad scholar Tristram P. Coffin called a "degenerate sadist" (qtd. in Reuss 287)—and made him into a folk hero, using the Robin Hood principle that he knew from the folklore associated with Jesse James and other midwestern outlaws. For example, Guthrie's peace-loving Floyd becomes an outlaw when he defends his wife's honor from a boorish deputy sheriff who accosts her "in a manner rather rude." Frequently the social bandit, as noted in the Robin Hood principle, becomes an outlaw because of similar injustice and the need to defend his own or someone else's honor. Guthrie's Floyd, forced to take "to the trees and timber" after he "laid that deputy down," turns to a life of crime. Although the ballad does not identify his victims, the beneficiaries of Floyd's deeds include "many a starving farmer" who finds his mortgage paid, hospitable householders who provide for "a stranger / That come to beg a meal" and find that he has left them "a thousand-dollar bill," and families in Oklahoma City who receive "a whole car load of groceries" on Christmas. The social bandit has left a note attached to his holiday gift:

> "Well, you say that I'm an outlaw,
> You say that I'm a thief.
> Here's a Christmas dinner
> For the families on relief."

Guthrie begins the ballad with a "come all ye" stanza, a commonplace device in traditional balladry, which he directs specifically at children. The lesson they are supposed to learn from the example of Pretty Boy Floyd contrasts this "man of the people" (a term often assigned to the social bandit) who robs from the apparently rich to give to the poor with those enjoying the privileges of the moneyed classes who will use a "fountain pen" to extract so much from the dispossessed as to "drive a family from their home"—a sentiment that Reuss believed to be a regional proverbial saying that Guthrie had poeticized (298).

Outlaw ballads that treat the social bandit according to the formula of the Robin Hood principle have long characterized the oral heritage out of which Guthrie emerged, and while "Pretty Boy Floyd" falls within that heritage, it also reflects the era of the Great Depression and the Dust Bowl. Floyd was one of several outlaws who rose to notoriety by preying largely on the financial institutions that many progressives during the 1930s demonized. Their crimes, many of which victimized the people with whose concerns Guthrie identified, often involved acts of bloodshed as well as economic consequences. The only violent act attributed to Floyd in Guthrie's ballad is his defense of his wife's honor. Nor does Guthrie deal with Floyd's death; in the expressive culture dealing with social bandits, the bandit's death is often attributed to betrayal. His narrative instead is a sanitized version, focusing on the social bandit's charity and on the class consciousness that defined Guthrie's political and social philosophy. For Guthrie, who used the social bandit formula in other compositions, Charles "Pretty Boy" Floyd is the embodiment of socially responsible values, especially defense of family and concern for other people even if it means exile from conventional society. For Guthrie such a figure epitomized the admirable "good man outside the law" (qtd. in Kaufman 28). Guthrie's recording did not appear with the other *Dust Bowl Ballads* in 1940; it was not released until 1964. Though that may be due to a variety of factors, one wonders if the memory of the real Charles Floyd was too recent for RCA Victor to publish a song depicting him as a model of social justice.

Guthrie drew on several folk song genres as the framework for the compositions that make up *Dust Bowl Ballads.* As noted, ballads figure prominently among his genre resources, as do blues, which he had learned as early as his Okemah days and later from recordings, and gospel music. Another genre that he exploited (and that eventually came to be closely identified with him) was the talking blues. Though probably derived from African American expressive forms such as field hollers as well as from the recitation tradition that characterized Anglo-American performance traditions, the first fully developed talking blues on record was that performed by Chris Bouchillon in 1926. Titled simply "Talking Blues," the record sold some ninety thousand copies and inspired Bouchillon to reuse the form several times. His piece is a rhythmic chant over guitar accompaniment consisting of six-line stanzas that relate a comic story filled with oft-narrated motifs and images. The first two lines of each stanza rhyme, as do the second pair of lines. The final lines, much more free and irregular than their predecessors, also rhyme and offer a commentary, sometimes in the form of a punch line, on what appears earlier in the stanza. Bouchillon's "Talking Blues" had no pretensions beyond the comic, but when Woody Guthrie took over this genre, he used it as a vehicle for his social philosophy, though couching his message in often bitter humor.

"Talking Dust Bowl Blues,"[14] which Guthrie apparently wrote in California and performed on his radio broadcasts, presents the misadventures of migration. The narrator and his family, who had been driven from their formerly prosperous farmstead somewhere in the Midwest by the sustained drought, cross the desert and mountains in a "Ford machine," for which they'd traded their acreage. Loaded with people and possessions, the automobile misses a hairpin curve, scattering "wives and childrens / All over the side of the mountain." The family finally arrives in California broke and "so dad-gum hungry I thought I'd croak." Up to this point in the song, Guthrie has offered no overt social or political comment. The family's plight stems from the climate and the speaker's own ineptitude behind the wheel, not from an unjust social system. But all they can afford to eat in California is "a spud or two" from which the narrator's wife makes a "tater stew." Guthrie extends his final stanza beyond the customary six lines to include a stew-based dig at the establishment:

We poured the kids full of it,
Mighty thin stew, though.
You could read a magazine right through it.
Always have figured
That if it'd been just a little bit thinner,
Some of these here politicians
Could have seen through it.

The double meaning of the last line introduces commentary into a comic narrative that to this point has not differed significantly in tone from the model provided by Bouchillon's recording. In order for dense politicians finally to understand the inadequacies of the American economic system, they need an especially heavy-handed indicator—something so obvious that even they cannot misapprehend it. Guthrie and his listeners would have been hard pressed to imagine something thinner than a stew through which one could read a magazine. They might think that dense politicians required evidences of systemic features equally extreme before they would take action. This talking blues—much more subtle than most of Guthrie's other examples in the form (e.g., "Talking Columbia," "Mean Talking Blues," "Talking Merchant Marine")—exploits the expectations of listeners familiar with the genre before introducing its sociopolitical message. They are enticed by the comic familiar before being "educated" about politicians.

Though perhaps not a "literary" device, another way in which Woody Guthrie drew upon folk tradition in *Dust Bowl Ballads* was his use of familiar melodies—often from folk songs—as the setting for his poetry. Sometimes, as in the case with "Tom Joad," he employs those tunes straightforwardly, adopting them without change. By using for "Tom Joad" the melody commonly used for the outlaw ballad "John Hardy," Guthrie suggests, to those familiar with the traditional song, that his protagonist is also a social bandit. Other traditional and popular melodies that Guthrie adopted and sometimes adapted for the songs that make up *Dust Bowl Ballads* include those he used for "Dusty Old Dust" (from the musical setting for Andrew Jenkins's "Billy the Kid"), "(If You Ain't Got the) Do-Re-Mi" (from "Hang Out Your Front Door Key," a British music hall song of the early twentieth century), and "Vigilante Man" (from "Today Has Been a Lonesome Day"). In these cases, uses of familiar tunes may not have functioned as specific aural allusions; instead they grounded Guthrie's radical, seemingly exotic messages in the everyday and commonplace. They alerted listeners that what they were hearing was not so out of the way that it could not be couched in the musical vehicles that they had heard all their lives. Somewhat disingenuously, Guthrie—writing under the name of his alter ego "Alonso M. Zilch"—claimed that his choice of tunes derived from indecisiveness: "At times I cannot decide on a tune to use with my words for a song. Woe is me! I am then forced to use some good old, family style tune that hath already gained a reputation as being liked by the people" (qtd. in Jackson 7). However, to accept this assertion or dismissively to suggest that "almost all his lyrics simply ride on the back of someone else's music" (Jackson 7) ignores that Guthrie may have been using the familiar melodies purposefully. Using ready-made tunes may have been "standard practice among topical songwriters" (Place 59), but it was an effective method of couching new ideas within the matrix of tradition.

That Woody Guthrie followed the practice of his predecessors and contemporaries in embedding radical political and social messages in a popular, folk aesthetic has often been noted in considerations of his work. But once that generalization has been made, the specifics of how he combined message and vehicle have largely been ignored. He drew upon the familiar in ways that allowed him to parody and allude to particular materials in the familiar repertoire. But even when there was not a clearly defined relationship between a song he composed and a specific model, his exploitation of familiar aesthetics, formulas, and genres allowed him to ground his work in tradition. Guthrie apparently saw himself within a truly American artistic and philosophical heritage—one that included not only Joe Hill but Walt Whitman. He ensured that what he did was clearly American by using traditional art forms as the foundation for his work.

The pieces that make up *Dust Bowl Ballads* had many successors in Guthrie's work. He continued to parody familiar songs and genres, he exploited the ballad aesthetic especially in narratives of disaster, and he set his compositions to familiar melodies. Moreover, he performed in a style consonant with that which he'd adopted as he was learning music as a youth and which dominated hillbilly records. His combining of an updated message applied to current events, often taken from daily headlines, with traditional musical and literary patterns generated plenty of imitators, especially the "Woody's children" who emerged in mainstream music in the early 1960s. And into the twenty-first century, his "grandchildren" have continued to do what Guthrie did to good effect in the songs that became *Dust Bowl Ballads.*

Protest song scholar R. Serge Denisoff has drawn a distinction between songs that have a "magnetic" purpose and those whose aim is "rhetorical." The former are calls to action, which usually involves joining a union or organizing in some way to combat the forces of oppression. Rhetorical songs, though, focus on raising awareness: on naming and describing situations, thus making people cognizant of conditions of political and social disenfranchisement (5–7). The songs that make up *Dust Bowl Ballads* fit the latter purpose. Though role models of active protest exist in the characters of Tom Joad and Pretty Boy Floyd, it is unlikely that Guthrie considered them figures to be emulated. He used them to transform "the dust bowl and the Okies into a heroic encounter. He took migrant workers and dispossessed farmers and transformed their ramblings into a voyage bound for glory" (Cohen 14). Along the way he showed his listeners the forces—climatic, economic, and political—that made their ramblings so difficult.

Notes

1. Two important book-length biographies (Klein and Cray) have explored Guthrie's life in detail. While they do not agree on all particulars regarding this complex, elusive artist, they both present the general outline of his life leading up to April 1940 that I have skimmed through here.
2. Whether Guthrie actually joined the Communist Party remains in question. Although he contributed to Communist publications such as *People's World* in Los Angeles and *The Daily Worker* in New York City and occasionally advocated party positions that were at best questionable (e.g., his support of the nonaggression pact between Nazi Germany and the Soviet Union), Guthrie probably lacked the discipline to adhere to the sometimes rigid ideological constraints that the party imposed on its members.
3. Guthrie had recorded earlier versions of more than half of the songs included on *Dust Bowl Ballads* during the Library of Congress sessions he did with Alan Lomax in March 1940. He rerecorded several of the songs, often with significant word changes, over the next several years. In this study I am using the versions recorded at the two Victor sessions, which are available on a compact disc version of the two *Dust Bowl Ballads* albums issued by Rounder Records (Rounder CD 1040). Specifics regarding those sessions are available in Logsdon (188–89). Logsdon also provides information about other reissues of the material.

4. "I Ain't Got No Home," words and music by Woody Guthrie. WGP/TRO–©Copyright 1961 (Renewed), 1963 (Renewed), Woody Guthrie Publications, Inc. & Ludlow Music, Inc., New York, administered by Ludlow Music, Inc. International Copyright Secured. Made in U.S.A. All Rights Reserved Including Public Performance for Profit. Used by Permission.
5. Cray (123) suggests a 1938 date for Guthrie's composing this song. This was a time when he and Missouri-born singer Maxine Crissman were introducing more socially conscious material into their repertoire of hillbilly songs performed on their radio program *The Woody and Lefty Lou Show.*
6. "Dust Pneumonia Blues," words and music by Woody Guthrie. WGP/TRO–©Copyright 1963 (Renewed), 1976 (Renewed), Woody Guthrie Publications, Inc. & Ludlow Music, Inc., New York, administered by Ludlow Music, Inc. International Copyright Secured. Made in U.S.A. All Rights Reserved Including Public Performance for Profit. Used by Permission.
7. Rodgers's commercial success in the late 1920s and early thirties inspired many imitators, including Guthrie's fellow Oklahoman Gene Autry, who began his professional career in music by attempting to replicate the Rodgers sound. Guthrie himself might have been tempted to do likewise, but apparently he could not yodel. Moreover, by the time he began to appear on California radio, Rodgers had been dead for several years, many potential imitators had come and gone, and the fad for his music had somewhat abated.
8. "Dust Storm Disaster" (aka "The Great Dust Storm"), words and music by Woody Guthrie. WGP/TRO–©Copyright 1960 (Renewed), 1963 (Renewed), Woody Guthrie Publications, Inc. & Ludlow Music, Inc., New York, administered by Ludlow Music, Inc. International Copyright Secured. Made in U.S.A. All Rights Reserved Including Public Performance for Profit. Used by Permission.
9. "Tom Joad," words and music by Woody Guthrie. WGP/TRO–©Copyright 1960 (Renewed), 1963 (Renewed), Woody Guthrie Publications, Inc. & Ludlow Music, Inc., New York, administered by Ludlow Music, Inc. International Copyright Secured. Made in U.S.A. All Rights Reserved Including Public Performance for Profit. Used by Permission.
10. The Carter Family, though, had recorded the song on May 10, 1928, so it is possible that Guthrie knew of it before his visit to Lomax. Moreover, Pete Seeger had performed it at the *Grapes of Wrath* concert in February 1940, the event that introduced Guthrie to the New York City folk song scene.
11. That Guthrie could indeed write rich descriptive passages is clear from his prose in the fictionalized autobiography *Bound for Glory* or in his posthumously published novels, *Seeds of Man* and *House of Earth,* as well as in many letters and other writings, published and unpublished. His failure to do so in "Tom Joad" derived from his conscious use of an aesthetic that eschewed such description.
12. "Pretty Boy Floyd," words and music by Woody Guthrie. ©Copyright Woody Guthrie Publications, Inc. (BMI). All rights reserved. Used by Permission.

13. Having grown up more or less contemporaneously with the outlaw in eastern Oklahoma, Guthrie had some personal affinities with Floyd as well. Moreover, Reuss believed that he had heard "numerous accounts of his real or alleged doings." Additionally, members of Guthrie's family claimed to have personally met Floyd (302).
14. "Talking Dust Bowl" (aka "Talking Dust Blues"), words and music by Woody Guthrie. WGP/TRO-©Copyright 1960 (Renewed), 1961 (Renewed), Woody Guthrie Publications, Inc. & Ludlow Music, Inc., New York, administered by Ludlow Music, Inc. International Copyright Secured. Made in U.S.A. All Rights Reserved Including Public Performance for Profit. Used by Permission.

Bibliography

Briley, Ronald. "'Woody Sez': Woody Guthrie, the *People's Daily World*, and Indigenous Radicalism." *California History*, vol. 84, no. 1, Fall 2006, pp. 30–43.

Coffin, Tristram P. "Mary Hamilton and the Anglo-American Ballad as an Art Form." *The Critics and the Ballad: Readings*, edited by MacEdward Leach and Tristram P. Coffin, Southern Illinois UP, 1961, pp. 245–56.

Cohen, Edwin. "Neither Hero nor Myth: Woody Guthrie's Contribution to Folk Art." *Folklore*, vol. 91, 1980, pp. 11–14.

Cray, Ed. *Ramblin' Man: The Life and Times of Woody Guthrie.* W. W. Norton, 2004.

Denisoff, R. Serge. *Sing a Song of Social Significance.* Popular Press, 1972.

Greenway, John. *American Folksongs of Protest.* A. S. Barnes, 1960.

Grider, Sylvia. "Black Easter–April 14, 1935." *Diamond Bessie and the Shepherds*, edited by Wilson M. Hudson, Encino Press, 1972, pp. 61–71.

Guthrie, Woody. *Dust Bowl Ballads.* Rounder 1040, 1988.

———. *Pastures of Plenty: A Self-Portrait*, edited by Dave Marsh and Harold Leventhal, HarperCollins, 1990.

———. *Woody Sez*, edited by Marjorie Guthrie et al., Grosset & Dunlap, 1973.

Hobsbawm, Eric J. *Primitive Rebels: Studies of Archaic Forms of Social Movement in the 19th and 20th Centuries.* W. W. Norton, 1959.

Hodgart, M. J. C. *The Ballads.* W. W. Norton, 1962.

Jackson, Mark Allan. *Prophet Singer: The Voice and Vision of Woody Guthrie.* UP of Mississippi, 2007.

Kaufman, Will. *Woody Guthrie: American Radical.* U of Illinois P, 2011.

Klein, Joe. *Woody Guthrie: A Life.* Random House, 1980.

Logsdon, Guy. "Woody Guthrie Biblio/Discography." Santelli and Davidson, pp. 181–243.

Olrik, Axel. "Epic Laws of Folk Narrative." *The Study of Folklore*, edited by Alan Dundes, Prentice-Hall, 1965, pp. 129–41.

Place, Jeff. "Woody Guthrie's Recorded Legacy." Santelli and Davidson, pp. 57–68.

Reuss, Richard A. "Woody Guthrie and His Folk Tradition." *Journal of American Folklore*, vol. 83, 1970, pp. 273–303.

Robbin, Ed. *Woody Guthrie and Me: An Intimate Reminiscence.* Lancaster-Miller, 1979.

Santelli, Robert. *This Land Is Your Land: Woody Guthrie and the Journey of an American Folk Song.* Running Press, 2012.

Santelli, Robert, and Emily Davidson, editors. *Hard Travelin': The Life and Legacy of Woody Guthrie.* Wesleyan UP, 1999.

Seal, Graham. *The Outlaw Legend: A Cultural Tradition in Britain, America, and Australia.* Cambridge UP, 1996.

———. "The Robin Hood Principle: Folklore, History, and the Social Bandit." *Journal of Folklore Research*, vol. 46, 2009, pp. 67–89.

Shumway, David R. "Your Land: The Lost Legacy of Woody Guthrie." Santelli and Davidson, pp. 128–37.

Simon, Bryant, and William Deverell. "Tom Joad: Thoughts on a California Dreamer." *California History*, vol. 79, 2000, pp. 180–91.

Szwed, John. *Alan Lomax: The Man Who Recorded the World.* Penguin, 2010.

5

Luis J. Rodriguez's *Always Running*

Between Chicano Nationalism and the Left

JOSÉ NAVARRO

"America Was Born in the Streets"[1]

Gangs and gang culture have long been a problem in the United States, but they have equally been prominently celebrated in the American cinematic and literary imaginations. For example, the original Howard Hughes *Scarface* film (1932) was subtitled "The Shame of the Nation." For the 1983 remake, however, director Brian De Palma dropped the subtitle and, given the cultural context of predatory capitalism and a renewed focus on the Cold War, the film became an incredible success through its depiction of a Cuban immigrant's rise to power through drug trafficking and his seemingly inevitable demise. Likewise, many people also looked fondly on the gangster figure Don Corleone in Francis Ford Coppola's *The Godfather* (1972). Perhaps the fondness was because Don Corleone was characterized as the Italian patriarch of a soon-to-be-assimilated *American* family—signaled by his son Michael Corleone's military service and political aspirations. Film critic Roger Ebert writes in one review of the film: "Don Vito Corleone (Marlon Brando) emerges as a sympathetic and even admirable character; during the entire film, this lifelong professional criminal does nothing of which we can really disapprove" (1997). In Ebert's review of the Martin Scorsese film *Gangs of New York* (2002), he similarly notes that the end result is "a considerable achievement, a revisionist history linking the birth of American democracy and American crime." He adds: "It is instructive to be reminded that modern America was forged not in quiet rooms by great men in wigs, but in the streets, in the clash of immigrant groups, in a bloody Darwinian struggle" (2002).[2] The list of such gang films continually grows, and the glamorized, nostalgic reviews by white film critics repeatedly also reveal Americans' fascination with gangsters and their stories.

Nevertheless, not all gang films and gangster stories capture the American imagination with the same "sympathy"; nor do many other of the gang figures seem as "admirable" as Don Corleone in the estimation of these same film critics. With few exceptions, Chicano/Latino gang films and Chicana/o gang narratives have merely underscored long-held racialized stereotypes of Mexicans historically portrayed in Hollywood films and in American fiction by white writers and directors. As such, the difference between the reviews and representations of Italian and Irish gang narratives (white ethnic gang stories) and Chicano/Latino gang narratives in the United States is evidence of a racialized logic that allows for a sympathy and admiration of particular characters based on their proximity to white Anglo-Saxon Protestant (WASP) identity. While the Irish and Italian immigrants portrayed in the films above reflect the difficulties of their specific incorporation into U.S. society,[3] in the late nineteenth century, twentieth, and early twenty-first centuries such identities are now largely claimed symbolically (see Gans). This process of integrating white ethnics happens not only because of the pressure to integrate African Americans during Reconstruction and in the post–World War II period but also because of the dominant black-white binary of racial politics in the United States. More importantly, such narratives of criminality and the subsequent inclusion of white ethnics in the U.S. body politics allow for disavowals of structural racism in the United States. This is especially true in the face of shifting immigration policies and the gains of the civil rights movement after 1964/1965.[4] The inclusion of white ethnics in the American body politic and the American workplace, and their representation in fiction and film, also solidifies tensions between black and brown workers and the white working class at this moment in history. This is because the unions formed and largely controlled by these white ethnics strategically privileged familial bonds (or whiteness by default) as the central entryway into the union and access to better paying jobs. The result is that, even among the Left, race and racism remained an unresolved element of the struggle for upward economic mobility. This particular historical context, as a result, seems to undergird the differences in reception of these gang narratives in both film and literature.

Gary Soto, in his review of Luis J. Rodriguez's *Always Running: La Vida Loca, Gang Days in L.A.*, for example, offers an assessment of gang narratives that contrasts with Ebert's. He writes: "We know Los Angeles gangs largely by what appears on television: squints of truth that we get in 10-second clips of black and Latino youths being pushed into the back of a police car or handcuffed and lying belly down on the sidewalk." "These images" he continues, "are brief and so fixed in their portrayal of right and wrong that they preclude any argument." Overall, then, Soto describes the role of the media in dealing with these particular narratives that continually represent Chicanos as "problems" and as resistant to incorporation into a "normal" American society. Soto, by contrast, understands these Chicano gangs and gang members in the same ways Ebert understands the white ethnic gangs in *The Godfather* and *Gangs of New York:* as products of a society that rejects and marginalizes them. Soto ends his review by suggesting that *Always Running* offers insight that could never be offered by the mainstream news media or Hollywood and writes: "In 'Always Running,' here's truth [that] no television set, burning night and day, could ever begin to offer" (Soto 26).

Soto's assessment of *Always Running*, moreover, contrasts with the nostalgia embedded in reviews of gang narratives like *The Godfather*. These white ethnic gang narratives underscore the eventual integration into American society of white ethnics as proof that the United States is an exceptional democratic nation-state. Soto's review, in fact, directly challenges the notion that these narratives offer proof that anyone—regardless of race/ethnicity—can integrate into the nation and realize the American Dream by highlighting the racial tension within the Left that is often subsumed into the broader class politics of gang stories like *The Godfather*.

It is also important to note that these mainstream Hollywood gang stories are told against the backdrop of the development of nationalist movements in the 1960s like the American Indian Movement (AIM) and the Black Power and Chicano Power movements, which responded to the historical role of race/racial formation as integral to the sociopolitical and economic stratification of the United States. These empowerment movements also recast the subsequent emergence of black and Latino gangs as a direct result of racial discrimination and marginalization they faced in the country rather than as an innate cultural or racial problem. Indeed, in many ways, the crux of the tension between the reception in these gang narratives underscores the tension between the Left and the Chicano and black nationalist movements of the 1960s and 1970s. These tensions also play out in Rodriguez's own sociopolitical development in his autobiography: his entry into a critical political awareness comes from attending leftist meetings organized by Chente Ramírez, and yet the majority of his political activism requires him to address issues related to structural racism in school and mass incarceration.

Chicano gang narratives like Rodriguez's *Always Running*, therefore, self-consciously recall the historical role of race as a specter of American imperialism in the formation of the American West and in U.S. national development in general.[5] Furthermore, his memoir not only implicates American imperialism and its legacies (the dispossession of lands, structural racism, state violence, etc.) in the creation of contemporary/urban areas that spawn modern gangs, but it also offers an implicit critique of the racial tension among the Left in the United States. This is why Rodriguez begins *Always Running* by narrating the different reasons his family migrated from Juárez, Chihuahua, México, to Los Angeles; and why, once they are in Los Angeles, he narrates their migrations from Watts to Reseda to San Gabriel. These constant "migrations," he notes, were the result of economic necessity and led to a general instability in his life and his identity. The majority of the book, nonetheless, focuses on his experiences and critiques of two primary institutions, the public education system and the police, rather than immigration and housing segregation—although Rodriguez continually suggests their linkages.

As a result, much of his narrative is a critique of State power in which he suggests that these negative interactions with the State are the impetus for him and other young minority men and women becoming gang members: that is, they form gangs as a response to racism but also as a response to state violence. Thus, if we understand the education system to be the system through which the State carries out a form of ideological control, and understand the police as the primary apparatus of repression (Althusser), then Chicanos who become gang members, criminals, and so on become so in response to State aggression and violence carried out by these specific apparatuses. Rodriguez's critique suggests that both apparatuses work in concert, as the education system disproportionately punishes young men of color and pushes them out of school and the police lock them up once they are out on the streets.

The New Left, of course, clearly understood these relationships between education, culture, violence, capitalism, and the State, and embraced Althusser's critique.[6] Rodriguez's memoir has a similar focus. In this respect, Rodriguez's work outlines and portrays radical responses (including processes of nationalist identity-formation) to State violence, and he records these processes in his own sociopolitical bildungsroman. His narrative, then, is about a Chicano gang member coming into a political consciousness and taking action on behalf of the larger Chicano community rather than simply being about the neighborhood gang and his personal involvement with it. It is as much about the life of an individual as it is the life of the barrio/community.

For Rodriguez, this process also involves an extension of the *carnalismo* that is central to gang membership rather than a complete disavowal of it. He also recognizes the salience of such familial bonds in the formation of his Chicano political identity. This stands in contrast with the adoption of a more "universal" leftist politics that is peddled by the "collective" with which he studies later in his memoir. In other words, Rodriguez's narrative relies on a lived experience that is informed by the histories of racial segregation and the socioeconomic and political formations of the barrio in the broader contexts of white supremacy and settler colonialism. When he narrates his life, therefore, he constantly toggles between his own individual sociopolitical development and the ways in which he remains a product of the conditions of the barrio. In the process, he offers insight into barrio life and its historical formation. This toggling embodies what I term "barriobiographics"—a form of life-writing that self-consciously privileges the barrio and the *barriological* (Villa 2000) as the site of and the cultural foundation for the Chicano/a gang member's epistemological and ontological formation.[7]

Nonetheless, the majority of scholarship on Rodriguez to date is focused on his experience with the education system, not these literary and generic considerations. As a result, this scholarship is focused on fields related to urban education.[8] Consequently, the literary scholarship on Rodriguez's text is less expansive. Monica Brown's *Gang Nation* (2002), for example, provides perhaps the most significant insights on questions about the nation, State violence, and citizenship in *Always Running* as a gang autobiography. In this framework, Brown argues that gang membership functions to reproduce forms of belonging and citizenship. She writes: "The gang members depicted in these works attempt to negotiate national spaces and places, fighting wars abroad and 'at home' all the while caught between the United States and Mexico, their gangs and their families" (Brown 37); and she adds: "Rodriguez analyzes in detail how he (and presumably other gang members) internalized…hatred" (69). Importantly, she also notes: "Reading Rodriguez's account of gang life in East LA, it is impossible to overlook the ways both gang life and cultural nationalism fulfill similar needs for urban youth—for community, loyalty, respect, and a sense of allegiance to specific territory or place out of which their identity arises" (70). Brown, in other words, understands gangs and gang membership to be alternative models of the nation and citizenship as both affect and effect a sense of "community" (i.e., as in Benedict Anderson's framework), "loyalty," "belonging," and then lead to a type of "nationalism." Indeed, the *placas*, or gang graffiti and gang monikers, that dot a particular barrio work in precisely the way Benedict Anderson argues a print culture works to help us imagine the nation.

Paula Moya argues likewise in her essay "'This is Not Your

Country!': Nation and Belonging in Latina/o Literature." Moya notes that Rodriguez's autobiography, "by exposing the dynamics of exclusion operative in the dominant conception of US nationalism, works to interrogate those dynamics and that conception, even as it contests the idea that Latina/os must forever be outsiders to the US national imaginary" (184). Moya's article is primarily a review and critique of three major works—one of which is Monica Brown's *Gang Nation.* She lauds Brown for articulating the way gangs have a particular social and economic function for their members—namely, providing an increased sense of community, citizenship, and belonging. Moya especially notes the way Brown is able to sympathize with Latina/o gang members without excusing or justifying their violent actions. Finally, Moya notes the critical contribution that Brown's work makes in examining the way "historical events have been narrativized or ignored, remembered or repressed" (193) for various political reasons.

Amaia Ibarraran Bigalondo, in her essay "Wolves, Sheep and *Vatos Locos:* Reflections of Gang Activity in Chicano Literature," compares and contrasts Rodriguez's *Always Running* to Yxta Maya Murray's *Locas* (1997). Bigalondo explores the differences in the "aggression" and "vision" of gang life and gang activity as those are informed by gender. She concludes that Murray's novel ends more "pessimistically" than does Rodriguez's memoir and notes: "Rodriguez's narration accounts for his own personal experience" and "renders [his] novel with a strength that widely surpasses Murray's work" (113). This article might suggest, at the very least, how a comparison of *Always Running* and *Locas* might create different readings of each text with respect to gender. The article, however, fails to get at any substantial reading and simply concludes: "reality is stronger than fiction" in this case (113).

Vincent Perez, in his article "'Running' and Resistance: Nihilism and Cultural Memory in Chicano Urban Narratives," highlights the difference between Palo Alto and East Palo Alto, California, to emphasize the relationship between gang membership, criminal activity, and class difference. Perez specifically makes literary comparisons between Richard Wright's *Native Son* (1940), Rodriguez's *Always Running* (1993), and Ronald Ruiz's *Happy Birthday, Jesus* (1994). Perez suggests the way in which Rodriguez's and Ruiz's texts offer an intimate look at "Chicano nihilism by positioning [their subjects] within the context of a racialized and carceral society that relentlessly engulfs urban minority youth with the threat of violence, imprisonment, and death" (134). In the end, Perez argues that Rodriguez's character/self internalizes and absorbs the racist attempt by the dominant culture to "negate him" and that such "acceptance of nihilism functions as a form of opposition against a racist and repressive status quo" (144).

The most recent literary scholarship on Rodriguez has been carried out by Josephine Metcalf. In her book *The Culture and Politics of Contemporary Street Gang Memoirs* (2012), she argues that the narrative arc of gang memoirs like *Always Running*, Sanyika Shakur's *Monster: The Autobiography of an L.A. Gang Member* (1993), and Stanley "Tookie" Williams's *Blue Rage, Black Redemption: A Memoir* (2004) "rests on conversion" or "the journey from violent young gangbangers, through punishment, on to political enlightenment and the renunciation of violence" (12). Metcalf also insightfully details the reception of these memoirs by educational stakeholders and the mainstream press. While Metcalf seems sympathetic to these writers and pays careful attention to their sociopolitical developments, she still manages to reproduce an outsider/normative framework for assessing these writers, their texts, and their critiques of broader socioeconomic and political structures that they argue give birth to gangs in America. For example, she argues that their "accounts of violence must be understood as an opportunist pop-cultural strategy to sell a product, as well as a serious portal into understanding marginalized young people struggling to survive in an extreme social environment" (12). Then, when describing their narrative arc, she describes these writers as beginning as "'ignorant' gangbangers" who eventually "mature" and become socially and "politically conscious" (12). Finally, she notes that these writers offer "sensationalist tales while simultaneously presenting the sober reflection of politicized hindsight" (14) and suggests that the violence in these texts stems from a masculinity based on the "warrior-style behavior of the narrators" in which "women are seemingly sidelined in the memoirs to permit room for boastful tales of machismo and male bravado" (14).

Describing such narratives as "sensationalist" tales, however, suggests that the experiences of these men of color are disconnected from an "objective" reality that can seemingly only be rendered by white male authors. Such a characterization resembles the ways in which literary critics and writers historically refer to early American texts written by women, like the old "captivity" narratives, or the way exceptional frameworks have been applied to writers of color like Phillis Wheatley. It is implicitly a pejorative characterization of autobiographical narratives by men of color.

Furthermore, Metcalf's understanding of the violence in these texts as rooted in "machismo" and "male bravado" fails to contextualize this violence, especially as it relates to race and gender in the United States. Rooting this violence in the stereotypes of the "macho" Latino figure and the menacing black figure implicitly and unconsciously ties such violence to Latinidad or blackness; it forgets that the violence perpetrated by these men is merely one facet of a broader (mostly white) phenomenon of violence that stems from a violent patriarchal structure and culture in the United States embodied, in these texts, by modern police forces. In short, to racialize such violence as Metcalf does in her analysis suggests a racial or cultural specificity to such violence while simultaneously ignoring the racist tenets of the violence committed by white police officers against men of color in these same narratives. One might argue that such State violence, committed disproportionately against men of color, and the very logics that perpetuate the notions of black "super-predators" and Latino hypermasculinity as "machismo," maintain the system of white supremacist heteropatriarchy and the existing socioeconomic and political orders by placing the sole blame for such violence on these men of color. It leaves unquestioned the framework of white men "protecting" women from the threat of black and brown men.[9]

In framing these writers and their texts in these ways, Metcalf also fails to understand the culture of African American and Latino gangs in which offering insights into or writing about gang life is akin to "snitching," not "an opportunist pop-cultural strategy to sell a product" (12). Additionally, the act of writing about gangs and gang life can never solely be for "personal fulfillment" (14), as she claims, because such writing always places the writer at risk of death from their homeboys.[10] Thus, the act of writing is part of a simultaneous process of leaving and disavowing gang life—including the violence that comes with it—because gang members cannot talk about their participation in gang activity, in general, and remain part of the gang. In the 'hood, this is called "dry snitching," and it comes with serious consequences. Therefore, to suggest that these writers tell "sensationalist tales" for "personal fulfillment" and money ignores and dismisses the very real risks they take in writing such truths about the barrio/'hood.

Nonetheless, I agree with Metcalf that these texts generally grapple with individual development and violence and the broader structural critiques of State power raised in and by their narratives. Rodriguez's *Always Running*, however, more than any other American street gang memoir, self-consciously focuses on the interplay between the broader structures of his society and his personal development from gang member to community activist and writer. In doing so, he specifically layers the histories of Spanish conquest, American westward expansion, and the modern formation of the barrio onto one another and, as a result, his autobiography simultaneously uncovers the colonial/imperialist roots of barrioization.[11] In addition, he privileges a barriological approach to understanding barrio life and barrio lives as a counter to neoliberal narratives of integration into the nation. These barriobiographics are exemplified by a type of life-writing in which writers like Rodriguez self-consciously offer themselves up as metonyms for other Chicanos/as and present their experiences as a result of the broader structural (socioeconomic, racial, etc.) inequities confronted by people similarly trapped in barrios across the United States, and they become the politically infused aesthetic and literary expression of choice of the Chicanx subaltern memoirist. The result is that Rodriguez ends up necessarily trapped between a historically specific Chicana/o nationalism and a broader leftist politics in his memoir that lead to a complicated, individual progression out of *la vida loca*/Chicano gang life through a messy intersectional class consciousness.

Barrio-Biographics

The representations in Rodriguez's memoir launch effective but troubling critiques of the legacies of U.S. imperialism, State violence, and white supremacy as they specifically relate to Chicanos in the American West. While his memoir focuses on his own interiority/subjectivity as it is shaped by racist, heteropatriarchal logics in the United States, he is simultaneously aware of the subjectivities of those around him. That is, his politicized Chicano autobiographics[12] require him to toggle simultaneously between his own subject formation and his community's formation because of the metonymic logics of race and class in the United States. The process of life-writing, therefore, is part of a complex negotiation for Chicanos like Rodriguez whose narratives all involve a coming to a political consciousness without so easily divesting themselves from the logics of coloniality and the accompanying traumas (e.g., the physical, psychological, sexual violence, etc.). At one point in the memoir, for example, Rodriguez illustrates this complex relationship by self-consciously writing about writing. He notes:

> The fact that I didn't know anything about literature. I had fallen through the chasm between two languages.... This was the predicament of many Chicanos.... We could almost be called incommunicable, except we remained lucid; we got over what we felt, sensed and understood. Sometimes we rearranged words, created new meanings and structures—even new vocabulary. Often everyday talk blazed with poetry.... Our expressive powers were strong and vibrant.... We needed to obtain victories in language, built on an infrastructure of self-worth. (219)

In this passage, Rodriguez describes his writing process after getting a contract to write for Quinto Sol Publications of Berkeley. He also describes the ways in which forced English monolingualism led him to an "incommunicable" state, but his resilience to remain "lucid" relied on his communicating what he "felt, sensed and understood" about the world. Rodriguez points out the process of creating "new meanings and structures"…"built on self-worth" in which "everyday" barrio talk is "blazed with poetry" as necessary to countering racist, nativist discourses that require English monolingualism and straight-line assimilation. In short, Rodriguez describes the most crucial aesthetic and political elements of barrio-biographics by pointing to the resilience and resistance of the community, and to the neologisms and rhythms of quotidian barrio-centric discourses that are always poetic to him. This barrio-biographics, in other words, is about a struggle that is waged on the basis of claiming and asserting one's individual subjectivity and self-worth through the genre of life-writing while understanding that the logics of race/racism continually challenge these very articulations of the self and result in a process of barrioizing/ghettoizing the community.

Thus, Rodriguez's memoir *requires* a focus on the life of the barrio (the barriological) *and* on Chicano nationalism as a political consciousness tied to notions of indigeneity and Aztlán. This is why he also details his participation in ToHMAS (the Chicana/o student organization) at Mark Keppel High School, the Chicano/a Movement in general, and the Chicano Moratorium in particular: to specify his return to Chicano nationalism and turn away from a purely leftist politics in his memoir. Of course, the consistent leftist/postnationalist strain in his text reminds the reader that national boundaries are generally superficial and necessarily encompass a diverse array of people based on a constellation of markers of identity such as class, race, and culture. In addition, Rodriguez's constant challenges to borders—literal and symbolic—are founded on the notion that they are, by nature, exclusionary.[13] Nationalism, nevertheless, still functions as the ideological basis for creating a forceful but fictive national cohesion for Chicanas/os, exemplified by the notion of Aztlán, which has been continually deployed since at least the 1960s as a response to anti-Mexican racism in the United States. Obviously, this deployment is "strategic" (Spivak) but also a necessary response to the processes of deterritorialization (Saldívar) and its subsequent social, political, and economic erasures of people of color by Anglo settlers.[14]

As a Chicano nationalist text, then, shaped by recounting acts of physical and epistemic violence, Rodriguez's memoir also reproduces a framework for life-writing that privileges a unified subject/subjectivity or at least one that is in "development" in the "conversion" narrative described by Metcalf. The version of Chicano male heteropatriarchal subjectivity represented by Rodriguez results in the formulation of what Rosa Linda Fregoso calls the "transcendental revolutionary Chicano subject"—a subject that simultaneously challenges and reproduces ideological forms of oppression. Fregoso, when reassessing the Chicano nationalism of the 1960s and 1970s, notes how the Chicano Movement ignored different subjectivities like queer and gender subjects in order to combat the fragmentation of the community perpetuated by racist and class-based structures in the United States. She adds: "The short-sightedness of the Chicano studies intellectuals was that they assumed that the construction of their own self-representations as subjects was equivalent to that of the totality of the Chicana/o experience, and that this shared representation could always be generalized in the interests of the entire group" (Fregoso, "Chicana/o" 29).

Generally, then, the danger with understanding Rodriguez's memoir as also engaging in a barrio-biographics is that this framework might reproduce similarly narrow forms of representation with regard to the Chicana/o community. Nonetheless, his autobiography remains a narrative of *both* the development of subaltern Chicano/a subjectivities as resistant to settler colonialism and racist State power. If his memoir were represented as the *only* or the *singular* voice of the Chicana/o experience in the Southwest, then it would reproduce the "short-sightedness" of the early Chicano nationalists. In addition, Rodriguez's memoir seems to implicitly reproduce a narrative of liberal development that resonates with a broader (mostly white) readership that is invested in reforming and reintegrating racialized gang figures like Rodriguez without committing to structural change. Overall, however, as Leigh Gilmore notes, these tensions are always embedded in the "politics of writing in the first person" (Gilmore, *Autobiographics* 4).[15] Consequently, then, memoirists of color attempt to work through a loss/desire of their individual subjectivities while maintaining their relationships to the communities for which they are forced to speak.

Furthermore, autobiography as a genre allows for the development of an ambiguous and contradictory subjectivity for Rodriguez—primarily through the development of a fantastical citizen/subjectivity (Brown, Metcalf) that reinforces the narrative of American exceptionalism through productions of a "national Other" (Pease 5). Donald Pease argues:

> As collectively experienced fantasies [i.e., the fantasies whereby subjects give up their power to the state to govern through various relations—democratic, authoritarian, socialist, etc.], these narratives extended the reach of state regulatory mechanisms into the individual psyche where these fantasies have historically performed functions that are both extensive and complexly interrelated. (5)

Importantly, Pease notes earlier in his essay:

> Metanarratives recast the reason of the state as teleology (a horizon of narrative expectations emanating from a national origin and organized by a national purpose) and thereby induce the state's subjects to collude in their own subjection. (4–5)

In other words, the development and articulation of Chicano autobiographies like Rodriguez's as *nationalist* narratives function to reinscribe the fantastical relations between the nation-state, however it is imagined (e.g., Aztlán, Latino gangs, or the United States), and its subjects. Therefore, these layered narratives of liberal development implicitly embedded in Rodriguez's autobiography reveal how these narratives reproduce and extend the "naturalized" reach of state power expressed through the writer's own subjectivity. Again, Monica Brown and others argue that this is one of the roles of violence among gangs and gang members in Rodriguez's memoir—that "these 'counter-nations' [gangs] simultaneously mirror and expose some of the most oppressive facets of dominant culture's construction of nation and an American 'national symbolic'" (Brown xvii).

Brown's argument, however, relies too heavily on the notion of citizenship that unquestioningly requires a legitimating structure (the nation-state) to concretize one's subjectivity (i.e., in forming a national subject). In this respect, Brown situates these narratives in a historicism that takes as its model a narrative of national and subject development that proceeds from "barbarity" (i.e., these figures as gang members) to civility and citizenship. Brown's analysis, then, ultimately seems to be attempting to write Chicano gangs, and by extension, Chicana/o communities, into a master narrative of the American (mythological) national development and, thereby, reinforce one of the great myths of its own development: that the United States has historically been an *inclusive* democratic nation and that inclusion into the body politic might solve the problem of gangs.

The Wild West: Chicanos/as as Strangers and Unassimilable Subjects

Leo Chavez's "Latino threat narrative" seems to underscore this point. He argues that the "threat" narrative consciously and implicitly situates Chicanas/os as foreigners in their own lands and as always criminal. In the process of layering the history of barrio formation/barrioization in his text, then, Rodriguez's narrative also challenges the Latino threat narrative. Some Chicana/o scholars likewise challenge such national formations by reimagining Chicano gang members as modern extensions of Mexican figures of resistance to Anglo encroachments in the Southwest, comparing them to legendary "bandits" like Juan Cortina and Joaquin Murrieta. This is precisely the reason that Hollywood, according to Charles Ramirez Berg and others, has made the figure of the bandido into an illiterate, bumbling idiot—to neutralize the revolutionary and political potential of such antecedents. These discourses are not new in the logics of American imperialism and settler colonialism. They offer justification for westward expansion and the myths that were created to make the violence of conquest palatable.

In addition, these logics and discourses of settler colonialism and racism have merely been transposed onto a "new American Congo" (Saldívar), now represented by the U.S.-Mexico borderlands and urban ghettos in the United States. Angie Chabram-Dernersesian argues furthermore: "Historically the border as a knowledge formation figures prominently within a critical vernacular pertaining to the cultures of imperialism, nationalism, and neocolonialism as well as the polyvalent cultures of resistance and affirmation." She adds: "Not surprisingly in the literature of Chicana/o (cultural) studies, the border is often intrusive or invasive; it designates a danger zone where state-sanctioned spaces of illegitimacy, nationality, nationhood, and citizenship are enforced from a positionality of conquest, domination, and privilege" (95–97). For Rodriguez, then, the connections between "illegitimacy," "nationality," criminality, and citizenship intersect at the foundational axis of his world in the greater east side of Los Angeles. Thus, the articulation of the "border [and the barrio] as a [site of] knowledge formation" is integral to the way Rodriguez conceives of his own identity and the community in the barrios of Los Angeles. He specifically notes how they are both products of socioeconomic displacements, multiple "border crossings," and the subject of efforts to contain the Latina/o "threat."

In this context, then, he details how his family "never stopped crossing borders" and simultaneously notes the way the LA river "became a new barrier, keeping Mexicans in their neighborhood over on the vast east side of the city for years" (19). When his family moved to San Gabriel, its particular history as an early Spanish colony in California is not lost on him either. He writes: "*Las Lomas* was an old barrio whose main rivals were to the west, in East Los Angeles, or the north in another barrio called *Sangra*." He adds, "Sangra was a corruption of San Gabriel, an incorporated city built around one of the Spanish Missions founded by Father Junípero Serra in the 1700s," and in this way sets the historical stage for the city's gang and police violence. Moreover, he notes that San Gabriel was originally a "major Indian village, Yang Na, [that] was once situated [there]"—adding, "later when the railroad linked many of the missions, they brought in Mexican laborers who became the first barrio residents" (40).

Again, this historical layering offers the reader a distinct connection between the complex processes of settler colonial violence involved with establishing the Spanish, Mexican, and then American West. More importantly, it should signal how the contemporary barrio and other urban ghettos are historically connected to these legacies of imperialism and conquest. In this historical context, the old military forces and systems of containment, like the reservation system during westward expansion, are now often replaced by modern militarized police forces and the prison system. This historical overlay in his text is perhaps best exemplified when Rodriguez and his homeboys give a sheriff's deputy the nickname "Cowboy." Through the lens of the American westward expansion, if the sheriff's deputy is the "cowboy," then Rodriguez and his friends symbolically become "outlaws," "bandidos," and "Indians" who might "go off the reservation"/barrio.

The framework of the American West also provides for understanding the historical continuities of the logics of white supremacy, Manifest Destiny, and Anglo settler colonialism in places like California. In another foundational moment of his memoir, for example, Rodriguez recounts his first experience of anti-Mexican racism in the United States. "Our first exposure in America stays with me like a foul odor," he writes. Then, he recounts the story of how, one day, on a visit to Will Rogers State Park, a white woman throws him and his family out, and suggests that his family does not belong in the United States. He writes:

> Once my mother gathered up the children and we walked to Will Rogers Park.... Mama looked around for a place we could rest. She spotted an empty spot on a park bench. But as soon as she sat down an American woman, with three kids of her own, came by.
>
> "Hey, get out of there—that's our seat."
>
> My mother understood but didn't know how to answer back in English. So she tried in Spanish.
>
> "Look spic, you can't sit there!" the American woman yelled. "You don't belong here! Understand? This is not your country!" (19)

The discourse of race and racism, for Rodriguez, also involves a discourse rooted in the context of settler colonial displacement of Mexicans in the Southwest. As a preface to this incident, he writes that the United States "seemed a strange world, most of it spiteful to us, spitting and stepping on us, coughing us up, us immigrants, as if we were phlegm stuck in the collective throat of this country" (19). In this way, Rodríguez exposes the most significant complexity and contradiction with regard to American westward expansion: that as the United States expands, it must also grapple with incorporating or exterminating the peoples whose land it takes. This "phlegm," as Rodriguez describes it, is the symbolic physiological reconfiguration of national corporeality in the American West with regard to subaltern subjects like Native Americans and Mexicans. Because of this, for Rodriguez, issues of citizenship, belonging, and community are literally written on the body, and the rigid racial formations of the United States do not readily allow much room to disavow such racist national formations.

Roberta Culbertson, in "Embodied Memory, Transcendence, and Telling: Recounting Trauma, Re-Establishing the Self," makes some critical distinctions between notions of memory, "proto-memory," and the ways in which we remember trauma through and on the body much like in this incident in Rodriguez's narrative. Culbertson suggests that there is something inarticulable about experiencing trauma—something that remains forever tied to the body. She writes: "Survivor writings make it clear that to be a survivor of one's violation is precisely this: to live with the paradox of silence and the present but unreachable force of memory, and a concomitant need to tell what seems untellable" (170). She adds, "It is the paradox of a known and a felt truth that unfortunately obeys the logic of dreams rather than of speech" (170). Culbertson also importantly points to the "ordered" nature of the way we remember and narrate in contrast to the ways we "dream"; she suggests that the narrative form and ordering process seem to present particular challenges to articulating trauma. Nevertheless, she ends by reiterating that despite the fact that narratives present particular structural and cultural problems to communicating violence and violation, the survivor feels a "compulsion to tell" precisely because telling becomes a symbolic mechanism for rebirth. Or, at the very least, the retelling becomes a place where the survivor can be fictively reborn because the narrative recasts the survivor as subject and object of the retold story. The moment above in Rodriguez's text, therefore, can also be read as a survivor narrative in which the focus on the corporeality in that scene signals the ways in which Culbertson's "felt truth" comes through his "ordered" narrative and represents his family and other immigrants as the "phlegm stuck in the collective throat of [the United States]." Rodriguez clues the reader into this framework for experiencing racist trauma when he ends this section by noting: "The refrain 'this is not your country' echoed for a lifetime" (19).

This framework for understanding Rodriguez's memoir as engaging in remembering and reconstituting traumatic moments is significant because, in retelling this incident of racist violence and in recounting incidents of sexual violence in the memoir, the "phlegm," "spit up," and later vomit he associates with these events become the literal and metaphorical markers of trauma in the text as well. In other words, these visceral responses become the literal representation of a symbolic "affective truth" (Million) that connects personal violence to broader forms of State violence (national formation and exclusion)—especially as these forms of violence embody the logics of conquest/colonialism in violence committed specifically against women.

As a result, the narrative of exclusion at the onset of his memoir, the various rapes he recounts later, and his love affair with a prostitute—all combine to connect racial and sexual trauma with a literal and symbolic trope of sickness and vomit. For example, Rodriguez recounts his mother's revulsion when she learns that he has become a gang member. He writes: "Mama hated the *cholos.* They reminded her of the rowdies on the border who fought all the time, talked that *caló* slang, drank mescal, smoked marijuana and left scores of women with babies bursting out of their bodies. *To see me become like them made her sick*, made her cringe and cry and curse" (48; emphasis added). In addition, these reactions to trauma by Rodriguez's mother and by Rodriguez himself suggest a chiasmatic internalization and reproduction of the very logics of coloniality, racism, and nationalism that they suffer as subaltern subjects because they reproduce this revulsion while disavowing it. In other words, Rodriguez's mother is made "sick" by his gang membership while Rodríguez is made sick by witnessing the rape of young women of color; and, both are made sick by their early experiences with racism in the United States.

Between Chicano Nationalism and the Left

All of the characterizations above point to significant and complex sociopolitical contexts: the histories of Spanish and American imperialisms related to Indigenous peoples in the United States and Mexico; and, later, these histories related to Chicanas/os like Rodriguez in the barrios/urban ghettos of California. Nevertheless, in his memoir, Rodriguez attempts to disentangle these historical phenomena in the making of his own subjectivity and transcend the "limits" of nationalism in order to develop a leftist/class solidarity politics for the barrio. He attempts to resolve such ideological ambivalences by actively critiquing and challenging ideological State apparatuses because these apparatuses actively function in the contemporary moment to negate his individual subjectivity and reduce him to the sum of the parts of an already constructed and contested racial self. Althusser notes, "the category of the subject is constitutive of all ideology, but at the same time and immediately [he adds]...*that the category of the subject is only constitutive of all ideology insofar as all ideology has the function (which defines it)* of 'constituting' concrete individuals as subjects" (171; emphasis in original). For Rodriguez, the ideological tensions in his memoir illustrate the ways in which *particular* ideologies (like those represented by the public school system and the police) function to concretize and constitute his subjectivity while community/barrio sociocultural relationships attempt to constitute another subjectivity.

In recounting one of the critical moments in the development of his political consciousness, for example, Rodriguez writes about how he inherited a literary and political lineage from books he found in the Pierce Community College library. He writes: "[The books] were primarily about the black experience, works coming out of the flames which engulfed many American cities in the 1960s," and he importantly notes how he came across Piri Thomas's *Down These Mean*

Streets (1967) among these texts. According to Rodriguez, Thomas's book became a "living Bible" (138) and arguably the model for *Always Running*. As such, even among a series of radical texts like Eldridge Cleaver's *Soul on Ice* (1965), Claude Brown's *Manchild in the Promised Land* (1965), and George Jackson's *Soledad Brother* (1970), Rodriguez identified the most with a Puerto Rican/Nuyorican who understood the process of navigating the black-white binary racial structure of the United States as a Latino. Rodriguez even calls Thomas a "barrio boy like me, on the other side of America" (138).

In another critical moment in his memoir, Rodriguez introduces the reader to Chente Ramírez, the "administrator, father-figure, counselor and the law" of the John Fabela Youth Center (146). Chente, Rodriguez writes, helped him to move beyond the political "trap" of nationalism by inviting him to a reading group called the "collective" in which Rodriguez and other students and community activists "studied politics, philosophy, economics" or "the dynamics of social revolution" (156). Later, Rodriguez details the political philosophy of the "collective" and writes: "Unlike others in the Chicano Movement who strove to *enter* the American capitalist system, [the collective] prepared for a fundamental reorganization of society"—a sentiment he will rearticulate in the epilogue of his memoir. Shortly after this initial description of the collective, he adds: "The collective explained how workers of all colors and nationalities, linked by hunger and the same system of exploitation, have no country; their interests as a class respect no borders." "To me," he emphasizes, "this was an unconquerable idea" (185). In an aside, Rodriguez writes that after his participation in the "collective," his homeboy Chicharrón begins calling him the "Chinmunist"—a "combination of Chin and communist" (194).

Thus, the discovery of revolutionary African American literature in the Pierce College library and his introduction to leftist thought and politics by the "collective" mark the two most significant moments of Rodriguez's sociopolitical coming-of-age. These engagements—both literary and political—begin the core process of transformation for Rodriguez. As I note above, however, there remains an ideological ambivalence as Rodriguez tries to unmoor race, racism, and later racial capitalism from a Marxist/leftist politics that is primarily focused on class/economic issues. Indeed, although he intends the description to be positive, Rodriguez unconsciously but accurately points out that such sociopolitical philosophies are "another culture" (156)—one that *might* ask him to throw off his racial/ethnic identity for a "universal" proletarian subjectivity. Such a subjectivity obviously runs the risk of ignoring the historically specific conditions of racial capitalism—especially in the United States—and the complex ways in which race, gender, and sexuality inform the history of imperialism/colonialism, the formation of the modern nation-state, and their "subjects/citizens." The result, again, is that Rodriguez attempts to address these broader structures of power—American imperialism, white supremacy, capitalism, and the nation-state—through the theoretical and political tensions of his own form of life-writing that I describe as "barrio-biographics."

Another result of his subscription to his Chicano nationalist identity, however, is that he begins to come to the realization that his own male subjectivity, as formed by these histories of conquest, might be unconsciously complicit with a white, racist heteropatriarchal social order (Fregoso, "Representation"). As a result, the most positive representations of women in the memoir often are those of Chicanas who are engaged in political activity, like "Skin" (158) or Esme (174). Ultimately, however, Monica Brown is right: in such memoirs as *Always Running*, the reader and perhaps writer are inadvertently invested in a narrative of liberal development that produces—through a collective investment in the nation—similarly racist, heteropatriarchal logics of domination. This tension, therefore, threatens to assimilate and co-opt these male writers of color insofar as they provide a cover for white supremacist, totalizing logics of heteropatriarchy by performing their own "culturally specific" hypermasculinities: machismo for Chicanos and its opposite, Marianismo, for Chicanas. This means that while Rodriguez positively represents these Chicanas because of their subscriptions to a radical politics, he also does not find them particularly suitable as romantic partners.

Nevertheless, Rodriguez still tries to resolve such ambivalences by relentlessly critiquing and challenging ideological and repressive state apparatuses *alongside* these women. He and Esme, as the leaders of ToHMAS, for example, demand that the school better serve Chicano students by teaching Chicana/o studies and hiring more Chicana/o faculty (Rodriguez 212). Rodriguez also levels the charge that the police in the barrio were "just another gang" (72) and, after the murder of Miguel Robles, leads a gang truce and community effort to unite the barrio. These actions are significant reminders in his memoir that the "social problems" in America cannot simply be blamed on Chicanas/os and other parts of the "laboring classes" in order to subsequently try to exorcise them by imprisoning or even "deporting" Chicanas/os and Mexican immigrants from the nation. Rodriguez even directly challenges basic notions of good and bad in the barrio. He writes: "Shootings, assaults and skirmishes between the barrios are direct results of police activity. Even drug dealing. I know this. Everybody knows this" (72). Despite Rodriguez's role in these efforts, it is important to note that these community-based actions are predominantly led by politically conscious Chicanas in his memoir and in the barrio.

Still, Rodriguez remains committed to critiquing the structural issues that constitute these various subjectivities—gang member, Chicana/o, or otherwise—in his memoir. Indeed, the memoir is bracketed by a preface and epilogue that contain his most focused critique of the larger structural forces that lead to the marginalization of all youth of color and their subsequent criminalization. In the preface, he writes: "'The Crazy Life' in my youth...was only the beginning stages of what I believe is now a consistent and growing genocidal level of destruction predicated on the premise there are marginalized youth with no jobs or future, and [are] therefore expendable" (6–7). With regard to drug dealing, he adds: "the values which drive gangs are linked to the control of markets, in a way similar to what has created borders between nations." Then, "The drug trade is business. It's capitalism" (8). He ends the preface by noting: "Criminality in this country is a class issue" (10).

Meanwhile, in the epilogue, in the wake of the 1992 Los Angeles rebellion, he argues that urban America and its largely black and brown residents are disproportionately subject to State violence and that this message is finally reaching "'mainstream' America" (250). Nevertheless, he qualifies this by claiming that mainstream America's problem is that it still sees young black and brown youth as the "problem" rather than the symptom of broader, structural problems of racism, class division, and so on in the country. After which, he rhetorically asks: "What to do with those whom society cannot accommodate?" "Criminalize them," he responds. "Outlaw their actions and creations. Declare them the enemy, then wage war. Emphasize the differences—the shade of skin, the accent in the speech or manner of clothes [as with Trayvon Martin, the teenager who was murdered on his way home in Sanford, Florida, in 2012]. Like the scapegoat of the Bible, place society's ills on them, then 'stone them' in absolution. It's convenient" (250).

This bracketing, therefore, also represents a key political, aesthetic, and ideological bracket to his personal life story contained within. That is, in "classic" autobiographies, one assumes the writer is presenting their life story without editorializing or without an active agenda. They are presenting their true life events. However, in recounting his life story, Rodriguez remains clear and focused with regard to the ways in which the nation-state and its various structures of power create and maintain an undercaste of society—in this case, Chicano gang members—and then represents *them* as inherently criminal. In the "magic" of classic autobiographies, dominant ideological premises require the reader to leave unquestioned the ways in which the law, the nation, criminality, and their exclusivity are all constructs of power. Rodriguez, as a result, is intentional about undermining the ways in which his autobiography might be used to suggest, in the dominant framework of autobiographical writing, that other gang members should simply follow his "model" of development by abandoning gang life and becoming "productive" members of society. Rodriguez could not make the function of his memoir clearer than in the preface, where he claims that the book is a call for the "reorganization of American society" (10), not a simple focus on singular Chicano subjects in the barrio like him.

Despite the liberatory potential of his memoir and its politics, however, the most poignant and effective criticism of Rodriguez's narrative is his treatment of women. They do not even seem to merit inclusion or focus in the preface or epilogue in the way racialized male and classed subjects are included. Given that these places are where he is most clear about his radical politics, one might expect him to address the question of sexism in either location. He does not. As I note above, his other major shortcoming is that, like other Chicano writers that are products of the 1960s and 1970s Chicano Movement, he reproduces rather than deconstructs these heteropatriarchal relationships. That is, these nationalist narratives reproduce masculinist, heteronormative constructions of the nation-state and its politics despite appearing to challenge them. Angie Chabram-Dernersesian argues that these Chicano men struggle with their own marginality and subjectivity and find themselves in a new "border state" where, as we see in Rodriguez's memoir, masculinist discourses give them some semblance of power/empowerment.

Still, his memoir functions as a cautionary tale whose message is that one should, at all costs, come to a political consciousness, as individuals and as a community, in order to stand a chance at challenging a racist State and its violence. He also suggests that the problems of marginalization and intercommunal and intracommunal violence can only be addressed by a restructuring of thought, and through reasserting one's subjectivity through a process of decolonization. To this point, Rodriguez does not argue, as some do, for a return to a mythical, nostalgic place of egalitarian Indigenous/pre-settler origins as a panacea for the problems of settler State violence; nor does he suggest that such an origin is somehow "outside" of the capitalist, racial, and patriarchal systems that operate today. Not in practical terms. In the end, Rodriguez's memoir offers us a partial model for decolonizing the individual barrio subject and for addressing State violence. In it, he suggests this methodology involves a process of recognizing the Other and the self and of recognizing the self in the Other as a conscious refusal to accept the material and ideological conditions of settler colonialism that affect us all. This is why Rodriguez begins with the histories of Spanish and American conquests—so that his memoir, as a modern individual and barrio biography, always reminds us of the sociopolitical and literary foundations of Chicanos and their troubling attempts to decolonize the mind/self and community.

Notes

1. This statement was the central advertising line for the film *Gangs of New York*.
2. Ebert's framing here seems to reveal a subconscious inclination toward a Eurocentric social Darwinist understanding of modern American society—one that suggests the brutality and criminality of "founding fathers" while ignoring the real victims of such violence (i.e., people of color in the United States). In his review, then, the assumption is that "modern America was forged" by white immigrants and people of color had little to do with its development.
3. Leo R. Chavez argues that while Latino and Mexican "migrations paralleled those of other immigrant groups...Mexicans in particular have been represented as the quintessential 'illegal aliens,' which distinguishes them from other immigrant groups" (Chavez 4).
4. The Civil Rights Act of 1964 barred discrimination based on "race, color, religion, sex, or national origin" and led to the development of "affirmative action programs." The Hart-Celler Immigration Act of 1965 removed country of origin quotas in U.S. immigration policy, ended country of origin discrimination, and changed the racial/ethnic demographics of immigrants into the United States such that approximately 85 percent of all immigrants entering the United States now are from Asia, Latin America, and the Caribbean (Portes and Rumbaut 2006).
5. Note Frederick Luis Aldama's decolonial/anti-imperialist analysis of *American Me* in "Penalizing Chicano/a Bodies in Edward J. Olmos's *American Me*."
6. See Althusser, esp. chapter 4, "Ideology and the Ideological State Apparatuses (Notes Toward an Investigation)."
7. It should also be noted, however, that *pinta/o* (prisoner) narratives are slightly different than Chicana/o street gang narratives because *pinto* narratives foreground the experience of imprisonment and the author's or main character's interactions with the carceral state as an added layer of their own epistemological and ontological formations in the barrio. For a more in-depth review of this term and framework, see my forthcoming essay, "Chicano/a Gang Narratives," in the *Oxford Encyclopedia of Latina/o Literature*, edited by Louis Mendoza, Ben Olguín, Sandra Soto, et al.
8. See articles by Darder, Katz, and Boyle-Baise as key examples.
9. This is an adaptation of Gayatri Chakravorty Spivak's articulation of this phenomenon in "Can the Subaltern Speak?" (originally 1983).
10. Rodríguez narrates the moment when his own homeboy, Topo, tries to kill him (237–38).
11. Many writers of color who engage in life-writing grapple with the ways in which place and space are formed of these racist histories of housing segregation, the reservation system (for Indigenous peoples in the Americas), and the barrio/ghettos in major metropolises across the United States. While each policy and system of segregation has its specific history, what unites these systems is an impulse, first, to exterminate (as with Native Americans), then, second, to contain or control these

people of color because they remain integral as the cheap labor that fuels a dual labor market economy in the United States.

12. I am borrowing this term from Leigh Gilmore's theory of feminist autobiography in *Autobiographics*.
13. For a good primer, see Nikhil Singh's *Black Is a Country* (Harvard UP, 2004).
14. Chicana/o and Latina/o scholars have leveled effective critiques of this form of cultural nationalism. Here, I am thinking of the scholarship of Elizabeth Martinez, Alma García, and Gloria Anzaldúa in particular. Importantly, these scholars also articulate and theorize a Chicano/a and Latina/o identity that is not constitutive of any notion of a homogeneous nation-state (especially not a masculinist nation-state). They imagine the nation as inclusive and culturally, ethnically, and politically constructed by a diverse and queer community of color (see Anzaldúa, Arteaga, Moraga).
15. See also Sidonie Smith, Genaro Padilla, and Norma Cantu on autobiography, ethnic/Mexican American autobiographics, and autoethnographies.

Bibliography

Aldama, Frederick Luis. "Penalizing Chicano/a Bodies in Edward J. Olmos's *American Me*." *Decolonial Voices: Chicana and Chicano Cultural Studies in the 21st Century*, edited by Arturo J. Aldama and Naomi H. Quiñonez, Indiana UP, 2002, pp. 78–97.

Althusser, Louis. *Lenin and Philosophy, and Other Essays*. 1971. Monthly Review Press, 2001.

Anzaldúa, Gloria. *Borderlands/La Frontera: The New Mestiza*. Aunt Lute Books, 1987.

Arteaga, Alfred. *Chicano Poetics: Heterotexts and Hybrities*. Cambridge UP, 1997.

Ashley, Kathleen, Leigh Gilmore, et al., editors. *Autobiography and Postmodernism*. U of Massachusetts P, 1994.

Berg, Charles Ramirez. *Latino Images in Film*. U of Texas P, 2002.

Bigalondo, Amaia Ibarraran. "Wolves, Sheep and Vatos Locos: Reflections of Gang Activity in Chicano Literature." *Journal of English Studies*, vol. 4, 2003, pp. 107–14.

Boyle-Baise, Marilynne. "Community Service Learning for Multicultural Education: An Exploratory Study with Preservice Teachers." *Equity & Excellence*, vol. 31, no. 2, 1998, pp. 52–60.

Brown, Monica. *Gang Nation: Delinquent Citizens in Puerto Rican, Chicano, and Chicana Narratives*. U of Minnesota P, 2002.

Cantú, Norma. "Memoir, Autobiography, Testimonio." *Routledge Companion to Latina/o Literature*, edited by Suzanne Bost and Frances Aparicio, Routledge, 2013, pp. 310–22.

Chabram-Dernersesian, Angie. "Introduction to Part Two: Chicana/o Cultural Studies 'On the Border.'" *The Chicana/o Cultural Studies Reader*, edited by Angie Chabram-Dernersesian, Routledge, 2006, pp. 95–98.

Chavez, Leo R. *The Latino Threat: Constructing Immigrants, Citizens, and the Nation.* Stanford UP, 2008.

Culbertson, Roberta. "Embodied Memory, Transcendence, and Telling: Recounting Trauma, Re-establishing the Self." *New Literary History*, vol. 26, no. 1, Winter 1995, pp. 169–95.

Darder, Antonia. "Latino Youth: Pedagogy, Praxis, and Policy." *Latino Studies*, vol. 4, no. 3, 2006, pp. 302–4.

Ebert, Roger. Review of *Gangs of New York*, directed by Martin Scorsese. *RogerEbert.com*, 20 Dec. 2002, rogerebert.com/reviews/gangs-of-new-york-2002.

———. Review of *The Godfather*, directed by Francis Ford Coppola. *RogerEbert.com*, 1 Jan. 1972, rogerebert.com/reviews/the-godfather-1972.

———. Review of *The Godfather*, directed by Francis Ford Coppola. *RogerEbert.com*, 16 March 1997, rogerebert.com/reviews/great-movie-the-godfather-1972.

Fregoso, Rosa Linda. "Chicana/o Cultural Representations: Reframing Alternative Critical Discourses." *The Chicana/o Cultural Studies Reader*, edited by Angie Chabram-Dernersesian, Routledge, 2006, pp. 26–32.

———. "The Representation of Cultural Identity in 'Zoot Suit.'" *Masculinities*, special issue of *Theory and Society*, vol. 22, no. 5, Oct. 1993, pp. 659–74.

Gangs of New York. Directed by Martin Scorsese, Miramax, 2002.

Gans, Herbert J. "Symbolic Ethnicity: The Future of Ethnic Groups and Cultures in America." *Ethnic and Racial Studies*, vol. 2, no. 1, Jan. 1979, pp. 1–20.

García, Alma M., editor. *Chicana Feminist Thought: The Basic Historical Writings.* Routledge, 1997.

Gilmore, Leigh. *Autobiographics: A Feminist Theory of Women's Autobiography.* Cornell UP, 1994.

Katz, Susan Roberta. "Presumed Guilty: How Schools Criminalize Latino Youth." *Social Justice*, vol. 24, no. 4, 1997, pp. 77–95.

Martinez, Elizabeth. "La Chicana." *Chicana Feminist Thought: The Basic Historical Writings*, edited by Alma M. Garcia, Routledge, 1997.

Metcalf, Josephine. *The Culture and Politics of Contemporary Street Gang Memoirs.* U of Mississippi P, 2012.

Million, Diane. "Felt Theory: An Indigenous Feminist Approach to Affect and History." *Wicazo Sa Review*, Fall 2009, pp. 53–76.

Moraga, Cherrie. *The Last Generation: Prose and Poetry.* South End Press, 1993.

Moya, Paula. "This Is Not Your Country!": Nation and Belonging in Latina/o Literature." *American Literary History*, vol. 17, no. 1, 2005, pp. 183–95.

Padilla, Genaro. *My History, Not Yours: The Formation of Mexican American Autobiography.* U of Wisconsin P, 1993.

Pease, Donald. "National Narratives, Postnational Narration." *Modern Fiction Studies*, vol. 43, no. 1, 1997, pp. 1–23.

Perez, Vincent. "'Running' and Resistance: Nihilism and Cultural Memory in Chicano Urban Narratives." *Melus*, vol. 25, no. 2, 2000, pp. 133–46.

Portes, Alejandro, and Rubén G. Rumbaut, editors. *Immigrant America: A Portrait.* 3rd ed., U of California P, 2006.
Rodriguez, Luis, J. *Always Running: La Vida Loca, Gang Days in L.A.* Curbstone, 1993.
Rodríguez, Richard T. *Next of Kin: The Family in Chicana/o Cultural Politics.* Duke UP, 2009.
Saldívar, José David. *Border Matters: Remapping American Cultural Studies.* U of California P, 1997.
Scarface. Directed by Brian De Palma, Universal, 1983.
Smith, Sidonie, and Julia Watson. *Reading Autobiography: A Guide for Interpreting Life Narratives.* 2nd ed., U of Minnesota P, 2010.
Soto, Gary. "The Body Count in the Barrio." *New York Times Book Review*, 14 Feb. 1993, p. 26.
Spivak, Gayatri. "Can the Subaltern Speak?" *Colonial Discourse and Post-Colonial Theory: A Reader*, edited by Patrick Williams and Laura Chrisman, Columbia UP, 1994, pp. 66–111.
Thomas, Piri. *Down These Mean Streets.* Vintage, 1997.
Treviño, Jesus Salvador. "Latino Portrayals in Film and Television." *Jumpcut*, no. 30, March 1985, pp. 14–16.
Villa, Raúl Homero. *Barrio-Logos: Space and Place in Urban Chicano Literature and Culture.* U of Texas P, 2000.

II

LEFT READINGS

Rewriting Region and Radicalism

6

Eschaton of Abundance

Ward Moore's *Greener Than You Think* as Transcendentalist Satire

ROBERT YUSEF RABIEE

"Progress," she repeated, looking from
the scythe-wielder to me and back again.
"Progress, Weener.
A remarkable conception of the nineteenth century."

—Ward Moore, *Greener Than You Think* (1947)

I do not belong to the poets, but only to a low department
of literature, the reporters; suburban men.

—Ralph Waldo Emerson to Thomas Carlyle (April 25, 1839)

Former used bookstore employee and WPA writer Ward Moore published his first science fiction novel, *Greener Than You Think*, at the beginning of the post–World War II real estate development boom that would forever alter the American landscape and collective imaginary. The novel is prescient, foreshadowing the mixed anxiety and optimism that would characterize the Cold War–era United States. The story follows salesman Albert Weener as he markets the Metamorphizer, brainchild of self-trained scientist and would-be global savior Josephine Spencer Francis. Miss Francis (as Weener calls her) develops the chemical, which allows grasses, including wheat, to grow indefinitely. She hopes in this way to end world hunger. Her utopian vision is undercut when Weener makes a fateful observation while passing by the bungalows south of Hollywood Boulevard: Francis's hunger-busting invention may best be used to revive dead lawns. The salesman applies an undiluted sample of Metamorphizer to a scraggly patch of Bermuda grass, and so initiates a weird environmental apocalypse as the mutated grass overwhelms the house, the block, the city, the western United States, and finally, the world. Weener and Miss Francis soon discover that the Metamorphizer's promise of ever-increasing yield cannot be curbed. As hypnotic, living tendrils choke the planet, Albert Weener becomes the most powerful oligarch in human history. It is a bleak vision of capitalist development run amok, and a canny satire of suburbanization.

Like so many works of speculative fiction, *Greener Than You Think* is largely forgotten today, a disappearance foreshadowed by a series of negative reviews for Moore's first and greatest science fiction novel.[1] Writing in *The New York Times*, reviewer Theodore Pratt praised Moore for conceiving a "perfectly wonderful idea for a work of fantasy," but finally dismisses him as "a totally undisciplined man with words" (Pratt 14, 16). The review concludes that Moore is "out of Hammett and Cain via James Joyce" (this is meant as an insult), an undisciplined writer "given to peculiar spellings and punctuation, to the telescoping of words" (16). Yet Pratt's dismissal of Moore's style misses a fourth target of *Greener Thank You Think*'s satire: the literary and intellectual heritage of Transcendentalism. Moore sets this up early on with Weener's description of Hollywood's lawns:

> I was suddenly lawn-conscious. There was probably not a Los Angeles street I hadn't covered at some time—magazines, vacuums, old gold, near-nylons—and I must have been aware of green spaces before most of the houses, but now for the first time I saw lawns. Neat, sharply confined, smooth-shaven lawns. Sagging, slipping, eager-to-keep-up-appearances but fighting-a-losing-game lawns. Ragged, weedy, dissolute lawns. Half-bare, repulsively crippled, hummocky lawns. Bright lawns, insistent on former respectability and trimness; yellow and gray lawns,

> touched with the craziness of age, quite beyond all interest in looks, content to doze easily in the sun. (13)

As in a Whitman poem or passage from Emerson's *Nature*, Weener offers an ecstatic catalogue based in a highly individual experience of the natural world.[2] That in this case the Transcendental subject is a door-to-door salesman in the suburbs and his rapturous experience of nature comes from observing lawns lays the groundwork for Moore's critique of American notions of progress, which as the epigraph to this essay shows, Moore pinned firmly in a nineteenth-century intellectual context. The "peculiar spellings and punctuations" and "telescoping of words" that Pratt argues distract us from the novel's satire are in fact an essential aspect of Moore's satire of the Transcendentalist legacy. Ward Moore seems to concur with Ralph Waldo Emerson that Transcendentalism is primarily a philosophy for "suburban men."

Moore's novel satirizes four imbricated subjects: the United States' boundless economic optimism, postwar suburbanization, Anglo-American indifference to western ecologies, and the intellectual tradition of Transcendentalism. *Greener Than You Think* argues that these elements of American social life must be viewed together, a concatenation of blunders and illusions encouraged by the United States' inability to grasp the global stakes of national development. The novel's eschaton of abundance—a state of perpetual global crisis spurred by unplanned development and overproduction—leads to stacked economic and ecological crises that Weener plays to his own advantage through sleight-of-hand on the stock market. By implicating both the scientist Miss Francis and salesman Albert Weener in his global apocalypse, Moore critiques capitalist development and its reckless industrial applications of scientific advances.

Moore approaches these issues from a broadly leftist perspective, an unsurprising fact given the shreds of biographical information to which we have access. According to Kenneth Rexroth's *An Autobiographical Novel* (1961), Moore ("Bard Major") was an active member of the Communist Party (311). The back matter of the first edition of *Greener Than You Think* affirms Moore's reputation as a radical. Among his many book-selling jobs, the sleeve notes, Moore worked for "Joe Kling's Pagan bookshop"; Kling was a well-known Greenwich Village socialist and publisher of the dissident newspaper *The Pagan*. There is also compelling evidence in *Greener Than You Think* that Marxist thought informed Moore's social vision. Again and again in the novel, characters speaking some sort of truth about the Bermuda grass situation are denounced as Communists. For instance, an assemblyman calls Miss Francis a "paid agent of the Communist International" for insisting that scientists "share with each other their advances from moment to moment and so add to the security of civilization from day to day" (95). Moore's work can thus be situated in relation to what Michael Denning calls the early twentieth-century "cultural front" of leftist class struggle. Moore was of a generation of socialist authors who understood that, as "mass consumer culture became a common ground of a new working-class culture," the Left must direct its propagandistic energies toward popular music, cinema, and fiction (Denning 48).

But the "cultural front" model can only take us so far when approaching a novelist such as Moore. The texts Denning takes up emerge, for the most part, from an eastern cultural scene that was directly connected to organs of political dissent and organization. Moore's *Greener Than You Think* does not come with the strong imprimatur of orthodox Communist Party ideology that a novel such as Mike Gold's *Jews Without Money* (1930) does, nor does Moore's novel evince the social democratic realism of Steinbeck or Odets. Instead, Moore attempts a leftist critique of culture situated in the very specific dilemmas of the American West—of land use, irresponsible suburbanization, the cult of the image, and the rhapsodic imagination of endless expansion that characterizes social life in the West in general and Los Angeles in particular. Moore's eccentric Marxism allows the author to skewer the West's settler colonial history and the ideology of Manifest Destiny that motored that history from the nineteenth century to Moore's own time. In Moore's world, fresh-faced adventurers who seek fortune and change in the West meet a place with no center whose anarchic logic, when abstracted out to the global stage, threatens to upend all hitherto existing social relations.

Given the political background out of which the book emerged, it is no surprise that interest in Moore's work was reignited by the Marxist ecologist Mike Davis, who gives *Greener Than You Think* a central place in his 1999 *Ecology of Fear: Los Angeles and the Imagination of Disaster*. My reading of the novel follows from Davis's observation that "Moore was the first writer to convincingly turn the tables on Los Angeles: the city that had for decades consumed nature in voracious bulldozer bites is itself bitten back and consumed" (318). For Moore, "turning the tables on Los Angeles" means demonstrating how logics of expansion and accumulation that we typically identify with Manifest Destiny and the American West threaten to homogenize the planet's environmental and social diversity. Davis calls this strategy, which he locates in a number of apocalyptic narratives, "ecogigantism," and argues that it is "the dominant allegorical device in environmental science fiction" (321). Michael Page further notes that this species of "apocalyptic environmentalism" skewers the "ecological complacency and self-assured and unexamined species triumphalism" that has led Western societies to "eat up the planet, poison and degrade its biosystems, and put into jeopardy the continued sustainability of the human species" (Page 52). Both Page and Davis accurately summarize the meaning of Moore's world-ending infestation, but neither explores the specific object of his critique: an American ideology of boundless expansion and self-development that is dogged by hints of that ideology's coming failure.

It is primarily *ideological* and not actual environmental apocalypticism that Moore's satire takes up as its target. Almost immediately after swallowing up the home of its first victim, the Bermuda grass also gains its first of many acolytes. The man is "Brother Paul," a radio evangelist who offers the following jeremiad to his listeners:

> The Lord has taken a simple and despised weed and caused it to multiply in defiance of all your puny powers and efforts. O my friends, do not fight this grass, but cherish it; do not allow it to be cut down for it is full of significance for you. Call off your minions and repent, lest if the holy messenger be injured a more terrible one is sent. But now, my friends, I see my time is

> up; please send your contributions so urgently needed to carry on the Divine Work to Brother Paul care of the station to which you are listening. (67)

The "doom-predicting, advent-prophesying graminophile evangelist" encourages his followers to find salvation through "The Sanctification of the Forerunner," or "self-immolation in the *Cynodon dactylon*" (243, 125). Eventually, Brother Paul—whose real name is the Hawthornean "Anthony Preblesham"—gathers a worldwide "graminophile" suicide cult. He also becomes an employee of the man who started it all, Albert Weener. Once the Bermuda grass has taken over the entire planet, Weener writes in his diary: "Brother Paul, ridiculous mountebank, was yet correct in this—the Grass chastised us rightly. Whatever sins mankind committed have been wiped out and expiated" (359). In just one line, Moore dramatizes a central theme in American cultural development: the lasting impact of the Puritan eschatological imagination on both visions of America's endless expansion and the demise (or decline) of that "dream."

If we worry that Moore's satire—and my reading of it—now threatens to sprawl like the grass at the center of the narrative, we should remember that the eschatological traditions of Puritanism and the secularization of millennial energies that Transcendentalist thinkers unleashed emerged from the same root. "In all matters except literal church polity," writes literary critic Wesley T. Mott, "Transcendentalism reconstructed the Puritan world view as it was concerned with the nature of the Spirit, human faculties and affections, moral conduct, and national mission" (Mott 243). "National mission" is particularly important here, especially as it concerns the intimate connection between Transcendentalism and westward expansion that Kris Fresonke elaborates on in *West of Emerson: The Design of Manifest Destiny*. The secret language spoken by both the Puritan eschatologists and the Transcendentalists is obvious in Henry David Thoreau's posthumous essay "Walking" (1862):

> We go eastward to realize history...; we go westward as into

> the future, with a spirit of enterprise and adventure. The Atlantic is a Lethean stream, in our passage over which we have had an opportunity to forget the Old World and its institutions. If we do not succeed this time, there is perhaps one more chance for the race left before it arrives on the banks of the Styx; and that is in the Lethe of the Pacific, which is three times as wide. (Thoreau 20)

Thoreau's enthusiasm for the history-effacing power of westward expansion recalls "A Modell of Christian Charity" (1630), John Winthrop's famous sermon written and delivered onboard the *Arabella*. The pieces share a basic premise: going into new lands enables a total erasure of the past, and opens up room for the creation of a civic being with a new and radical relationship to history, the state, God, and himself. Winthrop and Thoreau share a chiliastic social vision, one in which a new golden age may be brought about in the temporal realm. But if Transcendentalism and Puritanism can be said to share a dream of an imminent golden age, then they also share a nightmare: the possibility that the golden age may be indefinitely deferred, or worse, perverted into an age of horrors and persecutions. Immediately after the famous insistence that he and his shipmates "must Consider that wee shall be as a Citty vpon a Hill, the eies of all people...vppon vs," Winthrop warns that should the Puritans "deale falsely with our god in this worke wee haue vundertaken," God will "withdrawe his present help from vs" (Winthrop 195). Expansionist optimism comes prepackaged with its own principle of negation, the threat of divine abandonment and (finally) spiritual and material ruin. What finally did compromise this dream was, ironically, the necessary precondition for its existence: the coming age of global industrial capitalism. Per folklorist Robert St. George, "when Puritan communities encountered commercial capitalism, Puritanism lost" (St. George 381). Cotton Mather put it rather more bluntly: "Religion begat prosperity, and the daughter devoured the mother" (qtd. in Innes 26). Without capital's thirst for new territories and the raw materials that may be extracted from them, Winthrop and his fellow travelers would not have been granted a charter for the

Massachusetts Bay Company. But religious communities such as the Puritans' could not survive the tradition-effacing power of global trade, which demanded that their religious provisions be set aside in favor of secular markets and those markets' social logics.

While Thoreau does not predict an explicitly Christian millennium in his writing, his eschatological imagination sees a different kind of golden age on the horizon, one in which "the spirit of enterprise and adventure" will unleash a flowering of individualism in the territories west of the Mississippi. As historian Thomas Hietala puts it, the cultural and political architects of Manifest Destiny held "that territorial expansion would actually promote democracy within the nation" (Hietala 173). Like the Transcendentalists, expansionists were inheritors of a Puritan sense of errand. They too were haunted by a sense of that errand's potential end. The Jeffersonian "romantic agrarianism" at the root of Manifest Destiny required endless territorial expansion: "So long as American workshops remained in the wilderness...the reality of swift technological and economic change could be reconciled with the pastoral ideals of a New World Eden" (Hietala 262, 96). But the American workshops relied on capital from the East, and the demands of capital were often at odds with those of the self-styled yeomanry that sought to claim free land (so-called) in the West.

All of these forces—anxiety about the end of an era, fear of a new and uncertain industrial future—come to a head in the famous last lines of Frederick Jackson Turner's "The Significance of the Frontier in American History" (1893): "And now, four centuries from the discovery of America, at the end of a hundred years life under the Constitution, the frontier has gone, and with its going has closed the first period of American history" (Turner 60). As Harold P. Simonson suggests, the statement has a chilling effect precisely because it "brings back into the American consciousness what for two centuries had been denied," the double bind of the Puritan "errand" in the New World:

> Turner revived the eschatological question upon which the Puritans had looked with both dread and fascination. To speculate about last things is to accept the possibility of limitation.

> To accept this possibility is to contemplate the end of the long American journey and to discover, with shocking abruptness, that, as inheritors of Puritan theology, we have been committed to this end from the beginning. (Simonson 125)

The question is not, then, whether the logic of Manifest Destiny carried within itself the kernel of its own collapse. Of course it did. The question instead is, "What *kind* of declension will we witness? What will the 'once-free,' 'once-Wild' West become?" Simonson focuses on the fierier implications of the failed errand. Western literature and film has often relied on this variety of Puritan apocalypticism: the riotous climax of West's *The Day of the Locust* (1939), the freeway jam at the center of Karen Tei Yamashita's *Tropic of Orange* (1997), the earthquake that caps Robert Altman's *Short Cuts* (1993), or the biblical rain of frogs that falls in Paul Thomas Anderson's *Magnolia* (1999). But another type of eschatological anxiety has nothing at all to do with fear of being burned up in an instant (that would be some sort of relief, at least), but instead with being forced to live out the consequences of a failed covenant *in this life*. God's abandonment can entail more than epic final judgments or (to borrow a phrase from Melville's *The Encantadas*) a "penal conflagration." Often, the big spiritual letdown finds its first expression in the most quotidian ways: crops that won't yield, abnormal births, abandoned or defaced churches, and the horror (for Puritan father Increase Mather) of young men wearing hats to religious services. The Puritans were premillenialist Christians, and thus believed Christ's return would come through "the work of God's human agents," that "the coming of the Millennium will not be accompanied by a series of cataclysmic events; instead it develops and evolves through human history" (Court 43). What holds true for Christ's return holds true for His abandonment of humanity: it will play out within human history and events, not through that history's negation. The dream of westward expansion won't necessarily explode. It might do something even more terrible: go on expanding, monstrously and indefinitely.

Turner himself expresses this premillenialist view of the decline and decay of the "closed" frontier in "The Problem of the West" (1896).

Turner argues for a now hidden, now open struggle between the "primitive conditions" of an ever-shifting western frontier and "the older social conditions of the East" (Turner 62). The American West, he tells us, "began with the Atlantic coast" (with the Puritans) before "[passing] across the continent" (62). "Manifest Destiny" and the Puritan "errand into the wilderness" are leveled: Turner argues that the latter served as the model for the former. The essay soon shifts, however, from disinterested articulation of historical fact to poetic eulogy for the frontiersman. "In spite of his rude, gross nature," Turner writes, "[the frontiersman] was an idealist withal. He dreamed dreams and beheld vision" (69). The dream was one, as we have seen, of agrarian idylls, of pastoral democracy: "where everybody could have a farm, almost for taking it, economic equality easily resulted, and this involved political equality" (67).[3] After closing the West in "The Significance of the Frontier in American History" (1893), Turner now laments it; and by lamenting it, he pushes historical investigation into the register of eschatology. For the Turnerian frontiersman as for the Puritan, the ruin begins with the arrival of industrial capitalism:

> The free lands are gone, the continent is crossed, and all this push and energy is turning into channels of agitation. Failures in one area can no longer be made good by taking up land on a new frontier; the conditions of a settled society are being reached with suddenness and with confusion. The West has been built up with borrowed capital, and the question of the stability of gold, as a standard of deferred payments, is eagerly agitated by the debtor West, profoundly dissatisfied with the industrial conditions that confront it, and actuated by frontier directness and rigor in its remedies. (74)

Put another way, the frontiersmen begat the railroad, and patricide necessarily followed. "Free lands"—the idyllic Jeffersonian landscape at the heart of Manifest Destiny's imagination—become conduits for "channels of agitation"; the pastoral faces the industrial, and the former loses its grounding. If New England was damned by a vengeful and jealous Calvinist God, then the West faces a force much more dire:

bankers scorned. This is not the "end of the West" as violent disruption; it is the "end of the West" as bureaucratic nightmare. Moore's Cold War–era satire, with its *Dr. Strangelove*-like generals, grass-worshiping cults, and shady business dealings, captures this sense of a world of endless possibility stagnating in a circus of conflicting geopolitical, economic, and religious absurdities.

This imagined "end"—apocalypse as steady decline, not sudden collapse—is not strictly about privation, absence, and retreat. Indeed, as Marx and Engels argue, under capitalism, "the end" may play out in a much more curious manner:

> In these crises, there breaks out an epidemic that, in all earlier epochs, would have seemed an absurdity—the epidemic of over-production. Society suddenly finds itself put back into a state of momentary barbarism; it appears as if a famine, a universal war of devastation, had cut off the supply of every means of subsistence; industry and commerce seem to be destroyed; and why? Because there is too much civilisation, too much means of subsistence, too much industry, too much commerce. (Marx and Engels 226)[4]

The chaotic nature of capitalist production thus leads us to a bizarre conclusion: *an eschaton of abundance*. Marx and Engels's description of overproduction in the *Manifesto* prefigures the central place this crisis occupies in Marx's mature economic theory (Marx, *Grundrisse* 411–19). "In *competition*," Marx writes in his notebooks for *Capital*, "this inner tendency of capital appears as a compulsion exercised over it by *alien capital*, which drives it forward beyond the correct proportion with a constant *march, march!*" (413). Say's law, a core tenet of classical economics, holds that rational producers only make as much as they may reasonably discharge on the marketplace; Marx and Engels point out the evident error in this idea, emphasizing instead the irrational, voracious manner in which capital spreads its influence across the globe. The ideological field described by the three interrelated concepts "Puritanism," "Manifest Destiny," and "Transcendentalism"—all three the handmaidens of American capitalist development in its different stages—is likewise damned from the beginning by its own dream of limitless growth and expansion. This threat ("too much civilisation, too much means of subsistence") is what I see Turner, a non-Marxist Progressive, presaging in "The Problem of the West," and what Ward Moore pushes to an apagogical extreme in *Greener Than You Think*.

The eschaton of abundance's logic is the same as that of the Midas myth: those who long for endless riches are cursed by having their wish fulfilled. Moore's rapacious Bermuda grass is a living emblem of that anxiety at work. This becomes clear in the first of many long, lyrical descriptions of the grass:

> The Dinkmans had lived in a city block, an urban entity.... But now I looked upon no city scene, no picture built upon the substantial foundation of daddy at the office all day, fixing a leaky faucet of an evening, painting with woodwork during his summer vacation; or mom, after a pleasant afternoon with the girls, unstintedly opening cans for supper and harassedly watching the cleaning woman who came in once a week. An alien presence, a rude fist through the canvas negated the convention that this was a picture of reality. A cone-shaped hill rose to a blurred point, marking the burial-place of the Dinkman house. It was a child's drawing of a cone-shaped hill, done in green crayon; too symmetrical, too evenly and heavily green to be a spontaneous product of nature; man's unimaginative hand was apparent in its composition. (55)

Weener's assertion that the "alien presence" is like a "rude fist through the canvas" of a pastoral suburban scene calls to mind Ahab's "pasteboard mask" speech in the "Quarter-Deck" chapter of *Moby Dick*, which climaxes with Ahab ejaculating, "If man will strike, strike through the mask!" (Melville 161–62). For Ahab, "striking through the mask" will place him face-to-face with an absent God; for Weener, the "rude fist" punching through the canvas is that of humanity itself, whose "unimaginative hand" can be seen in the hypnotic hill of grass. Moore's description proceeds dialectically from the familiar (suburban family life) to the "alien" (the Bermuda grass tower), before demonstrating that the familiar and the alien share an identity in that they are both products of human overreach. This "city block" in the West could not exist without the dual ideological apparatuses of Transcendentalist optimism and Manifest Destiny. Both systems rely, as we've seen, on a dream of endless expansion, of continuous production. However, as inheritors of the Puritan eschatological imagination, both are also burdened with their own principle of contamination. The Dinkmans' lawn, opulent symbol of white European civilization's victory over Southern California, becomes that civilization's undoing.

Weener's description of the Dinkman plot is anchored in the material signifiers of an epidemic of overproduction, the suburban homestead and its manicured front lawn. The architectural character of Hollywood—converted from farmland to a model suburban utopia of single-family homes with self-contained lawns by the land developer H. J. Whitley in the early 1900s—is a product of the general trend toward suburbanization that overtook American cities after the Civil War. Historian Kenneth T. Jackson observes that the suburban homestead became a marker of American civilization precisely because it stood against urban planning logics from the Old World. Whereas "in pre-Napoleonic Europe, about 75 percent of the populace lived in squalid hovels, which were shared with unrelated individuals and farm animals," Americans opted for a planning style whereby the home would be a "self-contained unit," with the front lawn serving as a barrier—a kind of verdant moat separating the household from the threats and temptations of the city (Kenneth Jackson 47, 58). Ted Steinberg asserts that "the rise of the lawn to dominance in suburbia represents one of the most profound transformations of the landscape in American history," a transformation presaged by early settlers who found that indigenous grasses were not suitable for European-style husbandry (Steinberg 9–12). Importing European grasses, these settlers caused a material break from indigenous land-use traditions. Nowhere was this break more radical than in Southern California, a landscape that Anglo-Americans, against all logic, beat and transformed into an unsustainable paradise of miniature English-style country homes. Davis observes that "only Mexico City has more completely toxified its natural setting, and no other metropolis in the industrialized Northern Hemisphere continues to grow at such a breakneck pace" (Davis 318). As Christopher Isherwood rhapsodizes in his essay "Los Angeles," published the same year as Moore's novel, the city formed largely as "an uncoordinated expanse of townlets and suburbs, spreading wide and white over the sloping plain between the mountains and the Pacific Ocean" (Isherwood 157). Isherwood, a precise and knowing stylist, describes the suburban sprawl as "white" to underscore the racial nature of Southern California suburbanization, which relegated nonwhite residents to areas where the ecological toll of Anglo development was felt the most.[5] The Anglo-American settler did not so much eschew European models in favor of an autochthonic frontiersman aesthetic so much as adapt another European model, the manor home, to a smaller and thus more readily replicable scale.

Moore connects the material facts of Los Angeles's expansion to the ideological forces that helped motor that material development. He makes this aspect of *Greener Than You Think*'s satire explicit in the character of Joe Thario, a young employee of Weener's who becomes obsessed by the undulating fields of grass. Moore transforms Thario from an eager young industrialist into a doe-eyed, Whitmanian Transcendentalist, thereby skewering the use of Transcendentalist philosophical tenets to offer a respectable, mystical sheen to the crude economic and social realities of westward expansion. Thario's sham spiritual awakening begins after Weener sends him on a scouting mission to see if the Bermuda grass can be converted into a cheap fuel:

> [Thario] filled notebooks, those thick pulppapered volumes which children are supposed to use in school but never do, with his reactions. In idle moments when he was away, I glanced through them, but for the most part they were incoherent. Meterless poems, lists of adjectives, strained interpretations of the actions of the grass, and many musical notations which seemed to get no farther than a repetitive and faltering start.
>
> I reproduce a few pages of the less chaotic material for what it is worth: "The iceage drove the Cromagnon from the caves

> which prophesied Cnossus and Pithom and the Temple of Athena in the Acropolis. This grass, twentiethcentury ice, drives magnates from their twentyroom villas to their twentyroom duplexes. The loss was yesterday's. Walt Whitman." (207–8)

Again, as in Weener's first rhapsodic description of Hollywood lawns, Moore leans on a cataloging technique familiar to readers of Emerson's essays or Whitman's poems. But Thario, a more perceptive observer than Weener, takes the grass as an occasion to contemplate American history and social development. Thario's obsession grows from here, eventually leading him to leave his job in order to compose a symphony ("Thario's First") in honor of the grass. "My backside might be in a swivelchair, but my soul would be right up here [with the grass]," Thario tells Weener. "It's Whitman translated visibly and tangibly ...'Come lovely and soothing death, undulate round and round'" (210). Thario quotes from Whitman's "When Lilacs Last in the Door-yard Bloom'd" (1865), an elegy for Abraham Lincoln that also contains a pattern of images leading to an eschatological moment:

> When lilacs last in the door-yard bloom'd,
> And the great star early droop'd in the western sky in the night,
> I mourn'd—and yet shall mourn with ever-returning spring.
> O ever-returning spring! trinity sure to me you bring;
> Lilac blooming perennial, and drooping star in the west,
> And thought of him I love. (lns. 1–6)

If we trace Moore's allusion back to Whitman, we encounter a prime example of the eschatological imagination that haunts Transcendentalism's boundless optimism. "And yet shall mourn with ever-returning spring" (ln. 3) is precisely the logic of the eschaton of abundance: in this line, endless production and bloom breeds mourning, deprivation, and loss. Thario's specific citation comes from the "Death Carol" section of the poem, where Whitman invites "the sure-enwinding arms of cool-enfolding Death" (ln. 143), a forerunner to Moore's world-enwinding Bermuda grass. The Bermuda grass is not only "Whitman translated visibly and tangibly," but also a symbol of the apocalyptic imagination that rests at the heart of Transcendentalist optimism.

Thario finally embarks on a quest for "mystical union" with the grass. The whole journey is framed as a parody of Whitmanian poesy and Transcendentalist philosophy:

> I am the Grass and the Grass is me; in mystical union we have become a single entity. I speak with its voice and in the great cadences which come from its heart you can hear Thario's first, transfigured and magnified a hundred thousand times. (327)

Like the followers of Anthony "Brother Paul" Preblesham, Thario self-immolates in the grass. Later, as Weener roams the world on his yacht looking for a new home, he recalls Thario's desire for "mystical union." Weener sails off the coast of grass-covered Europe, "the home of civilization" (346), and contemplates his fallen employee's end:

> I have reserved the afterdeck to myself and as I sit here now, scribbling these notes, I think what impresses me more than anything else is the feeling of vitality which radiates from the herbaceous coast. The dead continent is alive, alive as never before—wholly alive; moving with millions of sensitive feelers in every direction. For the first time I have a feeling of sympathy for Joe's constant talk of the beauty of the Grass, but in spite of this, the question which comes to my mind is, can you speak glibly about the beauty of something which has strangled nearly all the world? (346–47)

Looking out on the wasteland of untamed beauty that was sparked by his experiment on a lawn in Los Angeles, Albert Weener has his first (and only) honest insight: to become enamored of endless production, to make oneself a devotee to the spectacle of infinite territorial expansion, is foolish, "glib." Weener finally reaches a moment of earnest ethical crisis. His apprehension of the beauty of the Bermuda grass is based on the deaths of millions and the ruin of the globe. Written during and published immediately after World War II, *Greener Than You Think* modulates in its conclusion from a broad science fiction satire of American salesmanship to a lament for civilizations that had self-immolated in the rush for accumulation and dominance. In this way, Moore's critique of the Transcendentalist self is not unlike that of C. L. R. James, the Trinidadian Marxist who saw in Melville's Ahab a figure of the West's imperialist mania and that mania's tendency toward apocalyptic self-destruction.[6]

Early in the progress of Moore's grass apocalypse, Weener scoffs at a gruff-talking military man with a disdain for Miss Francis's whole Metamorphizer project:

> I looked contemptuously at [the army captain], for he had that unimaginative approach which disdains Science and so holds Civilization back on its upward path. If the world's future rested with people like this, I thought, we should never have had dynamite or germ-theories or airplanes capable of destroying whole cities at a blow. (69)

This short passage demonstrates the genius of both Moore's creative imagination and his thick critique of American expansionism. Weener's ascension through the novel, predicated as it is on the destruction of the globe, vividly dramatizes Marx's famous insistence in *The Eighteenth Brumaire of Louis Bonaparte* (1852) that "all great world-historic facts and personages appear, so to speak, twice…the first time as tragedy, the second time as farce" (15). The farce in *Greener Than You Think* is an eschaton of abundance, a logical absurdity in which overproduction bred by a philosophy of endless upward progress crescendos not in a harmonious conclusion, the sustainment and elevation of the whole human species, but instead an abysmal, dissonant collapse. The West—where suburbs are born seemingly overnight, where the arms industry set up its largest factories, and where the cult of consumer culture finds its fullest expression—becomes a perfect theater for Moore's weird conception of American decline. From the Puritans onward, the notion that America's grandest aspirations and most deeply held ideals must inevitably lead to our mutual ruin has been central to our national mentality. The centrality of this myth and its continued hold on American political, social, and philosophical imaginations—along with the second-class status of such genre fiction in most literary studies—is, I believe, a major cause of *Greener Than You Think*'s continued obscurity. It is difficult to imagine a less heroic avatar for the "truly American" man, to adapt a phrase of Frederick Jackson Turner's from "The Significance of the Frontier in American History," than Albert Weener, an affectless con artist who would sell out global order for his own petty material ends. And yet, as Moore writes in his epigraph to the novel, this is precisely his satire's meaning for his nation: "Neither the vegetation nor people in this book are entirely fictitious. But, reader, no person pictured here is you. With one exception. You, Sir, Miss, or Madam…are Albert Weener. As I am Albert Weener" (6).

Notes

1. Not all of Moore's contemporaries dismissed his work. In a later *Los Angeles Times* piece on the literary heritage of Southern California, Lawrence Clark Powell mentions *Greener Than You Think* alongside Evelyn Waugh's *The Loved One* as a Southland novel that "bring[s] the acids of satire where they are needed" (Jordan-Smith D6). The highest praise for Moore's book comes from *Sunset Magazine* managing editor and LA literary maven Joseph Henry Jackson, who calls the book "as devilishly ingenious a yarn as I've ever come across," and even recommends that we "try Mr. Moore's 'Greener Than You Think' as a sort of companion piece" to Orwell's *1984*. He concludes, "Mr. Moore has a savage imagination, too, though to my mind he controls it a trifle better than Mr. Orwell" (Jackson A5–6).
2. For an exhaustive discussion of Transcendentalism's reliance on cataloging rhetoric, see part 3, "Word and World: Nature as a Model for Literary Form," in Buell.
3. The idea that America was primarily a land of small yeoman farmers is a foundational premise of the Anglo-American historical imaginary. However, as historian William Hogeland persuasively argues, Cold War–era historians such as Forest McDonald tended to overdetermine the economic and social importance of small freeholders in their analyses, overlooking the role played by large landholders who revived the English manor system in the young nation. While western lands would have provided a comparatively more "free" alternative for such tenants, few were able to establish successful claims there, and the same landholders who controlled the political and financial institutions of the East would soon exert their influence on the West. See Hogeland 24–26.
4. See Marx, *Grundrisse*, 411–19, for Marx's direct attack on Say's law and Ricardo's denial of the possibility of a crisis of overproduction.
5. Mike Davis discusses the importance of suburban homeowners associations and

restrictive covenants in maintaining the racial polarization of Los Angeles County in *City of Quartz: Excavating the Future in Los Angeles*, 160–69.

6. See James, *Mariners, Renegades, and Castaways*.

Bibliography

Buell, Lawrence. *Literary Transcendentalism: Style and Vision in the American Renaissance*. Cornell UP, 1975.

Carlyle, Thomas, and Ralph Waldo Emerson. *The Correspondence of Thomas Carlyle and Ralph Waldo Emerson, 1834–1872*, edited by Charles Eliot Norton, vol 1., 3rd ed., James R. Osgood and Company, 1883.

Court, John M. *Approaching the Apocalypse: A Short History of Christian Millenarianism*. I. B. Tauris, 2008.

Davis, Mike. *City of Quartz: Excavating the Future in Los Angeles*. New ed., Verso, 2006.

———. *Ecology of Fear: Los Angeles and the Imagination of Disaster*. Vintage, 1999.

Denning, Michael. *The Cultural Front: The Laboring of American Culture in the Twentieth Century*. Verso, 2011.

Fresonke, Kris. *West of Emerson: The Design of Manifest Destiny*. U of California P, 2002.

Hietala, Thomas R. *Manifest Design: American Exceptionalism and Empire*. Rev. ed., Cornell UP, 2003.

Hogeland, William. *Founding Finance: How Debt, Speculation, Foreclosures, Protests, and Crackdowns Made Us a Nation*. U of Texas P, 2012.

Innes, Stephen. *Creating the Commonwealth: The Economic Culture of Puritan New England*. W. W. Norton, 1995.

Isherwood, Christopher. *Exhumations: Stories, Articles, Verses*. Methuen, 1984.

Jackson, Joseph Henry. "A Bookman's Notebook: Notes on the Margin." *Los Angeles Times*, 8 Aug. 1949, pp. A5–6.

Jackson, Kenneth T. *Crabgrass Frontier: The Suburbanization of the United States*. New York, Oxford UP, 1987.

James, C. L. R. *Mariners, Renegades, and Castaways: The Story of Herman Melville and the World We Live In*. 1953. Edited by Donald Pease, Dartmouth UP, 2001.

Jordan-Smith, Paul. "Books and Authors: Dr. Powell's Discourse on Southland Fiction Inspires Discussion, Study." *Los Angeles Times*, 27 July 1952, p. D6.

Marx, Karl. *The Eighteenth Brumaire of Louis Bonaparte*. 1852. International Publishers, 1994.

———. *Grundrisse: Foundations of the Critique of Political Economy (Rough Draft)*. 1858. Edited and translated by Martin Nicolaus, Penguin, 1993.

Marx, Karl, and Friedrich Engels. *The Communist Manifesto*. 1848. Translated by William Reeves, edited by Gareth Stedman Jones, Penguin, 2002.

Melville, Herman. *Moby Dick or, The Whale*. 1851. Penguin, 2002.

Moore, Ward. *Greener Than You Think*. William Sloane Associates, 1947.

Mott, Wesley T. "Emerson and Antinomialism: The Legacy of the Sermons (1978)." *On Emerson*, edited by Edwin H. Cady and Louis J. Budd, Duke UP, 1988, pp. 216–44.

Page, Michael. "Evolution and Apocalypse in the Golden Age." *Green Planets: Ecology and Science Fiction*, edited by Gerry Canavan and Kim Stanley Robinson, Wesleyan UP, 2014, pp. 40–55.

Pratt. Theodore. "Strangler." Review of *Greener Than You Think*, by Ward Moore. *The New York Times*, 7 Dec. 1947, pp. 14–16.

Rexroth, Kenneth. *An Autobiographical Novel*, edited by Linda Hamalian, New Directions, 1991.

Simonson, Harold P. *Beyond the Frontier: Writers, Western Regionalism, and a Sense of Place*. Texas Christian UP, 1989.

Steinberg, Ted. *American Green: The Obsessive Quest for the Perfect Lawn*. W. W. Norton, 2006.

St. George, Robert. *Conversing by Signs: Poetics of Implication in Colonial New England Culture*. U of North Carolina P, 1998.

Thoreau, Henry David. *Walking*. 1851. Arc Manor Class Reprints, 2007.

Turner, Frederick Jackson. *Rereading Frederick Jackson Turner: The Significance of the Frontier in American History, and Other Essays*, edited by John Mack Faragher, H. Holt, 1994.

Whitman, Walt. *Leaves of Grass and Other Writings*. 2nd ed., edited by Michael Moon, W. W. Norton, 2002.

Winthrop, John. "A Modell of Christian Charity." 1630. *The Puritans: A Sourcebook of Their Writings*, edited by Perry Miller and Thomas H. Johnson, Dover, 2001, pp. 195–98.

7

Mari Sandoz

A Writer's Politics

BETTE WEIDMAN

Mari Sandoz's leftist politics was not an organizational party-inspired activity. It was a writer's politics, and it shaped and informed her novels, her histories, and her famous biography of Crazy Horse. The commitment emerged from conditions of her western homesteading childhood, her struggle to realize her vocation, and her keen observation of the Euro-American settlement of the West. Sandoz was a loner, not a joiner, and the severity of her leftist critique of American society brought her personal attacks and death threats. Writing left in the West, she was ultimately forced to leave her beloved Nebraska (Stauffer 131–32).

In twenty books, all still in print, Sandoz wrote a powerful condemnation of class stratification, urban and rural poverty, greed and profiteering, and genocidal attacks on Native Americans by U.S. government policies. In two of her novels, *Capital City* (1939) and *The Tom-Walker* (1947), she envisioned the dissolution of democratic government and its replacement by fascist dictatorship. These were the two cautionary tales that brought violent reprisals in Lincoln, Nebraska.

Mari Sandoz grew up in the Sand Hills region of northwestern Nebraska, not far from the Sioux reservation in South Dakota. By the time of her birth, in 1896, her father, Jules Ami Sandoz, a Swiss emigrant, had established a homestead, found a hardworking helpmate in his fourth wife, Mary Elizabeth Fehr, also Swiss, and begun his work as a locator of settlers seeking farms and struggling against ranchers and moneyed interests. Jules had begun the study of medicine in Switzerland; his father was a respected, prosperous veterinarian, so his emigration was not motivated by poverty. Rather it was a rebellion against the family that opposed his choice of a woman of a lower social class. Jules planned to emigrate with the young woman, but she refused to join him in the United States. Then an accident in the course of well digging made him permanently lame, adding another setback. Jules possessed an overbearing personality, a determination to dominate. Doubtless his powerful will contributed to his survival in the harsh conditions of the frontier, but it also made for a difficult family life.

As his oldest child, born disappointingly female, Mari witnessed her father's abuse of her mother and received her own share of beatings, especially when she sought reading matter or sent her stories to local newspapers. The admirable and the despicable were thoroughly mixed in Jules Sandoz; his courage, love of the country, commitment to locating and defending settlers, and interest in Indians were all valuable legacies he undermined by the fear he instilled in his family. For Mari, intellectual and emotional independence from the difficult father was a requirement for development, yet she was sharply aware of the cross-class distribution of the will to dominate and to use others. You might say she was raised to understand the human traits that both produced fascism and resisted it.

When a Mexican editor inquired about the sources of her political ideas, she referred to the European history of her family in a passage that merits full quotation:

> In regard to the origins of my social consciousness, the members of my Father's family were followers of Pedro Waldo in his pre-Reformation rebellion against the tyranny and corruption of the church. When the executions and recantations began, our family fled from Lombardy to France, and when the religious persecutions became too intense there, they crossed over into Switzerland, at the end of the nineteenth century, a model for new nations.
>
> The members of my mother's family were from the Canton

of Schwyz and took an active role in the formation of the original confederation of Uri, Schwyz, and Unterwalden in 1291, from which emerged the Confederation of Switzerland.

My own liberalism came from this fertile past as well as from a childhood of living in the midst of poverty. A continual caravan of the world's disinherited passed by our house in quest of free lands which my father helped them to find. Among them there was also the constant recognition of the exploitation of the Western states by the loan-bankers of the East. All this we heard talked about in our childhood as well as the history of the rapacious empires—of the expansion of Rome to all Europe, the expansion of Spain in the New World, the expansion of England all over the globe—and the expansion of the United States, which already at that time resembled England in its use of military power and financial capital.

Thus, having at an early age become aware of the long struggle to obtain and defend a small and decent portion of individual liberty, and of the recent pressures against this liberty—as society becomes more and more complex—the development of my social consciousness was logically inevitable. Moreover, there was another determining factor in my childhood: the daily presence of an expropriated race, the American Indian. I was attracted to them very much, as children are always attracted by men of grand bearing, graciousness, and wisdom. One of the greatest of these, old He Dog, brother chieftain of the great Crazy Horse, called me his granddaughter until he died around 1937. From him and others like him, I developed a feeling of the brotherhood with all things on earth, which is the essence of the ancient philosophy of the Sioux, and the foundation of the deep sense of responsibility which each Sioux feels for each member of his community. (orig. Bledsoe; trans. and qtd. in Sandoz, *Hostiles and Friendlies* 30)

Significantly, Sandoz's breakthrough as a writer came as the result of the biography she wrote at the surprising deathbed request of her father. After a lifetime of belittling writers and artists, discouraging her and driving her away from home, the dying man came to see the importance of telling the realistic, not the romantic, story of the settlement of the West. After fourteen rejections, *Old Jules* won the Atlantic Monthly Prize for Non-Fiction in 1935, freeing Sandoz to develop her life's work in both fiction and nonfiction.

IN THREE NOVELS WRITTEN in the ten years between 1937 and 1947, Sandoz shaped a critique of American society from the 1890s to 1945, the period of her own unfolding life. These novels represent a powerful and original confrontation with the failures of American democratic ideology. *Slogum House* (1937) represents the settler-rancher culture of the developing frontier in which she grew up. *Capital City* (1939) matches her own trajectory, leaving the circle of her rural family and moving to Lincoln, Nebraska, for work, education, and self-discovery. This urban novel was followed, after eight years, by *The Tom-Walker* (1947), a work with a longer historical perspective. It is the story of three men of the Stone family as each one returns from the war that shaped his generation: the Civil War, World War I, and World War II.

Slogum House is set in a fictionalized version of the Niobrara River region of Sandoz's northern Nebraska childhood. The land is dry prairie painfully farmed by settlers hoping to realize homesteads of their own. These settlers, many of them European immigrants, occupy the fringes of the novel and are rarely seen directly, only when their needs and possessions come into conflict with the wealth and power-hunger of Gulla Slogum. The novel begins with Gulla in mid-career, matriarch of a family she raised out of ambition to escape low-caste poverty. She is doyenne of a money-making establishment, Slogum House, where she accumulates land and cattle and combines her family home with a public eatery and a house of prostitution for passing freighters, ranchers, and politicians. She raises her own labor. Following her orders, two adult sons harass and steal from settlers, bringing their mother "Slogum purchases" of lumber and fencing wire. Her beautiful twin daughters, Annette and Cellie, are raised to sell sexual favors to powerful men, while another daughter, Libby, is assigned to do the cooking. A younger set of twins is also managed by the mother—Ward expected to follow his brothers and Fanny sent to boarding school to become a lady.

The father is Ruedy Slogum, the son of middle-class Swiss emigrant parents, not unlike that of Sandoz's European forebears. Although Ruedy is raised by his Schweitzer grandmother to love music, poetry, and gardening, there is no father figure substantial enough to save him from seduction by Regula Haber, one of twelve children in a river-bottom family of prostitutes and criminals. Gulla plans to achieve the fortune predicted for her by her mother through the shotgun marriage to Ruedy, but his family disinherits him when, despite his self-disgust, he refuses to abandon Gulla and the baby.

This is the first sign in the novel that two different systems of value are represented in one American family. But while Ruedy and Libby are powerless to defeat Gulla and suffer greatly at her hand, they outlive her and her despicable sons. The will to power, the desire to control, and the appropriation of the possessions of others are expressions of a personalized right-wing fascist ideology. There is, at the novel's end, a victory in the outliving, the endurance of Ruedy and Libby without loss of generosity or loyalty. Unfortunately, the political victory of Roosevelt's moratorium on mortgage foreclosures comes too late for many of Gulla's victims.

The Slogums are Sandoz's representative American family, one-third brutal, one-third good, and one-third victims. Although she claimed she was writing allegory in *Slogum House*, allegory implies a more abstract quality than this book has. These characters are so firmly individualized, even in their various kinds of brutality, victimization, or generosity, that the reader sees them as drawn to the realistic, rather than typical, pole of representation. Similarly, the political and economic landscape seems closer to that of the late nineteenth-century and early twentieth-century West than to an abstract "Hogback of Humiliation." Nor is social class simple in Sandoz; while crime and cruelty follow from the Habers, the will to shape a political response emerges from the community Gulla seeks to engulf, through the humane and educated Ruedy, distanced from his upper-class family and making common cause with a variety of neighbors.

In American literature, Gulla resembles no one so much as Nathaniel Hawthorne's Judge Pyncheon in *The House of the Seven Gables*, another novel about stolen land and ill-gotten gains. *Slogum House* comes to an end in a year of drought, the settlers losing their lands to the banks where Gulla has been collecting their mortgages. Rebellion is brewing in the people she has victimized, and they stop a scheduled foreclosure sale. Gulla's own weight, her unrestrained and symbolic self-indulgence, causes the stroke that finally kills her, just as the second Roosevelt president responds to economic upheaval with the saving grace of a moratorium on mortgage foreclosures.

The fortunes of the Slogums and their neighbors are interwoven with the cycles of the seasons, the responsiveness of the land to cultivation, the behavior of human beings working out their destinies against the background of community and regional and national politics. Politics is seen as a malleable force, ultimately but belatedly responsive to human needs. The Slogums we admire pay dearly for their freedoms, Libby at one point saving her father from suicide.

With its large and varied cast of characters, its setting on the Nebraska prairie, its violence and its tenderness, *Slogum House* would make an admirable film. Dominated by the unromantic image of the hogback, a low rise in the flat land to which Gulla sends her lookouts, the patched-together architecture of Slogum House represents a twentieth-century *House of the Seven Gables*, and its story, like that of its predecessor, is one of the tragic waste of American promise.

In *Capital City* (1939), written in the depths of the Depression, Sandoz reflected her own move, eighteen years earlier, from rural Nebraska to urban Lincoln. During the first of these years she lived economically on a small income earned by filling capsules for a pharmaceutical company at the rate of twenty-five cents per thousand, in order to pay for rent, food, and the leisure to study at the university. This Spartan existence, later supported by research work and then by her writing, marked her way of life. She could easily have modeled Hamm Rufe, the upper-class scion of the Hammonds, of the ruling class of Franklin, the fictional Lincoln, Nebraska, of the novel, on herself. A leftist political activist, Rufe left his prosperous family as a young man, bent on observing life. The reader first meets him in early middle age, after a prologue describing the physical and economic realities of the city, which lies "like a cluster of lice along the vein of a yellowing leaf" (*Capital City* 3). The narrative voice offers the hot, dusty September evening, along with the poor harvest season, as background to the town's celebration of its Fall Festival, an effort to stimulate business in a society sharply divided between the wealthy and the poor.

Hamm Rufe, from whose perspective we see the scene, is accompanied by Coot, or Asa Bruce Harcoot, once a bank president, now a derelict. The two live in Herb's Addition, a tarpaper Hooverville for the dispossessed, a vantage point from which they can observe the contesting forces in the city below them, under the capitol dome with its sculptured frieze dedicated to the people of the world. Like Coot, Hamm is a refugee from Franklin's version of prosperity, concealing his identity as one of the richest heirs of the city, Rufer Hammond, behind the pseudonym of Hamm Rufe.

Hamm has not only withdrawn from his family and the civic life of Franklin, he has withdrawn for a period of years from the political activism that resulted in his being beaten during his participation in a strike in Boston in 1919. That street battle gave him the facial scar and disfigurement that now enables his disguise. Hamm had been rescued from the street battle by a young Czech girl, Stephani, whom he subsequently married and still loves, but from whom he is separated. She cannot understand his withdrawal from activist political participation. Yet Hamm has really not withdrawn ideologically; he writes political commentary for *The Nation*, and he lives in the shantytown by way of maintaining his independent perspective, and particularly his independence from his mother and the Hammond wealth and social position. Living as a Hammond would make him a hypocrite to everything he believes.

Sandoz takes a risk in inventing so odd a hero, one who seems to have decided to give up most of the pleasures of life (except music) for the act of witnessing. Ultimately, Rufe completes his withdrawal from active life, bequeaths his beloved to a political activist, and sacrifices his life in a labor strike. This kind of "hero" is not unlike Ruedy and Ward Slogum; all three bear emotional scars that make full participation too painful. Ruedy has given hostages to Gulla, from whom he cannot withdraw his presence, although at one dark moment he arranges his suicide. All three are observers, Ward quietly seeking to protect the mortgagers, and draw into themselves the sufferings of others. All three have channeled their capacity for love into deeply felt ideas of social justice. The invention of this kind of hero, for whom the victory is an inward consistency of principle, should be counted as an achievement of Sandoz's modern novel. The sacrifice of the characters to whom the writer gives her fullest intellectual approval suggests that the rewards this world can give are insufficient for the costs full participation exacts.

Capital City starts with the suicide of Cobby Welles, once the boyhood comrade of Rufer Hammond. Cobby has played the Capital City game, married in his social class, served as bank president, and fathered a troublesome son involved in the protofascist Gold Shirts. But his life, even sweetened by a Polish lover, is still too bitter. At least Rufe gives up his life for a cause, instead of weltering in self-pity.

The cast of characters is large here, as in *Slogum House*, but with no dominating Gulla their stories emerge in more detail. Burt Parr and Molly Tyndale have to fight their parents for a cross-class marriage, but at the end, when democratic government has collapsed in Kanewa (Sandoz's blend of Kansas, Nebraska, and Iowa), the girl's father is grateful for the poor boy's devotion. The capital city of Franklin, the novel's version of Lincoln, Nebraska, has two families, university faculty, who adopt orphaned refugee children: a Spanish boy who survived the Spanish Civil War and a German-Jewish child. The boys become friends. They are deliberately killed by a hit-and-run driver never prosecuted, but whose red convertible is easily recognized as belonging to a Gold Shirt. Hamm has a friend in the historian Abigail Allerton, who has written a documentary history exposing corruption in Franklin's past, centered in the political headquarters of the Franklin House Hotel. Abigail's ostracism, reversed when her book achieves a movie contract, is another example of the self-serving hypocrisy of the city's social leaders.

In his excellent article "'The Ripening Fascism of the Corn Belt': Lost Democracy in Mari Sandoz's *Capital City*," Philip Dubuisson Castille notes the way Sandoz renders "class conflict as a spatial event" (Castille 131). In his description of the motorcade celebrating Franklin's Fall Festival, Castille shows that the city's main street, Philadelphia Avenue, "symbolically spans the entire city," laying out its regions of wealth and privilege and its periphery of poverty. Although it takes place on wheels, the motorcade is one of the notable processions in American literature, worthy to place beside the Election Day procession in *The Scarlet Letter.* Here the election being celebrated is not of the colonial magistrates, but of the pseudo kings and queens of a business-sponsored boosterism concealing a city with many unsolved problems resulting from an inequitable distribution of wealth.

Castille's spatial analysis carries over brilliantly to the novel's conclusion, also marked by a procession, but this time a disorderly confrontational one, like one of those painted by James Ensor. Here, too, an election is being celebrated, but it is the election of Charlie Stet, the fascist independent candidate who has drawn voters from two unsatisfactory choices. Anti-labor, anti-Semitic, Stet is an American Hitler. His election is marked by the converging of the football Homecoming crowd, the march of striking truckers, and the counter-march of Stet's Gold Shirts. In the ensuing confrontation violence erupts, and Hamm Rufe, in the midst of it, sees his mother approach to prevent the use of Hammond property for this violence. Leaping forward to protect her, he takes a deadly blow from a Gold Shirt's club, as the twenty-thousand football fans sweep all before them. When the crowd clears, there is a Hawthornesque pieta: the mother finally recognizes her dead son.

While democracy is undermined in Kanewa, the election to the U.S. Senate of the Farmer-Labor candidate has surprisingly succeeded. Hamm has willed his long-abandoned wealth to Stephani and the victorious Carl Halzer, and the young lovers Molly and Burt have fled across state lines, so there may be a future when the nightmare is over.

The novel's turning point comes late. Following an arsonist's fire in Herb's Addition that kills a trapped old cripple, Mrs. Hammond's liberal consciousness is raised, and she invites her as-yet-unrecognized son to a meeting to discuss rebuilding. She wants him to persuade the poor to leave their independent lives in the Hooverville for the regimented county farm. Hamm is infuriated:

> "Poor people they seem to you!" he shouted upon the astonished woman. "Misguided, people for charity! Have you forgotten that this was once a land of refuge for such people as these? A refuge from the need and the tyranny of charity? There was a man here once—a man who founded this town, who believed in the preservation of the earth for the common people; a man who fought to the end of his life against the selling out of his state. He was ostracized for his belief in human rights; he had his print-shop smashed, his desk rotten-egged for expressing this belief. Fortunately he died before he had to see this town, the city he named for a man whose greatness he could understand, protecting a lot of lawless hoodlums who openly whip and burn and murder, hoodlums that are backed by his own flesh and blood!" (*Capital City* 309)

He is speaking of his mother's father, his own grandfather, who named the town "Franklin." Hamm's indictment expresses the outrage of the leftists at the falling away from American ideology permitted by the wealthy. Hamm's mother doesn't recognize him or his ideas, dismissing him as a tramp, but her dog recognizes his old playmate and leaves the meeting with him.

Sandoz's concept of the hero as a self-acknowledged failure in spite of his journalistic writing is an interesting problem for readers. Why doesn't Hamm claim his name and his position? Sandoz doesn't see leadership emerging from the elite; her hope rests with the elected farmer, Carl Halzer, and with the processes of lawful government. Hamm cannot lead a violent revolution; he can only die as a sacrifice, a wake-up call for his contemporaries. We get a new kind of hero, one committed to an intellectual life, one who turns away from riches and toward a community of the like-minded.

In his study *Revolt of the Provinces: The Regionalist Movement in America, 1920–1945*, Robert L. Dorman includes Sandoz's work as an example of the regionalists' "delegitimizing the socio-economic system that had brought America to ruin" (153). He sees her "dark and disenchanted vision" as "a stoic, fatalistic embrace of politics, a rear-guard action against the coming of dystopia" (253). Sandoz, he wrote, "took the theme of betrayed exceptionalism the furthest of any regional writer." In discussing the figure of the locator in *Slogum House*, Leo Platt, Dorman writes of a character whose courage and will led to political action by the masses. In *Capital City*, Sandoz leaves space for this future through Stephani and Halzer, and makes of the sacrificial figure of Hamm a powerful image and argument. Dorman calls Sandoz the "Cassandra" of the regionalist movement, but in spite of her tough realism, she does not write to prophesy doom. Like all great writers, from Herman Melville to Eugene O'Neill, Sandoz writes to lift the consciousness of her readers to a new plane, in the confidence that truth can be told and received.

The Tom-Walker (1947) is her most ambitious postregionalist novel. Beginning in Ohio at the end of the Civil War, it continues through the aftermath of World War I in Nebraska and Wyoming, and concludes at the end of World War II in Washington, D.C. The most complex and least discussed of Sandoz's major novels, it offers a powerful anti-war argument based on the lives of three generations of the Stone family. Perhaps inspired by John Dos Passos's 1921 novel *Three Soldiers* and his *U.S.A. Trilogy* (1938), Sandoz produces a tour de force covering eighty-three years of American history. Her leftist politics not only embraces an anti-war theme, but each of the three sections deploys precise political analysis fitted to its time and place.

As in her previous novels, the texture of the prose is a rich weave of plotline and the characters' political interpretations of their situations. All are aware of their social, economic, and political contexts, in itself a political statement. There are no naïve pawns here, but citizens alert to and informed about their government. In this book the prose weave has the additional color of a vocabulary belonging to the time and place of the characters. Sandoz had to fight eastern editors to keep her westernisms, of which this novel's title is only one. Her concern for independence from East Coast publishing decisions is also political, a resistance to a moneyed establishment using the resources of the West for its own benefit.

Each of the major protagonists brings back a life-threatening war wound that only youthful vitality overcomes; the war experience, which is not dramatized in the novel, also exacts a psychological cost. The first Milton Stone returns from the Civil War an amputee. He ran away from home at fourteen to join Sherman's army, and when he returns, five years later, he does not send word of his injury ahead to the family. Poor farmers in Ohio when he left, they have prospered in the war economy by the time of his return. Milton understands this war profiteering as selling out the soldiers. His social-climbing mother has arranged his homecoming as a gala wedding, without knowing that her son has a surprise of his own—a missing leg.

Wartime prosperity does not last, and Milton's hopes to become a doctor or at least a pharmacist are reduced to his peddling patent medicine cures. He adjusts to the artificial limb, especially when he gets an iron post and is confident enough to turn cartwheels and make sparks fly. However, his larger-than-life escapades can't stem the tide of political corruption and economic woe:

> By then [1872] the country was hearing one scandal after another, stinks worse than a summer battlefield coming out of Congress, the Cabinet, the White House itself, the whole topped off like a bury wagon by the rotten corpse of the Credit Mobilier, the holding company of the Union Pacific railroad. Looked like the panic so long threatened was here, with the new banks going down like rootless trees in a Kansas twister—the starving and the homeless swarming the city dumpings. Maybe the monster guyascutus so long held up as a scare to the nation was really loose this time. (*Tom-Walker* 75)

"Guyascutus" and "tom-walker," circus talk for a stilt walker, are western slang terms with which Sandoz colors her dialogue and which make their way into the fiber of the book. Milton Stone is not the only tom-walker in the narrative; his sons, and in a sense, all who struggle against the overwhelming odds of greed, political power, natural disaster, and physical and psychological illness, earn the symbolic title. They tower over the corrupt, the haters, those who might take their hard-won gains but cannot destroy their resistance.

The narrative tells a quietly heroic tale of the first two Stone women: Lucinda, who struggles against the first Milton's drinking and straying, and Penny, who resists Martin Stone's rage to raise three children on a homestead saved only at the last moment by irrigation and Roosevelt's moratorium on mortgage foreclosures. Only the second Milton, the survivor of World War II, is unlucky in his wife, Hazel; ironically, just as prosperity is finally ending the years of struggle, the political scene shifts to a mood worse than conservative. Milton's Hazel is on the staff of a power-hungry senator, selling out until it is too late to turn back from the rising tide of corruption.

Subtly the narrative shifts from recognizable realism, pegging the characters' lives to documented events, to a breathtaking surreal turn to violent takeover by a fascist right wing. The Stones have recognized and fought corruption before, from the harassment of the KKK as they begin homesteading to banking practices favoring the wealthy. The elder Milton Stone, who lasts until his hundredth birthday and remains a great talker, always has a clear vision of political manipulation, but as he weakens and dies, the political situation deteriorates. With the suspicious death of a cabinet member and threats against the elected right wing's president, the younger Milton tries to extract his wife from the dangerous mess. Attending a congressional session, he recognizes the platform party:

> Western interests, sugar, packing, mine and oil; Eastern too, Wall Street, power, railroad, automotive, steel, coal, chemicals, even a sold-out labor lord—perhaps the most powerful two dozen men in the nation, and with their tie-ups, in the world. Men Hugo Dean called the Thyssens, Krupps and Schachts of American Destiny. (*Tom-Walker* 367)

The scene becomes surreal as the president of the United States denounces the senator who is demanding his resignation. Milton is tempted to use Hazel's gun, but suddenly there's a great blast, an A-bomb set off by the guyascutus himself, the ambitious Senator Potter. In the ensuing tumult Potter is sworn in as president, with Hazel beside him.

After this horror, Milton comes to consciousness again; he has had the surgery to remove the threatening bullet long lodged in his chest. As he realizes he is in a hospital room, the horror of the scene in Congress recedes, and he thinks it all a nightmare, drug-induced by anaesthesia, until he sees "a large gilt-framed color print of a man, like the cheap official pictures he saw blowing around the bombed-out streets of Berlin, or found hidden in good Nazi beds" (*Tom-Walker* 372). The novel ends as he identifies the picture as that of Boyd Potter. We are left to conclude that it did, in fact, happen here. It is a powerful end for a book that can be described as a leftist analysis of American history from the Civil War to the end of World War II.

While there are moments of some success for the Left in the West and honorable mentions of Sandoz's political heroes, William Jennings Bryan, Robert La Follette, and George Norris, the Every-American Stones are a representative mixed bag in their politics. Nothing fools or diverts the outspoken leftism of the original tom-walker, Milton Stone, always a defender of the rights of the humble. His grandson, Milton, the engineer, is further committed to an international vision of food and water for all, from his beloved Wyoming to China, where he works on irrigation projects and gets his potentially death-dealing bullet from a misguided Chinese reading anti-American propaganda.

The Stones are not politicians; they are homesteaders, dry-land farmers, seamstresses, cattlemen, engineers. With their creator, they look at politics as the dominant condition under which their lives unfold. Some of them lose their passion for equality and justice when they prosper (for example, the second, Martin); some, like the first Milton, lose direction in unmanageable rage. But all are fully human and attract the reader's identification. The novelist's central value is a commitment to the common people—labor, veterans, fathers and mothers—and her novel carefully dramatizes their lives, one by one, as they struggle.

Sandoz's attraction to nonfiction, so clear in the novels' historical references, evidently helped her to see that a blend of genres is an effective approach for a writer who understands the personal as enmeshed in the political and historical. She has been criticized, on the one hand, for inserting factual material into her novels, and on the other hand of "fictionalizing" her biographies and histories by introducing dialogue and fully dramatized scenes. This artistic choice can be understood as yet another of her leftist interventions. Her goal in each book is to put the reader into the scene and the moment, for the sake of producing a galvanizing impact. All the dramatizations in her histories have a documentary source; none falsify the written record. Castille remarks that this negative criticism has receded recently, as Sandoz is seen as anticipating the New Journalism and the nonfiction novel of the 1960s (Castille 131).

Sandoz had already paused in her novel-writing, on the way to *The Tom-Walker*, to write a biography of Crazy Horse (1942), which will be discussed at the end of this essay in connection with her later work *Cheyenne Autumn* (1953) and her activism on behalf of Native artists and communities. Immediately after completing *The Tom-Walker*, she turned her hand to a long-cherished project, the Plains Histories trilogy. Although she wrote these nonfiction histories out of chronological order, the three books cover the period from the seventeenth century to the early twentieth. Each book is centered on an animal whose exploitation made human life successful in North America. The stories of the hunters and herders are fully imagined.

Persistent leftist themes in the histories, *The Beaver Men: Spearheads of Empire* (1964), *The Buffalo Hunters* (1954), and *The Cattlemen* (1958), are the waste of resources and the destruction of environment. American beaver attracted Europeans, who had eradicated their own animal populations by the seventeenth century; this stimulated colonial activity, including the monopolistic Hudson's Bay Company and the explorations of Lewis and Clark. Sandoz notes the underlying struggle of Indians and Europeans in all three of these periods. In *The Buffalo Hunters*, the plans for transcontinental railroads and the struggle between land-hungry settlers and the ranchers who sought "free grass" caused the Plains Indians to lose their long-established herds of buffalo and their way of life. Sandoz shows how each of the four great herds moved toward extinction at the hands of wasteful buffalo hunters. Although these books have no novelistic plots, they have strong story lines, artistic structures, and many characters, including Buffalo Bill Cody and Wild Bill Hickok, whose reputations for heroism Sandoz undercuts thoroughly. She reveals George Armstrong Custer's blundering choices as he seeks to aggrandize his reputation to support a bid for the presidency.

Sandoz draws much of her fresh information from firsthand memoirs of the period, and when the narrative reaches her own part of the country, she calls on her knowledge of the Red Cloud Agency and the despairing Sioux who met the U.S. Army at Wounded Knee Creek. She writes of the unromantic development of the West, the wasteful and immoral behavior of the hunters, leading to an empire of wealth for some, but suffering and displacement for the Native people.

The last book in the Plains trilogy, *The Cattlemen* (1958), opens with a long perspective on the role of cattle in prehistory and history. Going back to ancient Egypt, the Golden Calf of the Old Testament, and the famous cave paintings at Lascaux in southern France, Sandoz creates a respectful framework for the later tale of violence and corruption in the western cattle industry. For her, animals are never simply commodities. Growing up as a homesteading settler, she observed her father, Jules, calling on Teddy Roosevelt to control the intimidating cattlemen; thus she is well placed to write leftist criticism of an industry that exposed the class struggle between wealthy, often foreign, ranch owners and impoverished settlers and cowboys. She describes the impact of the Kincaid Act of 1904, which opened 640 acres to settlers who filed properly and to some who filed improperly, effectively ending free range. Her story comes to a climax in the battles between ranchers and settlers at the KC Ranch, recorded in the journal of its last victim, Nate Champion.

ALTHOUGH SANDOZ'S LEFTIST POLITICS is present in everything she wrote, it boldly frames her understanding of the underlying failure of American ideology in the move to displace and exterminate the American Indian. Her perspective is a direct inheritance from her father, Old Jules, who befriended and hunted with members of nearby Sioux communities. Jules's interest in and respect for his Native neighbors was a positive expression of his freedom from racist preconceptions.

Sandoz researched her biography of Crazy Horse in the 1920s, when she was on the staff of the Nebraska State Historical Society and then spent two winters in the archives in Washington, D.C. She supplemented her exhaustive research by traveling with her friend Eleanor Hinman through Sioux country on a three-thousand-mile car trip, interviewing Native elders and friends and relatives of Crazy Horse. Her intention was to replace the "gaudy, bloodthirsty Sioux warrior of popular notion" with the serious, thoughtful man of the people who led them in self-defense (*Crazy Horse* ix). She also wanted to transmit her understanding of the Sioux in a literary style that would reflect their own patterns of thought and speech. Crazy Horse's life parallels the story of his people, from their first confrontation with U.S. Army soldiers in 1854 to his death in 1877. Thus we gain the unfamiliar point of view of Native people, witness and understand their own internal political divisions, and appreciate in an unromanticized way their adaptations to their beloved land. Crazy Horse is realized as a fully human man in this account, capable of making mistakes in love and of coping with disappointment.

But this remarkable biography was not the only product of Sandoz's leftist identification with the unjustly harassed and vanquished Native people. In *Cheyenne Autumn* (1953), she presents an account of the September 9, 1878, escape from U.S. government captivity in Oklahoma of about three hundred Northern Cheyenne men, women, and children. Under the leadership of Dull Knife and Little Wolf, they evade the pursuing soldiers for several months, trying to keep alive as many of their cultural practices as possible while they are on the run. Sandoz had the story not only from documentary sources, but from the lips of Cheyenne survivors. She includes in her acknowledgments this source:

> First of all I am indebted to Old Cheyenne Woman, who was

> one of those pulled wounded and bereaved from the Last Hole below Hat Creek bluffs. She lived with the Sioux of Pine Ridge and the neighboring whites and liked to talk in her pidgin English to a small girl on the upper Niobrara, particularly when the sun eased the old wounds received at Sand Creek, the Sappa, and above Robinson. She was the aunt of the sweet-singing Little Finger Nail and believed that he would have discovered the good new road for his people. But it was all blown away as by the wind, and so she lived out her days among strangers. She nursed many white children through the diphtheria epidemics and finally died, a pauper and alone, in a little white-man town. (*Cheyenne Autumn* xiv)

If ever there were a story of persecution and resistance fit to stand beside that of the Warsaw Ghetto, it is this richly detailed evocative American tragedy.

Sandoz did not confine her commentary on Indian affairs to her published books. In the collection of her correspondence there is ample evidence of her interceding on behalf of Native writers and artists. A fine collection of these letters is *"I Do Not Apologize for the Length of This Letter": The Mari Sandoz Letters on Native American Rights (1940–1965)*, introduced and edited by Kimberli A. Lee. The title of the collection is the first line of the October 18, 1949, letter Sandoz wrote to President Harry S. Truman, protesting poverty on the Tongue River Reservation of the Northern Cheyenne.

Even though she was diagnosed with bone cancer in 1964, suffering from pain and fatigue, Sandoz agreed to write an introduction to the pictographs of Amos Bad Heart Bull, publication of which she had recommended to the University of Nebraska Press. It appeared in 1967, her last published work.

If we understand leftist politics to be based on a moral and intellectual grasp of history and culture that values human life and the equal opportunity of all to pursue happiness and on the necessity of a critique of established ideas and government policy, Mari Sandoz stands far to the left of many non-Native Americans of her time and even of today. She saw the underlying injustice of colonialism as it shaped the history of the West and she strenuously opposed the genocidal politics that accompanied it. As Vine Deloria Jr. recognized, she stands in a very special small company.

Bibliography

Bledsoe, Tomas. "Guerra Ideologica y Militar: Cuatro Novelistas Contemporaneos de NorteAmerica." *Cuadernos Americanos*, vol. 11, Jan.–Feb. 1952, pp. 237–55.

Castille, Philip Dubuisson. "'The Ripening Fascism of the Corn Belt': Lost Democracy in Mari Sandoz's *Capital City*." *Storytelling*, vol. 5, no. 2, Winter 2006, pp. 131–42.

Dorman, Robert L. *Revolt of the Provinces: The Regionalist Movement in America, 1920–1945*. U of North Carolina P, 1993.

Kocks, Dorothea E. *Dream a Little: Land and Social Justice in Modern America*. U of California P, 2000.

Sandoz, Mari. *The Beaver Men: Spearheads of Empire*. Hastings House, 1964.

———. *The Buffalo Hunters: The Story of the Hide Men*. Hastings House, 1954.

———. *Capital City*. 1937. U of Nebraska P, Bison Books, 2007.

———. *The Cattlemen: From the Rio Grande Across the Far Marias*. Hastings House, 1958.

———. *Cheyenne Autumn*. 1953. U of Nebraska P, Bison Books, 2005.

———. *Crazy Horse: The Strange Man of the Oglalas*. 1942. U of Nebraska P, Bison Books, 1961.

———. *Hostiles and Friendlies: Selected Short Writings of Mari Sandoz*. U of Nebraska P, Bison Books, 1959.

———. *"I Do Not Apologize for the Length of this Letter": The Mari Sandoz Letters on Native American Rights (1940–1965)*. Introduced and edited by Kimberli A. Lee, Texas Tech UP, 2009.

———. *Slogum House*. 1935. U of Nebraska P, Bison Books, 1981.

———. *The Tom-Walker*. 1947. U of Nebraska P, Bison Books, 1984.

Stauffer, Helen Winter. *Mari Sandoz: Story Catcher of the Plains*. U of Nebraska P, 1982.

Villiger, Laura R. *Mari Sandoz: A Study in Post-Colonial Discourse*. Peter Lang, 1994.

8

"Poisons Up to the Waist in a Junkyard of Breaking Machines"

Peter Berg, Bioregional Ethics, and the Trouble with the Master's Tools

WILLIAM LOMBARDI

In significant ways, Peter Berg's character is particular to the U.S. West. He is the rogue embodiment of things falling apart. He was an outsider and an outlaw who surveyed the American scene and saw that we "live with poisons up to the waist in a junkyard of breaking machines" (*Envisioning* 172). Berg intended to make sure the machines were broken for good. Yet for this reason Berg is also the key environmental activist you have probably never heard of. He did not believe in the efficacy of environmental agencies or large organizations; he championed the grassroots, but by many accounts was a difficult and aggressive leader. For these reasons, perhaps especially his assiduous commitment to the grassroots, Berg is not a household name. His words, though, on behalf of becoming "borne-native," of "reinhabitation," and of "growing a life-place politics," from the mid-1960s until his death in 2011, have shaped the discourse of sustainability.

He began in San Francisco's Haight-Ashbury district attempting to break the capitalist machine by orchestrating the Diggers' "free store."[1] Then, among other key figures of 1960s rebellion, he brought the Left to the cause of environmentalism, only to quarrel with the boardroom politics of environmentalism's most influential groups. Finally, Berg became the champion of bioregionalism, the grassroots movement that acknowledged the inseparability of nature and culture. Bioregionalism is a profound view that has often been lost within an environmental politics that, according to historian Kirkpatrick Sale, usually divides itself philosophically between biocentric and anthropocentric agendas (Sale, *Green* 27).[2] In the main, this essay is both a recuperation of Berg as a significant figure in U.S. West counterculture, and a recovery of the bioregional ethic as a cornerstone of radical resistance worldwide. With this backdrop, the essay addresses the problems inherent in collective visions of subversive practice, the frictions between would-be countercultural allies as they confront ecological disaster on a global scale. Recovering Berg achieves two things imperative to understanding the internal issues facing contemporary leftist politics: it remembers the decolonizing potential and planetary reach of Berg's bioregional practice; and it exposes the philosophical impasse facing aspiring allies—how to respect the situational, material, and circumstantial differences specific to each of us while still presenting a united front against systems of oppression.

"Rough Beast"

As Joan Didion tells it in her preface to *Slouching Towards Bethlehem* (1968), a society that has lost faith in its narrative braces itself for a "rough beast" coming in the form of any number of countercultural monsters. Into this network of actors both known and unknown, and among the growing list of places forming the worldwide countercultural web emerging during this period, Berg and his crew of Diggers, a later, more extreme incarnation of the San Francisco Mime Troupe, introduced a kind of activist life-acting that Berg termed "guerrilla theater."[3] In Didion's episode the Diggers surround a black ally at a Holding Company show in Golden Gate Park. He is made to be an unwilling participant in their performance of black alienation. The rage they foist on a man who would otherwise be their ally suggests that their critique of dominant culture effectively but carelessly colonized his blackness for a second time. Didion exposes the Diggers' blindness to their own privilege. In blurring the boundaries between what is real and what is performance, the Diggers forget that only they, and not their temporary cast member, can leave the scene at will. While the Diggers' act today may be excused as poorly translated irony from the first wave of a cultural revolution, this scene underscores the basic crisis of faith in one another that attends allegiances among marginalized people, especially as it pertains to solidarity with white sympathizers. The crisis of coloniality and privilege that the Diggers' guerrilla theater still poses complicates the most compelling socioenvironmental arguments, the vanguard of which posits intersubjectivity and favors affinitive kinship as a rebellious, necessary, and possibly redemptive undertaking.[4] To paraphrase Audre Lorde, the Digger scene in "Slouching" can be said to underline how survival still depends on celebrating difference while finding common cause with other outsiders, especially in the context of dissenting political acts (Lorde 112). In her famous essay, Lorde also declared that "the master's tools will never dismantle the master's house." Patently, Berg and the Diggers were not using the master's tools to tear down the master's house. And yet it is plain, when Didion describes it, that Berg's new tools were not toys, either. The Digger ethos of "play" should remind us that newness makes such tools fraught, and easily mishandled.

Or perhaps, too, it is a matter of who wields the tools that determines how new they really are. Against the violent milieu of the Vietnam War, all types of revolutionaries under the influence of Frantz Fanon's writing were apt to respond to coloniality in the jarring way the Diggers had. After Fanon, activists of this era yet adhered to a rigid binary ill-equipped for the intersectionality of possible postmodern alliances. Radical kinships are formed and maintained among the world's disenfranchised on a knife's edge. Peter Berg, called "the Hun," not without some rancor, by his closest peers both for his subversive vitriol and his mainstream machismo, epitomized the "rough beast" Didion feared. As Didion puts it in "Slouching," Berg is "perhaps the only person in the District on whom a gold earring looks obscurely ominous" (124). Berg was an unofficial leader of the Diggers who also promoted grassroots food and health initiatives in the Haight-Ashbury district. Significantly, though, Berg steered the movement from fighting purely social issues to a larger activist commitment recognizing that social and environmental concerns are intrinsically related.[5] The roots of today's socioenvironmental activism—which feminist and bioregionalist Stephanie Mills calls "ecosocial" activism—can be traced to Berg's earliest articulations of the DIY ethos, his local environmental justice work, and his language of decoloniality and sustainability.[6] Still, firsthand accounts of Berg make it easy to imagine the hun, the rough beast, standing menacingly on what he called the "planetedge" (*Envisioning* 36) with hammer and crowbar in hand. In many respects, Berg may have been too ornery, too combative for the nature crowd.

Bioregionalism Is/Not a Decolonialism

Berg is responsible for a familiar and critical environmental lexicon that survives in various forms. This lexicon is applied by like-minded movements seemingly without awareness of Berg as its origin. He was among the first to deploy "ecology" with specifically activist connotations (Glotfelty and Quesnel 14). Berg popularized the use of "sustainability" in regard to human practice in the early 1970s. Perhaps his greatest contributions to the language of ecosocial activism come from the essay Berg wrote on behalf of the Frisco Bay Mussel Group, "Borne-Native in the San Francisco Bay Region" (1977), and the essay he co-authored with conservation biologist Raymond F. Dasmann, "Reinhabiting California" (1978). The Frisco Bay Mussel Group essay, for instance, confronted "live-in colonialism," a way of being under capitalism that Berg viewed as living "on top of" rather than "with" or "in" the land (*Envisioning* 74, 75). In addition to the concepts of live-in colonialism and its opposite, being or becoming "borne-native," in that essay Berg redeployed the term "reinhabitant," and began using "watershed" and "watershed consciousness" as keywords for a revised environmental consciousness.[7] The following year, with "Reinhabiting California," Berg and Dasmann laid much of the groundwork for what would become bioregionalism, or the practice of ecologically sound emplacement considerate of human and nonhuman actors. Bioregionalism, on their terms, complicates the many forms of regionalism, which are most concerned with regional culture, with "living on top of" in the traditional sense, rather than "in" or "with" outlined in

Berg's Frisco Bay essay. For Berg and Dasmann, bioregionalism meant "living-in-place," or "following the necessities and pleasures of life as they are uniquely presented by a particular site" (*Envisioning* 81). Berg and Dasmann established programmatic definitions for "reinhabitation," "living-in-place," "bioregion," and "watershed" (*Envisioning* 81–82), each of which stand, at least in spirit if not in name, at the core of interconnected localist practice today.

True to Berg's leftist sympathies, this decentralizing language was emblematic of distrust of governmental solutions. It challenged the authority of capitalism while simultaneously sidestepping the "Washingtonization of the environmental majors"—the Sierra Club, Audubon Society, and the National Wildlife Federation, among others—at a time when these organizations were most influential (Sale, *Green* 55). In fact, Kirkpatrick Sale sees an indirect connection between Berg's foundational work in radical environmentalism and the rise of the ecological grassroots in the decade that followed.[8] Sale points to bioregionalism, deep ecology, ecofeminism, and the Gaia hypothesis as key philosophies of the Left's response (*Green* 62–65). On the other hand, Carolyn Merchant underscores deep ecology, social ecology, and ecofeminism as the main concepts driving ecological consciousness at that time (*American Environmental History* 206), though elsewhere she includes bioregionalism among these (*Radical Ecology* 237–40). Still, essays on deep ecology, Gaia, and ecofeminism all appear in the bioregional reader *Reinhabiting a Separate Country*, edited by Berg for the Planet Drum Foundation in 1978. Social ecology, however, proposed by Murray Bookchin, argued against deep ecology. Sale describes Bookchin as an "anarchist in the old-left tradition" (*Green* 64). That Berg was in sympathy with deep ecology even as Bookchin quarreled with it positions Berg's ideas squarely among those driving the New Left.[9]

Yet those terms that speak most strongly to human culture—reinhabitation, living-in-place, and borne-native—suggest both/and potentials that are thornier than Berg intended, and for reasons he did not appear to foresee. For instance, influential regional historian Robert L. Dorman writes that in the 1970s bioregionalism and the Native

American occupations occurring across the West were not only part of the same cultural moment, but were sympathetic causes (Dorman 147). Likewise, everywhere in his work Berg himself points to Indigenous cultures as a key source for reinhabitation efforts. And yet, there is little evidence that Native peoples actively sought out Berg and his cohort or were interested in supporting bioregionalism's goals of sustainability as such.[10] There is an unavoidable patina of Native evanishment and pastoral idealism attending reinhabitation, for example, and borne-native is especially presumptive, damaging, and oblivious to the history and conditions of Native sovereignty. Still, Berg's indictment of live-in colonialism predates what contemporary critical discourse recognizes as settler colonialism by nearly twenty years. Further, Berg positions living-in-place in contradistinction to making-a-living, wherein living-in-place "keeps a balance with its region of support through links between human lives, other living things and the processes of the planet" (81). In other words, Berg's program of sustainable localized practice, his bioregionalism, both problematically adopts the settler colonial legacy of the privilege to co-opt or usurp, *and* presents an astonishingly prophetic blueprint for ecosocially sound decolonization across the many marginalized creatures, persons, and landscapes.

Bioregionalism Is a Decolonialism

As Berg and Dasmann define it, a bioregion is a "geographical terrain and a terrain of consciousness...a place and the ideas that have developed about how to live in that place" (*Envisioning* 82). Bioregionalism is an "approach to living on and with the land" that hinges on reinhabitation, or "a process that involves learning to live-in-place" (81). Bioregionalists believe that "all life on earth is interconnected in a few obvious ways, and in many more that remain barely explored. But there is a distinct resonance among living things and the factors which influence them that occurs specifically within each separate place on the planet" (82). That is to say, bioregionalists are reinhabitants who are committed to local activism in the interest of nonexploitative, sustainable lifeways; they acknowledge and celebrate difference while recognizing that the world's places are neither uniform nor discrete, but rather an entangled, differential web, the survival of which depends on all strands remaining intact. Berg imagined a "planetariat," a worldwide network of committed groups contingent on living-in-place in their bioregions for the good of the biosphere (*Envisioning* 51). Bioregion, then, is a decentralized cultural concept with biospheric reach.

Remarkably, Berg developed this ideology in the face of institutional environmentalism. Traditional environmentalism, Berg argued, offered a valuable service, but operated like "a hospital that consists only of an emergency room. No maternity care, no pediatric clinic, no promising therapy: just mangled trauma cases" (*Envisioning* 109). Berg enlarged the spirit of Wallace Stegner's "Wilderness Letter," for example, which was instrumental in galvanizing the environmental movement, by refusing to view nature as something "out there," nonhuman by default. Instead, Berg's bioregional vision remembered the basic animality of humans, and that all places—"untouched," manipulated, and urban alike—participate in "nature." Berg's bioregionalism, extending the environmentalism of the day, was linked to the belief that the social is inherently ecological, and the ecological is intrinsically social. Bioregionalism, as Berg envisioned it, intervenes at ground level, in everyday lives and mundane places. Exploding the binary of urban and wild, specifically in the context of environmentalism, was a tremendous leap in the ecological paradigm as well as the social justice paradigm, but was not immediately or readily received.[11]

Berg's outsider temperament set him at odds with the intellectual elite as well as the environmentalist establishment. From the beginning, as had been the case with the Diggers, Berg was determined that bioregionalism remain a grassroots movement, kept out of the hands of the government and academy. Kirkpatrick Sale's book *Dwellers in the Land* (1985), which was an attempt to legitimize and mainstream bioregionalism, was largely snubbed by Berg and other insiders as institutionalized, as taking possession of an ideology that should be kept in the hands of the people. Still, Sale's book is among the most often cited by those within the academy when confronting facets of bioregional principle, often sidestepping Berg entirely. Fairly or not, in part owing to his deliberate stance as an outsider, different aspects of Berg's argument have been elided in this manner, repudiated, or forgotten entirely by many scholars, and yet Berg's central positions—environmental justice, global interconnectedness, and everyday ecosocial practice—are precisely at the forefront of activist, environmental humanities, and ecocritical conversations in the present moment, especially as they pertain to creating allies among inclusive communities of dissent. Berg's understanding of the inseparability of nature and culture, his decisive interest in the betterment of all by including the human and the nonhuman in all decisions regarding inhabitation, and his formal plans to redirect environmentalism's energies from setting aside parklands to establishing green cities and fixing landscapes that have been ruined by exploitation speak to an ongoing effort to decolonize, or, in his words, to shift our orientation from "nation-world" to "local-planet" (*Envisioning* 51).

The local-planet sensibility of bioregionalism decentralizes authority and reorients emplacement toward empathy and responsibility. This decentralization and reorientation requires that we decolonize or rewire our collective social imaginary—that we tear down the master's house. Bioregionalism relies on being and becoming allies in interest of the preservation and celebration of difference, and is a direct challenge to enforced, exploited otherness. For instance, Berg was keenly aware of the homogenizing effects of globalization, and was resolved to change the way we think about environment and culture by adopting new language to circumvent global settler hegemony. Initially, he challenged settler culture head-on in works like "Amble Toward Continent Congress" (1976), which describes the North American continent as "studiously unknown" by explorers, and argued clearly that it "wasn't a trackless wilderness to 'Indian' inhabitants," claiming, "[Native Americans] were neither ignorant of the continent nor savage towards it" (*Envisioning* 61). He deemed the European settlement of the continent under these conditions to be a "biocidal beacon" to the world (*Envisioning* 63). Later, and more concretely, in "Borne-Native," Berg insisted that live-in colonialism "becomes its own worst threat," meaning that settler colonialism, by living artificially in places instead of within the parameters those places prescribe, moves steadily "through extinction of native life towards self-extinction" (*Envisioning* 74). Further, in "Reinhabiting California," Berg and Dasmann wrote succinctly: "we now know that human life depends ultimately on the continuation of other life" (*Envisioning* 81). In effect, over the course of a decade after the end of the Diggers, Berg's thinking developed from being dubious of colonial lifeways, to recognizing the implications of U.S. genocide and ecological imperialism, to understanding that global neoliberal capital deploys similarly destructive strategies, and finally that such strategies have made all living things vulnerable, perpetrators and casualties alike. Today, sadly, what Berg imagined as a successfully united biospheric planetariat remains instead a "precariat," defined socially but not always ecosocially, and not by its solidarity but by its unequal shares of vulnerability.

As he mobilizes vulnerable people against global ecological crisis, the decoloniality that Berg attempts demands mutual respect and an expanded sense of kinship among actors. He maintains: "WE'RE SPECIES-KIND. WE COME FROM EVERYWHERE (*Envisioning* 57; emphasis original). In widening environmentalists' ethos of care in such a manner, Berg registers an evolving challenge to the duress of new colonialisms across the course of national and postnational empire. Berg extended the base and tactics of decolonization through the language of kin and kind, in what he imagined as a "green guerrilla network" (Glotfelty and Quesnel 18). Within Berg's framework, network and kinship are central to action in "green cities," interconnected bioregions, spaces as vast as the Pacific Rim, and the entire biosphere. If settler colonialism fuels the exceptionalist narrative of conquest, then networks of affinitive kinship across and among vulnerable people and landscapes—planetariat and bioregions—serve as its counterbalance. Crucially, if "invader society" (*Envisioning* 82) and "industrial consciousness" (Glotfelty and Quesnel 3) in Berg's parlance are the engine and outcome of the systematic violence of capital, then the decoloniality articulated by Berg acknowledges the genocide of North America's Indigenous populations as one piece of a global struggle, while extending the roster of casualties to include all of us currently threatened by world environmental risk. As Berg had prophesied, the biocidal process has indeed spread beyond deliberate, global native extinction to the less overtly deliberate, but no less systematic, threat of extinction of all living things, whether catastrophic or slowly violent.

In this regard, it is worthwhile to revisit Patrick Wolfe's claim that "settler colonialism destroys to replace" through a "logic of elimination" (Wolfe 388) in the context of Berg and Dasmann's assertion that "reinhabitation means learning to live-in-place in an area that has been disrupted and injured through past exploitation" (*Envisioning* 82). Berg and Dasmann's plan is optimistic, in that they mean to rebuild anew from the materials at hand, however debased those materials may be. So, too, they convey an acute awareness of culpability, and a commitment to repairing the socioenvironmental damage that came before them. For example, they present strategies for clean water, sustainable forestry practices, and the redistribution of agricultural land to create small farms that make economic and ecologic sense (86). Within their reinhabitation project, there is a patent willingness to cede the centrality of humans, as well as answer for the rote abuse that settler society driven by extractive industry is predicated upon. And yet, Wolfe describes the structured dispossession of Native people from their traditional holdings by the settler state as an ongoing concern, while to reinhabit assumes a contentious past-ness that Native Americans, by their very existence, must refute outright. For Wolfe, genocide and removal, systematic killing and displacement, are material and enduring. Bioregional reinhabitation, on the other hand, assumes the same posture of earlier suppositions, that "watersheds" are as equally open and available for resettlement as territories had been under the imperial eye, Berg and Dasmann's best intentions to the contrary. It can be said that the bioregional eye, while refusing to destroy or eliminate, yet proceeds by a similar logic. These are not the same tools, but perhaps they build the same house. In this one critical move, bioregionalism fails to reverse, even as it recognizes, the settlers' custom of dispossession. Berg and Dasmann count, and rightly so, Native peoples among the "disrupted," "injured," and "exploited," surely; and, they make space in bioregional ideology for Native lifeways. However, the Indian her or himself must still conform to the reinhabitants' vision of what living-in-place entails. Unintentionally, Berg and Dasmann have recentered the white narrative back upon itself.[12] There is a whiff of the Diggers' oversight in this calculation, a lapse in sympathy, an omission of complicity left unaccounted for.

Bioregionalism Is Not a Decolonialism

As a conceptual impasse on par with the Diggers' miscue, Berg and Dasmann's oversight possibly reveals the grimmest reading of bioregionalism's aims, those of a program indisposed to fully grasp the unequal burdens of its stakeholders.[13] Too often in his writing, Berg defaults to the uncritical lens of pastoralism, to Rousseauian anecdotes concerning noble savagery, and to a troubling epistemology of "nature," "wild," and "rootedness" that are remiss in neglecting what we know of those terms' exclusionary histories. The paradox is staggering but not uncommon. Clearly and passionately Berg fights against the predictable deferrals related to what has been collectively rendered in other quarters as "the arrogances of imperialism" (Haraway 6), "the legacies of colonialism" (Byrd xi), or "the persistence of settler mythologies" (Brown and Kanouse ix) as they have played out variously upon and within disparate marginalized communities. And yet, there are glaring gaps in Berg's methodology: not in his posthumanism, not in his science, but in his identity politics; there are incongruences in those very claims of tribalism or comradeship or kinship that disqualify the logic of his vision for many outside of the white, heteronormative community.[14] These incongruences are typical of first-wave subcultural agendas; still, Berg's insensitivities remained unreconciled as his environmental worldview painstakingly evolved. There is an assumed, static subjectivity underlying bioregionalism that denotes "big tentism" in its best and worst incarnations. Without a doubt, Berg knows the world is queer—the "soft borders" of the bioregion that he argues for sanction all metaphoric forms of "trans"—but he is negligent in his honest attempts to account for them.

An unfortunate part of Berg's argument is that he seems to conflate Indian identity with a generalizable Pleistocene hunter-gatherer European counterpart, for instance, when he authorizes Pleistocene economies and social norms as models for reinhabitation culture (*Envisioning* 91–93). Berg maintains that "[Pleistocene civilization] is *wild* civilization. It is based on our interconnectedness with natural cycles and draws its morality, ethics, and values from that relationship" (93; emphasis original). Berg's claim is awkwardly demonstrative of Philip J. Deloria's concern that on the advent of postmodernity, "Indian" was mobilized to grab hold of any cultural contradiction: "Indians could be both civilized and indigenous. They could critique modernity and reap its benefits" (157). Add to this, too, the direct and indirect allusions to Native culture—totem animals, ecological Indians, the use of Native languages as the source for bioregions—by Berg and his comrades. These aspects of Native life are intended to remember and include Indigenous knowledge in the bioregional plan, but conflating Native and pre-Christian European serves primarily to justify the bioregional cause to a specifically *white* audience even as it suggests one source for kinship with racial others. It is plain that by recalling a European place-based ancestry, Berg's implied audience is white, and, by extension, that the audience for bioregionalism is white as well. A wild/civilized ancestry seems to justify bioregionalists' *re*settlement, which, by any other name, is settlement nonetheless. Berg's is an effort to recover an essential European-ness beyond the reach of imperial desire, an ancestry that seemed to live according to his notions of sustainability. Citizen of the Chickasaw Nation and literary critic Jodi A. Byrd writes explicitly of the Indigenous experience, stressing the present-ness and complexity of Native selfhood and self-determination in the context of coloniality. She expresses some of the volatility attending Native identity, not the least of which is the contested space of "Indian-ness" itself (xviii). Berg trades on the Indian imaginary in a manner to which Byrd and others take offense, wherein her "postindian" identity, in Gerald Vizenor's words, is overlooked. As Vizenor conceives of it, postindian denotes "an active sense of presence" rather than the *received idea* of the Indian, which is the result of centuries of white simulation, translation, and dominance (Vizenor vii–viii). In this respect, the bioregional Indian is one such simulation, reflecting cultural assumptions in the absence of firsthand experience with Indians themselves (Vizenor 1). On the one hand, Berg attempts to go back to pre-Christian sources to rupture the received procession of imperial, persecutory ideology; on the other hand, his thought bears the implicit hallmarks of orthodoxy. The Indigenous person, invested in their own worlding and active presence, is compelled to repudiate such dominance.[15] The charge against bioregional pastiche, however unflattering, might be that Berg and his cohort went from blackface as Diggers to redface as bioregionalists, inadvertently announcing the same insensitivity alongside their honorable intent.[16]

In this respect, bioregionalism is founded on unpardonable inattentiveness toward the "unmappable, ungrievable, and unapproachable" loss attending Indian survivance (Byrd xi). For instance, Deloria writes of the countercultural period of the 1960s and 1970s: "Many communes toyed with symbolic Indianness; they were in reality largely disconnected from Indian people." Furthermore, "although there were certainly exceptions, communalists tended to value Indian Otherness and its assorted meanings more than they did real native people" (159). Berg's experience with communal living influenced his bioregional agenda. His work and claims fit too neatly within the construct Deloria describes. It can be argued, however, that the body of bioregionalists who contributed to Berg's *Reinhabiting a Separate Country* (1978) and the writers who contributed to the largely Canadian bioregional anthology *Home!* (1990)—another indispensable bioregional document—surpassed this dismissive generalization in their earnestness and dedication. Even an unsympathetic reading should recognize Berg and his peers' diligence such that they can be placed among Deloria's "exceptions," even while we should recognize their problematic abstractions. For example, Christopher Plant writes in his essay in *Home!* of the ways in which retrospect has shown that the back-to-the-land movement had "matured" in significant ways since its early days ("In Pockets" 27), and Judith Plant remarks, in her introduction, "Growing Home," that her group of reinhabitants learned to preserve salmon directly from their Native neighbors, who had grudgingly allowed them on traditional ground (ix–x). The Plants' comments each suggest that abstraction, at least in some cases, became genuine compassion for and interaction with Native people, with an admission of mistakes along the way.

This does not, however, clear the troubled complexion of bioregional keywords like "future primitive." The term comes from Jeremiah Gorsline and Freeman House's essay of the same name and is meant to honor indigeneity as well as function programmatically. It was adopted in part by Ernest Callenbach in his bioregional novel *Ecotopia* (1975) and by Berg in "Bioregion and Human Location." Gorsline and House attest that the future primitive has been "awakened to the richness and complexity of the primitive mind which merges sanctity, food, life and death" (*Reinhabiting* 39). For them, it represents the postindustrial man modeled on the preindustrial, but there is a challenging sense of "play" to the endeavor that hearkens to Deloria and Vizenor even as it attempts to decenter Western consciousness. Similarly, Callenbach's future primitives are hypersexualized.[17] Berg, like Gorsline and House, views the future primitive as one who experiences "wholeness, magic, [and the] ability to perceive oneness" (*Envisioning* 94). In effect, the concept of future primitive draws freely from varieties of simulated global indigeneity while the actual Native person is for the most part only a marker, a museum piece who has vanished but is recoverable for white bodies to emulate in their sustainable practice. For Berg and his peers, the language of kinship exists all too uncomplicatedly alongside the problematic simulations discussed above, while at the same time it inadvertently assumes aspects of Mary Louise Pratt's innocent, imperial seeing-man.[18] While Ann Laura Stoler cautions critics about the too-easily distinct pastness of the colonial period disguised in the term "postcolonial," critics of bioregionalism should be cautious of "future primitive" or Berg's own "new settlers," which likewise neglect the harmful resonance of these words within the active presence of coloniality and indigeneity (Stoler ix; *Envisioning* 51).[19]

One of Berg's younger comrades, Seth Zuckerman, writing in tribute after Berg's death, commented: "For all of Peter's rustic visions of the urban landscape, he did not conceive it as a Jeffersonian idyll," but perhaps this is too generous (Glotfelty and Quesnel 261). Perhaps bioregionalism is not a decolonialism because its erasures of difference in the interest of well-meaning pluralism come too easily and its sympathies are too automatic. The language of magic, oneness, and nativeness *is* idyllic; the pastoral dream *is* Jeffersonian. Yet in a similar vein and context, in what she calls "staying with the trouble," Donna J. Haraway argues differently. To stay with the trouble of bioregionalism, it might be said, to see it through its essentializing and paternalism, we need to admit its failures and successes. In effect, Berg's writing inherited the "damages and achievements of colonial and postcolonial naturalcultural histories," and it bears unavoidable legacies even as it finds a way to tell "the tale of still possible recuperation" (Haraway 125).[20]

Against "Carbon-Heavy Masculinities"

Berg's influence and significance, it is clear, should be freestanding. We should use caution, though, in wedding the importance of Berg to environmental history as a matter of "firsting," since this is itself a masculinist and hierarchical conceit. As was the case with Berg's tacit coloniality, his generic masculine universal presents a further obstacle to his recuperation as a key figure and to the uniform worldview the bioregional community imagines itself to have generally. For instance, Haraway's recent arguments in *Staying with the Trouble* (2016) are in remarkable philosophical accordance with Berg's bioregionalism, right down to her expression of "trouble" through her love of neologisms and language play.[21] However, Haraway's work is evacuated of Berg's paternalism, or what she refers to as "the generic masculine universal" (47). Likewise, ecocritic Stacy Alaimo points to the overlooked importance of humor to offset what she thinks of as "carbon-heavy masculinities" at the source of denials that contribute to anthropogenic climate change, the result of new colonialisms. Alaimo's work, too, is rife with echoes of Berg's ideas, especially as she emphasizes the ecosocial advantages linked to "the ordinary practices of everyday life" (2). Yet while Haraway, Alaimo, and a host of other scholars argue, after feminist philosopher Karen Barad rather than Peter Berg, for the intersubjective composition of being, they are more careful than Berg to remember the social realities attending the differences between constituent actors.

Under the sign of coloniality and capital, the generic masculine universal—the source of carbon-heavy masculinity—views all things as available to a particularly masculine anthropocentric desire. Berg undoubtedly understood this problem, even as his writings bypass his own problematic universal subject position. He articulated an alternate path out of carbon-heavy masculinity this way: "I think the bioregion is going to continue to manifest itself in consciousness, even for those people for whom bioregion at this point is just an adjective. Pretty soon they're going to start saying the noun of it, and they're going to begin seeing that it is a life-place that they owe their allegiance to" (*Envisioning* 103). By this new allegiance, Berg extends principles of inhabitation beyond the usually masculine principle of domination; he argues beyond the scale of the expected rhetoric and practice of consumption and exploitation to include places, things, and humans as he had been doing for two decades. Berg continues: "As nation states become more desperate to control their situations, they impose more on the regions, bioregions, and ethnic peoples, and by so doing create in them a desire for a separate identity, and a feeling of deliberate repression of their values" (*Envisioning* 104). In renouncing the nation-state, in this interview with British Columbia's *New Catalyst* magazine in 1989, Berg expresses his belief in the collective strength of grassroots organization, which would usurp the central authority of the nation-state and upend its implicit masculinist hegemony (*Envisioning* 101). And yet, the bioregional identity he would replace it with, that "separate identity," appears to be wholly monolithic, relying on an unquestioned unanimity, a singular experience among disenfranchised people. Significantly, as diverse places and peoples are alienated, Berg understands that organized defiance requires unity; yet at the same time, the uneven distribution and messy conundrum of potential factionalism falls outside the pale of his argument. His presumption is that nature, society, and ecosocial activism look the same to all people. The generic masculine presumption of this position is easily brushed aside if we are attuned to Berg's message of collective strength, and yet it remains a critical stumbling block to many allies. Still, Berg concludes the interview powerfully, rendering the end of centrist authority in a decidedly egalitarian, horizontal rather than vertical mode: "Global doesn't mean that everybody talks to everybody; global means that somebody talks to everybody. Somebody controls 'global,' that's why that word is to be avoided in bioregional parlance" (*Envisioning* 106).

While Berg assiduously unhands the carbon-heavy, generic masculine universal in message and tone in staggeringly contradictory ways, some of the ominousness that Didion had documented in Berg in Haight-Ashbury still lingered perceptibly around him.[22] Cheryll Glotfelty and Eve Quesnel include a valuable selection of "Tributes" to Berg written by his activist peers in their recent book, *The Biosphere and the Bioregion* (2015). Glotfelty and Quesnel's book serves in many ways as the bioregionalist response to Ursula K. Heise's *Sense of Place and Sense of Planet: The Environmental Imagination of the Global* (2008), the paradigm-shifting ecocritical text that argued against localism as the appropriate response to global environmental crisis, largely at the expense of Berg and bioregional ideals.[23] The overall effect of the "Tributes" section of Glotfelty and Quesnel's book, however, is that it shows Berg's peers' grudging respect for him, especially his tension-filled sense of humor. Glotfelty and Quesnel's book exemplifies the paradox about Berg and bioregionalism the present essay makes: in many ways Berg's bioregional program is optimistic, pragmatic, and absolutely necessary to ecosocial activism in the Anthropocene, but it is heady with underlying tension.

For example, Peter Coyote, in remembering his days as a Digger with Berg, recalls that people "got" the Digger message immediately (Glotfelty and Quesnel 196). However, Coyote's reminiscence stands in blunt contrast to the blackface scene Didion recorded in "Slouching Towards Bethlehem." Coyote writes that people "loved [the Diggers] for expressing their lives and thoughts in such funky, comedic, and insightful ways," contending that their guerrilla theater drew on a sensibility that was "ancient but contemporary, if you can imagine indigenous myths enacted by Laurel and Hardy." Coyote's remarks, like Berg's, are delivered offhandedly, assuming the same general appeal. Yet there is no doubt about the insensitivity of his "indigenous myths enacted by Laurel and Hardy"; this is dubious language for ecosocial solidarity, leaving little room for "love" of Digger funkiness for many allies. Great Plains bioregionalist David Haenke described the Diggers' work as performances "of great and funny seriousness, real stuff dispensed for the benefit of living beings" (Glotfelty and Quesnel 201–2). Kirkpatrick Sale observed that Berg was "able to find humor in what was otherwise a moment of tension or difficulty" (226). Provocateurs or not, communities of dissent are unlikely to be founded on blackface, a masculine universal, and irreverence toward Native spirituality. Didion's revelation, then, is that the counterculture community of the period grasped its new tools with a master's resolve, deconstructing at will but presuming its own imperviousness.

Perhaps the most revealing tribute on this subject is by Digger coconspirator David Simpson, who explains that Berg's performances were "barrages…regularly unleashed on audiences, witting or otherwise," and were "sometimes thunderous and intimidating." Sans Coyote's inveterate slapstick, Simpson's summation concurs with Didion's portrait of the group. Soberly, Simpson concedes, "a factor contributing to the intensity of all of our actions and perceptions in the brief, fiery Digger incarnation…was an unspoken competition with one another—always the men" (Glotfelty and Quesnel 228). Still, Simpson describes Berg's attacks on normativity as "virulent, clever, and necessary" (229). The spirit of revolution is alive and well in Coyote's and Simpson's writing to this day. Like many, Coyote and Simpson seem to better understand in retrospect the inequities that had plagued that first wave. His "Laurel and Hardy" comment to the contrary, for instance, elsewhere Coyote consciously takes a chastened, more experienced tone.[24] Of Berg in particular, however, Simpson maintains that "modesty was not the first word you would use to describe Peter Berg or, for that matter, any of the young men and, in some ways, women who identified with the concepts and actions that defined the Diggers. The whole Digger ethos seemed at times to be founded to some degree in an unshakable certainty of purpose and a machismo elan" (Glotfelty and Quesnel 236–37). In striking terms Simpson grants the principal concern of kinship, that "certainty of purpose" founded on "machismo elan" threatens a truly collective countercultural, bioregional imaginary and the status quo alike. Coyote, however, hails a new way out of the macho logics of colonialism in and outside of heteronormative life. He allows that the Digger cohort eventually "made all sorts of explorations around the realm of feminism," because "a lot of men like [him] had a great deal to learn." He freely realizes that they had to "uproot thinking that was just self-indulgent" (interview). Of this group of male countercultural allies, and of Berg in particular, groundbreaking ecofeminist Susan Griffin recalls, "Peter was not a feminist in the early years. But he got there more quickly than many men.... I know Peter learned a great deal from feminism eventually, as did feminists from his work in ways both large and small" (Glotfelty and Quesnel 200). Griffin purposely establishes that Berg's "watershed" stood in stark contrast in her mind to the exploitative biopolitics of "oppression, power, and rape" linking land to the female body. This is not faint praise amid the language of virulence, immodesty, and self-indulgence used by others to describe themselves and Berg. Griffin's claim, along with similar examples from ecofeminists sympathetic to the bioregional worldview, signals hope for the masculine universal imaginary within the bioregionalist community.

"Poisons Up to the Waist in a Junkyard of Breaking Machines"

The chief worry of making kin is how and on what terms we interact with one another. The main purpose of bioregional practice is that we live according to the needs and limits of the places we inhabit. Berg brought these tangential aims to the forefront of ecosocial consciousness as analogous concerns. Since then, and parallel to Berg, revising the generic masculine in environmentalist terms has followed the lead of queer theorists.[25] Historian Michael Bronski reminds us, in fact, that much of the factionalism within the gay communities of the late 1960s and early 1970s stemmed from leadership who had come of age in the prefeminist era, thus harboring masculinist tendencies similar to those of the Diggers (Bronski 202). Yet he acknowledges, too, that the queer community adapted quickly and more ably than other marginalized populations to the needs of its inherently diverse community (212). Gloria Anzaldúa, writing against machismo among

Latinos, puts it this way: "Being supreme crossers of cultures, homosexuals have strong bonds with the queer white, Black, Asian, Native American, Latino, and with the queer in Italy, Australia and the rest of the planet.... Colored homosexuals have more knowledge of other cultures; have always been at the forefront (although sometimes in the closet) of all liberation struggles in this country" (Anzaldúa 106–7). Taken together, the queer model of border crossing, layered and interconnected subjectivity, and progressive loyalties provide a blueprint for the making of affinitive kin among vulnerable people, particularly as a grassroots cause. However, what Berg and other environmentalists by and large have not fully explored is that the concept of a bioregional homeplace as a unifying theme is overburdened from the first; "home" has been "viciously distorted," having already, in ecofeminist Helen Forsey's words, been "corrupted by patriarchy to mean a man's castle, where women and children are neither free nor safe" (Andruss et al. 83). In other words, a universalized sense of environment as home looks uncannily like the master's house.

Peter Berg's New Tools

Still, Berg's insistence on "from below" activism ignites local struggle everywhere. When he says, "We live with poisons up to the waist in a junkyard of breaking machines," he means for all people to recognize that the shared danger of environmental collapse can become our common cause. By "we" he means both the human and nonhuman. According to Gustavo Esteva and Madhu Suri Prakash, however, the problem with common cause as the foundation of global kinship is that it supposes "a secular and culturally neutral or transcultural" salvation (11). Like Forsey, they realize the danger of recolonization by any other name. Berg's contribution to the cause of sustainability and social justice, then, is his foundational work in recognizing that social space is grounded in a material, fragile world that demands the wholesale reconstruction of our way of being in it, even if he did not fully conceptualize the destructive nature of older patterns of social behavior. Nonetheless, the self-extinction Berg had prophesied seems much more clearly writ today, and it is all the more urgent to find ecosocial common ground. Berg asks: "Can we stop tearing the web apart, and consciously build a role as partners in all life?" (*Envisioning* 173). "Conscious building" patently denotes a partnership in which the labor of all hands works in collective interest against what Berg saw early on to be the "suicidal devouring attacks on the biosphere" as "society begins to eat itself." Forsey argues that if such a partnership is to succeed, "people in a community must be…vigilant and self-critical, as well as patient and generous, in addressing the group's internal dynamics" (Forsey 85). Each member, she concludes, must keep the "principles of respect, equality, cooperation and caring" constantly in mind. Berg's new tools, in other words, used for conscious building, require proper training, handling, and maintaining that successive generations of activists have, in part, made guarded attempts to learn.

Unlike Didion, my purpose is not to sell out Peter Berg. My aim is to illustrate, by way of Berg's important bioregional arguments, the sticking points that remain to be overcome within leftist politics in general, and the prickly countercultural alliances of the West's Left specifically. For all he has done in service of local struggles for sustainable practice, Peter Berg is inseparable from the bioregional ideal. As activists, critics, and would-be allies call for cooperation in the interest of full citizenship and self-determination, Peter Berg's bioregional model should not be overlooked or forgotten. When it comes to kin, we must decide on which points we are determined to maintain our differences, and at what costs, ends, and consequences, especially when planetary well-being is at stake.

Notes

1. Peter Coyote remembers that Berg remarked, "I feel like I gave a good tool to an idiot" when Abbie Hoffman published his book *Free* after a visit west to survey the Digger scene (Coyote, *Sleeping* 71). The Diggers were an anarchist group located in San Francisco in the 1960s. They were involved in street or "guerrilla" theater, as Berg called it, which challenged the norms and ideals of conventional society. The Diggers printed and distributed radical broadsides outlining their "free" philosophy, and they ran a Free Store in Haight-Ashbury. Works by members Emmett Grogan, Peter Coyote, and David Simpson, the Digger Archives online, and the Digger Interviews published on the Reinhabitory Institute website articulate the Diggers' lasting and pervasive influence on leftist culture.

2. On the one hand, traditional conservation groups worked to set aside wilderness and protect "natural" regions; on the other hand, social ecology and then radical ecology operated in service of primarily human needs.
3. The Diggers provide a vital touchstone and subtext to this essay. Their work links Berg and others to an earlier, East Coast leftist tradition and underscores the openness and fluidity of many subversive projects during the 1960s. The Mime Troupe was a politically charged radical theater group founded by R. G. Davis. The Diggers were an anarchist group determined to spread an anti-capitalist message that was formed by Emmett Grogan and Billy Murcott in intervening years. Berg left the troupe and joined the Diggers to pursue his concept of "life-acting," in which performers went into the streets, attempting to transform audiences into participants, blurring the lines of what is "real." Peter Coyote, a Mime Trouper and Digger, explains that the Diggers were an important part of the New Left, operating "at the edges of the counterculture, expanding it through alliances and recombinations that transformed our core group beyond recognition," thus positing a "Free Family" (Coyote, *Sleeping* 95–96). Eventually, this loose affiliation spread beyond the limits of San Francisco, manifesting itself in the network of backcountry and rural communes across the country. Berg was instrumental in the formation of this complex, and in significant ways his efforts to create a network between them form the roots of his bioregional philosophy. Emmett Grogan's *Ringolevio*, Coyote's *Sleeping Where I Fall*, Berg's *Envisioning Sustainability*, and David Simpson's reminiscences published online provide several interesting perspectives on the Digger experiment. See also *The Digger Archive* at diggers.org and Glotfelty and Quesnel's *The Biosphere and the Bioregion*.
4. See Barad 185, Bennett 21, Grusin xviii, and Haraway: "Making kin as oddkin... troubles important matters, like to whom one is actually responsible" (2); "we require each other in unexpected collaborations and combinations, in hot compost piles. We become-with each other or not at all" (4).
5. Berg was just as pivotal a figure between Beats and hippies as Gary Snyder and Allen Ginsberg had been. See Snyder and Ginsberg's *Selected Letters* 162, 165, 213, and Snyder's "tribute" in Glotfelty and Quesnel 248–49.
6. To my mind, Mills's "ecosocial" represents Berg's "planetary," grassroots aims. I distinguish between Berg's emphasis and the emphasis on "social" in the academy's "socioenvironmental" favored by Heise, Rob Nixon, and others who examine "from above," or "global" concerns.
7. Berg had deployed the term "reinhabitation" three years earlier in the first Planet Drum broadside, "Reinhabitation Message from the Pacific Coast, North America" (1974; *Envisioning* 53). Planet Drum is Berg and partner Judy Goldhaft's ongoing bioregional initiative.
8. Berg was both a "radical" and an "environmentalist," but he was not precisely a part of the "radical ecology" movement, which was more closely associated with the traditions of the Left at the time. Social ecology and radical ecology more precisely

represented the goals of the Left on behalf of labor. Thus, the Left and environmentalism had been and remains a fraught partnership. Berg and others, coming from a leftist tradition, used those tactics and strategies in their organization efforts, but often veered from the Left's ideology when it came to their ecological practice. For helpful context, see *The Anarchist Library*'s "Defending the Earth: A Debate," in which Murray Bookchin and Dave Foreman discuss the aims of radical ecology and other subversive groups.

9. Berg and Bookchin might be described as kindred spirits in the same cause, but they were often resolute rivals. Commemorating Bookchin's passing, Berg described their interactions as "contentious albeit intellectually respectful" (Berg, "Some Encounters with Murray Bookchin"). In the same essay Berg called Bookchin "a guidepost for a positive direction."
10. In his memoir *Sleeping Where I Fall*, Peter Coyote writes at length about Indian and hippie alliances, especially as they concern certain ritualistic activities. He likewise recalls problematic and troubling countercultural connections to the Black Panthers and Hells Angels.
11. To be clear: environmentalism since *Silent Spring* has acknowledged that a healthy environment is essential for human life. However, conceived in this way, the environment should be maintained in the interest of a human population. Environmental policy was still starkly drawn as either in the interest of the preservation of species or the health of human communities. Berg's writing and work stood at the vanguard of holistic approaches to humans and nature, in which people might live according to the pleasures and constraints of their given bioregions, in the best interests of all creatures/actors within that space.
12. The spirit of this language comes from Nicholas A. Brown and Sarah E. Kanouse, from their book *Re-Collecting Blackhawk: Landscape, Memory, and Power in the American Midwest* (14). They argue: "As non-Natives, we are uniquely situated to address [the problem of settler beliefs]. Any anticolonial project requires that non-Natives examine how our territorial claims, political processes, national narratives, and even senses of self are bound up first in genocide and then the resurrection and use of phantom Indians." They trace this language to Philip Deloria (note 73) and Sara Ahmed (note 74) (Brown and Kanouse 252).
13. My thanks to Krista Comer for first holding me accountable to this reading of bioregionalism in conversation during her brief stay at my home in Plumas County during the summer of 2016.
14. In fact, this is precisely Bookchin's radical ecology argument against deep ecology, if not against Berg directly. See Merchant, *Radical Ecology* 152.
15. See Vizenor, *Survivance* 11.
16. See Deloria's argument in the chapter "Counterculture Indians and the New Age," in which he writes: "whenever Americans have encountered crises of identity, some of them have inevitably turned to Indians"; "playing Indian . . . has been con-

stantly reimagined and acted out when Americans desire to have their cake and eat it too" (156, 157).

17. See Naomi Jacobs's critique of Callenbach's feminism, for example; see also Deloria, *Playing Indian*.
18. Pratt's "seeing-man" has the authority to "passively look out and possess" (9).
19. See Deloria's general argument on this point: "White radicals sought political power by appropriating and cobbling together meanings that crossed borders of culture and race. In the process, they devalued words like *Indian* and *nigger* and deemphasized the social realities that came with those words. Such attempts to create political solidarity worked to the benefit of whites, but they could have negative political consequences for Indians and African Americans. After all, those social realities underpinned civil rights protests. And if whites claimed and then diluted the very words that described those social worlds, they could offer in return only a power more linguistic than actual" (165). Writing about the New Age years following the counterculture sixties and seventies, Deloria argues that the unintended consequence of such dilution was a "gaping disjuncture between a cultural realm of serious play and the power dynamics of social conflict" (170).
20. Haraway goes further: "Materialist, experimental animism is not a New Age wish nor a neocolonial fantasy, but a powerful proposition for rethinking relationality, perspective, process, and reality without the dubious comforts of the oppositional categories of modern/traditional or religious/secular. Human-animal knots do something different in this world" (165). Haraway and others seem to advance a version of ecofeminism not unlike Berg's bioregionalism. She does so carefully, though, without terms like "future primitive" and "borne-native."
21. See "staying with the trouble" (Haraway), "dwelling in the dissolve" (Alaimo), in the context of "more than saving what's left" and "learning to live in landscapes that have been exploited, etc" (Berg).
22. Peter Coyote writes of Berg at this time that he was "subliminally menacing…he frightened people who did not know him well" (*Sleeping* 18).
23. See Heise 10; also, see Lynch, Glotfelty, and Armbruster's *The Bioregional Imagination* for an early bioregionalist response to Heise's argument (8–11).
24. To his credit, Coyote says as much elsewhere, conceding: "And just because we're breaking [norms and conventions] in one realm, we're not breaking them in the other," meaning the Diggers carried many of the biases of traditional culture with them into the counterculture. Coyote says, "We didn't know that we embodied all the problems we were trying to solve. We didn't know how to be skillful and gentle with each other." He continues: "if we had looked more deeply we would have understood that the counter-culture condemned us to marginality. That our attachment to the style of long hair, free sex, feral children, whatever, separated us from a lot of people who might have been our allies" (interview). For Simpson's part, the word "necessary" stands out. It has echoes of the Black Panthers' "by any means necessary," for example. We can see, however, that in the first-wave moment

solidarity was perhaps a matter of disparate groups talking past each other about getting along.

25. See Catriona Mortimer-Sandilands and Bruce Erickson's anthology *Queer Ecologies: Sex, Nature, Politics, Desire* (2010) as a landmark example.

Bibliography

Alaimo, Stacy. *Exposed: Environmental Politics and Pleasures in Posthuman Times.* U of Minnesota P, 2016.

Andruss, Van, Christopher Plant, Judith Plant, and Eleanor Wright, editors. *Home! A Bioregional Reader.* New Catalyst, 1990.

Anzaldúa, Gloria. *Borderlands/La Frontera: The New Mestiza.* 4th ed., Aunt Lute, 2012.

Barad, Karen. *Meeting the Universe Halfway: Quantum Physics and the Entanglement of Matter and Meaning.* Duke UP, 2007.

Bennett, Jane. *Vibrant Matter: A Political Ecology of Things.* Duke UP, 2010.

Berg, Peter. *Envisioning Sustainability.* Subculture, 2009.

———, editor. *Reinhabiting a Separate Country: A Bioregional Anthology of Northern California.* Planet Drum Foundation, 1978.

———. "Some Encounters with Murray Bookchin." *Planet Drum*, www.planetdrum.org/bookchin.htm. Accessed 2 July 2018.

Bronski, Michael. *A Queer History of the United States.* Beacon, 2011.

Brown, Nicholas A., and Sarah E. Kanouse, editors. *Re-Collecting Blackhawk: Landscape, Memory, and Power in the American Midwest.* U of Pittsburg P, 2015.

Byrd, Jodi A. *The Transit of Empire: Indigenous Critiques of Colonialism.* U of Minnesota P, 2011.

Coyote, Peter. Interview with Reinhabitory Institute. 2015. *Reinhabitory Institute*, www.reinhabitory-institute.org/2015/04/24/interview-of-peter-coyote/.

———. *Sleeping Where I Fall: A Chronicle.* 3rd ed. Counterpoint, 2015.

Deloria, Philip J. *Playing Indian.* Yale UP, 1998.

Didion, Joan. *Slouching Towards Bethlehem.* 1968. Farrar, Straus and Giroux, 1990.

Dorman, Robert L. *Hell of a Vision: Regionalism and the Modern American West.* U of Arizona P, 2012.

Esteva, Gustavo, and Madhu Suri Prakash. *Grassroots Postmodernism: Remaking the Soil of Cultures.* 1998. Zed, 2014.

Foreman, Dave, and Murray Bookchin. "Defending the Earth: A Debate." *The Anarchist Library*, theanarchistlibrary.org/library/murray-bookchin-and-dave-foreman-defending-the-earth-a-debate. Accessed 26 May 2017.

Forsey, Helen. "Community: Meeting Our Deepest Needs." Andruss, Plant, Plant, and Wright, pp. 83–85.

Ginsberg, Allen, and Gary Snyder. *The Selected Letters of Allen Ginsberg and Gary Snyder, 1956–1991.* Counterpoint, 2008.

Glotfelty, Cheryll, and Eve Quesnel, editors. *The Biosphere and the Bioregion: Essential Writings of Peter Berg.* Routledge, 2015.

Gorsline, Jeremiah, and Freeman House. "Future Primitive." Andruss, Plant, Plant, and Wright, pp. 39–41.

Grusin, Richard, editor. *The Nonhuman Turn.* U of Minnesota P, 2015.

Haraway, Donna J. *Staying with the Trouble: Making Kin in the Chthulucene.* Duke UP, 2016.

Heise, Ursula K. *Sense of Place and Sense of Planet: The Environmental Imagination of the Global.* Oxford UP, 2008.

Jacobs, Naomi. "Failures of the Imagination in Ecotopia." *Academia.edu*, academia.edu/RegisterToDownload#FindColleagues.

Lorde, Audre. "The Master's Tools Will Never Dismantle the Master's House." *Sister Outsider: Essays and Speeches.* Crossing, 2007, pp. 110–12.

Lynch, Tom, Cheryll Glotfelty, and Karla Armbruster, editors. *The Bioregional Imagination: Literature, Ecology, and Place.* U of Georgia P, 2012.

Merchant, Carolyn. *American Environmental History: An Introduction.* Columbia UP, 2007.

———. *Radical Ecology: The Search for a Livable World.* 2nd ed., Routledge, 2005.

Plant, Christopher. "In Pockets of Resistance: The Back-to-the-Land Movement Matures." Andruss, Plant, Plant, and Wright, pp. 26–28.

Plant, Judith. "Growing Home: An Introduction." Andruss, Plant, Plant, and Wright, pp. ix–xi.

Pratt, Mary Louise. *Imperial Eyes: Travel Writing and Transculturation.* 2nd ed., Routledge, 2007.

Sale, Kirkpatrick. *Dwellers in the Land: The Bioregional Vision.* 1985. U of Georgia P, 2000.

———. *The Green Revolution: The American Environmental Movement 1962–1992.* Hill & Wang, 1993.

Stegner, Wallace. "Coda: Wilderness Letter." *The Sound of Mountain Water.* 1969. U of Nebraska P, 1985, pp. 145–53.

Stoler, Ann Laura. *Duress: Imperial Durabilities in Our Times.* Duke UP, 2016.

Vizenor, Gerald, editor. *Survivance: Narratives of Native Presence.* U of Nebraska P, 2008.

Wolfe, Patrick. "Settler Colonialism and the Elimination of the Native." *Journal of Genocide Research*, vol. 8, no. 4, 2006, pp. 387–409.

9

Contact Points

The Roadside Diner's Machinery of Work in John Steinbeck's *The Grapes of Wrath*

JOHN SCHWETMAN

When twentieth-century literary critics examine road novels, they often construct their analyses around Jack Kerouac's *On the Road*, thus equating this subgenre of literary fiction with motifs of liberation and self-fulfillment. According to this paradigm, literary travelers set out to "find themselves" by cutting their ties to hometowns that relentlessly subject them to the expectations of other community members. In political terms, Kerouac's work, in spite of its association with Left-leaning "counterculture" movements that follow it in the 1960s, perpetuates an idealized notion of radical individualism that paves the way, rather, for the libertarian Right. The novel's rebellious male protagonists define travel as a means of asserting their autonomy and independence from larger community and government structures. For an alternative understanding of U.S. travel narrative, one may turn to an equally influential earlier work that defines travel much differently while nonetheless telling the story of Americans on the road: John Steinbeck's *The Grapes of Wrath*. Indeed, one senses Kerouac's uneasy regard for this important literary precursor in his central character Dean Moriarty's hostility to his own origins among itinerant farm workers, "these dumb, dumb, dumb Okies" (Kerouac 216).

In marked contrast to Dean Moriarty, Steinbeck's Tom Joad is proud to be an "Okie," and he leaves his rural home only with the greatest reluctance.[1] For Tom and the other Joads, the highway, which serves as Kerouac's idealized arena of libertarian self-fulfillment, is instead the site of strict limitations where they find themselves treated as less than human, branded by the derogatory term "Okie" and subsumed beneath the biases attached to it. For them, the highway is a place of deprivation and subjugation to the agendas of others and alienation from the communities that had once enabled them to thrive. Their understanding of life on the road contrasts remarkably with that of Jack Kerouac, and this contrast resonates with a general sense that the American idea of migration and cultural conflict is riddled with unresolved conflicts and contradictions. Elements of the American Left, especially in the West, have traditionally found Kerouac's journey of youthful rebellion appealing, with its open territory and distance from the older eastern American established communities. However, close consideration of Steinbeck's earlier work as a travel narrative reveals a concept of travel that is more consistent with the Left's goal to bring people of different social classes together on more equal terms with the help of policies supporting that end. Furthermore, through its incisive critique of technologies of production and mediation, Steinbeck's novel offers a potentially helpful corrective to the Left in the American West, and, more particularly, California, which was from its earliest days, as Carey McWilliams reports in *Factories in the Field*, a land in which "a few individuals and concerns got possession of the agricultural resources of the State" (22), and this large-scale landownership disconnected the policies from the needs of the workers and the land itself. Indeed, California's tendency toward large-scale land-holdings paved the way for a pattern of innovation in Silicon Valley laboratories whose computer and communications technologies further displaced dwelling and working on the land with more mediated and abstracting modes of relating to it and deriving value from it.

In the opening chapters of the novel, Steinbeck presents readers with an idealized account of the Joads' originary community as a place in which they feel a sacred and unquestioned connection to the land. This connection produces violence and sadness at times, but, in return, it provides the farmers with a confident sense of who they are. Much of this is evident in the discourse of Muley Graves, who defiantly refuses to leave and laments the fragmentation and dispersal of his farming community, saying, "Place where folks live is them folks. They ain't whole, out lonely on the road in a piled-up car" (55). Muley consistently upholds this belief by electing to stay on the land even when all of his friends and family join the highway exodus westward, leaving him completely alone. In Muley's lament, Steinbeck provides a vivid account of what the migrant farmworkers are giving up when they choose to migrate from Oklahoma to California in search of a livelihood. In the process, they spend several days in transit, and their experience on the highway foreshadows an existence of endless movement that awaits them in California. In the middle part of the novel are several representative scenes of the roadside experience of migrants on Route 66. As Jackson J. Benson has written, Steinbeck himself drove from Chicago to California in 1937, and this was his primary exposure to the plight of migrating farmworkers on the road: "the only traveling done along Route 66 during the period prior to the writing of the novel was on the last leg of the Steinbecks' return from Europe. Steinbeck and his wife had stopped off in Chicago to buy a car and drove back by way of Route 66 in September of 1937" (Benson 153). As tourists in Europe, Steinbeck and his wife had been able to travel for leisure, and the sight of the desperate economic migrants on Route 66 would have presented them with a striking contrast. Rick Marshall notes in "Steinbeck's Cognitive Landscapes in *The Grapes of Wrath*" that "the benign landscape that we now traverse at sixty to seventy miles per hour was once a formidable obstacle to those, like the Joads, wishing to migrate west in the 1930s, even though the highway is the technological answer to the desire to tame this environment" (62). Marshall's article defines the American highway as a "cognitive landscape," and argues that it is landscape in which tourists have the upper hand. As the site of the expression of so much hostility to the Joads' aspirations, Route 66 becomes a central setting for *The Grapes of Wrath*. It is the location of the migrant Oklahomans' transformation from settled farmers into itinerant labor seekers, and it is the job of leftist cultural critique to make this transformation visible to a community of readers who may not otherwise be aware of it.

The idealized agrarian existence depicted in the novel's flashbacks in Oklahoma becomes more vivid when situated alongside the industrial order that Steinbeck portrays in his highway scenes. Steinbeck has already introduced a thematic of "touch," which is a term that Muley Graves uses obliquely to define his traumatic response to dispossession. He asks: "You fellas think I'm touched?" (54). The shift from this thematic of "touch" to that of "contact" provides a framework for understanding the dramatic transformation of the Joads in this novel. Even before they depart Oklahoma, they encounter the threat of a new mode of contiguity, as is evident in Steinbeck's depiction of the bulldozer driver who destroys tenant farmsteads and assures that, when it "was harvested, no man had crumbled a hot clod in his fingers and let the earth sift past his fingertips. No man had *touched* the seed, or lusted for the growth" (38, emphasis added). In this passage, the spiritual qualities of touch become more pronounced through their opposition to the depredations of an abstracting industrial order. The key difference between the bulldozer driver and the more traditional tenant farmer in this passage is that the bulldozer driver's connection to the soil is mediated through the apparatus of the tractor. This mediation provides an analogue for a mediating ideology that enables the bulldozer driver to disavow the consequences of his actions while accepting his place "in his iron seat" within a matrix of machinery that "he could not control" (38). Renata Lucena Dalmaso offers a persuasive reading of the violence of the tractors in her 2015 article "'Modern Monsters,' Old Habits," in which she points out that Steinbeck has carefully distinguished human-constructed from natural disasters in his novel, aligning the human-constructed ones with Freud's notion of the *unheimlich*, or uncanny: "The uncanny refers, then, to the traumatic possibility that a human being might not be human at all. The frightful feeling associated with the tractor is made even stronger by the use of the word 'monster' to describe this machine" (28). In this reading, Dalmaso persuasively identifies Steinbeck's repeated opposition of the natural and unnatural in making his argument in the novel. I would add that the mediation of connections to the earth plays a significant role in producing this sense of the uncanny. Steinbeck makes it clear that much of the monstrosity of this form of farming is the result of technologies of mediation that confound the determination of who is culpable for the Joads' dispossession.[2]

The bulldozer is an advance guard for a conquering industrial order that quickly enfolds the Joads as they travel west, and the novel's central intercalary chapter about a roadside diner on Route 66 provides an important distillation of the shift from an old agrarian order into the new, more mediated, industrial one, as described in Carey McWilliams's *Factories in the Field*, that produces "an agricultural proletariat indistinguishable from our industrial proletariat" (48). It features a roadside diner whose primary characteristic is its interchangeability with all of the other roadside diners dotting America's highways: "Along 66 the hamburger stands—Al & Susy's Place—Carl's Lunch—Joe & Minnie—Will's Eats" (166). As part of the support system for an expansive network of interstate trucking, the hamburger stand contains the goods that this network makes available everywhere: slot machines, a jukebox, numerous mass-produced consumer items, and images advertising them. Rick Marshall defines the highway as a significant assertion of social organization through governmental power: "The highway is a product of modern engineering and manufacturing principles, made possible through the centralized coordination and detailed regional planning only a strong federal government could provide" (59). Such a complex system depends to some extent on the uniformity and interchangeability of its component parts, and the roadside diner embraces these features. Interchangeability is likewise a virtue to a traveling clientele that seeks familiar, predictable food and leisure in the shifting highway landscape. And the denizens of the stand—workers and customers alike—are as interchangeable as the objects around them. At first mention, Steinbeck names the waitress "Minnie or Susy or Mae" and the cook "Joe or Carl or Al" before settling on the last of these three in each case, thus emphasizing his point that their status as individuals is subordinate to their predetermined roles in the operations of the diner (167). The waitress Mae has also picked up the habit of identifying her customers more as types than as individuals. Stationed at her post behind the counter, typing, or stereotyping, customers allows Mae to protect her personal space behind a veil of ritualized, routine interactions with lonely truckers and aloof tourists, interactions that evoke a general sense of personal connection while protecting Mae from any deeper emotional entanglements.

This central chapter has come to represent much of what is most appealing about *The Grapes of Wrath*. Heidi Kim has written: "This vignette represents Steinbeck at his best: the ear for dialect, the vividly realistic writing, the sense of humor and irony, the local detail that aspires to the national and universal, and, most of all, his faith in the greatness of human nature, in spite of its intermingling with pettiness and stupid social convention" (Kim). Mollie Godfrey develops this analysis of "stupid social convention" further in her article "'They Ain't Human': John Steinbeck, Proletarian Fiction, and the Racial Politics of 'The People,'" in which she compares Al's diner to a service station that appears earlier in the novel and considers how interactions between the workers in roadside businesses and migrant farmers add nuances to Steinbeck's argument about social change. She points out that these roadside workers may momentarily identify with the migrants and perhaps even offer them acts of kindness, but "these acts of generosity don't shake their faith in the moral order of capitalism" (126). Godfrey presents a detailed analysis of how Steinbeck contributes productively to a leftist political movement when she argues that "his anticapitalism was more 'American' than [employers'] anticommunism" (110). In her analysis of Steinbeck's leftist stance in the novel, she claims that the diner scene includes one of several "'good guy' moments" in the novel that serve as counter-models for the more committed political activism that readers find later in the novel at the government-run Weedpatch migratory labor camp.

The diner scene nonetheless deserves further attention for its political valences because of the way Steinbeck uses it to provide readers with a literary petri dish within which the highway's three primary constituencies—truckers, tourists, and migrant farmers—can interact. At the chapter's outset, the migrants are absent from the scene, leaving the customers Mae serves to gravitate toward two extreme types: the good truck drivers and the bad tourists. The truckers, Mae knows, can make or break a roadside stand, because other travelers look to them as natives of the highway with inside knowledge of the quality of each stand: "Can't fool truck drivers, they know. They bring the customer" (167). Mae's mantra keeps her alert and ready to flirt with each entering truck driver and to make him feel at home. Her behavior is a performance for these customers, a performance that is fundamental to her position in the stand as the "contact, smiling, irritated, near to outbreak" (167). The term "contact" provides an emblematic contrast to the earlier term "touch," which is more direct. In this case, Mae is the "contact" between the cooking going on back in the kitchen and the customer at the "front of house," as restaurant lingo currently denotes it. She stands in an interstitial zone between the worlds of production and consumption, and her performance obscures the fundamental economic realities that govern the transaction of money for food. In other words, Mae puts a human face (her face) on an impersonal system of exchange, and, while she is a crucial point in the system, her work gives her no value outside of that system. To emphasize the mediated, mechanistic nature of Mae's status as a contact, Steinbeck repeats the term in describing the jukebox in the corner, wherein a "nickel drops from between the contact points into the box where the profits go" (171–72). Thus, Steinbeck maps the interpersonal dynamics of the stand onto the workings of this machine in a manner that parallels his depiction of the tractors in Oklahoma: as a mode of mediated interaction providing ethical and emotional cover for the cold, capitalist logic underlying it. His phrasing acquires political pointedness when he defines the work of conducting electricity between contact points as somehow more genuine than the implicitly more fraudulent work of carrying abstract economic value, which is the primary function of money. In so doing, Steinbeck adopts a skeptical stance on the ideologies of market-based exchange that would be familiar to most Marxist readers.

One term for this mixture of human flesh and the metal workings of the machine is *cyborg*, which serves as a basis for Donna Haraway's 1991 "Cyborg Manifesto." Whereas Steinbeck would regard the mixture of human and machine represented by the cyborg as intrinsically horrifying, Haraway sees the cyborg as a potentially liberatory figure, because the cyborg can accept her fate of perpetual entanglement with the machinery surrounding her and negotiate an assertive self-conception from there: "Cyborg writing must not be about the Fall, the imagination of a once-upon-a-time wholeness before language, before writing, before Man. Cyborg writing is about the power to survive, not on the basis of original innocence, but on the basis of seizing the tools to mark the world that marked them as other" (Haraway 175). Steinbeck writes persuasively against what later becomes Haraway's optimistic reading of the industrialization and technologization of the human body leading toward a series of complex interpenetrations of human bodies and machinery. *The Grapes of Wrath*, which is distinctly not "cyborg writing," looks back to the age of "original innocence" to which Haraway refers. Steinbeck's approach to the interactions between humans and technology thus runs directly counter to the approach for which Haraway argues. Furthermore, Steinbeck criticizes mediation of all kinds, including the mediation of value through money. Mae is a contact point, and the money that exchanges hands between her and the truckers is the electrical current running through her. Her performance is therefore as predetermined as that of the recording of Bing Crosby on the hamburger stand's jukebox. The truckers' nickels pay for Mae's hospitality act, just as they pay for the food she serves up. When Haraway writes her essay forty years later, she writes from a vantage point that has grown much more accustomed, or resigned, to the interpenetrations between human flesh and mechanical artifice and the commodification thereof. Her comfort with this mode of mediation accompanies an implication that the earlier mode of touch, of more authentic connections to the land, is merely a nostalgic fantasy hearkening back to a time of now-unrecoverable genuineness.

While Haraway's critique of such nostalgia is appealing and persuasive in many ways, the Left may wish to resist the temptation to follow Haraway down this particular path. Steinbeck's novel argues that faith in human connections is not something we can afford to lose, and the diner scene demonstrates this when the illusion of temporary community that Mae and the truckers have cultivated suddenly collapses. Tourists, for example, blunder into the stand on occasion, and they do not know the rules governing Mae's performance. They play the game poorly, and this reminds everyone of the artificial pretexts for their interactions. This may explain why tourists are inevitably the most unpopular characters in most settings. Whereas the truckers are single men, the tourists in chapter 15 travel as a married couple without children because of pharmaceuticals and treatments they take in order "to make their sexual intercourse safe, odorless, and unproductive" (168). The tourists are even deeper in the realm of mediated contact than Mae, and Steinbeck's criticism of them is extremely hostile in noting this quality. Whereas the women are grotesque blends of flesh and chemicals, the men are anxious defenders of the system that has dispossessed the Joads: "Beside [the women], little pot-bellied men in light suits and panama hats; clean, pink men with puzzled, worried eyes, with restless eyes" (169). In portraying these anxious businessmen, Steinbeck identifies their anxieties as the result of their awareness of their business as a form of "curious ritualized thievery" that may, one day, incite a populist uprising (169). Bourgeois tourists are an easy target for Steinbeck's barbs, and this characterization belongs to a long tradition of criticism of the managerial class.[3] The description seethes with hostility, and thus opens *The Grapes of Wrath* up to John Gardner's charge in *The Art of Fiction* that it is "a firm novel but a disappointing melodrama in which complex good is pitted against unmitigated, unbelievable evil" (10).[4] In its criticism of mediation, the passage evokes images of various bureaucratic apparatuses governing the flow of money around the country while calling attention to the complete detachment of this system from the material conditions of production that make it possible. The men are worried because their ideology does not adequately obscure the fragile nature of this chain of mediatory devices protecting them from poverty. And the desperation of these men introduces the theme of "ritualized thievery," which turns out to be crucial to the events that follow.

The disruption occasioned by the arrival of tourists is only momentary, and Mae's act can continue in spite of it. The greater disruption results from economic distresses of the Dust Bowl and the collapse of the southern tenant-farmer system, events that usher the migrant farmworkers into the scene as a dangerous third element in the transportation system that the diner represents. According to this chapter's symbolic logic, as natives of the road familiar with its rules, the truckers do not pose much of a threat to the migrants. This symbolic logic likely contradicts a historical reality in which massive trucks posed more danger to migrants than tourist cars, but it suits Steinbeck's overall argument to insist that, because of their incommensurabilities, contact between tourists and migrants will necessarily result in catastrophe. One truck driver's account of a collision demonstrates the violent outcome of such a meeting in which "one of them cut-down cars full a stoves an' pans an' mattresses an' kids an' chickens" collides with a luxury car "doin' ninety" (172). In a haunting, far more violent echo of the fusion of flesh and machinery in Steinbeck's earlier depiction of the bulldozer and its driver, the tourist ends up impaled on his own steering wheel, "a-wigglin' like a frog on a hook" (172). The trucker's language describing this accident emphasizes the inextricability of human flesh from the mechanical apparatus of transport. The tourist, speeding along in his "Big Cad," brimming over with confidence, and the migrant farmers crawling down the road in an old, overloaded "cut-down car" (172) make for a deadly combination because of the enormous variation in speeds. The crash thus symbolizes class disparities in this novel and their often violent consequences. In both cases, the roadside hamburger stand and characters like the truckers and Mae exist between the two extremes, just as the hamburger stand itself exists somewhere between Oklahoma and California.

What follows the introductory descriptions of the stand, the truckers, and the tourists is a peculiar interaction that draws attention to this central chapter. Having introduced the notion of thievery in his earlier description of the tourists, Steinbeck reminds readers that thievery is a constant concern for people who work and live near well-traveled routes. Mae talks about how the migrant farmers rarely buy anything from her store and adds, "People says they steal" (172). This comment, emerging from the nebulous realm of public opinion, sets the stage for the entry of an actual migrant farm family. Upon their arrival, Big Bill, one of the truckers, says, "Better tie your stuff down" when he notices a migrant family approaching the stand. After allowing the family to fill their radiator, Mae carries the joke further, saying, "I'll keep my eye on the hose" (173). The migrant farm family faces an unsympathetic audience at this moment. They are in a perilous position on the highway in the middle of the desert and at the mercy of these hostile "natives." Their clothing, their car, and their dialect set them off from their surroundings, and such stark differences pose significant obstacles to the fellow feeling that is a necessary precondition for a leftist political project to end their exploitation through pro-worker policies. This is why Steinbeck proceeds to stage a series of economic transactions in the diner that dismantle the hostile stereotypes of migrant farmers.

Though the farm family is not the Joads (the Joads never appear in the intercalary chapters), this family clearly comes from the same general background as the Joads and shares many of the same circumstances as poor migrants on a highway built for wealthier tourists and more experienced truckers. Like the Joads, it is a family of people who feel uncomfortable with mediation in their connection with the land and thus look back to a time when they were in touch with it. Etymologically, there are distinctions between touch and contact, but, for the purposes of my argument, *touch* expresses a less mediated, more spiritual mode of interconnection. Muley Graves touches the land as part of a religious commemoration of his departed past. To "have the touch" is to have a special ability, often with spiritual overtones. In contrast, as a mediated connection between elements, *contact* lacks these spiritual overtones. It is related to the Latin root for *contagion* and thus can represent a transfer not of spiritual energy but illness. In the example of the jukebox in the roadside hamburger stand, contact is the transfer of electrical energy, not spirituality.[5] Thus, in the realm of the hamburger stand, money represents a transfer along lines of contact. As Christ's encounter with the money changers in the Jerusalem Temple suggests,[6] few activities are traditionally more opposed to spiritual matters than the exchange of money.

For the migrant farmers, money nonetheless represents something real like bread and gasoline and the numerous possessions they have had to sell in order to fund their journeys west. Money is a symbol for them of an exchange of material goods taking place just beneath surface. At the other end of the economic spectrum, the tourists regard money as pure abstraction. According to Steinbeck's description, they know that business is "ritualized thievery," and the lack of concrete referents for their sums of money makes them "worried" (169). The tourists' conceptions of money reinforce what Steinbeck writes about the nickel that sits between contact points in the jukebox, both as a physical conduit for electricity and as a symbolic index of abstract economic value (171–72). In this light, the jukebox's equally mechanical neighbor, the slot machine, also merits consideration. It contains slugs as well as nickels, a reminder that machines ultimately only react to money as a material object and fail to recognize the immaterial value of money as a symbol. Consequently, when the farming family enters the scene and asks to buy a loaf of bread, they find themselves confronted with an alien system of value, in which experienced operators game the representational vagaries of money to their own advantage, sometimes fraudulently, as the slugs in the slot machine suggest.

Bread, for example, is worth fifteen cents per loaf, so the migrant farmer with a budget limiting him to ten cents asks Mae to cut ten cents' worth of bread off the loaf. When Mae offers him the entire fifteen-cent loaf at that price, he replies, "That'd be robbin' you, ma'am" (175). The farmer's insistence on paying full price despite his family's desperate need puts Mae's and the truckers' earlier joke about their thieving natures in a more serious light. It is easy to make generalizations about the migrant farmers in the abstract, but, here, face to face with actual migrants, the cruelty of their generalizations becomes more evident, especially when the farmers insist on completely compensating Mae for goods and services received. Rather than engaging in artful haggling, which they equate with "robbin' you," they insist on paying an objectively fair price. Once Mae notices this, her tone subtly shifts. She lets the farmer buy peppermint sticks for his sons at a fraction of their actual cost and lies about it to allow him to save face. On the one hand, she and the truckers admire these migrant farmers for their dogged adherence to principles in the face of hardship. On the other hand, to be reminded of their own callousness is quite irritating for them. After the farm family leaves, the truckers lightly parody Mae's act of charity by leaving her a one-dollar tip while telling her to "go to hell" (176). The scene is an adept example of audience manipulation. After establishing Mae, Al, and the truck-driving customers as an extremely hardened group of characters, Steinbeck depicts them grumpily helping out a family in need. By walking readers through Mae's changing attitude toward the migrants, Steinbeck models a process that, he hopes, will lead to a change in readers' attitudes toward the migrants as well. Or, as Mollie Godfrey argues, "the book teaches its middle-class readers to identify with the Okies in refutation of those dehumanizing strategies of racial othering that the novel shows were used to divide and denigrate the working class" (125). Godfrey establishes how in scenes such as this one hostile characters use racially coded language to justify harsh treatment of the Okies even though there is no racial difference between the Okies and those who label them in this fashion.

Once the family leaves, the hamburger stand seemingly returns to its earlier state as Al sits down to play the slot machine. Whereas the jukebox returns a song for a nickel, the slot machine returns the more abstract chance to profit from machine-generated probabilities. One of the presumed advantages of these machines is that they treat all players equally. Mae may treat truckers like gods and call tourists "shitheels" under her breath, but the slot machines do not discriminate according to appearance, class, or occupation. Anyone who pulls the handle has an equal shot at the jackpot, and that is the argument for the slot machine's brand of de-individualizing mechanization. As a sort of precursor to the standardized test in our education system, the machine cannot favor one user over another and merely provides a cold calculation of the user's success or failure to beat the odds. This example of the fairness and efficiency of mechanization is convincing until Al, taking advantage of the fact that he runs the stand and can monitor the machine's rate of pay, checks his crib sheet, goes over to one of the machines, saying, "Number three's ready to pay off," and collects his jackpot on the fifth spin (176–77). In other words, even the mechanically randomized formulas of the slot machine can become subject to the privileges of the native over the transient. Al's manipulation of the slot machine refutes the standard argument that the capitalist system provides a level playing field in which all participants have an equal chance at success. As Godfrey points out, in this conclusion to the diner scene, "Al immediately affirms the middle class's part in capitalist-sanctioned theft" (126). Steinbeck thus deflates any techno-utopian claims about the virtue of the machinery of impartial measurement. In his depiction of the slot machines, the playing field is never quite level. The machine merely drapes an ideological illusion of fairness over a rigged game. In this sense, though the mechanical contact point seems to replace more primitive spiritual superstitions associated with touch with a more enlightened form of rationalist judgment, it does so only in appearance. This is a distinction that the Left must continue to uphold if it is to produce a workable counternarrative to the neoliberal narrative of individualist accomplishment unfettered from community or government restrictions. Disconnection from place actively assists a conservative political project that insists on individual responsibility and seeks to sow distrust of anything acknowledging one's dependence on a larger community, such as the ties that bind people together through their geographical proximity.[7]

The roadside-diner chapter of *The Grapes of Wrath* shows that the increasing mechanization of the United States is a phenomenon entwined with changing transit networks and new attitudes toward travel. It conveys this through a carefully crafted opposition between the terms "touch" and "contact," and it provides a microcosm of the overall drama of the novel pitting the travelers against the landed natives.[8] The transient nature of the hamburger stand results partly from its location between places. However, in other ways, the hamburger stand is representative of what the Joads will experience in California, where, instead of stable communities like the one they left in Oklahoma, they will find squalid Hoovervilles and the more orderly Weedpatch migratory labor camp, as well as a law enforcement apparatus that is intent on keeping them moving along. Throughout their peregrinations, traditional notions of kinship and acquaintance fail to hold up, compelling friendship and family to give way to temporary alliances. Steinbeck's language describing their temporary encampments is vivid, defining them as "a world created, complete with furniture—friends made and enemies established... and every morning the world torn down like a circus" (213). In this situation, even the most traditionally esteemed affinities of family come under enormous pressure. The Joads can no longer take this group identity for granted. Instead of group identity emerging organically from their material conditions as it did in their idealized agrarian past, it becomes something the Joads must work hard to establish and maintain.

The story of the Joads' journey west is one of continual erosion of the family unit in spite of Ma Joad's efforts to prevent this erosion. In one memorable exchange, she threatens to beat her husband with a jack handle to prevent the family from leaving some of its members behind to help another migrant family fix its car (185). And despite her strong stand, the family does fracture. The grandparents, who have the strongest ties to the land, both die before the Joads reach California. Eldest son Noah wanders off just as the Joads cross over into California. Jim Casy gets arrested in the first Hooverville, and Tom leaves the family at the end of the novel to protect them from the danger of police retribution because of their connection to him. These departures are the direct result of the fact that the Joads have no house or property to keep them together. The family's unity depends on the connection to a physical location, and in the absence of such a connection, it falls to pieces. Indeed, one of the most dramatic and tragic elements of *The Grapes of Wrath* is its failure to land the Joads in any kind of stable endpoint. Though history tells us that migrant workers did eventually find a place in California, partly due to the flourishing of the defense industry during World War II, Steinbeck finished writing this novel before that development. So, he leaves the Joads afloat in an economically precarious state at the novel's conclusion. That said, he provides a symbolic sense of closure around yet another portrayal of touch in Rose of Sharon's benevolent act of breastfeeding an ailing old man,[9] and he offers some hope of future community for the Joads in the government-sponsored resettlement camp at Weedpatch and in the possibility of a global political movement against the forces of free-market labor exploitation that are arrayed against them. Nonetheless, the forces of mechanized commodity-exchange and mediated contact so evident in Al and Mae's roadside diner prove to be significant obstacles for the Joads to overcome as they seek to reestablish a stable footing in California. By calling attention to the intervention of machines in this context, Steinbeck seeks from a Marxist perspective to denaturalize elements of structural inferiority that his readers might otherwise accept as components of a natural, free-market order.

Having established a mediated, mechanized industrial order as the source of the Joads' hardship, Steinbeck then must work through their various options for adaptation and resistance. In *The Harvest Gypsies*, a series of articles that Steinbeck wrote for the *San Francisco News* that provided the basis for *The Grapes of Wrath*, he phrases the problem a bit differently, and his word choice is instructive: "If, on the other hand, as has been stated by a large grower, our agriculture requires the creation and maintenance at any cost of a peon class, then it is submitted that California agriculture is economically unsound under a democracy" (*Harvest Gypsies* 61). In other words, industrialized agriculture, as it is practiced in California in the 1930s, is destructive because of the way it reduces the migrant farmers to a state of peonage. Instrumentalization of workers, treating them like machines, is one means of creating this state of peonage, and abusive stereotyping of them reinforces such treatment. To understand this more thoroughly, it helps to consider Steinbeck's earlier novel *In Dubious Battle*, which offers its own comprehensive analysis of labor organization. The two main characters of *In Dubious Battle*, Mac and Jim, are labor organizers for the Communist Party, and they pride themselves on being used like machines to further the cause of the workers and work toward a more widespread uprising against the farm owners. Mac educates Jim to be an organizer with very pragmatic insights about how to motivate workers to organize themselves to resist farm owners, and he emphasizes the practical advantages of shared sacrifice. When Mac and Jim first arrive at a rough camp of apple pickers, they stumble into a stressful situation in which the daughter-in-law of the natural group leader, London, is giving birth without a doctor present. Mac seizes the advantage by falsely claiming to have medical expertise and then taking charge of the delivery, ordering the men to find clean white cloth wherever they can. When some men literally offer the shirts off their backs to help the farmworker's daughter, Mac uses those items before ordering that they be burned, even though, as Jim points out, Mac "didn't need all that cloth" (67). Mac explains that "we've got to use whatever material comes to us" (66), and that every needless sacrifice will serve his end of turning this disorganized band of fruit tramps into a well-oiled machine of collective action: "Every man who gave part of his clothes felt that the work was his own. They all feel responsible for that baby. It's theirs, because something from them went to it. To give back the cloth would cut them out. There's no better way to make men part of a movement than to have them give something to it. I bet they all feel fine right now" (67). In this example, *In Dubious Battle* dramatizes Steinbeck's theory of the "group man" in its clearest form and in greater depth than in the later *The Grapes of Wrath*, in which his theories of group formation become more abstract.

Like the "monster" referred to by land agents explaining the banks to the Oklahoma tenant farmers in *The Grapes of Wrath*, group man is a mass of people possessing a single personality and motives distinct from those of its individual members. As the two labor organizers in *In Dubious Battle* are painfully aware, they can motivate the men to organize against the landowners, but they ultimately have little control over what this organization will do. From Steinbeck's point of view, the labor organization in *In Dubious Battle* does not resolve the main problem for the workers, which is the alienation that keeps them pitted against one another for limited resources. The solution portrayed in *In Dubious Battle* depends on its own mode of somewhat mechanized organization, turning activists into replaceable parts in a large machine that fights for workers' rights against the organizations of landowners. One key instance of this occurs after London confronts Mac about his membership in the Communist Party and Mac somewhat reluctantly acknowledges his status as a professional organizer. London pointedly questions Mac about this, and the tension is high because of the widespread propaganda suggesting that Communists are using local laborers to advance a larger agenda that will actually do harm to workers at the local level. In response to London's question about what he gets out of it, Mac says,

> "Well, it's hard to say—you know how you feel about Sam an' all the guys that travel with you? Well, I feel that way about all the workin' stiffs in the country."
>
> "Guys you don't even know?"
>
> "Yes, guys I don't even know." (265)

Among American novelists, few have used dialogue as effectively as Steinbeck to convey crucial nuances about the conflicts driving the characters and the historical context in which they are operating, and this exchange is a great example. London's question is a direct and dangerous challenge to Mac's credibility as he attempts to guide the apple pickers through an incredibly tense, potentially violent confrontation with the landowners. Any hint that Mac's motives are impure will possibly destroy London's faith in him and, in turn, undo the whole strike. At this key moment, suggesting his hesitancy by awkwardly repeating the word "well" twice in two sentences, Mac declares that his loyalty is to something more abstract than the group of men around him. He claims, in essence, an affinity with "all the workin' stiffs in the country" that is just as strong as London's affinity with the men he has been traveling with for a year. In other words, Mac advances an argument for an expansion of loyalty outward in defiance of the traditional logic of locality. While Mac's phrasing here defines this expansion as outward to the boundaries of "the country" and is therefore nationalist, it nonetheless aspires to an international level of unity, and Communist Party rhetoric reinforces this sense that Mac engages in a battle on behalf of the workers of the world. As the conversation progresses, London accepts this explanation, saying, "I got nothing against reds" (265). However, London never exactly signs onto the larger program. There is no evidence that he will ever be ready to accept the cosmopolitan argument that he, like Mac, should act on interests beyond the local or regional.

The discussions of a national or international labor movement in *The Grapes of Wrath* are notably hazier and ill defined. In the absence of labor organizers, Steinbeck depicts a different sort of resistance to the landowners emerging from the activities of the workers themselves. The logic of unity in the face of oppression is the same in Jim Casy's formulation as it is for Mac in *In Dubious Battle.* However, Jim Casy and Tom Joad develop a different kind of resistance, an approach to group formation that is perhaps less straightforward. When a vigilante murders Jim Casy for "talking too much," Tom Joad kills another vigilante in response, then finds that he must leave his family to protect them from retribution. In disappearing, Tom elects to turn himself into a representative figure for all of the migrant farmworkers. In this way, the novel does not provide a literal answer to the plight of the farmworkers, but rather a symbolic answer, as Tom explains it in a farewell oration to his mother in which he repeats the phrase "I'll be there" after each of a series of descriptions of the people's hardship as they travel in search of work and community (463). On the literal level, Tom will not "be there" because he is disappearing into the landscape to become a solitary itinerant laborer, but, figuratively, Tom is establishing himself as a symbolic character who will unite people through his absence. Tom envisages a new community forming, a collectivity that defines itself instead of accepting the definition imposed on it from outside through the word "Okie." If the shiny metal gadgets of Al's diner represent the soulless mechanized forces against which Tom is striving, then this mystical statement, with its spiritual undertones anchoring people to the earth through "the houses they build," represents an effective repudiation of that order of *contact.* In comparison with the alternate machinery of labor organization of *In Dubious Battle*, this seemingly more ambiguous mode of political engagement represents the more truly revolutionary one.

Notes

1. In his article comparing *The Grapes of Wrath* to *On the Road*, Jason Spangler has produced a useful collection of references to Okies in Kerouac's novel and argued that the wandering Beats of *On the Road* have more in common with Steinbeck's

migrant farmers than is at first evident. Spangler adds that "while one was written in a time of cultural famine and the other in a period of hyperkinetic capitalist feasting, these novels mutually lament the price of existence paid by the individual in modern America and gesture toward an antidote for the incivilities of civilization" (309).

2. Conservative critics Charles Shindo and Keith Windschuttle offer a very different take on the renegotiation of connection to the land that has dispossessed the Joads, and both critics argue that the collapse of the southern tenant farmer system merits closer consideration than Steinbeck's novel provides. In *Dust Bowl Migrants in the American Imagination*, Shindo points out that the farmers reject New Deal solutions to their plight because of their desire to return to their status as yeoman farmers. And, in "Steinbeck's Myth of the Okies," Windschuttle argues that misguided New Deal programs hastened, or even caused, the collapse of this system.
3. Jackson J. Benson writes in "'To Tom, Who Lived It': John Steinbeck and the Man from Weedpatch" that the prototype of *The Grapes of Wrath* was a work titled "L'Affaire Lettuceberg," which consisted of "a series of brutal caricatures of prominent Salinas citizens" and was the result of Steinbeck's anger "at the fat smug people who waved their flags and willingly let other Americans starve in the mud" (185). This depiction of tourists is plausibly a remnant of that earlier effort to explain the forces arrayed against the migrant farmworkers. But "the grossness of his attack sickened him and although he had completed a sixty-thousand word manuscript, he couldn't go forward with its publication" (186).
4. In *The Art of Fiction: Notes on Craft for Young Writers*, Gardner depicts Steinbeck's hostility as directed primarily at the "California ranchers," whereas I would argue that the worried tourists bear more of it. The "California ranchers" are more accurately farm owners, and while some are callously exploitative, others are quite sympathetic to the plight of the Joads. Steinbeck's portrayal of the farm owners is more nuanced than that of the tourists.
5. The spiritualist movement in the nineteenth-century United States demonstrates ambiguities in the distinction between electrical and spiritual transference that once existed, which is why I hesitate to suggest too much about the distinction between "touch" and "contact" beyond the bounds of my own argument. Suffice to say that the two terms still carry some of their nineteenth-century connotations, but that the meanings of the two terms as I use them are distinct in both their etymologies and in the way Steinbeck uses them.
6. In a passage that most migrant farmers would readily have recognized, Jesus says, "Take these things hence; make not my Father's house a house of merchandise" (*Holy Bible*, John 2.16).
7. In his analysis of the political stance of *The Grapes of Wrath*, William Conlogue opposes two models of agriculture: the *yeoman* farm, with its emphasis on cooperation between farming neighbors of equal status, and the *entrepreneurial* farm, consisting of "independent individuals who discipline themselves and others in

vertical relationships based on monetary exchanges" (114). Conlogue notably opposes Steinbeck's *The Grapes of Wrath*, as a leftist critique of the industrialization of agriculture, to Ruth Comfort Mitchell's conservative rejoinder to Steinbeck in *Of Human Kindness*, a novel in which those "vertical relationships" become prominent because the "migrants must be made obedient citizens of a class-stratified entrepreneurial farm community" (Conlogue 101).

8. Mimi Reisel Gladstein's "Immigration Issues: Steinbeck's Continuing Relevance" argues that, in our current age of repeating immigration crises, *The Grapes of Wrath* is more politically relevant than ever. She writes that "Steinbeck had hoped that his presentation of the plight of the Joads and other migrant workers would serve as a call for understanding and sympathy, perhaps an impetus for humane policies," and that the global community tragically still falls short in this respect (24).
9. In his extensive analysis of the Joads' awakening as members of a larger, more abstract community, Joseph Fontenrose writes about Rose of Sharon's controversial act of charity, stating that in it "the Joads' intense feelings of family loyalty have been transcended; they have expanded to embrace all men. Another image could have symbolized this universality, but, for Steinbeck, perhaps no other could have done it so effectively" (Fontenrose 69).

Bibliography

Benson, Jackson J. "'To Tom, Who Lived It': John Steinbeck and the Man from Weedpatch." *Journal of Modern Literature*, vol. 5, no. 2, April 1976, pp. 151–210.

Conlogue, William. *Working the Garden: American Writers and the Industrialization of Agriculture*. U of North Carolina P, 2001.

Dalmaso, Renata Lucena. "'Modern Monsters,' Old Habits: Nature, Humans, and Technology in John Steinbeck's *The Grapes of Wrath*." *Steinbeck Review*, vol. 12, no. 1, 2015, pp. 26–38.

Fontenrose, Joseph. *Steinbeck: An Introduction and Interpretation*. Holt, Rinehart and Winston, 1963.

Gardner, John. *The Art of Fiction: Notes on Craft for Young Writers*. Vintage, 1983.

Gladstein, Mimi Reisel. "Immigration Issues: Steinbeck's Continuing Relevance." *Steinbeck Review*, vol. 12, no. 1, 2015, pp. 16–25.

Godfrey, Mollie. "'They Ain't Human': John Steinbeck, Proletarian Fiction, and the Racial Politics of 'The People.'" *Modern Fiction Studies*, vol. 59, no. 1, Spring 2013, pp. 107–34.

Haraway, Donna J. *Simians, Cyborgs, and Women: The Reinvention of Nature*. Routledge, 1991.

The Holy Bible. King James Version. American Bible Society, 1999; *Bartleby.com*, 2000, www.bartleby.com/108/. Accessed 3 Jan. 2017.

Kerouac, Jack. *On the Road*. 1957. Penguin, 1976.

Kim, Heidi. "An Appreciation of John Steinbeck's *The Grapes of Wrath.*" *Ethos: A Digital Review of Arts, Humanities, and Public Ethics*, www.ethosreview.org/cultural-interventions/an-appreciation-of-john-steinbecks grapes-of-wrath/. Accessed 21 Dec. 2016.

Marshall, Rick. "Steinbeck's Cognitive Landscapes in *The Grapes of Wrath.*" *Steinbeck Review*, vol. 8, no. 1, 2011, pp. 57–76.

McWilliams, Carey. *Factories in the Fields: The Story of Migratory Farm Labor in California.* 1939. Archon, 1969.

Shindo, Charles J. *Dust Bowl Migrants in the American Imagination.* UP of Kansas, 1997.

Spangler, Jason. "We're on a Road to Nowhere: Steinbeck, Kerouac, and the Legacy of the Great Depression." *Studies in the Novel*, vol. 40, no. 3, fall 2008, pp. 308–27.

Steinbeck, John. *The Grapes of Wrath.* 1939. Penguin, 2006.

———. *The Harvest Gypsies: On the Road to* The Grapes of Wrath. Heyday, 1988.

———. *In Dubious Battle.* 1936. Penguin, 2006.

Windschuttle, Keith. "Steinbeck's Myth of the Okies." *The New Criterion*, vol. 20, 2002, pp. 24–32.

10

"The Queen of the Mad Frontier"

Settler Colonialism and Jack Spicer's Queer Politics

ALEX TRIMBLE YOUNG

In 1955, Myrsam Wixman, a one-time member of the Mattachine Society, the now famous California pre-Stonewall gay civil rights organization founded in Los Angeles in 1950, wrote poet and fellow Mattachine activist Jack Spicer to thank him for a gift. Spicer had apparently given him an LP of the soundtrack for Disney's now famous 1954–55 miniseries, *Davy Crocket: King of the Wild Frontier*. Wixman responded with a review:

> [I] have just heard for the first time that "Duvid Crockett" [*sic*] which you have left me. It's very good. By the way, I've made up my own version, the first verse of which follows:
> Born in a privy in Tennessee
> Started jackin' off when he was only three!
> Became passive anal at the age of four
> Went down to Nashville, workin' as a whore.
> Davy, Davy Crockett
> Queen of the Mad Frontier!
> [...............]
> Beardless still at thirty-three
> Went up to New York, kinda on a spree
> Walked into Times Square an' 'fore he knew

> Got picked up by a wealthy ole Jew.
> Davy, Davy Crockett
> Hustler without a peer! (Wixman to Spicer)

Wixman's appropriation of frontier rhetoric for a poetic rendition of *Midnight Cowboy* avant la lettre is self-evidently campy, and deftly parodies both the image of the impenetrable frontiersman as the figure for national masculinity and the pseudo-psychology that attempted to pathologize homosexuality. While breaking down certain conceptions of normative masculinity, however, Wixman's parody reinforces others, celebrating a mode of (queer) western American masculinity that defines itself against Jewishness and East Coast urbanity.

The queer frontier imagined in Wixman's parody, with its seemingly contradictory blend of camp, masculinist rhetoric, and anti-Semitism, makes an appearance five years later in the iconic first stanza of one of Spicer's most celebrated poems, *Billy the Kid:*

> Let us fake out a frontier—a poem somebody could hide in with a sheriff's posse after him—a thousand miles of it if it is necessary for him to go a thousand miles—a poem with no hard corners, no houses to get lost in, no underwebbing of customary magic, no New York Jew salesmen of amethyst pajamas, only a place where Billy The Kid can hide when he shoots people. (*My Vocabulary* 185)

In *Billy the Kid*, we are presented with the frontier as a site of queer desire (Billy is explicitly figured as an object of homoerotic fantasy later in the poem), but also the site of violence and of a specific racial and sexual exclusion (with the Jew once again figured as an effeminate outsider). In *Billy the Kid*, the frontier also becomes the poetic itself: Spicer's late-career poetic practice, which his friend and fellow poet Robin Blaser would later dub "The Practice of the Outside" in an influential essay of that title, is allegorized as a process of figurative frontiering.[1]

While it has often been cited as an important touchstone in the genealogy of postmodern American poetics, *Billy the Kid*, like Spicer's work generally, has been largely neglected by western regionalist critics.[2] However, Spicer was a writer whose sense of himself as a westerner was never far from his sense of himself as a gay man and as a leftist. His conflation of regional identity, queer sexuality, and radical political commitment was a frequent theme in his poetry, and it was an orientation that he encouraged among his circle of friends and fellow poets. Spicer's unlikely mode of regionalism queered normative conceptions of western American masculinity, but it also indexed the tendency of Spicer's poetry and activist rhetoric, as well as that of much of his circle, to reproduce modes of misogyny and racial chauvinism endemic to the mode of western masculinity this rhetoric otherwise critiqued.

When Spicer's engagement with frontier allegory and strong sense of regional identity are noted by critics and his fellow poets, they are almost always cited as confirmation of his postmodern bona fides and his commitment to an indeterminate form of radical politics. Poet Peter Gizzi picks up on Spicer's identification with California and the West in his introduction to Spicer's collected lectures, arguing that, for Spicer, "California is America *in extremis*. It combines and locates his sense of limit in poetry, his questioning of grand narratives, and his sense of living out a posthumous existence in a post-apocalyptic, image-making, border culture" (Gizzi 201). Michael Davidson, on the other hand, reads Spicer's frontier rhetoric as a means of distancing himself from U.S. nationalism, arguing that "unlike Ginsberg, who often speaks for the nation, Spicer absented himself from it" (Davidson, *San Francisco* 171).

The seeming disjunction between Gizzi and Davidson's readings of Spicer's engagement with the American West—Gizzi reads Spicer's identification with the West as a space that is "America *in extremis*," whereas Davidson reads Spicer's frontier rhetoric as a move that absents his work from the symbolic space of the nation—speaks to the fundamental tension at the heart of Spicer's politics, a tension that is also manifested in the jarring juxtaposition of emancipatory and exclusionist rhetoric in his poetry. This tension between anti-statism and nationalism, emancipation and exclusion, becomes more legible if we read Spicer's western regionalism, and the political and poetic work it informed, beyond its national context.

In the readings that follow, I will argue that a transnational tradition of frontier popular sovereignty—a political tradition constitutive of, but not coterminous with, U.S. ideology—was a central force in shaping Jack Spicer's literary politics. American literary studies has long regarded frontier rhetoric as the exclusive domain of U.S. state ideology. However, for Spicer, and indeed for many radical literary figures during the period in which he wrote, frontier rhetoric gave voice to a failed but nonetheless radical politics of resistance to the United States and its cultural norms. Spicer's use of frontier rhetoric to describe his literary practice and literary community crescendoed in the wake of a long string of disappointments he experienced as a leftist activist. Understanding Spicer's politics as settler colonial, rather than either nationalist or revolutionary, is crucial, I will argue, for understanding how his politics during this period articulated its radical potential, but also, ultimately, for understanding how his political project failed.

Scholars of transnational settler colonialism have noted that the ambivalent relation to the nation-state that marks Spicer's regionalism marks the rhetoric of a broad range of settler colonial projects around the globe. Theorist Lorenzo Veracini argues that the ambivalent relationships between settler colonies and their colonial metropoles are indicative of a distinct political tradition. Settlers are colonists that "carry their sovereignty with them," and see themselves as representatives of the sovereign authority of the colonial metropole but also as founders of their own autonomous sovereign traditions. "The sovereignty claimed by settler collectives does not focus on the state and insists on the law-making corporate capacity of the local community, on its self-constituting ability" (Veracini 72). The forms of autonomy engendered on the settler frontier may be read as circumscribed forms of popular sovereignty, but emerged because, rather than in spite of, colonial violence. More often than not, settler colonists' demands for local autonomy were fueled by the desire to exercise sovereign violence in the expropriation of Indigenous lands and the management of racialized labor.

My focus in tracing the political traditions of settler colonialism in Spicer's work will not be his poetry per se, but rather an archive of correspondence, interviews, and political ephemera that map Spicer's political life in the years after his self-described "birth as a poet" in 1947 and the publication of *Billy the Kid* in 1958. Spicer famously worked to blur the lines between his literary, personal, and political lives, and his correspondence and the records of his activist work during this period constitute a vital archive for understanding the formal breakthrough that Spicer achieved with his celebrated "dictated" serial poems. As critic Daniel Katz pithily put it, speaking of the necessity of incorporating Spicer's correspondence when considering his oeuvre, "his love for the letter as form, his desire that poems and letters each work as the other, testify to this: the catastrophe of his life must also be read as *part* of the work" (Katz 8). Any understanding of the radical transformation of Spicer's poetics that occurred during this period is incomplete without an understanding of the "catastrophe of [Spicer's political] life" that was unfolding at the same time.

The Language poets' readings of Spicer, influenced by Marxist formalism, have given much attention to how the anti-normative modes of representation in his poetry can be read as gesturing toward alternative models of political representation. These readings have not, by and large, taken up the question of how the modes of political representation Spicer championed in his work as an activist during this period engaged with and informed the same issues of identity and representation he explores through his radical poetics (see Rasula). Conversely, poet and independent scholar Kevin Killian's groundbreaking work on Spicer's activist practice is largely focused on how that shaped the representation of sexuality in his poems, and what it tells us about his beliefs regarding "the homosexual in society" more broadly (Killian 23–24). My contention is that Spicer's activism in the Mattachine Society provides an insight into his politics that extends beyond its direct considerations of homosexual identity. Spicer's queer politics worked to make the Mattachine an organization that could represent the political concerns of a broad coalition of individuals on the local and national stage while still respecting alterity within that coalition:

he quickly found that goal to be impossible. Understanding Spicer's activism and ultimate failure within the Mattachine thus sheds invaluable light on Spicer's often perplexing experiments in poetic form: just as he had in his political life, Spicer, as a poet, worked to envision a nonnormative form through which a pluralist mode of life could be represented. The frontier emerged as the vexed allegorical vehicle through which Spicer pursued this goal in his poetry.

However, Spicer's engagement with politics and frontier rhetoric began long before he attended a meeting of the Mattachine Society. When Spicer arrived at Berkeley as an undergraduate in 1945, the campus was rife with leftist political activism of all stripes, ranging from "a strong socialist party, various factions of Stalinists, Trotskyists, anarchists, and pacifists... all, [Spicer] noted ironically, at war with each other." While he consorted with members of all these groups, Spicer found himself most attracted to the anti-statist "Libertarian Circle" in San Francisco, the group of "philosophical anarchists" led by Kenneth Rexroth (Ellingham and Killian 10). It was here that Spicer began his lifelong friendship (and rivalry) with Robert Duncan and where Rexroth claimed (somewhat hyperbolically) that "the ideological foundations of the San Francisco Renaissance had been laid—poetry of direct speech of I to Thou, personalism, anarchism" (Rexroth 508). Despite Rexroth's claim, Spicer's politics never fully embraced anarchism, but rather seemed to vacillate between something approaching anarchism and something closer to Marxism. Poet George Stanley, a Spicer acolyte, summed up this ambivalence neatly in an interview with Spicer biographer Lewis Ellingham:

> Jack believed in decentralization, he was a kind of anarchist in that way. I remember him saying "it would be good if every little place had its own government that was quite different from every other place's government: San Francisco, San Mateo, Oakland, lots of little tiny principalities," he liked that idea. But then, he also had a streak in him, what you might call kind of a Marxist animus, one based... ultimately upon hatred and revenge against these capitalists. And so we used to have these ar-

> guments about, you know, "if we have a revolution, then the revolutionary party will create a tyranny that's even worse than the one that preceded it" and at one point I remember Jack saying "it doesn't matter. It doesn't matter. At least *we* would have won." (Stanley)

The attempt to reconcile his quasi-anarchic desire for local autonomy and his revolutionary leftist commitments was a task that preoccupied Spicer throughout much of his career. From his earliest writings onward, he saw this task as tied not only to a (possibly mythic) family history—he often claimed his father had been a member of the Industrial Workers of the World (the Wobblies)—but also to his regional identity. In one of his early unpublished story fragments, Spicer imagined a romance of Wobbly resistance grounded in the romantic landscapes of the West: "the story of a wobbly, a bindle-stiff who had fought for Big Bill Heywood in Colorado, who was beaten and crippled by the thugs of Anaconda Copper in Montana, who had been jailed in ten states and been shot in five others, who had followed the IWW from its start to the day thirty years from then when everybody deserted it" (Spicer, "Pilgrimage").

Spicer's leftist commitments produced consequences in his early career that would force him to abandon the western spaces that were always, for him, spaces of resistance. Spicer followed his faculty mentor (and noted political theorist) Ernst Kantorowicz in refusing to sign the infamous University of California loyalty oath, and UC Berkeley refused to renew his position for the fall 1950 term. Spicer was forced to take a position as a research assistant in linguistics at the University of Minnesota, where he spent nearly two miserable years before returning to Berkeley, which had since modified its loyalty oath, excising references to Communism. On his return, he immediately joined a Trotskyist group with Robin Blaser but soon abandoned it when he and Blaser were kicked out after making a joke at a meeting (Ellingham and Killian 46).

Humor seemed to define Spicer's engagement with the Berkeley Left during these years: in one of his most vaunted stunts, he organized an intramural football team called "The Unpopular Front," brought together explicitly to beat the "Students for Wallace" team, which was, at least according to Spicer's friend Sam Hardin, a Communist front. Much to Spicer's delight, his team was able to accomplish this goal in its only game (Ellingham and Killian 30).

As anecdotes such as these suggest, Spicer was never able to commit himself in any meaningful way to the task of political organizing during his early years at Berkeley, despite his passion for leftist politics. However, Spicer's attitude toward political organization changed substantially when he became involved with the Mattachine. The meticulous minutes of the East Bay Chapter of the Mattachine Society, in combination with the correspondence of Gerard Brissette (who was elected the chapter's first area chair), offer a fascinating glimpse into Spicer's evolving political sensibilities as he played a part in the meetings of the East Bay Chapter, the statewide convention of 1953, and the bitter dispute that eventually led to the dissolution of the East Bay Chapter by the Mattachine's leadership. Tellingly, the archive of Spicer's engagement with the Mattachine contains few signs that he saw frontier allegory as a particularly compelling rhetorical mode for the organization. Rather, the frontier rhetoric of Spicer and his circle emerges with a new force in the months following the dissolution of the East Bay Chapter of the Mattachine and Spicer's consequent break with the society. The frontier became the figurative ground on which Spicer could imagine an alternative to the political failure he suffered when the Mattachine Society's most radical chapter collapsed under the threat of FBI investigation.

While archival evidence of Spicer's participation in the East Bay Chapter meetings doesn't appear until the meeting of April 20, 1953, the chapter, from its inception, was keenly aware of the necessity to maintain a fine balance between solidarity and respect for difference within its small coalition. Ken Burns, an activist involved with the Mattachine's LA-based leadership, wrote Gerry Brissette in the early days of the East Bay Chapter, responding to Brissette's anxieties about this issue in a paradoxical series of statements typical of the East Bay Chapter's image of itself at the time: "The organization should be bigger than any individual. This, of course, is not to say that the individual is not the most important part of the organization. However, we are working for the group as a whole" (Burns). Burns's anxiety came from the fact that the East Bay Chapter was an especially contentious and independently minded group—in no small part thanks to Spicer's contributions. As early as their second meeting, on April 6, 1953, it was clear that the East Bay Chapter was less than thrilled by the Mattachine's centralized power structure, which, at the time, concentrated power in the hands of five of the original founders, the so-called Fifth Order, all of whom lived in Los Angeles. As the minutes of that meeting put it, "We reserve the right not to have a fifth order. We reserve the right to be an autonomous group. (The feeling generally was that a fifth order system intimated dictatorial rule.)" ("Meeting Minutes, April 6, 1953"). Even as the group spoke up for local autonomy, the East Bay Chapter also seemed to endorse a general attempt to balance solidarity and difference, as this particularly poetic statement from the conclusion of the minutes of their second meeting attests: "All were in accordance with the general aims and purposes and quite eager to contribute their own potentialities.... Our organization is loose at present, but the general thought of the actively interested is of unification" ("Meeting Minutes, April 6, 1953").

In fact, however, the "loose organization" of the East Bay Chapter was to continue until its veritable dissolution in late 1953. The amorphous nature of the group seemed to be Brissette's primary concern in his correspondence with the LA leadership: in an April 26 letter, he goes so far as to bemoan his own election as area chairman as premature and blames a coalition of Spicer and his allies for electing a slate of representatives over-hastily:

> What I had in mind was a high level discussion group in which I could get to know better the leaders of the area, so that we could work together in better understanding and evolve the highly qualified Mattachine leaders I dream of. But unfortunately, under the influence of Paul and his friend, Jack Spicer, the meeting went far beyond any of my modest expectations, so

> that by the time the smoke had cleared, the group had elected an Area Council into existence with me as its chairman. (Brisette to Rowland, 26 April 1953)

The following months saw a continued and often futile attempt by Brissette to mediate between the LA leadership's desire to "evolve" "highly qualified Mattachine leaders" and a chapter, often egged on by Spicer, that was happy to "[contribute] their own potentialities" however they saw fit. Their meetings were a strange combination of grassroots political organizing and, as Robin Blaser put it, something "strikingly like present-day group therapy" (qtd. in Ellingham and Killian 48). Ellingham and Killian argue "the Mattachine offered Spicer a base of identity politics—a human face—that Spicer missed in his other radical connections" (ibid. 47). A close examination of Spicer's contribution to the East Bay Chapter meetings, however, reveals that what seemed to animate Spicer most about the Mattachine's unusual blend of the personal and the political was not that it "grounded" his politics in an authentic identity, but rather that it allowed him to pursue a more radical mode of queer politics precisely because the early Mattachine did *not* try to "ground" its community in a normative conception of identity. Instead, the Mattachine offered Spicer a space in which he could explore a radical politics that was not dominated by the notion that liberation required the sort of prescriptive attempt at class formation that Spicer and Blaser witnessed in the Trotskyist club.

While, as publications chair of the chapter, Spicer was helping to distribute *One* magazine and other literature advocating for the homosexual's essential assimilability into the mainstream culture, within Mattachine meetings he was advocating for an understanding of homosexuality that did not see sexual orientation as a static marker of identity, but rather a socially malleable phenomenon. As Kevin Killian notes in "Spicer and the Mattachine," and as the meeting minutes of the East Bay Chapter make even more explicit, Spicer argued vigorously against the growing consensus within the chapter that gay men should embrace their homosexuality as their essential identity as early in life as possible, instead suggesting that the Mattachine should work to promote the notion that humans are essentially bisexual and that both heterosexuals *and* homosexuals are socially conditioned to prefer one sex over the other. Killian notes Spicer's dubious historical analysis in advancing this argument in a discussion group meeting: minutes show that Spicer argued that he "believes children should be shaped toward bisexuality. Ex: Hawaii: in old days absolutely free of prejudice" (qtd. in Killian 35n31). While the last claim on indigenous Hawaiian life is obviously unfounded, the notion that the homo/hetero binary and its attendant prejudice is a product of European modernity rather than an essential feature of human society is one that has been borne out in contemporary postcolonial and Indigenous studies interventions in queer theory, such as Joseph Massad's *Desiring Arabs* and Mark Rifkin's *When Did the Indians Become Straight?*

Spicer often advocated, as an alternative to an obsession with the issue of the homosexual's relation to the mainstream, the question of the relationship between "in groups and out groups" within the Mattachine. He rejected the almost Marxist rhetoric of class formation advocated by many in the Mattachine leadership and argued for a more pluralist conception of the Mattachine community. Whereas Brissette's correspondence to the leadership often complains about the "queens" who he felt didn't understand the broader goals of the Mattachine's supposedly better educated leadership, Spicer spoke up for building a community that would seek to integrate "with the homosexual culture first, our relations with those who are belles, butches, etc" (Brissette to Rowland, 6 May 1953; "Meeting Minutes of the May 26, 1953"). Spicer is also the only recorded advocate in the chapter for the active recruitment of racial minorities into the East Bay Chapter. For the Mattachine leadership, the task of political organizing was about forging a normative "Mattachine character" that could properly represent "the homosexual" on the national stage, even if that meant a mode of political engagement that refused, by means of an indefinite deferral, a recognition of intersectionality, or solidarity with other minorities and political causes (Brissette to Rowland, 6 May 1953).

This rift that was developing following the 1953 convention between the East Bay Chapter and the leadership over the nature of community evolved in tandem with a much more concrete and immediate schism developing in the Mattachine thanks to anti-communist agitation spearheaded by a member of the San Francisco chapter named David Finn. Finn had threatened, at the constitutional convention, to "turn over the names of all in attendance [to the FBI] if the convention failed to reject the 'communistic' principles of the old leadership" (D'Emilio 85). Finn's point of view gained increasing support within the more assimilationist San Francisco chapter, until tensions came to a head at an area council meeting at which Spicer requested Brissette to call for Finn's immediate ouster from the society. The dispute over Finn's involvement ended acrimoniously, with the majority of the East Bay Chapter—including Spicer and Brissette—resigning en masse and under pressure (Killian 31). Ironically enough (since he never identified as a Communist), Spicer's experiment in organized political activism was thwarted by the same anti-Communist paranoia that forced him from Berkeley three years earlier.

One of Spicer's most prominent (and humorous) conflicts with the Mattachine leadership serves as a convenient segue into a discussion of how Spicer's political activism within the Mattachine Society translated into poetic practice (and frontier allegory) after his resignation. As publications chair of the East Bay Chapter, Spicer proposed that, instead of contributing to *One* (the Mattachine publication that now lends its name to the National Gay and Lesbian Archives), he start a new publication, local to the Bay Area, called *Two*. This brought a swift rebuttal from the LA leadership. Chuck Rowland, writing to Brissette, objects:

> [The idea of *Two*] seems utterly mad to me (with, perhaps, *Three* in Seattle, *Four* in Denver, *Five* in New York, *Sixty-nine* in Dallas).... The staff of *One* has performed a magnificent service in promoting the first publication of its kind in the U.S., and to issue another in competition with it seems to me the most unfortunate things that could happen. (Rowland)

However serious Spicer was about *Two*, he was certainly serious about the form of political organization it suggested: for Spicer, a *serially* organized Mattachine—decentralized yet still linked in a network—was clearly not the most unfortunate thing that could happen. For Spicer, solidarity did not have to mean a hierarchical structure and unified representation, but rather could be imagined more metonymically.

This political commitment to a social organization that respected alterity and fostered solidarity without imposing a singular identity on its subjects translated into Spicer's poetics over the course of the next year, as he went to work on his first "serial poem," *After Lorca*, which reflected on the life and death of another failed queer revolutionary. In a letter to Robin Blaser reproduced in Spicer's 1957 book *Admonitions*, Spicer reflected back on this period and the shift that occurred in his writing:

> Halfway through *After Lorca* I discovered I was writing a series of poems and individual criticism by anyone suddenly became less important [. . .] there is no single poem [. . .] Poems should echo and reecho against each other. They should create resonances. They cannot live alone any more than we can. (*My Vocabulary* 163)

While commentators have noted the formally iconoclastic nature of this striking formulation, insofar as it forces us to think differently about the relationship between poems, what has not been acknowledged is the extent to which these poetic formulations cleave so closely to Spicer's political thinking during his engagement with the Mattachine (see, e.g., Rasula 73). Just as Spicer rejected the notion that *One* should serve as a singular voice for the organization, he rejects the idea that the lyric can or should serve as a paean to the (supposedly) unified and singular subject.

This critical shift in Spicer's poetics occurred contemporaneously with his increasingly strident declarations of his own western regionalism. In the wake of his resignation from the Mattachine Society, Spicer moved out of California for a stint on the East Coast; it was during this time that he began to represent his poetic community as a cohesive movement with an identity firmly rooted in the West and its frontier past. It was also during these years, however, that Spicer's prejudices began to surface more frequently, in sharp distinction to the embrace of difference he espoused as an activist within the Mattachine.[3] In Boston, writing in collaboration with Blaser, Spicer conceived of a memoir entitled "The Playboys of the Last Frontier" that was intended to describe the years of poetic collaboration with Blaser and Robert Duncan in Berkeley and San Francisco, 1946–1955. This memoir, which was alternatively titled "Gunmen of the Last Frontier," was abandoned (like many of Spicer's prose projects) in its earliest stages, but its evocative titles are exemplary of the odd blend of camp and sincerity with which Spicer and his circle self-represented as "frontiersmen." In a laundry list of ideas for the project is the line "Sorry, no Jews" (Blaser and Spicer).

This affective identification with the frontier and the West pervades Spicer's letters to his West Coast poet friends during this period and is intermingled with the idiosyncratic vocabulary that he would later employ in both his poems and lectures to describe his poetic method. Writing to Allen Joyce from New York in July 1955, Spicer offers the following thoughts on his new city:

> New York is both better and worse than I suspected it would be. I hoped it would be frightening and it just isn't. The people seem so damnably innocent like the Americans that Henry James writes about. I hadn't realized how old California was.
>
> All the Westerners here know each other, even if they didn't there, and form an exotic foreign population. We are like Jews I think. But I suppose you know about this already.
>
> Like most primitive cultures, New York has no feeling for nonsense. Wit is as far as they can go. That is what I miss the most, other than you, and what is slowly pulling my identity apart. No one speaks Martian, no one insults people arbitrarily, there is, to put it most simply and leave it, no violence of the mind and of the heart, no one screams in the elevator. (Spicer to Joyce)

Of the many oddities of this passage, perhaps the most striking is the temporal and cultural inversion whereby New York becomes "primitive" and California becomes "old," upending the familiar Turnernian, progressive understanding of the development of the United States moving along an east-to-west trajectory (from "old" New York to the "virgin land" of the West). This temporal reframing of the West as old speaks to the fact that Spicer's frontier rhetoric was a mode of nostalgia, a rhetorical mode that speaks to Spicer's increasing longing, in his rhetoric of this period, for a community marked by Anglo ethnic purity. This temporal inversion is complicated, however, by the fact that it is "old" California that people perceive as full of nonsense (always a positive characteristic for the avant-gardist Spicer), with "a violence of the mind and of the heart"; whereas it is in "primitive" New York that people have the urbane wit of Henry James characters. This unusual vision of America is further complicated by Spicer's claim that westerners are like "an exotic foreign population" in New York. For Turner, the frontier becomes "more and more American" as it moves westward, farther from "the influence of old Europe," but every region, including the East Coast, "still partakes of [the] frontier characteristics" that were fostered during original settlement (Turner 34). For Spicer the difference between East and West Coast seems more categorical: westerners outside of the promised land are abjected "like Jews." The difference between residents of "the last frontier" of California and New Yorkers is not one of degree, but of kind: the New Yorkers are not simply less American, they are like citizens of another country, incapable of the affective and intellectual violence that could offer an alternative to normative American life.

If Spicer in some sense inverts the trajectory of the East to West development and rejects the national horizon of significance found in Turner's frontier narrative, he embraces an analogous mode of anxiety about the end of the frontier. In a letter from Boston to Myrsam Wixman, Spicer elaborated on his animus toward the East Coast:

> All the people I want to come back to are doomed people—people who will not accept the roles that God offers them—not doomed because they are Westerners but Westerners because they're doomed. New York is the only true reality. History someday will teach us that. You may not understand this part of it,

> being concerned with local problems, doomed problems—like how you live and how your heart manages to exist—but I have been among the hews of time and civilization. I have seen the emperor of Byzantium and wanted to spit in his face.
>
> It all comes down to this, honey. Nobody out here has a heart or a sleeping bag. Everybody knows where things are supposed to go and so there's no need for them. Your Bohemia (the SF-Berkeley Heart and Sleeping Bag Bohemia) is the last Bohemia the world will ever see. After that will merely be Chinamen and advertising. (Spicer to Wixman)

Here New York as Byzantium is pitted against the "Heart and Sleeping Bag Bohemia" of the West Coast; New York may be the "one true reality," but it is the nightmare that Spicer seeks to escape by returning to a West where romantic reenactments of frontier mobility are still close to the heart. Spicer's American tragedy pits an idealized frontier past against an inexorably advancing modernity, and as the ugly slur at the end of this passage indicates, Spicer saw "Eastern" modernity as a betrayal of his own ethno-cultural values.

It does not take much of an analogic leap to understand one reason why Spicer found the frontier a powerful mobilizing allegory for countercultural community following his resignation from the Mattachine Society. Spicer had a vision of the Mattachine as a "networked" assemblage of localities, "a single political community across separate jurisdictions" to which each local polity held only "a conditional type of loyalty" (to borrow Veracini's description of a settler "isopolity"). Spicer believed this community could nonetheless pose a radical challenge to the state's cultural and sexual norms. In that effort, Spicer failed (Veracini 70, 72).

The answer, for Spicer and his circle, was to attempt to evade the state and its norms rather than confront them. Their poetic "practice of the outside" became a figurative mode of escape. Several of his friends and acolytes moved to Vancouver, where, as poet George Stanley explains in an interview with Lewis Ellingham, "Robin [Blaser], and then Stan [Persky], and then myself went off to Vancouver and so we—I think we are kind of like the colonists who went off to found the colonies somewhere. You know, in the American imperialistic sense" (Stanley). These poets and Spicer referred to their artistic community as a "Pacific Republic" or "Pacific nation." Poet Stan Persky, also in conversation with Ellingham, said of the "Pacific Nation" that "we knew it was a mystical nation—but nonetheless we believed it had a reality. That this particular geographic space was coherent.... From Northern California through to British Columbia, including British Columbia" (Persky). Veracini notes that settler colonialism's transnational tendencies toward local autonomy are "constantly reconfigured in different settings and survive even the emergence and consolidation of a globalised international system of sovereign states after the Second World War" (Veracini 71). While Spicer's formation of a transnational literary community is certainly a quixotic example of this phenomenon, it is nonetheless a striking example of this political tradition in action.

It was during this later period in his career, too, that Spicer started publicly identifying himself as descended from Blackfoot Indians, a claim that his surviving brother believes to be almost certainly spurious.[4] Spicer's most notable public claim on Indigeneity—made in a 1965 interview at the end of a long rumination on California as a space of resistance to industrial capitalism—stands as an egregious example of the mode of "ventriloquism" Jodi Byrd identifies as endemic to so many formations of leftist intellectualism, in which "the left intellectual...steps forward to ventriloquize the speaking Indian by transforming the becoming- into *replacing*-Indian" (Byrd 16). This form of settler colonial ventriloquism is the inevitable apotheosis of any politics that imagines the path to freedom as a frontier movement.

Spicer's performance of a putatively Indigenous identity is only the most extreme example of his embrace of a settler colonial political tradition that emerged "precisely in the context of slavery and native expropriation," in the words of legal scholar Aziz Rana (Rana 14). Those historical "pioneers" who imagined the frontier as a space of escape from the state or capitalism more often than not accepted as a matter of course the Indigenous dispossession and the oppression of racialized exogenous labor that made such an "escape" possible. Likewise,

Spicer and his poetic circle often seemed blithely unaware of the contradictions between the radical politics they espoused and the casual misogyny, Indigenous erasure, anti-Semitism, and racism that inflected both their interpersonal relationships and their writing. We should recognize that Spicer's problematic qualities were not incidental to his celebrated poetics of "the outside," but rather constitutive of them.

To read Spicer's frontier allegory as grounded in a settler colonial political imaginary differentiates it from the "homonormative" or "homonationalist" rhetoric described by theorist Jasbir Puar (Puar xxvii). Spicer's frontier was not imagined as a space where a positive gay identity could be embraced within the framework of the U.S. nation-state, but rather as a queer space—albeit an exclusive one—in which normative categories of identity could be rejected. We should resist the binary logic that would force us to imagine Spicer's frontier allegories as either a radical rejection of their settler colonial origins or as symptomatic of the ideological interpolation of queer bodies into normative U.S. culture. Instead, we should recognize in Spicer's poetic frontiering a contradictory yet powerful allegory that attempts to articulate a vision for a radically inclusive politics even as it reinscribes certain specific aspects of the power structures it ought to have opposed. In our present moment, scholarship on avant-garde poetics still tends to equate anti-expressive poetics with anti-hegemonic politics, and queer anarchism is being theorized through the rhetoric of the "wild beyond." Recognizing the Janus-faced politics at the heart of Jack Spicer's poetics is an important step in the project of locating radical literary production and political rhetoric in relation to the structures of power that these discourses seek to transform.[5]

Notes

Portions of this essay are taken from *The Frontiers of Dissent: The Settler Colonial Imaginary in U.S. Literature After 1945* by Alex Trimble Young and are used by permission of the University of Nebraska Press (forthcoming fall 2019, University of Nebraska Press). The research undertaken for this chapter was supported by a grant from the Huntington-USC Institute on California and the West. The author would like to thank Kevin Killian, the staff at the ONE Archives, Mandeville Special Collections Library, and the Bancroft Library for their invaluable assistance in pursuing this research.

1. Several contemporary queer studies readings of Spicer have focused on how his camp aesthetic distances him from the sources of his collage-like poems. Unlike these readers, I do not read the campy aspects of Spicer's engagement with frontier rhetoric as an implicit critique that exceeds the more sincere aspects of his frontier nostalgia. See, e.g., Marie Damon, *The Dark End of the Street: Margins in American Vanguard Poetry* (U of Minnesota P, 1993), p. 144.
2. Among critics associated with western regionalism, Neil Campbell offers the most substantive reading of the "practice of the outside," representing Spicer's poetics as a particularly western cultural practice analogous to Deleuze and Guattari's "rhizomatic West," a writing practice that stands as "a strategy for opening up and scrutinizing established ideologies and languages, canonical practices and texts, resilient and official mythologies." *The Rhizomatic West: Representing the American West in a Transnational, Global, Media Age* (U of Nebraska P, 2008), p. 14.
3. In addition to the rhetoric documented here, it is important to note that, despite his anti-racist rhetoric in Mattachine meetings, Spicer's poetic circle was almost exclusively white and male.
4. In recorded remarks sent to Lewis Ellingham, Jack's brother Holt stated in 1983 that "I had heard some stories in the family that maybe there was Indian blood on one side of the family, or not. I don't know if this is a fact. But it was discussed on occasion. I always thought that it probably was more mythology than reality, but I certainly am not sure" (Holt Spicer).
5. Regarding queer studies and the concept of the wild, see Halberstam.

Bibliography

Blaser, Robin. "The Practice of the Outside." *The Fire: The Collected Essays of Robin Blaser*. U of California P, 2006, pp. 113–63.

Blaser, Robin, and Jack Spicer. Manuscript notes for "Playboys of the Last Frontier." Papers of Jack Spicer, The Bancroft Library, University of California, Berkeley, box 7, folder 5.

Brissette, Gerard. Letter to Chuck Rowland. 26 Apr. 1953. Mattachine Society Project Collection, Coll2008-016, ONE National Gay and Lesbian Archives, Los Angeles, California, box 1, folder 9.

———. Letter to Chuck Rowland. 6 May 1953. Mattachine Society Project Collection, Coll2008-016, ONE National Gay and Lesbian Archives, Los Angeles, California, box 1, folder 9.

Burns, Ken. Letter to Gerard Brissette. 9 June 1953. Mattachine Society Project Collection, Coll2008-016, ONE National Gay and Lesbian Archives, Los Angeles, California, box 1, folder 9.

Byrd, Jodi. *The Transit of Empire: Indigenous Critiques of Colonialism*. U of Minnesota P, 2011.

Davidson, Michael. *Guys Like Us: Citing Masculinity in Postwar Poetics*. U of Chicago P, 2003.
———. *The San Francisco Renaissance: Poetics and Community at Mid-Century*. New York, Cambridge UP, 1989.
D'Emilio, John. *Sexual Politics, Sexual Communities: The Making of a Homosexual Minority in the United States, 1940–1970*. U of Chicago P, 1998.
Ellingham, Lewis, and Kevin Killian. *Poet Be Like God: Jack Spicer and the San Francisco Renaissance*. Wesleyan UP, 1998.
Gizzi, Peter. "Jack Spicer and the Practice of Reading." Afterword to *The Collected Lectures of Jack Spicer*, Wesleyan UP, 1998.
Halberstam, Jack. "The Wild Beyond: With and for the Undercommons." Foreword to *The Undercommons: Fugitive Planning and Black Study*, by Fred Moten and Stefano Harney, Minor Compositions, 2013, pp. 2–13.
Katz, Daniel. *The Poetry of Jack Spicer*. Edinburgh UP, 2013.
Killian, Kevin. "Spicer and the Mattachine." *After Spicer: Critical Essays*, edited by John Emil Vincent, Wesleyan UP, 2011.
Massad, Joseph. *Desiring Arabs*. U of Chicago P, 2007.
"Meeting Minutes of the Tuesday, April 6th, 1953, Discussion Group." Mattachine Society Project Collection, Coll2008-016, ONE National Gay and Lesbian Archives, Los Angeles, California, box 4, folder 52.
"Meeting Minutes of the May 26, 1953, Discussion Group." Mattachine Society Project Collection, Coll2008-016, ONE National Gay and Lesbian Archives, Los Angeles, California, box 4, folder 52.
Persky, Stan. Interview with Lewis Ellingham. 1983. Mandeville Special Collections Library, University of California, San Diego, box 3, folder 9.
Puar, Jasbir. *Terrorist Assemblages: Homonationalism in Queer Times*. Duke UP, 2007.
Rana, Aziz. *Two Faces of American Freedom*. Harvard UP, 2010.
Rasula, Jed. "Spicer's Orpheus and the Emancipation of Pronouns." *Jack Spicer*, special issue of *boundary* 2, vol. 6, no. 1, Autumn 1977, pp. 51–102.
Rexroth, Kenneth. *An Autobiographical Novel*. Doubleday, 1966.
Rifkin, Mark. *When Did the Indians Become Straight?* New York, Oxford UP, 2010.
Rowland, Chuck. Letter to Gerard Brissette. 5 May 1953. Mattachine Society Project Collection, Coll2008-016, ONE National Gay and Lesbian Archives, Los Angeles, California, box 1, folder 9.
Spicer, Holt. Recorded remarks sent to Lewis Ellingham. 1983. Lewis Ellingham Papers, Mandeville Special Collections Library, University of California, San Diego, box 4, folder 4.
Spicer, Jack. Letter to Allen Joyce. 11 July 1955. Jack Spicer Letters to Allen Joyce, 1955–1956, The Bancroft Library, University of California, Berkeley.
———. Letter to Myrsam Wixman. 20 May 1956. Jack Spicer Papers, 1939–1982, The Bancroft Library, University of California, Berkeley, box 12, folder 7.

———. *My Vocabulary Did This to Me: The Collected Poems of Jack Spicer*. Edited by Peter Gizzi and Kevin Killian, Wesleyan UP, 2008.

———. "Pilgrimage." Undated fragment. Papers of Jack Spicer, 1939–1982, The Bancroft Library, University of California, Berkeley, box 20, folder 7.

Stanley, George. Interview with Lewis Ellingham. 1982. Lewis Ellingham Papers, Mandeville Special Collections Library, University of California, San Diego, box 4, folder 4.

Turner, Frederick Jackson. "The Significance of the Frontier in American History." *Rereading Frederick Jackson Turner*, edited by John Mack Farragher, Henry Holt, 1994, pp. 31–60.

Veracini, Lorenzo. *Settler Colonialism: A Theoretical Introduction*. Palgrave Macmillan, 2010.

Wixman, Myrsam. Letter to Jack Spicer. 19 Aug. 1955. Papers of Jack Spicer, 1939–1982, The Bancroft Library, University of California, Berkeley, box 4, folder 20.

III

LEFT IN TRANSIT

Success and Limitations

11

New Bohemias, California Style

The Intimate and Global Networks of Photographic Modernism

AUDREY GOODMAN

Although Henri Murger, French author and inventor of the notion of Bohemia in the mid-nineteenth century, proclaimed that "Bohemia only exists and is only possible in Paris," manifestations of resistance to bourgeois life and values in New York, San Francisco, Los Angeles, and Mexico City in the early twentieth century challenged such a provincial conception.[1] In North America, "Bohemia" became a set of sites at the boundaries of bourgeois life, places where ideas about art could be debated, and a means of designating artists' cosmopolitan sensibility, class consciousness, and opposition to corporate culture. The location of California at the western edge of America, geographically distant from European cultural capitals but open to ideas and artists migrating across the continent and around the Pacific Rim, intensified bohemian formations of artists asserting their autonomy within a globalizing bourgeois world system; its bohemian communities reveal many "ways in which California functions as a microcosm of national and global sociopolitical developments," epitomizing and often anticipating national and global trends (Salvioni 1–2). Far from isolated enclaves, urban bohemias in San Francisco and Los Angeles incorporated a wide range of cultural influences and generated distinctive aesthetic forms, often focused intently and closely on the landscape, the body, and the materiality of everyday life; they also negotiated tensions between artistic innovation and commercial patronage and advocated for the recognition of immigrants.

In this essay, I explore how groups of artists formed and intersected through the 1930s, paying particular attention to how their intimate associations and art responded to the emergence of the political Left in California and Mexico, redefined the practice of American modernism, and provided visual vocabularies for post–World War II political activism. I begin with an overview of the spaces that promoted bohemian cultures in each city from the 1910s through 1920s—sites such as neighborhoods, exhibition spaces, and arts institutions—and assess the relations between such informal associations and each city's developing public and political identities. Then I consider the private spaces in which intimate relations between photographers created productive conditions for aesthetic experimentation and political engagement, and argue that California modernism thrived due to these spatial arrangements and their many scales of association. Caroline Levine proposes in her recent book *Forms* that scholars in literary and cultural studies expand the study of form to include sociopolitical experience in order to "dissolve" the boundary between content and context (2); here I analyze both aesthetic and social arrangements to explore relations between communal patterns, innovations in visual art, and collective forms of protest. This method reveals patterns of creative collaboration at many levels. If "one of the principal challenges facing the study of global modernisms, as of any transnational cultural phenomenon, is the question of scale," as Harsha Ram argues in his analysis of the bohemian milieus of Paris, France, and Tiflis, Georgia (1372), a study of modernist bohemias requires close analysis of intimate, local, regional, national, and transnational formations and their intersections.

Photographers led the way toward new political and cultural perspectives in the 1920s and 1930s, a time when photography "played a crucial role in eliciting questions about the forms of ethical responsibilities and the promises of innovative aesthetics" (Gabara 1). The lives and work of West Coast modernist photographers not only linked European and immigrant experience with an emerging bohemian network but also introduced ways of seeing that shaped and interrogated the relations between artist and subject, observer and observed; the camera, once considered a tool for the objective recording of visual facts, "came to serve as one of modernity's most powerful emblems of the subjectivity of perception and knowledge" (North 3, 11). Edward Weston was "the prime modernist photographer on the west coast, if not the nation," William Deverell confirms in his introduction to *LA's Early Moderns: Art, Architecture, Photography* (12), and the camera networks linking Weston with the women photographers he mentored, and from whom he learned, serve as a case study in the emergence of a distinctive regional aesthetics and the mobile and improvisational nature of West Coast bohemian life, art, and politics. Weston taught and was inspired by Margrethe Mather, Tina Modotti, and Alma Lavenson, among others, photographers he met through camera clubs in Los Angeles, gallery spaces in Mexico City, personal relations, and the group f.64. Such collaborations led to an artistic practice committed to exploring the expressive potential of the body, the function of surfaces and edges as routes of access to erotic or irrational knowledge, the city as public political space, and the autonomy of art. The relationships between Weston, Mather, and Modotti exemplify the importance of attending to the smallest scales of association when analyzing the impact of California's new bohemias, because through their intimate relationships they taught each other to look at the material conditions of everyday life, to put their own bodies at the center of their experience, and to visualize collective formations within the urban and natural environments of the U.S West and Mexico. Through examining the various and interconnected lives and works of these major modernist photographers, we can see how such exchanges of ideas, images, bodies, and places actively challenged bourgeois values and constituted new bohemias, California style.[2]

Metropolitan Bohemias

Raymond Williams famously argued in "Metropolitan Perceptions and the Emergence of Modernism" that "the most important general element of the innovations in form is the fact of immigration to the metropolis" (Williams 45). He claimed that new and intimate encounters among artists speaking different languages and working in different styles led to the transformation of aesthetic and social forms; through immersion in the "novel and dynamic common environment from which many of the older forms were obviously distant, the artists and writers and thinkers of this phase found the only community available to them: a community of the medium; of their own practices" (45). This is, of course, the cosmopolitan and "genuine society within a society" that Pierre Bourdieu identified as bohemia's social form in nineteenth-century Paris, constituted by those "young people aspiring to live by art, and separated from all other social categories by the art of living they are in the course of inventing" (Bourdieu 55). If "there are decisive links between the practices and ideas of the avant-garde movements of the twentieth century and the specific conditions and relationships of the twentieth-century metropolis" (Williams 37), then we can productively examine the earlier California avant-garde through "the new and specific location of the artists and intellectuals of this movement within the changing cultural milieu" (44) of San Francisco and Los Angeles.

In both cities, immigration and rapid urban development created commercial, artistic, and private spaces where workers, artists, photographers, patrons, and audiences could meet, enabling the formation of creative networks that later led to political engagement. Art historians have noted the absence of traditional art markets in San Francisco, a distinctive feature of the cultural field that promoted artistic autonomy and independent publishing and sustained artists' belief in their power to resist East Coast interests and institutions. Historians such as Richard Cándida Smith have located "the ideological, socioeconomic, and historical roots" of the region's political ferment and the rise of the New Left in the Beat culture of the 1950s and 1960s. Others have looked back to the politics of San Francisco's major revolutionary movements (such as the Wobblies and the labor protests leading to the Great Strike in 1934),[3] or to the resistance Los Angeles artists mounted to early twentieth-century boosters intent on manufacturing a conservative future that would protect bourgeois interests.[4] However, the beginnings of West Coast bohemia can be found much earlier, in the formation of official clubs and unofficial spaces; as Smith argues, in California the line between avant-garde and popular cultures "took place earliest, most clearly, and most systematically" (xx), with ideas and institutions developing at the margins becoming mainstream much faster than elsewhere. This early twentieth-century avant-garde set in motion a process of interrogating how westerners saw their social world that would intensify with the rise of the popular front in the 1930s.

A key example of the formation, dissemination, and assimilation of bohemian values in the West can be found in the history of San Francisco's Bohemian Club. Established in 1872 as an open and democratic organization where "workers in the arts" could meet, it soon became a pillar of the city's cultural establishment. According to Oscar Lewis's classic account *Bay Window Bohemia:*

> In its beginning its members met at different restaurants of the area; later they shared quarters for a year or two with a carefree group who—appropriately, it would seem—called themselves the Jolly Corks. Finally, in 1877, the Bohemians moved into rooms of their own on Pine Street, above the California Market. (72)

Lewis provides an extensive list of the writers and artists who either belonged to the club or joined temporarily when they passed through the city; the visitors then "spread abroad the fame of the town's unique literary and artistic club" (73). When it acquired a redwood grove north of the city for its summer retreats, it became known for its original productions created by members who otherwise "earned their living as doctors, lawyers, merchants, artists, and the like" (74). The Bohemian Club thus quickly epitomized the type of association Max Weber defines as a "metropolitan plutocracy," as membership constituted "a ticket of ascent" into the city's ruling class, while the club's activities "served to diffuse and to maintain the bourgeois capitalist business ethos among the broad strata of the middle classes" (Weber 308–9). To maintain high social status in San Francisco, businessmen needed to promote art, and by cultivating the relation between artists and professionals, the Bohemian Club soon became an inextricable "part of the city's heritage."

In her memoir *Where I Was From*, Joan Didion also tells of the club's rapid shift from an informal alliance of writers to a strategic association of artists and businessmen, confirming the rapid incorporation of bohemian values into San Francisco's dominant culture. "The Bohemian Club of San Francisco was founded, in 1872, by members of the city's working press, who saw it both as a declaration of unconventional or 'artistic' interests and as a place to get a beer and a sandwich" once the writers had met their deadline and put their papers to press (83). Original members, such as Frank Norris, Joaquin Miller, George Sterling, Ambrose Bierce, Jack London, John Muir, and Joseph LeConte, epitomized "real," artistic men, but very soon they realized that money was essential for membership. By the 1910s, many of them had left the club, replaced by a new group of artists, writers, and philanthropists eager to support the arts and camp at "Bohemian Grove." San Francisco's Bohemian Club was already becoming the establishment, Didion contends, and by the 1970s "one in five resident members and one in three non-resident members... was listed in *Standard & Poor's Register of Corporations, Executives, and Directors*" (84). Didion came to see that

> the transformation of the Bohemian Club from a lively if frivolous gathering of local free spirits to a nexus of the nation's corporate and political interests in many ways mirrored a larger transformation, that of California itself from what it had been, or from what its citizens preferred to believe that it had been, to what it is now, an entirely dependent colony of the invisible empire in which those corporate and political interests are joined. (87)

While the club may have started as an improvised and miscellaneous association of men at the margins of the city's dominant masculine corporate culture, it soon became not only complicit with that culture but a way to "compensate" for its demands; as Joanna Levin puts it, the club, "in the name of Bohemia, proposed to supplement or transcend bourgeois work, gender roles, family relations, racial identities, and spiritual life" (Levin 204).

Other gathering places in San Francisco promoted more egalitarian and cosmopolitan communities of artists and audiences—and provided greater opportunities for women artists. For the thousands of Italians in San Francisco (almost forty-five thousand first- and second-generation immigrants were recorded by 1920), churches anchored their neighborhoods and hosted cultural events like Italian national holidays and religious celebrations. Banks, pharmacies, bakeries, and hotels served to sustain Italian traditions and support the city's Italian-American communities.[5] In the early 1900s, other "ethnic" neighborhoods, such as Chinatown and the Mexican or "Spanish" Quarter, also constituted some of the "new and specific locations" Williams described as formative for artists and intellectuals, even as they became commodified tourist attractions, thanks in part to the work of local writers. By exploring some of these neighborhoods and conveying his impressions in his published "Bohemian Papers," Bret Harte substantially invented a West Coast "Bohemia" for readers and tourists, and Frank Norris set scenes in *The Third Circle* and *Blix* in ethnic restaurants to dramatize the role contact with other cultures played in his protagonists' quests for self-definition and romance.[6]

Those who fashioned themselves as bohemians might congregate in particular neighborhoods, but they also moved freely from one part of the city to another, seeking out affordable restaurants, specialized performance spaces, or artistic clubs. For middle-class and lower-class San Franciscans, ethnic restaurants offered the best access to the heterogeneity and spectacle of metropolitan experience. Visitors seeking to brush against local artists consulted guidebooks to find places like Coppa's Italian Restaurant, "the most favored den of bohemia."[7] At Coppa's, writers and painters gathered to talk, joke, and otherwise perform for other patrons, and the regulars took advantage of the establishment's willingness to let them run a tab. Jessica Sewell, who researched the everyday habits of women in early twentieth-century San Francisco, claims that Coppa's was the "most prominent bohemian restaurant," a place where a single woman could arrive by herself and order wine (86–87)—in great part because everyone else was paying attention to the central table, the elaborate murals, and the wall inscriptions that created the restaurant's distinct atmosphere. Additional "bohemian" restaurants like Luna's (Mexican) and Sanguinetti's (Italian) "served an ordinary lower-middle-class clientele as well as bohemians and society folks" who found excitement in sharing tables with writers and painters, impersonating artists, and tasting exotic dishes (Sewell 87, 89). These restaurants catered both to upper-class thrill seekers and to working men and women seeking camaraderie and affordable tastes of home. In San Francisco the negotiation of "intricate processes of liberation and alienation, contact and strangeness, stimulation and standardization" (Williams 45, 47) was simultaneously formalized by the Bohemian and other clubs and accomplished informally in "bohemian" neighborhoods.

In Los Angeles, commerce and culture were intertwined from the start. Due to early and relentless marketing, Los Angeles seemed "an artistic and cultural backwater at the same time that the visual arts became central to local political debate and scrutiny" (Shrank 13). Lacking the "bohemian" neighborhoods of San Francisco, artists and émigrés found their own public and private spaces. Downtown restaurants, like Musso & Frank and the Brown Derby, and clubs, like the Author's Club and, later, the Zamorano Club, initially provided alternative spaces to those controlled by the city's power brokers, such as the California Club on Flower Street in downtown LA, which "was then and still is," according to Didion, "the heart of Southern California's old-line business establishment, the Los Angeles version of [San Francisco's] Bohemian and Pacific Union Clubs" (97). Along with restaurants, bookstores constituted the center of Southern California's bohemian culture—anticipating the revolutionary effect of City Lights in San Francisco in the 1950s. Shops that provided meeting, performance, and gallery spaces included Louis Epstein's Pickwick Bookshop (where Fitzgerald, Faulkner, Chandler, and Huxley were all patrons); Stanley Rose's two stores (one next door to Musso & Frank); and Vroman's in Pasadena. Adam Clark Vroman established his bookstore in 1894 and also used it as a Kodak agency; by the 1920s, it was the West's largest bookstore for trade books. Complementing Vroman's emphasis on current books and photography was Ernest Dawson's antiquarian book business, operating by catalog and through stores at Broadway and then South Grand Avenue, where Dawson worked hard to keep his wide-ranging stock turning over into the hands of curious browsers eager to encounter and recycle cultural materials. Finally, Zeitlin's bookstore, located first down town and then in Echo Park, a prominent bohemian neighborhood in the 1920s and 1930s, generated the most vital "circle" of professional and amateur painters, engravers, photographers, composers, animators, and writers. According to Kevin Starr, while the group was not associated with "a movement or an ideology in the formal sense of the term," it created "a sense of movement and place, of things happening or about to happen in literature, architecture, the fine and performing arts, and scholarship. It was a bohemia with a left wing and a right, with dissident and established elements intersecting within the Zeitlin radius" (Starr, *Material Dreams* 311).[8]

While such bohemian spaces promoted the complex and mobile alliances that shaped California's metropolitan perceptions, modernist aesthetics, and activism, the intimate relationships between photographers and the practice of photography itself also played a crucial role in foregrounding the politics of gender and place and in making visible immigrant and exile sensibilities. California's art and photography clubs provided opportunities for amateur artists to mingle, exchange ideas about art, and plan for the public display of their work. The San Francisco Art Association offered classes and exhibition space as early as 1871 in rooms next to the Bohemian Club (Lewis 229–30). The California Camera Club, founded in San Francisco in 1892, and the California Pictorialists, founded in 1894, provided social and professional support for working and aspiring photographers. Similar groups soon emerged in Southern California. These camera clubs developed out of amateur enthusiasms and were usually founded by affluent men, but they became more populist and accessible to women with the rise of the Kodak camera and the expansion of membership to include professionals. When the California Camera Club changed its criteria for membership to include anyone with an interest in photography and began to organize exhibits and produce magazines to share practices and knowledge of the craft with a wide readership, it suddenly became "a livelier group...and it soon lured most of the members of the older club into its own ranks" (Mann 15), claiming a membership of four hundred after two years. Members exchanged work with those in other clubs, held popular monthly slide programs, and ventured out on weekend excursions.[9] These informal associations created improvised communities of artists within and beyond California's metropolitan centers.

California Camera Networks

It was during a Los Angeles Camera Club outing to Griffith Park in 1913 that Margrethe Mather met Edward Weston; subsequently, they formed the Camera Pictorialists, designated "for serious camera artists only," the next step in developing a bohemian community based on a shared commitment to the practice of art. Weston "fell in love with art and with Margrethe Mather at the same time," according to Nancy Newhall, "and for some eight years could not separate them. It was a strange and troubling love" (Weston xix), as well as an intensely productive partnership. Weston explored his desire for his fellow photographer through a series of elaborately staged portraits: Mather modeled and masqueraded for him beginning in 1913, playing such roles as Empress Carlotta; an Asian figure posed with pine branch, fan, or plum blossoms (as in *Margrethe Mather in Chinese Slippers with Feather Fan*, 1923); or a nude bather in repose (*Margrethe Mather on Sand, Redondo Beach*, 1923).[10] A notorious proponent of aesthetic autonomy, Weston eschewed most political alliances, but he demonstrated through his photography of Mather and the California environment his opposition to the commercial values of bourgeois portraiture and a rigorous commitment to recognizing and protecting the West Coast's landscapes.

Mather's personal history, ambitions, and desires, however, remained less visible. Historian Beth Gates Warren claims that after leaving her Mormon parents in Salt Lake City for San Francisco's Nob Hill in 1910, Mather worked as a prostitute and continued to do so in Los Angeles, where "her favorite haunts were the lobbies of the posh Alexandria and Lankershim Hotels" downtown (Warren, *Margrethe Mather* 13). She lived near the top of Bunker Hill, on West Fourth Street, probably supported by her "mentor and protector," and lover,

Florence Reynolds (16–17). Mather's location in the center of Bunker Hill, her connections with a wide range of political activists (including the labor activist Emma Goldman), and her association with writers and actors made her an ideal person to introduce the more conservative Weston to bohemian Los Angeles and to establish photography as an enterprise that linked aesthetics and politics. Around 1916, three years after meeting Weston, Mather set up a studio in her carriage house and made rapid artistic progress. Starting in 1918, she worked with Weston in Glendale, met dancer Ramiel McGehee, made strikingly composed portraits of another friend, Chinese poet Moon Kwan, became acquainted with Charlie Chaplin and infatuated with actress Florence Deshon—and received notice that four of her photographs would be exhibited at the prestigious Pittsburgh Salon. Together Mather and Weston were photographed by Imogen Cunningham and made portraits of the Marion Morgan Dancers, Carl Sandburg, and Max Eastman on the beach; these prints were signed by both of them, marking Weston's only public collaboration.

Between 1919 and 1921, Weston and Mather created intimate portraits that reveal their ongoing experiments with form and perspective—and dramatize their emerging differences in ways of seeing interior spaces and each other's bodies. Some of Weston's portraits of Mather feature the style and compositional elements of Japanese woodblock prints and Noh stage designs, following models Arthur Dow presented in a lecture in 1919. In the photograph *Epilogue* [Margrethe Mather], 1919, for instance, Weston positions and illuminates a vase of flowers so as to amplify the size of its shadow, overpowering Mather, who is posed in the lower left corner of the frame with an open fan. By combining soft-focus technique with dramatic stylization, this work casts Mather as a flattened, enigmatic figure. By contrast, Mather's slightly later portrait *Edward Weston*, 1921, captures her partner and mentor just emerging out of the shadows into the frame of a doorway.[11] While Weston's position in the frame alludes to a private sanctuary above, the soft focus and tonal subtlety of this image communicates an interior space shared by subject and observer, and Weston's facial expression indicates his anticipation of a continued conversation. Even as these portraits reveal how Weston and Mather shared working methods and an aesthetic sensibility that sought to integrate influences from other media into their compositions, Weston's static arrangement of his model and Mather's seemingly candid image display striking differences in their approaches to framing the other's body and representing their intimacy.

In 1921, however, the personal and working relationship between Mather and Weston suddenly changed from that of lovers and model/artist to that of an "art partnership"; it was also the year that Weston met Modotti. When Weston left for Mexico in 1923, Mather managed his Glendale studio but returned to work in her own space on Bunker Hill. Perhaps in response to this break, Mather's work in the mid-1920s pushed earlier than Weston's against the conventions of the bourgeois portrait and the still life; neither pictorialist nor realistic, Mather's images heightened the artificial elements that structure her viewer's way of seeing objects and bodies, manipulating scale and adjusting the frame to heighten the tension between model and background. In *Semi-Nude* [Billy Justema Wearing Kimono], 1923, she playfully centers the image on her model's belly button to bring the viewer's attention to the body's origin and the circular repetitions in the kimono's pattern. Justema's hyperextended wrists create a sharper angle, testing the balance of ease and tension. While Mather posed nude for Weston, here Justema is "semi-nude"; the extended fingers of his left hand barely secure the kimono's fabric to his skin. Mather's portraits and nudes from this period are striking for the ways that they either locate their subjects at the corner or bottom of the image or move in very close. She also reveals the distinctive individuality of her subjects through composition, focus, and gesture, building layers of intimacy into the images.

Along with such magnification of the body's surfaces, Mather continued to experiment with form through studies and arrangements of objects like clam shells, combs, jelly molds, and fans. In a project that Mather and Justema called "Exposé of Form," she rendered natural and mass-produced objects into vibrant formations, revealing the affective power of contact with the modern physical world. For example, *Fan Strip*, 1930, aligns fans along a vertical axis while heightening the contrast between the jagged edges of each blade and the plaid surface beneath. In *Jelly Moulds*, 1930, the clustered arrangement animates manufactured forms into a lifelike bouquet, while *Japanese Combs*, 1930, heaps and layers the combs to suggest a texture like handwoven cloth. Mather also explored the expressive possibilities of gesture, creating images that isolate a single hand, arrange hands into a stylized grasp, or capture the beginnings of a caress. With her photographs from this later period, Mather thoroughly explored the tensions that arise at points of contact between bodies, objects, and environments and made such private interrogations visibly public. Such fascination with sites where interiority and exteriority meet—whether located in urban spaces or in the imagination of migrants, immigrants, and exiles—would become defining features of literary Los Angeles as well, evident in such key works of the late 1930s and early 1940s as Nathanael West's *The Day of the Locust*, John Fante's *Ask the Dust*, and Bertolt Brecht's *Journals*.

As Tina Modotti's itinerant creative life intersected with Weston's, her work provided another demonstration as to how intimate exchanges redefined the symbolic significance of gendered and working bodies. A first-generation Italian immigrant from Udine, Italy, Modotti became an actress and model in San Francisco, a textile artisan in Los Angeles, a photographer and political activist in Mexico City, and an exile in Germany, Russia, and Spain. In San Francisco, she met and fell in love with an exemplary California bohemian, Roubaix de l'Abrie Richey. They lived in North Beach, an educated and hardworking immigrant community, a center for Italian American music and theater, and the city's unofficial Bohemia. Italian theater groups flourished there, beginning in 1905 with the legendary performances of Neapolitan opera singer Antonietta Pisanelli at the Apollo Theater and Enrico Caruso's first performance at the Tivoli Opera House, located downtown just north of Market Street. This was the neighborhood endorsed in 1914 by the guide *Bohemian San Francisco* as a place that would reverse capitalist values: "Go there, and you learn why San Francisco is a Bohemian city. You will find out that so many things you thought important are not at all worth while" (qtd. in Albers 24).

Modotti's acting appearances in Italian plays in 1917 and 1918 at the San Francisco Liberty and Washington Theaters marked the beginning of her stage career, which also brought her roles in Ibsen's *Ghosts* and Niccodemi's *La nemica*. When she "married" Richey, the Italian newspaper *L'Italia* reported the wedding in order to account for her lack of recent roles. Richey, meanwhile, painted and wrote poetry, searching for the best medium for his aesthetic ideas.

Seeking new opportunities for their creative work, Modotti and Richey moved to Los Angeles in 1918, and there the couple encountered different kinds of bohemian spaces. They joined informal gatherings at architect Rudolph Schindler's home and also created their own cosmopolitan circle, holding frequent soirées for artists, performers, and photographers. Together the Richeys "gathered around them a circle of bohemian spirits," such as Weston, who had recently transformed himself into "a fashionable bohemian," wearing "knickers, a soft blouson shirt…a pince-nez, walking stick, and cape" (Warren, *Margrethe Mather* 15); Mather; dramatist, film, and photography critic Sadakichi Hartmann; British poet John Cooper Powys; and Mexican poet Ricardo Gómez Robelo, who became director of the Department of Fine Arts in Mexico under the supervision of José Vasconcelos. They thrived as members of Los Angeles's fluid but marginal community of artists and experimented with many forms of art. Richey adapted traditional batik techniques to design his own fabrics, "tapestries of illusion" used on film sets (Hooks 35). Modotti made costumes and styled dolls; she also continued to pursue her acting career, working at MGM and performing in three silent movies between 1920 and 1922. While she neither wrote nor practiced photography during this period, she inhabited the generative environment of Los Angeles's bohemian artists, absorbed the city's literary and visual cultures, and prepared to extend and transform the aesthetic practices of its most innovative practitioners of modernist photography, Weston and Mather.

When she followed Richey to Mexico City in 1922, Modotti discovered rich indigenous cultures and new artistic models, and she came to know those artists and activists engaged in creating Mexico's modern, postrevolutionary cultural identity, as did other North American and European women artists and writers like Katherine Anne Porter, Anita Brenner, Frances Toor, and Leonora Carrington. Modotti found in Mexico more powerful cultural networks linking artists and audiences that encouraged affiliations—and fostered obligations—beyond those of family, friends, or nation.[12] Although Richey became fatally ill with smallpox and died soon after his arrival, Modotti stayed, pursued her own photography, and become a major figure in the Mexican Communist Party. She organized an exhibit of Weston's photographs, and in 1923 they set up a photography studio and a common household. In their first year together in Mexico City, Modotti and Weston attended many dinner parties hosted by Americans Oscar and Beatrice Braniff ("interesting mélanges of money, intellect, and radicalism all garnished with a good sprinkling of posing," according to Argentieri 74); associated with muralists Lola Cueto, Diego Rivera, and José Orozco; and socialized with Vasconcelos and Gómez Robelo. But they "also worked hard and took their photography very seriously," Margaret Hooks insists (8).

As in the working relationship between Mather and Weston, Modotti and Weston developed distinctive styles as they posed for each other, Modotti nude on the roof of their building and Weston fully clothed, often next to his camera. In such photographs as *Nude, Tina Modotti*, 1924, Weston flaunts the strength and erotic appeal of Modotti's body as he displays his mastery of composition and tonality. In *Tina on the Azotea*, 1924, Modotti props herself on a woven blanket, her weight on her elbows; she projects her hips and buttocks into the viewer's space, her body contorted into a pyramid. In this portrait's play with exposure and concealment, and with organic and architectural forms, Weston reveals the essential role Modotti played in his own efforts to develop a photographic language at once pure and capable of sublimating emotion and desire. Meanwhile, in addition to posing as a model, Modotti was learning to manage a dark room, make portraits, compose landscapes, and find her political voice. They both exhibited work at a show at the Palacio de Minería in 1924, inaugurated by President Obregón and attended by Diego Rivera; Modotti showed ten prints and Weston won first prize (Argentieri 72–73). At the same time, Modotti was preparing herself for a more politically active role through and beyond her art. She translated anti-fascist articles written in Italian and contributed "street photography" to *El Machete*, the radical newspaper founded by Mexican muralists and other artists, and it was while at the newsroom located next to party headquarters that she met Cuban revolutionary Julio Antonio Mella (Folgarait 84; Hooks 147). She also joined International Workers' Aid, the International Red Aid, and the Anti-Imperialist League; soon she was delivering public addresses, leading meetings, and heading the local organizing committee.

For Weston, photography was a means to explore the relations between visual and other kinds of knowledge that he described in his writing as confined to matters of craft or aesthetics; he claimed that in his hands, the camera "transformed" facts "from things *seen* to things *known*" in a universal, objective sense (Weston, *Daybooks* II 241). By the early 1920s, Weston had already developed compositional strategies for controlling the relation between subject and viewer, and he extended his technical mastery in such works as *Tres Ollas de Oaxaca*, 1926, and *Two Swan Gourds*, 1924. For a time Modotti aligned herself with the avant-garde Estridentistas, a group inspired by Italian futurism and committed to the celebration of industrial innovation, machines, telecommunications, and spatial geometry, and she continued to approach modernist and revolutionary subjects from a variety of angles and scales, thus incorporating into her photography "the elements of strangeness and distance, indeed of alienation" (45) that Williams identified as the constitutive creative condition of metropolitan modernism. Modotti's work in Mexico reveals techniques that allowed her to isolate the figures and symbols of Mexico's class struggle, communicate the force of collective formations, and visualize the power of indigenous women. While she learned from Weston how to work close up, Modotti chose subjects explicitly charged with political significance, as in *Bandolier, Corn, Sickle*, 1927, the year she joined the Community Party.

When she worked in Mexico City, Modotti also explored the power of perspective to bring attention to the urban environment and to the transformative political power of the masses. She came to demonstrate the pleasure of form learned from Weston while experimenting with ways the camera might provide access to the affective dimensions of urban and technological modernity. Rubén Gallo claims that Modotti was "the first photographer in Mexico to view photography as a radically new form of aesthetic representation" and "deployed techniques such as close-ups, sharp focus, and oblique perspectives that could only be achieved with a mechanical instrument" (Gallo 232). Some of Modotti's most famous photographs celebrate the city's built environment from below, as if grounding the viewer's perspective in the body while elevating her eye to see wires above, those technological means of connection slicing through and beyond the clouds (*Telephone Wires, Mexico*, 1925). Other photographs survey the urban scene from above, such as those of a May Day procession taken from the rooftop apartment of her friend, painter Pablo O'Higgins (Paul Higgins). The perspective of *Workers' Parade*, 1926 (fig. 11.01), unifies this formation of agricultural workers and secures the distance from the crowd that allows the viewer to make sense of the scene. As it surveys and blurs their nearly identical sombreros, their proximity to one another, and their common ways of moving, the image creates a visual vocabulary for expressing class solidarity. It also reveals Modotti's emerging leftist activism through the way it draws the viewer into its social and spatial fields, demanding that viewer engage with the procession and recognize the city street as a political stage.

Throughout their partnership, Weston and Modotti professed devotion to pure art but lived and embraced many contradictions. "I consider myself a photographer, nothing more," Modotti wrote in her only published manifesto, "On Photography," which appeared in the 1929 issue of *Mexican Folkways;* "if my photographs differ from that which is usually done in this field it is precisely because I try to produce not art but honest photographs, without distortions or manipulations" (qtd. in Heron and Williams 260). She protested against photographers who try to produce "artistic" effects by "imitating other mediums of graphic expression" and instead create an inferior "hybrid product." She concluded by defending photography's value

FIGURE 11.01. Tina Modotti, *Workers' Parade*, 1926. Courtesy of Throckmorton Fine Art, New York

in terms of its ability to create a true document capable of recording life "in all its aspects."

Modotti's perception of cultural and class differences in Mexico had awakened her to her responsibility as an artist, and she expressed this emerging political consciousness through the photographs she made in Tehuantepec, Oaxaca.[13] She wrote to Weston in 1929 that she felt an obligation "to the country to show, not so much what I have done here, but especially *what can be done*, without recurring to colonial churches and *charros* and *chinas poblanas*" (Modotti to Weston, 17 Sept. 1929, qtd. in Folgarait 135). Her new way of working with "snapshots" in Tehuantepec sought a more honest relation with her moving subjects. Several images show women with their backs to the camera, either walking quickly away or immersed in activity (see, e.g., *Woman with Child at Market Carrying Basket*, ca. 1929, and *Children in River*, ca. 1929). Others depict market or fiesta scenes, clearly rendering the photographer a distant and impersonal observer (*Fiesta in Juchitán, Oaxaca, Mexico*, 1927–29). Still other photographs from Tehuantepec simultaneously intensify women's associations with traditional artifacts, such as ollas and the painted gourds called *jicapexle*, and assert women's independence and mobility.

Perhaps the finest example of Modotti's later work is *Tehuantepec Type*, ca. 1929, a portrait that focuses intently on the woman's dress and face while also drawing the viewer's attention to the shape, volume, and intricate decoration on the *jicapexle* (fig. 11.02). Unlike Weston's portraits of Modotti, this portrait maintains a modest but compelling distance from its subject and shows the woman looking into the distance, poised to walk on. By contrast, the *Self-portrait, Tehuantepec* that Modotti made at about the same time projects a more tentative claim to belonging. Posing herself in a costume against an adobe wall, Modotti appears relaxed but not fully comfortable, trying out an identity rather than fully inhabiting it. In the interval between Mella's assassination in Mexico City in January 1929 (which led to an intense period of police scrutiny and incriminating newspaper reports) and her own deportation to Germany in February 1930 (in the wake of suspicions that she conspired to kill the newly inaugurated president, Pascual Ortiz Rubio), Modotti struggled to define her purpose and her identity. Her final letters to Weston from Mexico in September 1929 and February 1930 continue to question how Mexican culture could be visualized honestly, without the interfering ego of the photographer or the official narratives of the government, even as they praise the support given by friends throughout her ordeal and her thirteen days in jail. Once in Berlin, Modotti bemoaned the lack of such a network, recounting to Weston her vain efforts to make arrangements with other photog-

FIGURE 11.02. Tina Modotti, *Tehuantepec Type* (woman holding bundle on head), c. 1929. Gelatin silver print, 8¼ × 7⅜". Courtesy of the Museum of Modern Art, New York.

raphers to share darkroom and studio space (Modotti to Weston, 23 May 1930, in Heron and Williams 257–60). She resisted offers to do newspaper work, struggled to keep up with current styles of "propaganda pictures," and failed to find a new artistic direction: "I feel there must be something for me but I have not found it yet," she confessed to Weston. "And in the meantime the days go by and I spend sleepless nights wondering which way to turn and where to begin.... If only I had somebody with whom to tell all my troubles, I mean somebody who could understand them" (259). Without the extensive and intimate connections that supported her life and art in San Francisco, Los Angeles, and Mexico City, Modotti could not sustain her transformative political vision.

Seeing Straight, California Style

My last example of how bohemian spaces, photographic networks, and intimate relations intersected and contracted to generate a distinctive regional aesthetics also expressive of opposition to commercial culture and global capitalism revolves around the formation of Group f.64 in San Francisco in the 1930s. The idea for the group and its name emerged at a party at the 683 Brockhurst Gallery in Oakland; after trying out several names, the group settled on Ansel Adams's suggestion to adopt the term used for the diaphragm setting that produces the maximum depth of field and the greatest image clarity. Adams also liked the design of the name as written: "that beautiful f followed by a 6 and 4," he exclaimed, as he drew out the curves in the air (Heyman 252). Weston noted in a *Daybook* entry that the group's primary purpose was to stimulate "interest in real photography" and support new talent. "The original plan was to rent a room in S. F. and give a series of exhibits," he wrote; but eventually the photographers agreed to exhibit at the M. H. de Young Memorial Museum, out of consideration for director Lloyd Rollins. Weston continued, "Some have expressed astonishment that I should join a group, having gone my own way for years. But I see it as purely educational. We are all friends, free from politics; and I have no desire to be the founder of a cult!" (Weston, *Daybooks* II 264–65). At a time when other West Coast photographers used a documentary style to dignify workers and protest against economic injustice, Group f.64 resisted both commercial tastes and the influence of politics and social realism with a renewed assertion of artistic autonomy.

While photo-historians such as Beaumont Newhall have described f.64 as an "informal society," a provisional association of like-minded photographers (Heyman, Alinder, and Rosenblum viii), it was also a group determined to distance art from politics. Members wanted to distinguish their photographic art from other avant-garde expression and codified their mission in a six-paragraph statement. Together they believed that "photography, as an art-form, must develop along lines defined by the actualities and limitations of the photographic medium, and must always remain independent of ideological conventions of art and aesthetics that are reminiscent of a period and culture antedating the growth of the medium itself" (qtd. in Heyman, Alinder, and Rosenblum 53). The group sought to publicize the "best contemporary photography of the West" and display only "pure" photography, which they "defined as possessing no qualities of technic, composition or idea, derivative of any other art-form." Their common method was explained in more detail later by Van Dyke as the skillful calibration of distance:

> They believed that everything in the picture should be in focus, and to achieve this they used small lens openings, with their cameras on tripods, because of the necessarily long exposures. There is a law of physics which makes it possible to have objects close to the camera, as well as distant objects, both in focus at the same time only when the lens opening is small. (qtd. in Heyman, Alinder, and Rosenblum 64)

Many f.64 members already knew each other, having first gathered when Weston was in San Francisco in the mid-1920s. Among them was Alma Lavenson, a self-taught photographer based in Oakland who achieved modest success in the camera competitions she entered in the 1920s and had contacted Weston at the suggestion of her patron, Albert Bender, whose letter of introduction provided an entrée into Weston's circle of photographers. Weston praised her composition but critiqued her still-pictorial style (Ehrens 5), leading her to change her approach almost immediately: "after I left…I kept thinking about it and I began to realize he was right. I quickly restored the clear, sharp lens that came with my camera. From then on I was a dedicated non-pictorialist," she claims (Novakov 18).[14]

The works exhibited in the f.64 show proclaimed the straight photograph as the epitome of the autonomous work of art. They dramatized the beauty of their vision of California by exaggerating surface textures, isolating objects from their environments, and defining the precision of edges. Therese Thau Heyman categorizes the photographs as "ordinary" in their choice of subjects, displaying "bits of landscape, posts, bones, and sky; a few industrial buildings; portraits, and nudes or figure studies," but "commanding" in effect. "The emerging aesthetic proved broader than the group's manifesto," she concludes (Heyman 257). We see the effects of Weston's example in photographs that explore intimate encounters with the surfaces and shapes of everyday structures, such as in Lavenson's *Composition f/64*, in which the geometries of a gas tank's cylinder and the diagonal lines of the stair, pulley arm, and structural frame seem arranged in dynamic balance. Henry Swift's *Banana Plant* and *Tree-Lobos* and Weston's *Artichoke Halved* reveal the delicate forms and hues contained within the leaves of a succulent, the twisted trunk of a tree, or the choke of a vegetable. Adams exposed with equal clarity the astonishing symmetry of a pinecone and the geometric structural balance of a factory building, while with *Frances* Consuelo Kanaga offered a tender portrait of a black child. Overall, the show marked a collective effort among the f.64 photographers to demonstrate the power of the camera both to suspend observational moments in time and to provide direct, unmediated views of the modern environment and ordinary people, countering those imperial visions of the West so often put to promotional use. With f.64, West Coast photographers achieved a clear, if short-lived, alignment of aesthetic and social purpose.

Conclusion

Bohemian formations in early twentieth-century California functioned as nodes in networks that connected artists with each other, their audiences, and sources of economic support. As the networks expanded across the continent, they created conditions for artists to test avant-garde techniques and revolutionary perspectives with local subjects and forms. We can describe such intersections of people, classes, and ideas effectively through sociological analysis of the cultural field, following the methods of Raymond Williams and Pierre Bourdieu, and trace the "patterns of interconnection and exchange that organize social and aesthetic experience" (Levine 113) through applying network theory. However, to grasp the subtle power of visual aesthetics created in response to bohemian artists' negotiation of regional politics and globalizing cultural fields, we should also pursue the intersections of art and society at every scale and continue "attending to specific patterns of contact between forms" (113). When artists such as Weston, Mather, and Modotti redefined the subjects of portrait photography to include everyday objects, urban landscapes, workers, and indigenous women, they focused public attention on the material conditions of modern life and charged the relations between places, things, and people with personal and political significance. Simultaneously aesthetic and social, global and intimate, California's many modernist bohemias introduced models of cosmopolitan encounter and visual vocabularies of resistance with which artists in the postwar period would protest against social inequalities, war, and environmental crises. Weston wrote in his *Daybooks*, "One's work must have social significance, be needed—to be vital" (Weston, *Daybooks* II 210). Instead of being "falsified in 'Bohemian' attics," such work breathes when connected "to represent needs, or to future hopes," he believed. As they practiced what Bourdieu called the art of living that they were in the process of inventing and opened what Weston referred to as "new roads for those who were ready to travel," California photographers generated vital forms of communication and living languages of dissent.

Notes

1. Murger, "The Bohemians of the Latin Quarter: Original Preface, 1850," qtd. in Levin 1.
2. Davidov makes a persuasive case in *Women's Camera Work* for reorienting histories of photography in California around women photographers, attending to "the conformity as well as the originality of their techniques and subjects; the ways in which they both borrow and distance themselves from each other and from their male colleagues; and the ways in which they associate and distance themselves from dominant models of respectability and from what they perceive as national culture" (31).

3. Consult "Countering Cultures: The California Context," Susan Landauer's overview to Peter Selz's *Art of Engagement*, esp. pp. 1–7.
4. For a lucid overview of the cultural field of early twentieth-century Los Angeles, see Deverell.
5. See Argentieri, chap. 2, for a detailed account of Italian immigration to San Francisco and of the cultural institutions that sustained the city's Italian culture.
6. Harte first applied the term "bohemian" to these neighborhoods in the "Bohemian Papers," a series of "Town and Table Talk" columns published in the *Golden Era*, the city's literary weekly, beginning in 1860. For a detailed analysis of Harte's "Bohemian Papers," see Levin, chap. 2.
7. See Edwords, *Bohemian San Francisco* (1913). The quote is from Starr, *Americans and the California Dream*, 254.
8. Zeitlin's circle included Phil Townsend Hanna, a literary journalist who became night city editor of the *LA Times* at age twenty-one, then general manager of the Associated Press for greater LA, and finally editor of *Touring Topics* (Auto Club of Southern California), which became *Westways* in 1934. In *Westways*, Hanna promoted California writers such as M. F. K. Fisher, Carey McWilliams, and Lawrence Clark Powell and photographers like Weston, Ansel Adams, and Grace Clemens. He also explored California's wine and food culture under the pseudonym Savarin St. Sure and through Fisher, while also editing *Bohemian Life*, a monthly publication devoted to food and drink.
9. The California Camera Club organized its first exhibition in 1892, featuring mostly landscapes and pastoral scenes, and began to publish the *Pacific Coast Photographer* the same year. Meanwhile, *Camera Craft*, published in San Francisco for amateur and professional photographers beginning in 1900, offered commentary on contemporary photography and reviews of current exhibitions. For a detailed discussion of the history of California camera clubs and women's roles in them, see Davidov 88–93.
10. According to Warren, Weston made these hyperrealistic and erotic images after seeing Stieglitz's portraits of Georgia O'Keeffe in New York; they were his best-selling photographs and admired by Diego Rivera (Warren, *Margrethe Mather* 31).
11. For digital versions of these photographs by Mather and Weston, access the Online Gallery at the Center for Creative Photography, University of Arizona, ccp-emuseum.catnet.arizona.edu/.
12. For a close analysis of Modotti's position in relation to expatriate and native women in Mexico City, see Adams, chap. 3.
13. While acutely aware of the distortions of feminine identity that could result from self-conscious posing for a camera, Modotti discovered greater personal and artistic freedom as she explored the region. In his nuanced study of this period in her career, Folgarait analyzes the relation between Modotti's life, her photographs, and the stages of her commitment to Mexico's Community Party (PCM) between

her arrival in Mexico in 1922 and her deportation in 1930. For more details, consult Folgarait chap. 2.

14. By the end of 1931, Lavenson's work had been featured in over twenty group exhibits, in places ranging from Los Angeles to Chicago, Paris, and Turin, and in 1932 she had her first one-person show at the California Camera Club. With a sharp perspective and impressive technical control, she depicted subjects ranging from industrial sites to abandoned mining towns, cityscapes to flowers. Weston continued to champion her work by inviting her to show four prints in the inaugural f.64 exhibition. For a complete history of Lavenson's career, see Ehrens. For digital versions of some of Lavenson's photographs, access the Online Gallery at the Center for Creative Photography, University of Arizona, ccp-emuseum.catnet.arizona.edu/.

Bibliography

Adams, Rachel. *Continental Divides: Remapping the Cultures of North America.* U of Chicago P, 2009.

Albers, Patricia. *Shadows, Fire, Snow: The Life of Tina Modotti.* Clarkson Potter, 1999.

Argentieri, Letitia. *Tina Modotti: Between Art and Revolution.* Yale UP, 2003.

Bourdieu, Pierre. *The Rules of Art: Genesis and Structure of the Literary Field.* Translated by Susan Emanuel, Stanford UP, 1995.

Brenner, Anita. *Avant Garde Art and Artists in Mexico: Anita Brenner's Journals of the Roaring Twenties.* Edited by Susannah Joel Glusker, U of Texas P, 2010.

Davidov, Judith Fryer. *Women's Camera Work: Self/Body/Other in American Visual Culture.* Duke UP, 2012.

Debroise, Olivier. *Mexican Suite: A History of Photography in Mexico.* Translated by Stella de Sá Rego, U of Texas P, 2001.

Deverell, William. Introduction. *LA's Early Moderns: Art, Architecture, Photography*, edited by Victoria Dailey, Nathalie Shivers, and Michael Dawson, Balcony Press, 2003, pp. 7–14.

Didion, Joan. *Where I Was From.* Knopf, 2003.

Edwords, Clarence E. *Bohemian San Francisco: Its Restaurants and Their Most Famous Recipes. The Elegant Art of Dining.* Paul Elder, 1913.

Ehrens, Susan. *Alma Lavenson: Photographs.* Wildwood Arts, 1991.

Folgarait, Leonard. *Seeing Mexico Photographed: The Work of Horne, Casasola, Modotti, and Álvarez Bravo.* Yale UP, 2008.

Fryer Davidov, Judith. *Women's Camera Work: Self/Body/Other in American Visual Culture.* Duke UP, 1998.

Gabara, Esther. *Errant Modernism: The Ethos of Photography in Mexico and Brazil.* Duke UP, 2008.

Gallo, Rubén. *Mexican Modernity: The Avant-Garde and the Technological Revolution.* MIT Press, 2005.

Harte, Bret. "Bohemian Days in San Francisco." *A Treasure of the Redwoods and Other Tales*. Houghton Mifflin, 1903.

———. "Town and Table Talk: A la Bohemian." *Golden Era*, 12 Aug. 1860.

Heron, Liz, and Val Williams, editors. *Illuminations: Women Writing on Photography from the 1850s to the Present*. Duke UP, 1996.

Heyman, Therese Thau. "Modernist Photography and the Group f.64." *On the Edge of America: California Modernist Art 1900–1950*, edited by Paul J. Karlstrom, U of California P, 1996, pp. 243–70.

Heyman, Therese Thau, Mary Street Alinder, and Naomi Rosenblum. *Seeing Straight: The f.64 Revolution in Photography*. Oakland Museum, 1992.

Hooks, Margaret. *Tina Modotti: Radical Photographer*. Da Capo Press, 1993.

Karlstrom, Paul J., editor. *On the Edge of America: California Modernist Art, 1900–1950*. U of California P, 1996.

Levin, Joanna. *Bohemia in America, 1858–1920*. Stanford UP, 2010.

Levine, Caroline. *Forms: Whole, Rhythm, Hierarchy, Network*. Princeton UP, 2017.

Lewis, Oscar. *Bay Window Bohemia: An Account of the Brilliant Artistic World of Gaslit San Francisco*. Doubleday, 1956.

Mann, Margery, editor. *California Pictorialism*. San Francisco Museum of Modern Art, 1977.

Mraz, John. *Looking for Mexico: Modern Visual Culture and Mexican Identity*. Duke UP, 2009.

Noble, Andrea. *Photography and Memory in Mexico: Icons of Revolution*. Manchester UP, 2010.

North, Michael. *Camera Works: Photography and the Twentieth-Century Word*. Oxford UP, 2005.

Novakov, Anna. "Alma Lavenson at 90." *The Museum of California*, vol. 10, no. 6, May/June 1987, pp. 18–19.

Ram, Harsha. "The Scales of Global Modernisms: Imperial, National, Regional, Local." *PMLA*, vol. 131, no. 5, 2016, pp. 1372–85.

Salvioni, Daniela. Introduction. *Art/Women/California 1950–2000*, edited by Diana Burgess Fuller and Daniela Salvioni, U of California P, 2002, pp. 1–13.

Seigel, Jerrold. *Bohemian Paris: Culture, Politics, and the Boundaries of Bourgeois Life, 1850–1930*. Penguin, 1986.

Selz, Peter. *Art of Engagement: Visual Politics in California and Beyond*. U of California P, 2006.

Sewell, Jessica Ellen. *Women and the Everyday City: Public Space in San Francisco, 1890–1915*. U of Minnesota P, 2011.

Shrank, Sarah. *Art and the City: Civic Imagination and Cultural Authority in Los Angeles*. U of Pennsylvania P, 2009.

Smith, Richard Cándida. *Utopia and Dissent: Art, Poetry, and Politics in California*. U of California P, 1996.

Starr, Kevin. *Americans and the California Dream, 1850–1915*. New York, Oxford UP, 1973.

———. *Material Dreams: Southern California Through the 1920s.* Oxford UP, 1990.
Tejada, Roberto. *National Camera: Photography and Mexico's Image Environment.* U of Minnesota P, 2006.
Warren, Beth Gates. *Artful Lives: Edward Weston, Margrethe Mather, and the Bohemians of Los Angeles.* J. Paul Getty Museum, 2011.
———. *Margrethe Mather and Edward Weston.* W. W. Norton, 2001.
Weber, Max. "Protestant Sects and the Spirit of Capitalism." From *Max Weber*, translated and edited by H. H. Gerth and C. Wright Mills, Oxford UP, 1946, pp. 302–22.
Weston, Edward. *The Daybooks of Edward Weston*, edited by Nancy Newhall, Aperture, 1990.
Williams, Raymond. *The Politics of Modernism: Against the New Conformists.* Verso, 2007.

12

"Backward in Time and Forward in Dream of Unknown Memory"

Deborah Miranda's Unsettling Colonial Genealogies

LISA J. UDEL

Our personal histories are the shorter versions of the tribal histories we have endured.

—DEBORAH MIRANDA, "THE BLESSINGS AND THE GENOCIDE"

In a recent work, *Bad Indians: A Tribal Memoir* (2013), Esselen/Chumash poet/scholar Deborah Miranda creates a multimodal and polyvocal document to deeply explore the constitutive relationship between history, epistemology, and identity. Using the practice of memoir to chart the author's personal/familial lineage as a starting point, then moving to contextualize that lineage alongside the settler colonialism of the California missions, Miranda enriches the form. Reflecting Indigenous communal subjectivities in its polyvocality and Indigenous narrative methods in its mixture of oral, written, and pictographic textualities, Miranda employs the tropes of genealogies and inheritance to explore the meaning of identity for herself, her community, and those she describes elsewhere as "differently Indianed" in the second decade of the twenty-first century (Miranda, review 150). In doing so, she articulates a key principle of much contemporary Native literature: that examinations of the interrelations of the literary and political, the past and present, are necessary to Indigenous intellectual and cultural sovereignties.

Miranda argues that personal genealogies of family—both material and epistemic—are interwoven with national genealogies of settler colonialism. Histories, genealogies as particular types of histories, and epistemologies operate as narratives that produce and reproduce culture. Understanding these intersections and specific contingencies and exposing those relationships promotes a viable identity for Miranda as a tribal writer and her community and leads to possible change. Such change occurs in contemporary personal and tribal practice and their corresponding narratives as well as in their colonial nation-building counterparts. Recent theorists have argued for an Indigenous critical theory that challenges us to "reconceptualize space and history to make visible what imperialism and its resultant colonialisms and diasporas have sought to obscure" (Byrd xxx). Miranda's text does this work and explores what Julia Emberly terms a "philosophical disposition toward bringing about an interface between Indigenous epistemologies and contemporary political debate" (Emberly 4). Miranda provides a reading of the attitudes and practices characterizing the settler colonialism that shaped the American West and pervade the current moment. That Miranda subtitles her text a "tribal" memoir points to the correlation of self with communal subjectivities and histories characteristic of Indigenous life writing, while her skillful use and analysis of multiple materials signals her awareness of ethnographic and historiographic contingencies and practices that inform the genre. Miranda addresses both *what* is told and *how* it is told.

Miranda's application of decolonizing Indigenous methods shares some approaches with leftist literary and political theories. If Indigenous histories have been characterized as "unfortunate casualties of the larger and inevitable American metanarrative of progress from savagery to civilization" (Wilson 133), it is the work of Native writers and theorists to report those histories and epistemologies, insist on their "hemispheric persistence" (Bernardin 15), and promote an alternate future. In this way, they share some aspects with leftist radicals, whom Alan Wald calls "the emancipatory heart" of social movement (Wald 25). Such activists, Wald notes, must work toward the "transformation of the culture they oppose" (27). Attending to histories that "chronicle...repressed national memory" equips radical workers with the knowledge and "creative inspiration" to envision the "unscripted future" (27). Similarly, Maori theorist Linda T. Smith has famously observed, learning the histories, "coming to *know* the past," is foundational to decolonizing intellectual praxis (L. Smith 36). Both approaches recognize the transformative potential of their movements.

Indigenous writers produce work that deviates from dominant narratives of nation-state unity—what Michael Wilson terms a "pedagogy of the indivisible nation" (Wilson 152)—pervasive in educational, political, and social systems. Such work, however, inevitably leads to a clash of narratives that must be addressed (Magdaleno). Wilson observes that

> the destiny of indigenous peoples is connected to the destiny of America—legally, politically, and globally. But these destinies are not necessarily the same; indeed, the national American pedagogy of the indivisible nation impedes those tribal nations that wish to affirm their own narrative destinies, many which pre-date the existence of the US. (Wilson 153)

To employ decolonizing methodologies, in Smith's terms, to "overturn...systems...and culture[s] they oppose," in Wald's terms, or to "affirm their own narrative destinies," as Wilson writes, serves as a disruptive assertion of Indigenous survival, memory, and potential sovereignty.

Miranda explores these themes in both recursive and linear structure. With a frontispiece, opening prayer, acknowledgments, and nine-page introduction, Miranda lays out the linkage between a colonized inheritance, personal and communal identity, and narrative that the body of her chronologically organized text explores. The multiple prefatory apparatuses—packed with information and references—contribute to a sense of multiple beginnings and perspectives informing Miranda's comprehensive study. Her extensive research spans the late eighteenth century to the present. Using diaries of priests and explorers, the words of California Native people missionized by the Spanish and colonized by European Americans (some of whom are her ancestors), government documents, BIA forms, newspaper articles, ethnographic field notes, tourist pamphlets and photographs, ancestry charts, Indian blood quantum charts, family stories, conversation, and memory, as well as her own poetry and journals (some published previously), Miranda argues that the work toward tribal identity becomes an imaginative act that partially reconstructs obscured, ignored, and falsified histories pervasive in the American West and, in turn, describes contemporary realities and asserts possible futures for contemporary California Native people.

Her use of blood quantum charts illustrates Miranda's multimodal approach to her themes. Inside the front and back covers, under the heading "Things You Can Do with Your Chart for Calculating Quantum of Indian Blood," Miranda includes four such charts and attending notations that are now colored in and labeled as, respectively: a "Wannabe Creations/fake 'Indian' design"; a "Hand of God" that asks what God's blood quantum would be, if "He" were human; "Patriotism Percentages" designed as an American flag; and a multicolored square cross of "Blood Quantum: The Four Sacred Directions." As the book's first and final linguistic/graphic hybrid images, the charts clearly bookend Miranda's text, both foreshadowing and reinforcing her focus. Miranda's caustic visual and verbal reinscription of blood quantum charts points to their deployment as one of many modes of hegemonic narrative that constructs identity while enacting a kind of bureaucratic genocide that affects her as a descendant of the Esselen tribe erroneously terminated in the 1905–6 census. The blood quantum charts, implemented in the nineteenth century, had consequences that continue to affect Native people in the United States today overall, and Miranda in particular. Miranda's mocking repurposing of the charts disrupts their historic use as narratives that determine and reify Indigenous identity, invalidates their authority, emphasizes their hegemonic and constructed nature as taxonomies, and demonstrates the methodology that she employs throughout the text.[1]

Miranda situates discussion of her lineage within these larger issues. The book's frontispiece opens with a photograph and dedication to her parents "who survived each other" (*Bad Indians* x–xi). Describing her mother, descended from English and French ancestry, as the "colonizer" and her father, descended from Chumash/Esselen ancestry, as "Indian," Miranda highlights one critical dialectic that characterizes her familial experience (12). Accompanying this photograph and quotation with Linda Hogan's inscription "I am the result of the love of thousands," Miranda conflates a larger community's surviving hardships with love, and immediately sets up several important themes: surviving a legacy of "intergenerational trauma" through reclamation of inherited narratives and creation of new narratives to pass on to future generations (77, 202, 123). Writing that her body is infused with "the full force of two separate streams of human history and story," Miranda foreshadows the violence of her parents' future relationship and its physical and psychological consequences on her family (xiii). Situated at the confluence of the two "separate streams," Miranda understands herself as the product, victim, and potential interpreter/mediator of this violence. Further, Miranda's overt linkage of "history and story," history *as a form of* story, along with her recognition of various versions of that coupling, articulates the relationship of genealogy/identity, epistemology, and narrative that I examine.

Miranda repeatedly draws the reader/viewer's attention to the ways both historic and contemporary narratives—often in contestation with each other—contribute to the construction and unsettling of nation-states and their various populations. Miranda examines the Spanish/Catholic missionization and subsequent EurAmerican colonization of Indigenous peoples of what later becomes California. She opens the section termed "The End of the World: Missionization, 1770–1836" with "Genealogy of Violence, Part I." Miranda assigns "Spain/Catholic Church" as the parent heading, which begets "Soldiers/Rape," which begets "Murder/Floggings, Stocks, Manacles," which begets "Incarceration/Prison with Suicide Rates" and "Domestic Violence/Child Abuse," among others (*Bad Indians* 2). Like her work with blood quantum charts, Miranda's repurposing of a genealogy, traditionally used to chart familial descent, here used to *visually* chart inherited systems and practices of oppression common in the American West, allows her to demonstrate the widespread and ongoing consequences of colonization. With the "Genealogy of Violence," Miranda provides a visual narrative of her argument about the legacy of settler colonialism that she and other descendants of missionized Native peoples have inherited. "Part I," of course, suggests that more violence is to come, which, in fact, it does. Later in her text, Miranda follows up with "Part II" to describe her family legacy of colonial violence, which I discuss in more detail below.

Miranda uses assorted materials to explore the nuances of those legacies. In her depiction of colonial epistemologies, Miranda draws on the words of Junípero Serra (the Spanish Franciscan who founded ten California missions in the eighteenth century), illustrations from clerical histories of the missions, and tourism booklets and photographs produced by amateur historians. In her poem "Fisher of Men," one of several based on Serra's journals, Miranda articulates the mission founder's attitudes toward the Indigenous people he encounters and forcibly converts. Characterizing them five times as "entirely naked / as Adam in the garden before sin," the speaker/Serra asserts that like fish "caught / in the apostolic and evangelic net," the "savages" will soon serve as a "plentiful harvest, ripe / for the reapers" of God (4–5). Echoing the language and imagery that Christ uses to recruit the apostles, Miranda subverts traditional Biblical references to reflect the view of Indigenous people as sinful savages needful of conversion into commodities to exploit and expend.

Miranda also draws on a 1922 clerical mission history to expose the exploitation of Indigenous labor that built the missions and laid the foundations of what would become the American West.[2] Miranda opens the section covering missionization with the etching "Padre Directing Mission Indians to Build," which she locates under the heading "Adobe Bricks." In the voice of the missionary, Miranda writes a text accompanying the illustration as a recipe instructing the reader how to build the bricks necessary for a mission, noting:

> Gather your Indians...you need dirt, water, straw.... Your

> Indians might have to haul some dirt in, which could take days, and no mules, a cart if they're lucky, baskets if not.... All in all, adobe is cheap—the ingredients free for the taking—but you will certainly go through a lot of Indians. More lazy creatures on earth we have never seen. (*Bad Indians* 7–8)

Miranda's assumed persona reflects perceptions of Indigenous populations as labor commodities and dehumanized ingredients, necessary to, and yet derided in the colonial enterprise. The narrator's callous attitudes toward Indigenous lives and their perceived value jars Miranda's reader, emphasizing epistemic practices and narratives of missionization and settler colonialism.

Miranda spends considerable attention on the priests' physical abuse of the neophytes and draws from several sources: the seventeenth-century Peruvian Indian Felipe Guáman Poma de Ayala's chronicle to the king of Spain decrying the violence inflicted by the Spanish (ca. 1615); the Mexican "Notebooks of Tonayuca" (1567), with drawings of Spanish colonists flogging Mexican citizens; a Spanish illustrated instruction sheet (1794) on the use of the *corma*, a hobbling device; and illustrations and descriptions of a cat-o'-nine-tails and cudgel (*Bad Indians* 7–8). Miranda's detailed visual and written descriptions of these torturous implements convey the extent of controlling practices and breadth of tools deployed against Indigenous peoples and represent what Jacqui Alexander has described as "itineraries of violence that are given other names such as democracy and civilization" (3). Miranda's study reveals the fetishistic array of methods used to enact and enforce hegemonic attitudes. Both Guáman Poma's chronicle and Tonayuca's notebooks convey the suffering of Indigenous people at the hands of Spanish invaders and articulate their point of view in an effort to stop such behavior. Guáman Poma narrates Peruvian and Andean history as a way to convey a shared understanding of culture and civilization to the king who, he believes, controls the actions of his military. Like Miranda, both authors are examples of writing as witness and protest. Their works model early efforts to unsettle colonial logics and practices that Miranda foregrounds here and explores in her tribal memoir.

In her discussion of the mission system, Miranda contrasts the competing narratives of the colonizer and colonized. She articulates both the ethnocentrism of the Spanish colonizers and the rage of the Indigenous witnesses and survivors. Miranda describes the mission as a "Massive Conversion Factory centered around a furnace constructed of flesh, bones, blood, grief, and pristine land and watersheds, and dependent on a continuing fresh supply of human beings, specifically Indian…" (*Bad Indians* 16). Poorly managed, unsuccessful and unsustainable as independent economic organizations, the mission system, Miranda notes, contributes to the death of "80 percent of California Indians…in a sixty-year period" (17). Her choice of "factory" underscores the mercenary aspect of missionization, its attending exploitation and endless consumption of human capital, along with its final failure to maintain a profit. Miranda's language deliberately brings to mind the Nazi death camps, an analogy I discuss later.

Miranda examines the various characteristics that Franciscan missionaries projected onto the Indigenous populations coerced into serving the mission structure. As a colonizing tool, this system of religious and cultural indoctrination obviously included replacing Indigenous names with Spanish names, religious beliefs and practices, attitudes about sexuality, sociopolitical systems, arts, languages, and agricultural traditions, among others. Miranda's study supports what Indigenous queer theorist Chris Finley describes: colonial powers enforce their domination of Native peoples when they make "sexuality, gender, and race key arenas of the power of the settler state" (Finley 31). Franciscan clergy and soldiers brought the denigration, torture, and ultimate disappearance of differently gendered or two-spirit people, whom Miranda describes here as "in-betweens" (*Bad Indians* 31). Traditionally recognized and respected in the tribal communities that Miranda discusses, such individuals fulfilled important spiritual responsibilities. Later labeled "sodomites," "monsters," and "*joyas* (jewels)" by the Spanish, they disappear, go underground, and their correct Chumash appellation "*aqi*" is forgotten. In "Cousins," Miranda allies herself with the *aqi* and speaks in their voice: "we disappeared, murdered or heartbroken, and the end of the world came anyway" (31).

Such indoctrination, Miranda points out, incurs internalized oppression and self-hatred that Indigenous communities continue to grapple with (19). Miranda captures the clergy's paternalism toward the neophyte: "subhuman, animal-like being[s].... *Bestias.* Lazy. Meek. Submissive. Humble. Timid. Docile. Obedient. Superstitious. Stupid. Ignorant. Children" (17–18). Miranda immediately follows this list of negative attributes with the names of nine Indigenous people who, she tells us, are her ancestors, thus situating herself in this history and its account. Critical in establishing and maintaining the settler colonial narrative, colonizing attitudes and practices continue after the mission system is long finished, throughout subsequent decades to the present.

In part 1 of the "Genealogy of Violence," Miranda identifies "rape...incarceration...domestic violence...child abuse...racism/internalized racism...and post-traumatic stress disorder" as the by-products of the Spanish mission system that proliferate over the centuries into Miranda's life (*Bad Indians* 2). Part of this violence is enacted through representations and nomenclature: their distortions, inaccuracies, and omissions. Looking at late nineteenth- and early twentieth-century histories, newspapers, and tourist documents, Miranda identifies continued settler narratives in varied representations of Indigenous people. Her father recounts being called "Diggers—like nigger," a term she researches and finds was applied to "Northern California Indians, peoples who had not been missionized by the Franciscans but instead endured the gold rush" of the nineteenth century that devastated California's Indigenous peoples (44–45). Miranda discusses the trajectory of the word, its various applications, connotations, and ultimate demise.

Looking at an illustration from an 1894 memoir of David Leeper, a Gold Rush miner, Miranda examines the profound contrast between Leeper's depiction of the subject and her own. Leeper presents the image of a bare-breasted young woman, calling her "A Digger Belle." Offering no contextual commentary except the jarring label of racist derision combined with feminine charm, Leeper conveys sentiments common at the time. Miranda, in contrast, studies the image and notes that the picture "tells a story...with devastating strokes" (*Bad Indians*

45). Based on the woman's cropped hair and facial expression, Miranda concludes that she had likely shorn her hair as "a traditional act of mourning" (45). Noting that in 1851 and 1852, Congress "appropriated and paid out over one million dollars in bounties to white men who harvested Indian scalps from the California goldfields—scalps taken from men, women, and children," Miranda provides the context absent from Leeper's treatment of the subject (45). Many other California Native peoples were sold as slaves by bounty hunters, working in mining camps, missions, ranchos, and white-owned homes and businesses (46–47).[3] Given the historical circumstances surrounding the image, Miranda surmises: "If this woman was in or near the goldfields in '49, she was in the middle of one of the bloodiest genocides ever documented, one approved and funded by the United States government" (45).[4] Miranda recognizes the material realities that the Gold Rush, along with systemic cultural degradation wrought by the missions for past centuries, created for the woman in the picture. She foregrounds this history to flesh out the woman's story and to emphasize distorted representations popular during the time of their production.

Viewing histories, photographs, and popular postcards from the turn of the century, Miranda also addresses common debased depictions and misrepresentations of Indigenous women. Of Leeper's label "Digger Belle," Miranda notes: "Belle...seems to have been a widespread joke in California—sarcasm, irony, mean-spirited derision of Indian women" (*Bad Indians* 47). The pun of "Belles" with mission "bells" is frequently used throughout this period. The California mission trail uses the image of mission bells to designate the twenty-one missions for tourists traveling along the Camino Real. A popular 1895 photograph, later reproduced as a postcard and described in a local tourist publication as "The Belles of San Louis Rey," features three older women—all described as over one hundred years old—sitting "in the ruins of Mission San Louis Rey" (48). Just as the bells symbolize a tourist route, the use of "Belles" in this context symbolizes non-Native perceptions and derisive representations of Native women. Like countless images of Native people commodified to suggest an experience or emotion, the three women undoubtedly received no remuneration for the photograph or its countless reproductions. Miranda confesses: "exorbitant amounts of money are made from the ruins of Native lives, and that angers me.... If a 'Mission Bell' is an icon of touristic pleasure, then to be a 'Mission Belle' is to also be marked as a commodity, female (thought not human): marketable, a product for brief enjoyment" (48–49). Although Miranda reports that the BIA later discontinued using the term "digger" in response to the protests of Miwok Indians who burned a Digger effigy in 1922, the derisive use of "Belle" continued well into the twentieth century.[5]

Miranda consistently links historical material and the rhetorical violence of settler colonialism with her family. During her discussion of the Belles/bells, for example, Miranda includes a photograph of her grandfather posing under the bells of Mission San Miguel from 1925 (*Bad Indians* 8). Arguing that these contemporary attitudes and practices are by-products of colonization, she creates the second part of the "Genealogy of Violence" to discuss the effects of her father's violent behavior in her own life. Although set during the 1960s–70s of Miranda's youth, this second genealogy appears early in the text under "The End of the World: Missionization," underscoring its continuing part as her inheritance (33–35). This three-page section alternates narratives describing her father beating her four-year-old brother with passages from several mission reports criticizing Indigenous parenting habits as overly lenient and undisciplined and their love as "extravagant," "excessive" bordering on "vice" that requires punishment (34–35). Miranda lays out the text in eleven blocks, each separated by horizontal lines and using different fonts to distinguish her personal memory from the various mission narratives. Miranda visually overlaps the two narratives to emphasize their causal relationship and recalls the following in a segment worth quoting at length:

> the arc of my father's arm is following a trajectory I know too well...the instrument of punishment coming from two hundred years out of the past in a movement so ancient, so much part of our family history that it has touched every single one of us in an unbroken chain from the first padre or the first *soldado* at

> the mission to the bared back of the first Indian neophyte.... Flogging. Whipping. Belt. Whatever you call it, this beating, this punishment, is as much a part of our inheritance, our legacy, our culture, as any bowl of acorn mush.... More than anything else we brought with us out of the missions, we carry the violence we were given along with baptism, confession, last rites... my father's arm rises and falls in an old, savage rhythm learned from strangers who came with whips and attack dogs, taught us how to raise our children. (34–35)

Miranda wonders if it is possible to elude the psychological effects of this history, what John Borrows calls "colonial pathologies,"[6] an "illness" that Miranda and others call a form of "postcolonial stress disorder" (Miranda, "The Blessings" 35; Duran, Duran, and Yellow Horse Brave Heart). As survivor of and heir to this legacy, Miranda highlights the continuum of settler colonialist practices in both broad and intimate terms.

Miranda tells us of her intent to write the memoir "to create a space where voices can speak after long and often violently imposed silence" and to voice "the antidote to lies" (*Bad Indians* xx). Her identification and analysis of the mission violence as one form of colonizing behavior that is taught, enforced, and ultimately passed along through generations becomes an act of decolonization. Along these lines, Miranda examines the 1935 field notes and published documents that Smithsonian ethnographer J. P. Harrington assembled from his chief informant and Miranda's ancestor, Isabel Meadows. Meadows's material allows Miranda to discuss several aspects of settler colonialism common throughout the American West: the high rate of sexual violence against Native women by non-Native men and its history's erasure, but also, crucial to Miranda's project, the unsettling and supplanting of those heteropatriarchal narratives with intentional narratives of survival, naming, and resistance.

Working from photocopies of Harrington's notes, some reproduced in the memoir, Miranda studies Meadows's words and imagines her motivations for repeatedly speaking with a white, male ethnographer whom she would normally view with suspicion. In one interview with Harrington, Meadows forcefully recounts the story of a Carmel Mission priest who raped a young Indian woman one hundred years earlier. Naming both the priest—Father Real—as rapist and the young woman—Vicenta Gutierrez—as survivor, Meadows insists that this story be told, acknowledged, and recorded.[7] We learn that immediately after the rape, Gutierrez reported the crime and Father Real left the Carmel area. Miranda celebrates Gutierrez's and Meadows's respective acts of breaking silence about heteropatriarchal sexual violence against Native women by non-Native clergymen. Miranda writes "Dear Vicenta," a letter addressed to Gutierrez, and describes Meadows's narrative:

> Isabel didn't forget you, though. One hundred years after the padre raped you in the church, Isabel told your story to Harrington. She told it like it happened yesterday. And she was *mad*...Vicenta, she used the priest's *name*.... And she used your name. She made certain we knew which family you belonged to.... Isabel told that story like it happened to her, or to her daughter. She told that story like she could bring down the wrath of God just by finding the right words. (*Bad Indians* 24)

Miranda's letter praises Gutierrez's bravery in reporting the rape at a time when the clergy wielded power far greater than did individual Native women whom they viewed as sexually available and expendable: "I have to tell you, girl, that was brave. I didn't tell for years and years" (24). Her use of the more familiar "Vicenta" and "girl" rather than "Gutierrez" indicates Miranda's identification with her as both a witness to and survivor of rape. She seeks to console Gutierrez and herself while also angrily acknowledging the heteropatriarchal attitudes that permit rape within the colonial regimes: "it happens all the time, right? It's not just that we're women; we're Indian women... poor Indian women. The statistics on *that* are predictable. Thirty-four percent of us raped; one in three! And ninety percent of the rapists are non-Indian" (23). Miranda identifies rape as a settler strategy that plagues Native women and threatens their communities still. In this way, "gender violence…marks the evisceration of Indigenous nations" (Million 7). As theorists Andrea Smith, Sarah Deer, and Dian Million assert, sexual violence against Native women is both an ideological and physical tool of settler colonialism. Miranda traces gendered violence—both material and epistemic—from her own experience and that of women like Vicenta Gutierrez, back through the eroticized depiction of a bare-breasted "Digger Belle" and the derogated mission "belles" of postcards and ultimately to the earliest Spanish colonists.

Miranda raises several overlapping issues with her handling of the Vicenta/Isabel narrative. She applauds both women's work in breaking the silence surrounding heteropatriarchy. Vicenta challenges clerical supremacy in identifying a priest as her rapist; and, nearly a century later, Isabel relays an event that she deems crucial to the history of Indigenous people and colonization. Naming Vicenta's *family* also provides the communal context of identity that is specific to Native subjectivity and might have gone unacknowledged by a white ethnographer. Moreover, like both women, Miranda relates the events and identifies the speakers as a way to inform the reader. Miranda, however, complicates the notion of bearing witness when she questions the efficacy of recounting stories over a century old: "Vicenta, I don't know if the fact that your story survives, that Isabel's angry words fight for your dignity and honor, really brings any kind of justice to you. Not the kind of hands-on justice I'd like, anyhow.… Maybe nothing can bring you justice after all this time, Vicenta" (*Bad Indians* 25). Certainly Father Real was never charged with a crime; he simply left the Carmel Mission area to resurface later at the Mission Santa Cruz ("where he tried to sell the church's land illegally"), and then he permanently disappears from historical accounts (25). Miranda continues: while such reports of abuse typically went unacknowledged or were overtly repressed during their time, now such history has become "legitimate research" for academics who study Indigenous cultures and European contact, transforming what was a "shameful wound" into an "outrageous…weapon of colonization" (23). Where non-Native interlocutors may have ignored accounts of misogynist and racist violence, recent scholars, Miranda included, study heteropatriarchal norms and practices of settler colonialism.[8] After all, Miranda reminds us, the statistics of sexual violence that she cites are contemporary. Settler culture continues to wield this particular "weapon."

Miranda asks, what do we tell and why? Miranda's discussion of this issue, at this point in her text, exemplifies crucial aspects of her argument throughout the memoir: Who controls the narratives of such events, their extrapolation and dissemination? Does the act of telling past events that affected people long dead change current realities? Miranda asks: "the scribbling of an obsessed white man trying to record the memories of an aging Indian woman attempting to tell the story of an Indian girl's rape one hundred years before—can *this* change the world?" (*Bad Indians* 25). How does modern Indigenous memoir, created, in part, to correct misreadings, omissions, distortions, and erasures, also simultaneously comment on the very nature of historiographic narrative and twenty-first century indigeneity for those whose tribe has been terminated? In response, she notes: "I hold on to this: Isabel remembered your story, and she told it to Harrington, and he told it to me, and I'm telling it to everyone I can find" (25). A powerful aspect of Miranda's memoir lies in her intentional approach to narrative. Miranda recounts several layers of the Vicenta/Isabel account: Vicenta's *experience* and her *narrative* of that experience; Isabel's explicit and determined recounting of both to Harrington; Miranda's identification with Vicenta as a rape survivor and with both women as recorder/witness to criminal acts against Native women. Miranda rightfully inserts herself into this history, drawing the reader's attention to the Vicenta/Isabel/Deborah recovery narrative as part of her legacy.

Miranda characterizes Isabel Meadows as a savvy woman who determinedly used her work with Harrington to recover the erased narratives of Native women precursors and to document their history "in between the language lessons and Coyote stories Harrington was after" (*Bad Indians* 28). Like many "salvage anthropologists" of his time, Harrington sought to record languages and cultural narratives of tribes he believed would soon be defunct, in this case Ohlone and Esselen. Miranda pointedly notes that Isabel was no mere informant; she had her own agenda with Harrington: inserting "the stories *she* wanted to salvage," to ensure their inclusion in the historical record (28). As a contemporary "tribal memoir," Miranda's text comments on aspects of the earliest forms of Indian autobiography, subsequently termed "as-told-to" narratives that were usually shaped by their white editors for a non-Native audience and that powerfully told a narrative of colonization in the American West. Miranda attributes great importance to Gutierrez's history and to Meadows's insistence on conveying this history, as it includes the common occurrence of non-Native men's sexual assault of Native women, the clergy's abuse of Native people and of their power in their interactions, Gutierrez's refusal to remain silent, and her decision to identify her attacker.

Miranda identifies Meadows as both an ancestor and literary precursor whose ethnographic collaboration becomes "her body of work: her engagement in the creative use of words, literacy, and empowerment on behalf of her community" (*Bad Indians* 28). She interprets the Gutierrez/Meadows narrative as "a precursor to modern Native Literature, a stepping-stone between oral literacy and written literature" that captures Indigenous women's experience and conveys it centuries later (28). Adding, "this means that Isabel herself knew the power of that story, and believed in our survival—in the future, there would be Indian women who would need this story!" Miranda recognizes Meadows's strategic use of this story to articulate a Native female subjectivity necessary to future generations. The story survives because it is "passed down through California Indian women to California Indian women" determined to maintain its memory (29). Miranda contextualizes the narrative as both "a teaching device for contemporary California Indian women—for me, my sisters, our daughters"—and as a sacred "ceremony" with the potential to heal (29). Miranda understands Meadows's work as a form of activism, as "Indigenous practice: that of storytelling as education, as thought-experiment, as community action to right a wrong, as resistance to representation as victim" (29). Miranda's characterization of Meadows's strategy reflects her own deconstruction of settler narratives and representations of Native women such as "digger belles." Finally, Miranda characterizes Meadows's recounting of Gutierrez's story as a conscious form of recovery work for

Native women, conveying the message: "We are valuable human beings, she tells other Native women: our bodies are sacred, and we *have a right* to speak out against violence and violation" (29). Miranda describes such acts of "collective memory…[as] the source of our power, our potential inheritance" ("The Blessings" 35). As enriching and powerful forms of resistance to epistemic and material violence, Isabel's and Vicenta's narratival acts function as elements of Miranda's legacy as a Native woman writer.

Miranda positions herself within this lineage of Native women storytellers and writers whose "intergenerational Indigenous memory" (Bernardin 18–19) unsettles colonizing narratives to articulate and create alternate, Native subjectivities. Early in her memoir, Miranda uses her poetry (such as "Fisher of Men") to articulate various settler perspectives as a way to expose and critique those perspectives and also to assume a limited authorial control over those narratives. As she progresses through both the chronology of colonization and its shaping of California Indigenous experience, Miranda includes verse to articulate Indigenous perspectives that unsettle those colonizing logics and articulate various Indigenous responses. The poem "Lies My Ancestors Told for Me" addresses Native peoples' intentional use of subterfuge to protect their children in post-mission California. Posing the question "when is a lie the truth? / when is the truth a lie?" the Indigenous speaker responds, "when a lie saves the lives / of your children, grandchildren / and five generations forward" (*Bad Indians* 38). Just as Isabel Meadows recounts events of a century prior to an audience of future generations, the poem's speaker addresses the present moment with an eye to the future. Commanding the listener to tell "lies that deflect genocide," the speaker acknowledges that while future generations will despise their ancestors for their subterfuge and assimilation, "lie anyway / so they'll be alive / to complain" (39). These "lies" provide alternate stories or versions of identity. The speaker finishes:

> Tell the lies now and maybe later
> your descendants will dig
> for the truth in libraries,

field notes, museums,
wax cylinder recordings,
newspaper reports of massacres
and relocations, clues you left behind
when you forgot
to lie
lie lie lie. (40)

Admiring the strategic use of these lies and acknowledging their necessity to ensure survival, the speaker also reveals her ambivalence as she describes the ramifications of such obfuscation on future generations like Miranda's whose archival work of recovery becomes the major means to identify and understand her collective and personal history. Like Isabel Meadows, Miranda creates and uses her writing to assert control over the narrative while pointing out the various ways that Indigenous people have deployed narrative as a form of survival.

Like many contemporary Native writers, Miranda rightfully characterizes her ancestors as survivors of a "great holocaust" and she their beneficiary (*Bad Indians* 76). As described in the poem above, she uses the Harrington/Meadows "field notes," audiotapes ("recordings") of her paternal grandfather Tom Miranda recounting his experiences from the early twentieth century, and "newspaper reports" as material to rework in her verse and prose. Transcribing her grandfather's tapes allows Miranda to study and present his experiences. She notes, "I want Tom's voice to come through, his stories to chronicle and give Indian testimonio to part of California's past that has been erased or subsumed under that catchall 'assimilation'" (78). Miranda repeatedly places her family narratives within the settler context. An article published in the *Los Angeles Times* in 1909, around the time of her paternal grandfather's birth, describing the "drunken rampage" of a "Bad Indian," inspires Miranda to write one of her strongest pieces, "Novena to Bad Indians" (96–99). The poem praises and acknowledges many of the Native precursors whose resistance to and rejection of colonialism earned them the moniker of "Bad Indian." Miranda subverts the novena genre—a Catholic form of prayerful petition over nine days—

to proudly recognize the Indigenous people who fought against religious and political settler domination. Praising specific individuals, the speaker claims them as heroic "ancestors" and requests that they "illuminate the dark civilization we endure. Teach us to love untamed, inspire us to break rules, remind us of your brutal wisdom learned so dearly" (98–99). This titular piece serves as homage to a lineage of resistance that Miranda inherits, embraces, and continues in her revision of settler genres (blood quantum charts, tourism pamphlets, ethnography, Catholic prayer, etc.) and values (good/bad, obedient/resistant) in order to assert Native epistemologies and subjectivities.

Miranda also uses her memoir to trace the development of her inheritance as a tribally conscious lesbian writer and LGBTQ2 scholar. In its final section, Miranda deepens her focus on her use of writing to explore matters from her own life. She explores her rage, its emergence, development, and reformation in the poem cycle *Silver*, one of the memoir's most powerful pieces (*Bad Indians* 108–18). Each of the poem's seven parts presents an experience of material or epistemic violence from Miranda's life and her response. "Forge" presents her "earliest memory": that of her father holding a knife to her mother's throat while the infant Miranda watches and cries. She recalls, "The knife—a kitchen knife, silver and bright—is my fear" (108). That initial image/memory becomes a trope Miranda uses throughout the poem. Subsequent sections cover childhood experiences: anti-Indian comments from her stepfamily, her anger over her father's increasing violence toward his family, and in "Whetstone," her rage sharpened while recounting her rape at age seven by "Buddy," a family friend, and her resulting guilt when she realizes that he has raped one of her friends. When her mother tells Miranda that she shares her father's blood and toughness, she worries that she carries his potential for violence. Mundane events are ruined forever by their associations with her rapist. Miranda writes, "My problem is that I can't forget. Instead of growing dull and faint, my anger gets sharper and sharper. Like a knife. Like a big silver knife" (112).

Into marriage and motherhood, Miranda writes to understand and stem her enraged response to her children, worried that her violence is an inevitable inheritance. In this fifth section, "Cutting," Miranda acknowledges that the act of writing does not bring immediate relief or clarity: "The more I write, the further backward my words take me. I don't go easily or willingly" (*Bad Indians* 114). Haunted by shame and grief, Miranda shares her personal writing with a lesbian couple who encourage and validate her experience and testimonial. Exchanging their "stories of lost families, abuse, and healing" enables Miranda to express the rage that "cut[s] a way out of layers of scar tissue," to finally discard the metaphoric blade and begin her process of recovery (115). Miranda's decision to speak/write of her rape and name her rapist involves that backward view that overwhelms her previously, as it affirms her place in the Vicenta Gutierrez/Isabel Meadows lineage. The penultimate section, "Crucible," acknowledges the painful difficulty conveyed by the title: "Getting rid of the blade is not so easy. I try to hide it by plunging the damn thing, hilt and all, into my own chest" (116). Writing her "story" and acknowledging her emerging "truth" means leaving her marriage and rejecting "the fiction of a healing that doesn't cost but doesn't transform" (116). Miranda tells us that she avoids "this story for nearly a decade…fight[ing] transformation tooth and nail" (116). However, the need to break silence, to both articulate and live her "story" in all of its implications, becomes the inexorable route to recovery and her "old friend Truth" (116).

After she is finally able to "embrace" her truth, "Reforged" portrays Miranda's transformation of her life's raw materials. She notes that leaving her marriage and entering her loving relationship with another woman poses tremendous risks: "writing words that might have the power to take away my children permanently" (117). Yet, like the many examples of Native imaginative assertion she invokes throughout this memoir, Miranda recognizes their necessity and beauty. "[T]raveling through a place where no map exists," Miranda acknowledges the risks and potential freedom of her newly articulated lesbian identity (118). Miranda's maps, evident in both her memoir and earlier poetry, are, as poet and critic Janice Gould observes, "constructs that symbolically provide direction or describe a known, remembered, imagined, or longed-for terrain" (Gould 22).[9] Miranda enters new "terrain" at this juncture in her life. Gould's observation, that this impulse becomes particularly urgent among Native writers whose tribal communities were forcibly displaced from their traditional homelands, characterizes Miranda's experience as well (Gould 25).

Throughout the poem, Miranda traces how colonization and all of its by-products have forged the blade of rage. Up to this point, Miranda imagines plunging the knife of rage into her "own chest"; however, now she transforms the knife to a pen, "forged out of grief and violence" (*Bad Indians* 118). She begins what Jacquie Alexander terms the "healing work" of "body praxis" that is essential to "mapping…subjectivity" (Alexander 316). She recognizes the empowering potential of "sacred rage" ("The Blessings" 36). Miranda tells us that it becomes the work of "each woman telling her truth in a language forged from every knife ever held to her throat, or wielded in self-defense. It's not about destruction or forgetting, but transformation. The crucible is love" (*Bad Indians* 118). It is within this discussion that Miranda notes: "My mother, whose name means 'dove,' tells me Indian languages originate from the gleaming throats of birds" (117). As Miranda confronts her personal "Truth," recognizing it as her "old friend" rather than foe, she is able to link language with action, articulating her identity lovingly and taking action to ensure that identity. Miranda portrays her maturing self-awareness and ability to fulfill that awareness, underscored by her mother's words about language and indigeneity. At this crucial point of transformation in Miranda's life, her mother provides a metaphor of sound, flight, and freedom that shines in its beauty. Miranda's inclusion of her mother's knowledge provides a "mother tongue" and situates her work squarely among a lineage of women writers/storytellers who have worked to transform and flourish.

Following the poem cycle, Miranda traces the role of writing throughout her life. "Petroglyphs" depicts the maturation of Miranda's childhood writing. Staying with her maternal grandparents in the Tehachapi Mountains after her father is incarcerated for eight years, her mother "had run away," and her siblings placed in foster care, a three-year-old Miranda writes her name ("Deby") as a way to assert some kind of permanence, to create a "written record of myself, my name, my existence" at a time of tremendous family upheaval, her "Armageddon" (*Bad Indians* 119). This temporary home—her grandparents ultimately refuse custody of their biracial granddaughter—grounds Miranda: "I had staked myself to this world. I had created a space for myself.... I recreated that moment when I came into being" (120). Seeking permanence, Miranda uses language to inscribe herself, like a petroglyph, into that particular place, "always connected...to that mountain" (120). In the absence of an Esselen/Chumash story that would situate the culture in a specific place, linking identity and tradition with that place, Miranda writes her own narrative of emergence at the age of three, an act that is crucial to Native peoples' identity formation and its articulation, as Robert Nelson has famously observed (Nelson).

No longer writing only to assert an individual identity and stave off personal invisibility, Miranda now writes to assert broader subjectivities to successive generations. She tells us that she becomes the writer/creator for future descendants: "through this mark you will know I was here, and I know you are coming after me. We have stories to exchange about this difficult gift, life, and those stories will never disappear" (*Bad Indians* 122). Like her characterization of Gutierrez's and Meadows's work, Miranda's writing is intertextual, tribally functional, and grounded in specific historical contingencies, serving what Jace Weaver has termed a "communitist" function (Weaver xii). As a seventh-generation descendant of Indigenous people missionized in the 1830s, Miranda tells us that she writes out of generational trauma like her ancestors and precursors and for "the next seven generations" (123). She uses her writing as a form of "symbolic repair" of long-standing trauma (DeSalvo 34).

One way that Miranda accomplishes this repair is through her examination of how the settler story of the California missions is reproduced in contemporary American public education, specifically the "Mission Project" assigned as part of the fourth-grade curriculum. The project reveals the way educational systems still manifest what Walter Hixon describes as "fantasy, rationalization, narcissism, projection, and guilt [that] permeate[s] the...mind of the colonizer, enabling genocidal violence as well as historical denial" (Hixon 21). Redubbing it the "Mission Mythology" and "Mission Fantasy Fairy Tale," Miranda revises her daughter's school assignment and develops her "Post-Colonial Thought Experiment" (*Bad Indians* xvii, 186–91). Miranda divides the "experiment" into three projects, each with the assignment description and corresponding worksheet to resemble the mission project still assigned. The three segments—"Carmel Mission Project," "Birmingham Plantation Project," and "Dachau Concentration Camp Project"—demonstrate Miranda's belief in their equivalent positions as settler colonial eugenic practices. Miranda creates and maintains a blog on this topic that conveys her assessment. Her alternate assignment highlights the "clash of narratives," provides a "chronicle of repressed national memory," and insists that students "come to *know* the past," as it seeks to subvert the kind of ignorance that Dian Million terms a form of "knowledge production" still actively enabled in contemporary schools (Million 47).

Miranda acknowledges that writing for future generations is an act of imaginative faith. Drawing on the foundational work of Native lesbian feminist scholar Paula Gunn Allen and Chicana lesbian feminist scholar Gloria Anzaldúa, Miranda envisions a "future mythology of the Mestiza Nation" (*Bad Indians* 123). Just as Miranda uses Allen's intersectional metaphor of the "confluence," situating herself at the "confluence" of competing streams of history early in her memoir, Miranda here deploys Anzaldúa's metaphor of Mestiza Nation as a way to "heal…from our childhoods…[and] larger histories" (123).

The "scars" of history—Anzaldúa's "borderlands" within the Mestiza—provide new material for creation. Given the history of colonization, tribal disenrollment, language loss, land appropriation, deculturation, homophobia, and trauma, Miranda posits a Mestiza Nation of tribal reinvention rather than reformulation, using the painful shards that remain in order to create a new design, a new wholeness as a "mosaic" (*Bad Indians* 136). Miranda warns: "sometimes something is so badly broken you cannot recreate its original shape at all. If you try, you create a deformed, imperfect image of what you've lost" (135). Such impulses, Miranda argues, keep one focused on and situated in the past, rather than using the past to reimagine and build a future. She notes:

> If we allow the pieces of our culture to lie scattered in the dust of history, trampled on by racism and grief, then yes, we are irreparably damaged. But if we pick up the pieces and use them in new ways that honor their integrity, their colors, textures, stories—then we do the pieces justice, no matter how sharp they are, no matter how much handling them slices our fingers and makes us bleed. (135)

This metaphor of contemporary tribal and personal identity reflects that history while imagining its future form. Like a potter reusing "the broken shards of pots to make new pots," Native people are "*obligated*" to "honor and re-integrate…tribal truths" as they work to unsettle colonizing systems ("The Blessings" 36).

Miranda acknowledges the necessity of such a project, stating, "My own identity as 'Indian' stares right into the mouth of extinction.… Who am I, if my community can no longer function as a community?" while simultaneously questioning the efficacy of a metaphor—"an artificial construct"—to heal a broken community facing the deadly potential of "extinction" (*Bad Indians* 136). Miranda, however, allows all competing elements of her position: "I am not whole. And yet, I *am* whole. What the hell? I'm a whole mosaic" (136). Creating wholeness from fragmentation, Miranda reinvents herself in "this Post-Colonial Art Project" that she identifies as her inheritance (136). She uses her "family history as a means of collective self-creation, giving voice to the past" and envisioning the future (Watson 316). Qwo-Li Driskill, LGBTQ2 theorist and Miranda's co-editor of the two-spirit anthology *Sovereign Erotics*, suggests that "instead of seeing decolonization as something that has a fixed and finite goal, decolonial activism and scholarship ask us to radically reimagine our futures…that speak to our present colonial realities" (Driskill 70). Part of Miranda's talent lies in her ability to understand and convey how to craft the fragments of settler colonialism into a viable Indigenous identity. She incorporates "self-representation" into her theory of decolonization (Driskill, Justice, and Miranda 6).

Early in her memoir, Miranda posits the dialectic of her parents that shapes her experience: her mother as colonizer and father as colonized; however, as she works through her narrative, Miranda also reveals the rich legacy that her parents bequeath, despite their failings. Her mother provides much of the genealogical material she has collected over years that is necessary to Miranda's research, and her father passes on his Esselen/Chumash lineage. Miranda also acknowledges her parents' influence on her artistry, portraying her mother's initiation to the "Mother Tongue" at a key point in her personal narrative and her father's "creative urge" and appreciation for the "restorative power of language" (*Bad Indians* 77).

In this eloquent memoir, Miranda traces the generative capacity of storytelling, echoing writers like Leslie Silko and Thomas King when she observes: "story is everything we are: human beings are made of words and the patterns we construct out of words" (*Bad Indians* 193). Structured recursively, the memoir demonstrates Indigenous narrative structures and reveals the many ways that the past continues to resonate for contemporary tribal communities. Miranda locates herself within the lineage of ancestors like Isabel Meadows who engaged in "the work of making story out of disaster, a story that preserves Indigenous history, heartbreak, and hope" (201). In thinking about her life and tribal identity, Miranda understands Meadows as a model of narrative creation and survival. As a Native LGBTQ2 scholar, Miranda inherits the decolonizing task, telling us "I have tried to honor [Isabel's] words and her work as a storyteller, activist, historian, and intellectual" (207). Miranda understands her family stories as theories of identity and praxis, like other Native writers, such as Choctaw author LeAnne Howe (Howe 333). Miranda also claims a form of literary inheritance from many writers in addition to Allen, Anzaldúa, Silko, and Thomas King, including Elizabeth Cook-Lynn, a founding scholar of Native studies and Native nationalist theory, whose insistence that "a nation which does not tell its own stories cannot be said to be a nation at all" underlines the intersection of nation-building, narrative, and agency integral to Miranda's position (*Bad Indians* 193).

Miranda often describes her ancestors as the "story-bridge" that ensures her existence and her memoir, giving them voice as her return (*Bad Indians* xx, 74). She develops what Ronald Niezen calls the "rediscovered self...the articulation of collective being that...is brought back from an imposed condition of oblivion and forgetting" (Niezen xvi). Miranda uses the memoir to trace personal, tribal, and national lineage, noting the ruptures and bridging the gaps, recording "the good, bad, and ugly," however painful ("The Blessings" 36). She tells us: "California Indians...have many...stories. They aren't easy, they are fractured. To make them whole, what is needed is a multilayered web of community reaching backward in time and forward in dream, questing deeply into the country of unknown memory—an extremely demanding task" (*Bad Indians* 193–94). In its multimodal and polyvocal form, Miranda's memoir is itself the communal mosaic that she describes. As the bridge "reaching backward in time and forward in dream...of unknown memory," Miranda's text powerfully and deliberately affirms the rich legacy of a contemporary indigeneity.

Acknowledgments

I would like to express my gratitude to Mary Pipino, who read several versions of this piece and consistently offered valuable and speedy feedback. I also wish to thank Jan Goggans, who provided thoughtful commentary on this project in its earliest form.

Notes

1. For a discussion of blood quantum's continued effects on contemporary Native people, see Schmidt 1–9. For a discussion of blood quantum and the Maidu of California, see Tolley and Sarris.
2. From 1769 to 1823, Franciscan missionaries established twenty-one missions accompanied by military outposts in Alta California running from Sonoma to San Diego. Created to convert Native people and create settlements for Spain, the missions relied heavily on military presence to enforce their goals. See Dartt-Newton and Erlandson; Jackson and Castillo; Panich; and Sandos.
3. In fact, historians estimate approximately twenty thousand California Native people "worked in various forms of bondage post 1846." See Madley, "'Unholy Traffic.'"

4. Clifford Trafzer and Michelle Lorimer echo Miranda's assertions, noting that "the California militia, supported by the U.S. Army and state government, committed genocide against the Native Americans of California" during the Gold Rush era of the 1850s–60s (64). Like Miranda, they write to include that history in the broader narrative. See Alvarez, *Native America and the Question of Genocide*; Lindsay, *Murder State*; Madley, *An American Genocide*; Trafzer and Hyer, *Exterminate Them!*
5. For more on this, see Trafzer and Hyer.
6. Borrows, qtd. in Calloway 5.
7. For further history of sexual violence against Native women and missionization, see Hurtado 1–20 and Woodworth-Ney 82–92.
8. See Deer, A. Smith, and Amnesty International USA.
9. In her discussion of Jaune Quick-to-See Smith's map art and Miranda's poetry, Susan Bernardin suggests that through their histories and "political, spiritual, storied geographies," Indigenous maps offer "new frameworks" for reading western American literature (17).

Bibliography

Alexander, Jacqui M. *Pedagogies of Crossing: Meditations on Feminism, Sexual Politics, Memory, and the Sacred.* Duke UP, 2005.

Allen, Paula Gunn. *Off the Reservation: Reflections on Boundary-Busting, Border-Crossing Loose Canons.* Beacon Press, 1998.

Alvarez, Alex. *Native America and the Question of Genocide.* Rowman & Littlefield, 2014.

Amnesty International USA. *Maze of Injustice: The Failure to Protect Indigenous Women from Violence in the USA.* Amnesty International USA, 2007.

Bernardin, Susan. "Indigenous Memories and Western American Literary History." *A History of Western American Literature*, edited by Susan Kollin, Cambridge UP, 2015, pp. 15–30.

Byrd, Jodi A. *The Transit of Empire: Indigenous Critiques of Colonialism.* Minnesota UP, 2011.

Calloway, Colin G. "My Grandfather's Axe: Living with a Native American Past." *Reflections on American Indian History: Honoring the Past, Building a Future*, edited by Albert L. Hurtado, U of Oklahoma P, 2008, pp. 3–31.

Dartt-Newton, Deana, and Jon M. Erlandson. "Little Choice for the Chumash: Colonialism, Cattle, and Coercion in Mission Period California." *American Indian Quarterly*, vol. 30, no. 3–4, 2006, pp. 416–30.

Deer, Sarah. *The Beginning and End of Rape: Confronting Sexual Violence in Native America.* U of Minnesota P, 2015.

DeSalvo, Louise. *Writing as a Way of Healing: How Telling Our Stories Transforms Our Lives.* Beacon Press, 1999.

Driskill, Qwo-Li. "Doubleweaving Two-Spirit Critiques: Building Alliances Between Native and Queer Studies." *GLQ: A Journal of Lesbian and Gay Studies*, vol. 16, no. 1–2, 2010, pp. 69–92.

Driskill, Qwo-Li, Daniel Heath Justice, and Deborah A. Miranda. *Sovereign Erotics: A Collection of Two-Spirit Literature.* U of Arizona P, 2001.

Duran, Bonnie, Eduardo Duran, and Mary Yellow Horse Brave Heart. "Native Americans and the Trauma of History." *Studying Native America: Problems and Prospects*, edited by Russell Thornton, U of Wisconsin P, 1998, pp. 60–78.

Emberly, Julia V. *The Testimonial Uncanny: Indigenous Storytelling, Knowledge, and Reparative Practices.* SUNY P, 2014.

Finley, Chris. "Decolonizing the Queer Native Body (and Recovering the Native Bull Dyke): Bringing 'Sexy Back' and Out of Native Studies' Closet." *Queer Indigenous Studies: Critical Interventions in Theory, Politics, and Literature*, edited by Qwo-Li Driskill et al., U of Arizona P, 2011, pp. 31–42.

Gould, Janice. "Poems as Maps in American Indian Women's Writing." *Speak to Me Words: Essays on Contemporary American Indian Poetry*, edited by Janice Gould and Dean Rader, U of Arizona P, 2003, pp. 21–34.

Hixon, Walter. *American Settler Colonialism: A History.* Palgrave, 2013.

Howe, LeAnne. "Blind Bread and the Business of Theory Making, by Embarrassed by Grief." *Reasoning Together: The Native Critical Collective*, edited by Craig Womack et al., U of Oklahoma P, 2008, pp. 325–39.

Hurtado, Albert L. *Intimate Frontiers: Sex, Gender, and Culture in Old California.* U of New Mexico P, 1999.

———. "When Strangers Met: Sex and Gender on Three Frontiers." *Writing the Range: Race, Class, and Culture in the Women's West*, edited by Elizabeth Jameson and Susan Armitage, U of Oklahoma P, 1997, pp. 122–42.

Jackson, Robert H., and Edward Castillo. *Indians, Franciscans, and Spanish Colonization: The Impact of the Mission System on California Indians.* U of New Mexico P, 1995.

Lindsay, Brendan C. *Murder State: California's Native American Genocide, 1846–1873.* U of Nebraska P, 2015.

Madley, Benjamin. *An American Genocide: The United States and the California Indian Catastrophe, 1846–1873.* Yale UP, 2016.

———. "'Unholy Traffic in Human Blood and Souls': Systems of California Indian Servitude Under U.S. Rule." *Pacific Historical Review*, vol. 83, no. 4, 2014, pp. 626–67.

Magdaleno, Jana Sequoya. "How! Is an Indian: A Contest of Stories." *Postcolonial Theory and the United States: Race, Ethnicity, and Literature*, edited by Amritjit Singh and Peter Schmidt, UP of Mississippi, 2000, pp. 279–99.

Million, Dian. *Therapeutic Nations: Healing in an Age of Indigenous Human Rights.* U of Arizona P, 2013.

Miranda, Deborah. *Bad Indians: A Tribal Memoir.* Heyday, 2013.

———. *Bad NDNS*, badndns.blogspot.com/.
———. "The Blessings and the Genocide: Or, Ten Reasons Why This Issue of *News from Native California* Is Necessary." *News from Native California*, 2014/15, pp. 34–36.
———. "Dildos, Hummingbirds, and Driving Her Crazy: Searching for American Indian Women's Love Poetry and Erotics." *Frontiers: A Journal of Women Studies*, vol. 23, no. 2, 2002, pp. 135–49.
———. "Extermination of the Joyas: Gendercide in Spanish California." *GLQ: A Journal of Lesbian and Gay Studies*, vol. 16, no. 1–2, 2010, pp. 253–84.
———. Review of *Sovereign Bones: New Native American Writing, Vol. II*, edited by Eric Gansworth. *American Indian Culture and Research Journal*, vol. 32, no. 2, 2008, pp. 147–50.
———. "'Saying the Padre Had Grabbed Her': Rape Is the Weapon, Story Is the Cure." *Intertexts*, vol. 14, no. 2, 2010, pp. 93–112.
Nelson, Robert M. "Place, Vision, and Identity in Native American Literatures." *American Indian Studies: An Interdisciplinary Approach to Contemporary Issues*, edited by Dane Morrison, Peter Lange, 1998, pp. 265–81.
Niezen, Ronald. *The Rediscovered Self: Indigenous Identity and Cultural Justice.* McGill-Queen's UP, 2009.
Panich, Lee. "After Saint Serra: Unearthing Indigenous Histories at the California Missions." *Journal of Social Archeology*, vol. 16, no. 2, 2016, pp. 238–58.
Sandos, James A. *Converting California: Indians and Franciscans in the Missions.* Yale UP, 2004.
Schmidt, Ryan W. "American Indian Identity and Blood Quantum in the 21st Century: A Critical Review." *Journal of Anthropology*, 2011, pp. 1–9. doi.org/10.1155/2011/549521.
Smith, Andrea. *Conquest: Sexual Violence and American Indian Genocide.* South End Press, 2005.
Smith, Linda Tuhiwai. *Decolonizing Methodologies: Research and Indigenous Peoples.* 2nd ed., Zed Books, 2012.
Tolley, Sara-Larus, and Greg Sarris. *Quest for Tribal Acknowledgment: California's Honey Lake Maidu.* U of Oklahoma P, 2006.
Trafzer, Clifford E., and Joel R. Hyer. *Exterminate Them! Written Accounts of the Murder, Rape, and Enslavement of Native Americans During the California Gold Rush.* Michigan State UP, 1999.
Trafzer, Clifford E., and Michelle Lorimer. "Silencing California Indian Genocide in Social Studies Texts." *American Behavioral Scientist*, vol. 58, no. 1, 2014, pp. 64–82.
Wald, Alan. "Reaching for Revolution." Review of *Radicals in America: The U.S. Since the Second World War*, by Howard Brick and Christopher Phelps. *Against the Current*, vol. 79, Nov./Dec. 2015, pp. 25–29.
Watson, Julia. "Ordering the Family: Genealogy as Autobiographical Pedigree."

Getting a Life: Everyday Uses of Autobiography, edited by Sidonie Smith and Julia Watson, U of Minnesota P, 1996, pp. 297–323.
Weaver, Jace. *That the People Might Live: Native American Literatures and Native American Community*. New York, Oxford UP, 1997.
Wilson, Michael D. *Writing Home: Indigenous Narratives of Resistance*. Michigan State UP, 2008.
Woodworth-Ney, Laura. *Women of the American West*. ABC-CLIO, 2008.

13

Leaving the West for the Left

Louise Thompson Patterson, the New Negro Movement, and Black Women's Activism

EMILY LUTENSKI

In the late 1980s, Louise Thompson Patterson began to write a series of letters to professors, historical society curators, and state archivists throughout the American West. She identified herself simply as an African American woman living in Oakland, California, who was then approaching ninety years old, and asked them to send her any information they had on African American history in the region. She had, she reported, lived in Goldfield and Tonopah, Nevada; Seattle and Walla Walla, Washington; Boise, Idaho; Ogden, Utah; and Marshfield (today Coos Bay), Oregon. She moved to Sacramento, California, and then to Oakland as a teenager. She stayed in the Bay Area through her undergraduate training at the University of California, Berkeley, from which she graduated in 1923 with degrees in economics and Spanish. But two years later, she left the West because she felt that as a black woman she could not obtain a job there that would appropriately utilize her skills and training. She did not return until the 1980s, after the death of her husband, which compelled her to relocate closer to her daughter. At that time, with the help of Margaret Wilkerson, a professor of African American Studies and Theater at Berkeley, she began to compile her memoirs. This is when she wrote to archivists in search of information to place her childhood experiences in the West in context. She ended her letters by imploring her interlocutors, "I feel that the life of black people in the Far West has never really been put together and I hope I can make some contribution towards that end" (letter to Fitzgerald 1).

In letters she sent to aid with the project, Wilkerson explained, "Mrs. Patterson has lived an incredibly rich and productive life," and the "story of her years as a young, black child in the far West offers a fascinating portrait of American life during the early part of this century" (letter to Nylen 1–2). Wilkerson was correct on both counts. Thompson's memoirs, however, were never published, and substantial examination of her life and work has been infrequent in comparison to many of her contemporaries. On these occasions, the attention she has received has been twofold: first, as a figure in the Harlem Renaissance, and second, as a committed leftist from the 1930s until her death in 1999. These narratives have not, however, been brought together with her early years in the U.S. West. Indeed, it would seem difficult to do so, given how both the New Negro movement and black internationalism have been so closely associated with Harlem and, more recently, with metropolitan networks stemming to Paris, London, and elsewhere in the black Atlantic (see Brent Hayes Edwards's *The Practice of Diaspora: Literature, Translation, and the Rise of Black Internationalism* and Minkah Makalani's *In the Cause of Freedom: Radical Black Internationalism from Harlem to London, 1917–1939*). Thompson's experience would seem to bear out the focus on these other geographies; she insists that she left the West because it was so anti-black during her years there, and she suggests that this discrimination, coupled with the West's relatively small black population, made the region a difficult place to consolidate radical black political solidarity. As her efforts to compile memoirs later in her life reveal, however, Thompson was never able to entirely leave the West behind. To examine her archive on the black West complicates a vision of the region as politically retrograde—a vision that made it possible for American studies scholar Henry Nash Smith to make the provocative claim in a 1980 interview that "there is nothing more anathema to a serious radical than regionalism" (qtd. in Steiner 11). Instead, Thompson's archive suggests that her leftist, feminist, pro-black activism emerged from a long history of black women's western experiences with what she would later term the "triple exploitation" of race, class, and gender—as well as their efforts to resist it.

Thompson was born Louise Alone Toles in Chicago, Illinois, in 1901. Her parents divorced when she was a toddler. Afterward, her mother, Lulu Brown Toles, sought a fresh start and moved to Seattle with four-year-old Louise in tow. Mother and daughter first stayed in the home of newspaperman Horace Cayton Sr. and his wife, editor and writer Susie Revels Cayton (Thompson, "Chapter 1" 6–9). Thompson was only slightly older than their son, Horace, who had been born in 1903. As an adult, Horace Cayton Jr. would attend the University of Chicago and be trained as part of the Chicago School of urban sociology, which would influence the work of radical black social realist writers like Richard Wright. Cayton would famously publish, along with St. Clair Drake, *Black Metropolis: A Study of Negro Life in a Northern City* (1945). Thompson's experience with the Caytons, however, was relatively short-lived. In 1906, the Toleses left Seattle for Goldfield, Nevada, which was then a mining boomtown, in hopes of gaining an independent financial foothold ("Chapter 1" 9–15). But by 1910, the mines had busted, and mother and daughter were already gone, forced to board with a black family, the Davises, in Oakland, California, while Lulu worked as a waitress (U.S. Bureau of the Census, *Thirteenth Census*, Oakland 5A). In Oakland, Lulu remarried to a man named John Thompson. John's search for work, which Thompson later described as driven by misguided get-rich-quick schemes, led the family all over the West throughout the 1910s—through Washington, Idaho, Utah, and Oregon—before the family returned to California. When Thompson was in high school, her stepfather left the family to chase what he thought was another opportunity. This time mother and daughter refused to follow, and they never had contact with him again (Thompson, interview by Wilkerson 17–21). This refusal—and the enduring bond between mother and daughter—was the foundation for Thompson's later conviction that networks of black women were central to leftist organizing. When she and her mother severed ties with John Thompson, their act was more than a refusal to follow a man; it was a refusal to follow a man as he chased fictions of individual capitalist success engendered by the powerful myths of the West.

In 1925, two years after her Berkeley graduation and after a brief sojourn in Chicago, Thompson accepted a teaching position in Pine Bluff, Arkansas. It was a disheartening experience, with most of the teachers themselves undereducated, and the students often unable to attend school because of the exploitative working conditions in the southern sharecropping system ("Chapter 2" 7–35). Thompson subsequently left for a job at Virginia's Hampton Institute, a storied and better-supported institution. She thought it would deliver higher-quality education, but she was again disappointed. Hampton, of course, was where Booker T. Washington had been educated, and its model of vocational and industrial training informed his view on higher education for African Americans. Thompson, in contrast, was inspired by W. E. B. Du Bois, whom she had once seen speak at Berkeley, and who promoted black education in the liberal arts and insisted on black equality. During the period when Thompson taught at Hampton, students began to chafe against the administration, which they saw guided by a white paternalism that dictated both their limited curriculum and insulting disciplinary practices on campus. In 1927, the students instituted a strike protesting their conditions. On October 13 of that year, Thompson wrote an anonymous letter to Du Bois imploring him to investigate the practices at Hampton: "You will never forget your doing so," she wrote, because "this is a chance to free us from the clutches of the 'white man's almighty dollar'" (letter to Du Bois 1). This letter reveals that Thompson's early resistance to white paternalism also recognized the racial contours of U.S. capitalism built, as historian Edward E. Baptist has insisted, on the foundation of enslaved black people's labor. Unable and unwilling to continue working in the manner that Hampton demanded, Thompson made her way to New York City in 1928, where she had obtained a fellowship to study social work through the National Urban League ("Chapter 3" 5–7).

Once in Harlem, Thompson became involved in the New Negro movement, a context in which she is perhaps best known in connection with writer Wallace Thurman, whom she married shortly after her arrival in New York. Heady with her immersion in the vibrant world of black arts and politics that pulsed around her, when Thompson met Thurman, who was also a relatively recent transplant from the West, the pair became caught up in the dizzying nightlife and rich culture of the city, having a lot of fun in the process ("Chapter 3" 9). Thurman's novel *The Blacker the Berry*, incidentally, features an African American woman protagonist who also arrives in Harlem from the West. The Thompson-Thurman marriage, however, was not a success. Within six months the couple had separated, owing to, according to Thompson, homosexuality, a topic he wrote of frequently, including in *The Blacker the Berry*, but an orientation that, Thompson insisted, he tried to repress in himself. Although she moved to Reno, Nevada, in 1929 in order to obtain a quickie divorce, she was called back to New York when her mother, who had moved there to be nearer to Thompson, fell ill. Thurman and Thompson technically remained married until Thurman's death from tuberculosis in 1934; during his illness, Thompson tended him at the hospital ("Chapter 3" 11–12).

When Thompson returned to New York she and her mother began to share an apartment. By this time Thompson's Urban League fellowship was over. During it, she had conducted research on African American high school girls that documented how their teachers encouraged them to pursue particular vocations, such as domestic service or nursing. Her research sought to uncover systemic bias, but ironically this interest in structural inequality led her to dislike the field of social work. She thought social workers were expected to treat their cases as though they were the result of individual pathologies, rather than of systemic practices of racism, classism, or sexism, which went woefully unexamined ("Chapter 3" 12–14). This experience increased her interest in Marxism, which offered the structural analysis of inequality she desired. Even before she moved to New York, Thompson had been interested in Communism. She had even gone as far as to apply to a program that would have sent her to the Soviet Union to study leftist revolutionary principles. But when she was accepted, she decided she wasn't ready to commit; she was still only exploring leftism with an "open mind" ("Chapter 3" 4–6). The letdown of her Urban League fellowship had helped her, instead, to build her leftism from the ground up, through experiences with triple exploitation, rather than be indoctrinated from the top down.

Thompson chose not to renew her fellowship for a second year, but this meant that she needed to find work. Philosopher Alain Locke referred her to wealthy white widow Charlotte Osgood Mason, whose patronage supported Langston Hughes and Zora Neale Hurston during these years. Mason paid Thompson to serve as their secretary, a role in which Thompson typed much of what would become Hurston's *Mules and Men* (1935) and Hughes's *Not Without Laughter* (1930) ("Chapter 3" 17–24). As time wore on, however, Thompson, like Hughes, would become more and more dissatisfied with the tenor of Mason's employ. Hughes would ultimately break with Mason during the Depression as he began to write poetry that boldly expressed working-class concerns, rather than portraying African American experience in ways that could be interpreted as simple, natural, and folk-influenced—in other words, the paternalistic, primitivist vision of black life that Mason idealized. Mason had hoped to turn Thompson into a writer as well, but Thompson never saw herself in this light. Indeed, as late as a 1989 oral history interview, she claimed, "I don't consider myself a writer" (Patterson, Burdine, and Rutherford [Part 2] 35). She did, however, increasingly chafe at Mason's demands that, for example, she write thank-you notes to "Godmother," as Mason insisted on being called, after receiving the paychecks she earned with her labor. She made a clean break from Mason before Hughes did, when the dowager accused her of not being a "true Negro" ("Chapter 3" 27). In *Primitivist Modernism: Black Culture and the Origins of Transatlantic Modernism*, literary critic Sieglinde Lemke offers racial primitivism as an alternative to the modernism creation stories of Marxist scholars like Fredric Jameson, who propose "modernism is a reflection of transatlantic capitalism" (6). But when primitivism is clearly linked to patronage, as it was in Thompson's experience with Mason, the logics of racism and capitalism are not alternatives, but inextricable. Indeed, historian Mark Naison has insisted that Thompson's experiences with "white philanthropy"—with the Hampton Institute, the Urban League fellowship, and Mason—resulted in her "migration to the left" as she grew to understand the "prejudice she experienced as the logical outgrowth of capitalism" (43). The mutuality of racism and capitalism would be brought together with sexism in Thompson's later analyses of structural inequality as triple exploitation. And her consideration of gender, in particular, had earlier experiential roots—her life in the American West.

In scholarship on the Harlem Renaissance, Thompson remains best known as Thurman's erstwhile wife, Hughes's and Hurston's secretary and friend, and Mason's beneficiary. But Thompson's most significant contributions were as a leftist activist and intellectual. While in Harlem, she spearheaded a Marxist salon called "The Vanguard" with sculptor Augusta Savage. It ultimately became the Harlem branch of the Friends of the Soviet Union. In 1931, she joined the National Committee for the Defense of Political Prisoners, which had been organized as an auxiliary to the International Labor Defense (ILD), the American legal aid section of the Communist International. The ILD was one of the leading advocates for the defense of the Scottsboro Boys, whose trials had begun that year. With Scottsboro, Thompson became fully invested in the Left. In 1932, she threw herself into organizing a trip to the Soviet Union taken by a group of black intellectuals and artists—including Hughes and a young Dorothy West—with the goal to make a film about U.S. racism titled *Black and White.* The project fell apart because of a screenplay that Hughes, in his memoir *I Wonder as I Wander*, characterized as "improbable to the point of ludicrousness," lack of funding, and infighting among the travelers (76). While the leftist fervor of some of Thompson's compatriots became assuaged as a result, Thompson, along with Hughes and Loren Miller, defended the endeavor. She returned to Harlem even more committed to the Communist Party, earning her the nickname "Madame Moscow," according to Hughes's biographer Arnold Rampersad (248). Throwing herself into the work of organizing, she spearheaded the "Free the Scottsboro Boys" march on Washington in 1933, during which she walked arm in arm with Ruby Bates, the white woman who recanted her rape accusation in the case. She became a card-carrying member of the CPUSA and the International Workers Order, in which she served in several leadership roles. Thompson visited Spain during the civil war, and upon her return to the United States helped found the Harlem Suitcase Theater with Langston Hughes in 1938. The company sought to create proletarian dramas, such as Hughes's *Don't You Want to Be Free?*, based on the people's theaters Hughes and Thompson had seen in the Soviet Union (Maxwell 141–43).

In 1940, Thompson married William L. Patterson, who was twelve years her senior, a lawyer with the ILD, and a leader in the CPUSA. He had grown up in Oakland, and Thompson remembered once crossing paths with him there at an NAACP lecture by writer James Weldon Johnson, who was then serving as the organization's executive secretary ("Chapter 3" 3). The pair lived in Chicago and New York during most of their lives together, as both continued their work on the radical Left. At the height of anti-Communist efforts in the United States, Thompson remained unabashed about her political affiliations. In the 1950s, she and other African American women founded the radical civil rights organization Sojourners for Truth and Justice. In the 1960s, she served on the executive board of the National United Committee to Free Angela Davis (Maxwell 141–43). These actions epitomize her lifelong commitment to considering gender, race, and class together.

The most comprehensive biography of Thompson is Keith Gilyard's 2017 *Louise Thompson Patterson: A Life of Struggle for Justice*. Further documentation of her copious work as an organizer appears in recent histories of the black Left, particularly those focused on black women, such as Dayo F. Gore's *Radicalism at the Crossroads: African American Women Activists in the Cold War* and Erik S. McDuffie's *Sojourning for Freedom: Black Women, American Communism, and the Making of Black Left Feminism*. In literary scholarship, however, she has received less serious attention. This is despite William J. Maxwell's laudable attempts to recover her in *New Negro, Old Left: African American Writing and Communism Between the Wars*. As Maxwell notes, black radical women were especially marginalized due to the multiple axes of oppression they faced, which may have resulted in their omission from later scholarship. And further, black women's proletarian literature was uncommon during the interwar period; it did not appear with any regularity until the 1940s, in works such as Margaret Walker's *For My People* (1942) and Ann Petry's *The Street* (1946). In his examination of Thompson, Maxwell rejects characterization of her as unworthy of literary study because she has not been recognized as a creative writer, and he attends to Thompson's article "Southern Terror," which was published in *The Crisis* in 1934. In his treatment of this essay on Scottsboro, he argues for the "value of rediscovering black women's writing in a journalistic genre where brevity was a revolutionary credential" (144). Along these lines, McDuffie highlights Thompson's essay "Toward a Brighter Dawn," which he contends is one of the earliest instances when a theory of multiple oppressions that today might be termed "intersectional" appeared in print. Published in 1936 in *Woman Today*, the publication of the CPUSA's Women's Commission, "Toward a Brighter Dawn" called "the Negro woman" the "most exploited section of the American working class population." "Over the whole land," Thompson noted, "Negro women meet this triple exploitation—as workers, as women, and as Negroes" (14; McDuffie 112). To name triple exploitation—and to work relentlessly against it—was perhaps Thompson's greatest achievement as an intellectual and an activist. Her experiences in the West were foundational to this project.

Thompson's roles on the Left and as a writer have perhaps been understudied, but, save for biography, her engagement with the U.S. West has been entirely overlooked. Indeed, when she and Wilkerson began the research for her memoirs, the Nevada State archivist, who passed on the scant information he had on blacks in Goldfield and Tonopah, followed up by saying, "I guess the message I am trying to convey is that you have your work cut out for you." As mining communities, he wrote, the towns did have significant black populations prior to their busts circa 1908, but these populations had been segregated and marginalized. They were difficult to document, and their traces in early newspapers of the region seemed to associate them only with crime, rather than report on their daily lives (Rocha 1–2). Such revelations were likely unsurprising to Thompson, whose recollections of her youth in the West were largely of segregation and poor treatment at the hands of the whites who were the vast majority of the population in all of the towns where she lived.

These attitudes arose from the hostile political environment that sanctioned them. During the years that Thompson lived in Nevada, for example, Francis G. Newlands, who was then a state senator, published an essay titled "A Western View of the Race Question," where he suggested rolling back the Fifteenth Amendment and implementing, instead, "a humane national policy which…shall recognize that the blacks are a race of children, requiring guidance, industrial training, and the development of self-control, and other measures designed to reduce the danger of that race complication, formerly sectional, but now rapidly becoming national" (269). He was, furthermore, convinced that without the immigration restrictions by then in place, Asians would "quickly settle upon and take up possession of our entire west coast and intermountain region." Integration, he thought, was impossible—it would end in either "amalgamation" or "race war," both fates that were, to him, equally undesirable (270). The only option, he contended, was to "prevent the immigration of all peoples other than those of the white race," and "start immediately upon serious consideration of a national policy regarding the people of the black race now within our boundaries, which, with a proper regard for humanity, will minimize the danger which they constitute to our institutions and our civilization" (271). Hand in hand with his white supremacy, Newlands was also one of the most ardent supporters of westward expansion. Earlier, as a U.S. representative, he had been the author of the Newlands Resolution (1898), which annexed the Republic of Hawaii to the United States, and also the Newlands Reclamation Act (1902), which funded irrigation projects throughout the arid U.S. West, often by compromising Native American treaty rights.

Given contexts like this, where the West became tightly associated with white supremacy, it is not surprising that the majority of Thompson's recollections of the region are negative. "Goldfield," she recalls, "was a boomtown built overnight; it consisted mainly of tents and wooden shacks. The streets were unpaved. The populace was comprised of prospectors and whores with only a few families. The whores' cribs were right on the main street." Not only that, but it was racially segregated, as were most of the western towns where Thompson lived. In Goldfield, she and her mother resided in "a shack on the edge of town" ("Chapter 1" 10). Furthermore, her schooling was patterned by taunts and ridicule from other students on account of her race. She was turned away at venues from swimming pools to Sunday schools, neglected by white adults in moments when she was in physical danger, and asked to participate in a Fourth of July parade dressed as a savage ("Chapter 1" 21–23).

These experiences were made all the more painful for Thompson because they were in locations still without sizable black communities in which she could find support. It was not until a short trip to Portland, Oregon, Thompson records, that she gained knowledge of black culture and institutions: "In Portland I found my first black community.... In all of the other communities that I remember, we were isolated—either the only black family in town or too few to form any meaningful black community" ("Chapter 1" 29). Thompson would have visited Portland sometime in the 1910s. During the course of that decade, the black population grew from 1,405 to 1,556—but this was of a total population of 207,214 and 258,288, respectively (U.S. Bureau of the Census, *Thirteenth Census*, Population 95; U.S. Bureau of the Census, *Fourteenth Census* 843). Nonetheless, it was in Portland, she recounts, where "I had my first experience attending a black church. I was both amazed and frightened because I had never seen people shout in church nor had I heard such inspiring singing.... Here the singing and preaching was joyful. It was like a new world to me, a world I knew nothing about." She continued: "There was a black newspaper, a black barbershop, and other black businesses. Although we were only there three days, I saw black people doing things that I had never dreamed of" ("Chapter 1" 30).

When Thompson initially moved to the Bay Area in the late 1910s, there was not yet the sizable African American population that would spring up around the World War II years. Her experiences there, as elsewhere in the West, tended to be characterized more by the discrimination she faced than by the sense of community she idealized.

When her memoirs detail her search for a job after her college graduation, they note that blacks were only welcome in service industries, except for "those few blacks who were light enough...to pass for white" ("Chapter 2" 1–2). But doing this, Thompson asserts, lending support to historian Allyson Hobbs's argument in *A Chosen Exile: A History of Racial Passing in American Life*, could only come at an exorbitantly high cost. "If you had dark-skinned friends as I did," Thompson insists, "passing meant leading a double life.... If you had any pride in your history and family, that was no alternative" ("Chapter 2" 2–3). Both Thompson and her mother were light-skinned enough that in the 1910 U.S. Census both were demarcated "white" by the enumerator (U.S. Bureau of the Census, *Thirteenth Census*, Oakland 5A). Yet neither Lulu nor Louise endeavored to pass—save for once, after Thompson's college graduation, when, she relays, "I never thought I was light enough to pass as white, but I got a job by saying I was Mexican" ("Chapter 2" 3). To do so, though, made her already tenuous relationship to other African Americans even more fraught, and she determined to "leave the West Coast not only to get a job, but to satisfy my longing for... other blacks" ("Chapter 2" 5). She did this by taking on her teaching positions, and then finally by moving to New York City, a place she had fantasized about since she was a young girl thumbing through her mother's magazines back "in the dusty, crude gold and silver towns of the West." She would gaze longingly, in particular, at the Tiffany advertisements, which to her "symbolized travel, going places," more than "money and luxury" ("Chapter 3" 1). New York, she thought, would satisfy her dream; it was a place not only to find other blacks generally, but in particular other blacks "interested in travel and intellectual pursuits" ("Chapter 2" 6).

Although she longed to leave it in order to find a larger black community, the West contributed to Thompson's developing class-consciousness—particularly via her memories of the labor of black women in the region. Indeed, her memoirs describe Goldfield as a "classless society," because "the only thing that mattered in this new society was money." As a result, she insists, "my mother would not feel shame about being a chambermaid, cleaning floors and emptying chamberpots.... Dress, parentage, background—none of this mattered here." Thompson continues: "As I look back over those years, I am amazed at my mother's courage and strength, living as a single woman and supporting a young child. She even managed to reach out and help other women" ("Chapter 1" 13). Retrospectively, Thompson can see her mother as the inspiration for her radical consciousness. This consciousness—an awareness of triple exploitation—emerged from Lulu Thompson's commitment to claiming her racial identity even when she could have denied it, to her life of work, and to her efforts building support networks with other women. Thompson notes that her stepfather did nothing to provide for her "physical well-being" or "future." Instead, "he was just there sometimes" ("Chapter 1" 28). While Thompson's experience in the U.S. West was certainly difficult because of her race, class, and gender, what emerged from that experience was a roadmap for black female leadership and solidarity that she would apply to her later activist work.

As Thompson continued researching her memoirs, she began to understand the existence and importance of black female networks—if not what she would consider full-fledged black communities—in the West. Friends in the Bay Area referred her to an African American woman in Portland named Kathryn Bogle, whom they described as "one of the pioneers of black people in the Far West" (Thompson, letter to Bogle, 16 Sept. 1987 1). Bogle was born Kathryn Hall in Oklahoma in 1906. She moved throughout the Pacific Northwest as a child before her family finally settled in Portland. In 1937, she attained some notoriety when she published an article titled "An American Negro Speaks of Color" in the *Sunday Oregonian*. The article lambasted the West for its discriminatory practices, particularly in schools and employment, and crafted a picture of black life that ran counter to the stereotypical representations of blacks that she saw often featured in the newspaper (Bogle 70–81). Bogle had also once lived in Marshfield, and she told Thompson that she "remember[ed] coming to [her] house and that I played the piano for her" (Gordon 25). When Thompson and Bogle came into contact in their later years, they discovered they had other common acquaintances from their Marshfield days. Both had known another black family: the Burdines. Maggie and Earl Burdine, along with their older children, had moved to Oregon from Oklahoma in 1913. They eventually had seven children: daughters Dolores, Helen, Verdell, Audrey, and Erma Jean, and sons Earl and Alfred. On realizing that Bogle also knew the Burdines, Thompson implored her to notify Verdell, who was also living in Portland, that she would "like very much to meet her" (letter to Bogle, 4 Nov. 1987 1).

Becoming reacquainted with Verdell Burdine, now Verdell Rutherford, was a turning point for Thompson's research, and for her understanding of her own past in the West. Burdine had taken on the role of her family's historian, and had collected photographs, newspaper clippings, letters, and mementos, and had even written a brief family history. Among her belongings, she preserved a letter that a teenage Thompson had written to her older sister, Dolores, as well as an exchange of letters between Lulu and Maggie, all dated shortly after the Thompsons had left Oregon for Sacramento. Thompson reminded Dolores to "Be a good little girl and help your mother all you can" (letter to Burdine 3), and Lulu joked with Maggie, "I heard that Mrs. Anderson turned out to be quite a pugilist and that she beat her husband up in fine shape. Ha! Ha!" (Lulu Thompson to Burdine 5). These letters reveal the female-centered networks that these black women nurtured as they sought solidarity in resistance to triple exploitation. The experiences Thompson had with this female-centered network would impact her later thinking as a leftist organizer. Indeed, when she recalled the "Free the Scottsboro Boys" march on Washington, she noted that one of its successes was the participation of so many women. Led by three women—Janie Patterson (mother of accused Heywood Patterson), Ruby Bates, and herself—the march brought to the "very heart of the nation" both the "fight for the Scottsboro boys" and its "many women" supporters: "Negro and white, grandmothers and mothers, children and students." "Time and time again on this trip," she continued, "it had been the women who scoffed at hardship, demanding the right to share the difficulties with the men" ("And So We Marched" 6).

This female solidarity was perhaps first suggested to Thompson by her mother, and then consolidated by her memories of the Burdine women in the West. After the Thompsons left Oregon, the Burdines remained there—but only for a time. They had a successful farm, but when Earl heard that Washington had even more fertile land, the family moved to Yakima in 1920. No sooner had they settled there than a terrible flood hit their property. The family lost everything. They were forced to begin sharecropping until they could save enough money to purchase their own land again. Soon afterward, in 1925, Maggie bore her seventh child. Only three years later, her husband died. Maggie was forty-three years old, and she had no choice but to work both on her own property and outside of the home in order to make ends meet for the large family (Burdine, "Pioneering Oregon" 3). She labored on the farm during the day, and at a cannery at night, staying in the latter position until she was seventy years old. On her ninety-seventh birthday, a profile in the *Yakima Valley Sun* opened by noting, "She is a hard-working woman...always has been," and described her legacy as a "life of toil" (Brown 16). Indeed, their experience as laborers is something Lulu Thompson and Maggie Burdine shared. In a letter Maggie wrote to her husband in 1916 while he was away driving a herd to Nevada, she mentions, "Mrs. Thompson and Louise is gone up Coos River to work for the Chandlers for $60.00 per month" (letter to Earl Burdine 3). A year later, Lulu fretted to Maggie that although she and her husband both had jobs in Sacramento, of the two of them she was the one "so anxious to work and help pay on the place" (1). Late in her life, Thompson remarked that her mother had "worked most of the time" (Gordon 21).

Black women's labor, as a result, was central to the lives of both Thompson and Burdine, and foundational to their understandings of their mothers' imprints on them. Burdine reflected that when she was growing up, "We all worked.... I had my first job when I was ten years old.... [W]e were all taught to work very young" (Patterson, Burdine, and Rutherford [Part 1] 45). Thompson, in contrast, recalled, "I would have liked to work, because my family was a very poor family, and my mother worked very hard. However, in the areas of the country in which I lived, there was little or no opportunity for a Negro girl to get other than a very menial job. So my mother preferred that I try not to earn the money that would have been very much needed at home" (Thompson, interview 2). Although a youthful Thompson did not perform the same kind of menial labor that Burdine describes, she shared a vision of black mothers as workers, particularly because of their emplacement in the West. This vision would contribute to her later commitment to organizing on behalf of proletarian African Americans, and women in particular.

Her interests in race and labor certainly brought Thompson together with her second husband, whom she called Pat, with whom she shared a lifelong devotion to the African American freedom struggle and the radical Left. While they were not as far to the Left politically as the Pattersons, Verdell Burdine and her husband, Otto Rutherford, were also activists with interests in race and labor; Otto, for example, had served as a president of the Portland NAACP and had been a union organizer (Hopkins). In contrast to Pat and Otto, however, the prior generation provided a dimmer view of husbands. Maggie Burdine had faint praise for Earl, simply describing him as "not unkind" ("Pioneering Oregon" 1). John Thompson never received even this lukewarm a description; Louise went as far as to call him "mean" (Thompson, interview by Wilkerson 18). As a result, in the archives collected by Thompson and Burdine, men rapidly fall out of the picture, and mothers emerge instead as western heroes—indeed, they are often called "pioneers."

In a 1980 recollection that Maggie Burdine contributed to the *Portland Observer*, titled "Pioneering Oregon," she attributed the decision to move to Oregon to being "an early women's libber, I guess" (1). She never characterizes the hardships that befell her family as due to her bold decision to move to the West, but rather to her husband Earl's poor business sense, which often ran counter to Maggie's desires. Thompson writes of her stepfather as equally financially inept; he spent money on things simply because he thought they were a bargain, and he steered the family relentlessly through the West as part of his naïve fantasy that he would somehow strike it rich. In the face of this, Lulu Thompson, according to her daughter, would "pretend to like" whatever her husband bought, but Louise grew resentful of his frivolity (Thompson, interview by Wilkerson 19).

When Thompson and Burdine met and exchanged memories and documents, the archive they constructed served to bring into focus a new view of the black West as a woman-centered place. Verdell gave Thompson a history of her family that she wrote for her granddaughter, and Maggie was clearly the protagonist: "Maggie Boles," she wrote, notably referring to her mother by her maiden name, "decided it was time to go West.... This sturdy pioneer woman lived to be 100 years plus 6 months, despite the windstorms, draughts, floods and the eruption of Mt. St. Helen's.... This lady was strong of character" (Rutherford 1). In 1988, Thompson also interviewed Nattie Boles Gordon, a cousin of Verdell's who had also lived in Marshfield. Gordon commented, with some befuddlement, perhaps, on Maggie's strength: "I know she was always quite a...," Gordon paused, looking for appropriate language to describe Maggie, and then failed to find a precise noun to accommodate her empowered black womanhood before continuing, "well, [she] had quite an initiative about doing things. And she was the one that initiated the move in the main, to begin with to come out to Oregon" (12). Verdell agreed that westward relocation was her mother's decision. Moving to Oregon, she insisted, was "Mama's idea.... [S]he didn't know a soul out here but she said that she had been reading flyers and things about the state of Oregon and I think at that time that people were homesteading and she just decided that she was going to come as far West...as [she could] go without going in the ocean" (Patterson, Burdine, and Rutherford [Part 1] 26–27). While Lulu Thompson sometimes seemed like a pushover to her daughter, Maggie Burdine provided a vision of black western woman's agency and independence.

As a result, with Maggie as a model, Thompson could reinterpret her mother's past as the story of a pioneer. She remarked, in an interview conducted with Verdell, "You know my mother was very much in a way like your mother. I think your mother might have been more spunky than my mother. But in terms of making do" (Patterson, Burdine, and Rutherford [Part 2] 23–24). The fantasy that Thompson constructed of Maggie Burdine could have buttressed the way she imagined the motivations for her own mother's westward journey. She speculates in her memoirs: "Perhaps she caught the fever of others in the country who responded to Horace Greely's call, 'Go West, young man! Go West!'...Moving to 'virgin' territory represented a new start and new opportunities." She continues: "I do not know whether her choice of such an adventure into the 'wild and wooly West' in 1905 was an act of courage or desperation. But West we went" ("Chapter 1" 7). Indeed, black women's survival was often both courageous and desperate. As Nellie Y. McKay's foundational work has insisted, for "generations of black women," "the center of their life stories remains black survival," and these stories are as "politically significant as more overt modes of protest" (McKay 104–5). By reconstructing black women as pioneers and survivors, Thompson is able to find a model for black women's activism akin to the "struggles for group survival" outlined by Patricia Hill Collins in *Black Feminist Thought: Knowledge, Consciousness, and the Politics of Empowerment.*

As Collins notes, "struggles for group survival" include "actions taken to create Black female spheres of influence within existing social structures," such as the family (204). Although heteropatriarchal families can limit women's agency, Collins suggests that black women have nonetheless been able to use their influence as mothers, for example, as a way to exert political power. As she writes, "women's activism within Black families" has traditionally "meshed activism as community othermothers in the wider Black community as 'family'" (210). This extended motherhood is interdependent with the "struggles for institutional transformation" that Collins defines as "changing the rules"—in "housing, employment, education, public accommodations, and political representation"—that "circumscribe African American women's lives" (216). An emphasis on motherhood as a transportable model for activism—from families to communities to institutions—is evident in Thompson's treatment of black western womanhood. It is exemplified not only by her own mother, but also by Maggie Burdine, whose stories undergird Thompson's leftist activism.

Verdell Burdine, too, explicitly connects the story of her "spunky mother" to traditions of black women's social protest. "There were five of us," she comments—here, focusing on her sisters, since there were seven Burdine children in total, with two boys—and her mother "always taught us to stand up for our rights" (Patterson, Burdine, and Rutherford [Part 2] 23–25). This was not only retrospective. In 1929, Burdine, who was then fifteen years old, wrote a poem celebrating her mother and her sacrifices, and envisioned carrying on her mother's legacy:

> How much I owe to Mother dear
> That I can never repay.
> My loving, sweetest Mother here,
> So near in every way.
> And now that I am older grown,
> I'll do my best to see
> That all her work was not in vain,
> And make her proud of me.
> (Patterson, Burdine, and Rutherford [Part 1] 43)

When they spoke with Thompson in 1989, Verdell and Otto told her about the next generation of Burdine women, including their daughter, Charlotte, who had graduated with a JD from Howard University. This, too, they attributed to Maggie. Charlotte "wanted to go to a Black school," Verdell told Thompson about her daughter. She continued, "After all these years of attending white schools she wanted to go to a Black school." "She was Maggie Burdine's," Otto added, indicating, once again, that the black western woman and the networks she created were wellsprings of empowerment (Patterson, Burdine, and Rutherford [Part 1] 42), particularly in terms of consolidating black community and institutions.

Verdell was not the only Burdine daughter with activist impulses born of her mother's example. Her older sister, Dolores, whom Thompson had reminded to "be a good little girl and help your mother" back in 1917, was profiled in the *Yakima Herald-Republic* sixty years later. The article noted that she was "chairman of the Yakima Human Relations Commission; president of the Yakima chapter of the National Association for the Advancement of Colored People;

past president of Elite Hobbyite, an arm of the National Association of Colored Women," among a litany of other roles. She once homesteaded in Alaska. She wrote poetry. The same article quoted Dolores saying, like Thompson would, that she could have obtained a job she was trained for had she been willing to pass—but "I'll never deny my heritage. That's why I'm so active now" (Gosney 2). When Thompson asked Verdell if Dolores was like her mother, Verdell answered, "She's worse than Mama. I have to show you some of the things that she's been busy with.... [S]he was very, very active in the community.... She was everything in the community." Her husband, Otto, added, "She was very liberal" (Patterson, Burdine, and Rutherford [Part 1] 50–51). The Burdine women, indeed, centered black politics and identity in their lives. Unlike their brothers, Verdell noted in an interview, "all the girls married Black" (Patterson, Burdine, and Rutherford [Part 1] 48).

Thompson's rediscovery of the Burdine women provided her with a way to understand her own experience in the West. It also enabled her to reframe her memories of her mother; by interpolating the Burdines' "spunkiness" into her vision of her mother's life, she could imagine her as a paragon of resistance rather than suffering. By coupling Maggie Burdine and Lulu Thompson, black western womanhood became for Louise a model for action in the face of triple exploitation. When Thompson turned to organizing, this would have made sense not only to her as a black woman, but also to others on the Left. Indeed, the Left had its own tradition of seeing female organizers as "mothers" of the movement. The most famous example of this is probably labor organizer Mary Harris "Mother" Jones, but "Mother" was also an honorific applied to Communist leader Ella Reeve Bloor. In 1937, Thompson wrote an article about Bloor in which she noted that Bloor had "four children to care for and support," and that she "educated these children in the ferment of the class struggle, taking them along to the picket line, to meetings and even to jail." Thompson figured Bloor as a mother to her biological children, and as a figurative mother to workers as well, for whom she likewise models class struggle. Bloor's "courage, devotion and life of struggle," Thompson claimed, "have won for her the name of 'Mother' to America's toilers" ("America's Mother" 15).

Thompson's interpretation of black western womanhood, and motherhood in particular, as the wellspring for leftist struggle was not only in retrospect. Archival evidence suggests that Thompson had been mulling over the figure of the black western woman for many years. When Thompson asked Bogle to reintroduce her to Verdell Burdine in 1987, she commented, "I would be very much interested in getting the story of her family as I remember them so vividly from our Marshfield experiences" (letter to Bogle, 1). This is a bit of an understatement. The Burdines, and Maggie in particular, actually meant much more to Thompson than a few vivid memories. Indeed, over a decade after the last time Thompson laid eyes on Maggie Burdine, but half a century before she began to do research for her memoirs, Maggie was on her mind. Indeed, during Thompson's initial years in Harlem, as she was surrounded by the creative outpourings of Thurman, Hughes, Hurston, and other colleagues, she made her only known foray into creative writing. Between 1929 and 1930, around the same time that Verdell Burdine wrote her poetic homage to her mother, Thompson conceptualized and began to draft a manuscript that she tentatively titled "Maggie the Courageous." As this title suggests, the manuscript focuses on Maggie, the matriarch of the Burdine family, and her efforts, as part of her search for a better life than the one possible on a sharecropping plantation in drought-riddled Oklahoma, to move her family to Oregon to homestead. The manuscript is unfinished, consisting of only three short chapters, a summary of the plot, and descriptions of the main characters. Thompson described her protagonist as "fearless, ambitious—thrifty, industrious—endowed with high sense of sacrifice for her children." Among these children, in Thompson's rendition, "the only one in the family with any appreciation for her mother's sacrifices" is Verdell, whom she describes as an "earnest, hardworking girl" ("Maggie the Courageous" 1).

In her draft, Thompson's third-person omniscient narrator is focused on Maggie, often inhabiting her perspective. As the family rides the train on the five-day-long journey from Oklahoma to Oregon:

> The woman fingered for the hundredth time the well-worn

> folder sent to her by the enterprising, boosting Chamber of Commerce of Bend, Oregon. She knew every glamorous word, but a warm tingle of pleasure pulsated within her and two crimson spots inflamed each freckled cheek as she re-read the pages. "A farm of one hundred and fifty acres; richly timbered, virgin soil; rich pasturage; ample water; ideal climate...." Free to all who cared to take up a homestead and make themselves a new home! One hundred and fifty acres! ("Promised Land" 2)

Thompson's fictional reworking of Maggie's story imagines Maggie in much the way that Maggie seems to have imagined herself, and in much the way that her daughter, Verdell, envisioned her. She is an agent, a go-getter, and the character around whom the plot circulates. She incites all the action in the narrative. The move to Oregon is her decision, and it is a clear act of subversion—both of her husband and of the exploitative practices of sharecropping that her family endures in Oklahoma. In Thompson's manuscript, when Earl meets Maggie as she flees Oklahoma, she is not concerned in the least about his whereabouts. She tells him, "I'm takin' my children and goin' North.... You can come if you wanta, or you can stay—but I'm goin' jest the same" ("Goin' North" 4). She can no longer endure, she insists, the droughts and the "debt to the white folks," and she is "goin' to take my children North where they'll have some chance to get an education and be somethin'" ("Goin' North" 5–6). "I knew you wouldn't do nothin' bout" the family's oppression in Oklahoma, she tells him, "[s]o I jest went ahead by myself" ("Goin' North" 7). When she rejects the conditions of her labor, the authority of her husband, and the discrimination leveled at her race, Maggie's move West, as Thompson represents it, is an effort to throw off black women's triple exploitation.

Indeed, in Thompson's prose, Maggie's westward journey is patterned after the biblical Book of Exodus, the tale of Israelite emancipation, which, as African American religious studies scholar Eddie S. Glaude Jr. has pointed out, has long been embraced by black Americans who sought pathways from enslavement to freedom. It is a revealing slippage when the geography referred to as the "far West" throughout

Thompson's oeuvre is in this manuscript also the "North." First, this embeds "Maggie the Courageous" among the more traditional trajectories of the Great Migration common during the Harlem Renaissance years; second, it harks back to the bifurcated geography of North and South that emerged from the sectional crisis over slavery—due, in part, of course, to westward expansion. Thompson engages in this tradition of allusion to the Book of Exodus at the end of her second chapter, titled "The Promised Land," when she describes how after arriving in Oregon, Maggie "bowed her head in a prayer to the blessed Lord who had led her out of bondage into this land of promise" (9). As a result, Thompson's Maggie follows in the tradition of black migration most famously embodied by the Exoduster Movement to Nicodemus, Kansas, and other points West in the 1870s, a mass migration of thousands of African Americans out of the South in search of a promised land for black freedom, some of them guided by millenarian religious beliefs. Oregon subsequently appears as an Edenic paradise to Maggie, whose first glimpse of the countryside is of the "land of her dreams," replete with thickly timbered mountains and…the blue-red of…dawn." She wakes her husband, hoping he will share this utopian moment with her. But Earl drowsily rebuffs her after she hastily explains, "It's so pretty it makes me ache all over with joy." It is never him, only Maggie, who is convinced the West will give her family "[t]heir chance, thank God!" ("Promised Land" 8).

Unfortunately, once Maggie's family arrives in Bend, they are immediately subjected to racism. When they step off the train they are greeted by "rude, curious stares" and the vicious hiss of racist taunts by "the usual crowd of station loafers" ("Promised Land" 4). They are unable to find a restaurant that will serve them. They are finally forced to take up residence on the margins of town in a "tiny cottage" that "reared itself up as the last outpost of the village" ("Maggie the Courageous" 31). Even Maggie's first breathtaking glimpse of the lushly forested landscape can happen only after she makes herself quickly skim over the "garbage cans and ash heaps" that are at the foreground of her line of vision, due to the fact that the only place the Burdines could find to stay their first night in Oregon is in the "shack" of a porter the townspeople call "Nigger Jim," little more than a ramshackle lean-to adjoining the kitchen of the hotel where he works ("Promised Land" 7).

While Thompson's manuscript endeavors to understand the forces that would have driven black women West, the West never becomes the space for black female freedom for which her character, Maggie, hoped. This reality forced Thompson to participate in an exodus of her own, leaving the West for the East—and for the Left. In his study of the black West, historian Quintard Taylor has lamented the tired representation of "'motherly but single' elderly black female pioneer[s]," the "sturdy but silent *black* women" who, he argues, prop up the "stereotype of the black westerner as a solitary figure loosened from the mooring of family, home and community" (Taylor 22). Thompson's representation of black western women is suggestive of these images, but also undoes them. These women are autonomous actors, but they are not entirely alone. When she constructed her memoirs, Thompson treated her middle name, "Alone," as a prophecy of her western childhood: "When I was born, my mother's best friend came into the birthing room and announced that my name would be Louise Alone. Little did any of us know at that time how appropriate that name was for me.... As a black girl...growing up in the far West...I would live...in the loneliness of a person without community" ("Chapter 1" 2). But at the same time that her name portends this loneliness, her archive consistently undermines solitude by mapping multigenerational networks of black women survivors and activists. As a result, when Thompson imagines a range of black women in the role of the sturdy pioneer—the Burdines, her own mother, Kathryn Bogle, and even, perhaps, herself—she finds a way not only to disrupt deracinated images of western womanhood, but also to render black women's courage as well as desperation in their struggles for group survival. In doing so, Thompson creates a usable western past from experiences that could otherwise be shattering. By repurposing images of self-sufficient black pioneer women, she discovers models for black women's resistance to triple exploitation.

Indeed, attention to the nexus of gender, race, and class was crucial to Thompson's organizing for the Communist Party. She was perhaps the Left's earliest and most distinctive spokesperson for what today is called "intersectionality"—not only as a theoretical lens with which to analyze structural inequality, but also as a "critical praxis" (Collins and Bilge 31–32). In a 1937 article titled "Negro Women in Our Party," she remarks somewhat obliquely on the "extra special conditions"—sexism and racism—"that have kept [black women] up to now out of the labor movement entirely" despite their proletarian experiences and sympathies. This marginalization has, she asserts, made black women "feel strange" at party functions—as alienated in the Left as Thompson once was in the West. She encourages her comrades to create personal contacts with black women, which, she says, may not appear "so political, but they do mean a great deal." She goes on to contend, forecasting later slogans of the women's liberation movement, that "political life and personal life tie up together." With a "human approach," and with the ascent of black women to party leadership roles, Thompson suggests, black women will be better able to see themselves as part of the organization. Without women, she warns—without the mothers and community othermothers whose struggles for group survival are so crucial to African American politics—"our work in the Negro territories is going to be seriously hampered." "Getting large sections of Negro women is going to root the Party among the Negroes," she insists. But to do so will require "special attention be given to Negro women on the basis of their special problems"—their triple exploitation (25–27). Although Thompson left the West for the Left, she never left the lessons she learned there about triple exploitation and woman-centered activism; indeed, her western experiences were foundational to her vision of black women as a revolutionary vanguard.

Bibliography

Baptist, Edward. *The Half Has Never Been Told: Slavery and the Making of American Capitalism*. Basic Books, 2014.

Bogle, Kathryn Hall. "An American Negro Speaks of Color." *Oregon Historical Quarterly*, vol. 89, no. 1, Spring 1988, pp. 70–91.

Brown, Patricia. "Memories of 97 Years Light Birthday Cake for Margaret Cash." *Yakima Valley Sun*, 9 Sept. 1982, 16+.

Burdine, Margaret [Maggie]. Letter to Earl Burdine. 8 Aug. 1916. Louise Thompson

Patterson Papers, Stuart A. Rose Manuscript, Archives, and Rare Book Library, Emory University, box 4, folder 1. Manuscript.

———. "Pioneering Oregon." *Portland Observer*, 22 May 1980, pp. 1–3.

Collins, Patricia Hill. *Black Feminist Thought: Knowledge, Consciousness, and the Politics of Empowerment*. Routledge, 2000.

Collins, Patricia Hill, and Sirma Bilge. *Intersectionality*. Polity Press, 2016.

Dolinar, Brian. *The Black Cultural Front: Black Writers and Artists of the Depression Generation*. UP of Mississippi, 2012.

Edwards, Brent Hayes. *The Practice of Diaspora: Literature, Translation, and the Rise of Black Internationalism*. Harvard UP, 2003.

Gilyard, Keith. *Louise Thompson Patterson: A Life of Struggle for Justice*. Duke UP, 2017.

Glaude, Eddie S., Jr. *Exodus! Religion, Race, and Nation in Early Nineteenth-Century Black America*. U of Chicago P, 2000.

Gordon, Nattie Boles. Interview by Louise Thompson Patterson, Margaret Wilkerson, and Beverly John. Louise Thompson Patterson Papers, Stuart A. Rose Manuscript, Archives, and Rare Book Library, Emory University, box 27, folder 15. Typescript.

Gore, Dayo F. *Radicalism at the Crossroads: African American Women Activists in the Cold War*. New York UP, 2011.

Gosney, Jim. "Dolores Goodman: She Still Holds Out for a Racial Cure." *Yakima Herald-Republic*, 1 Nov. 1977, p. 2.

Higashida, Cheryl. *Black Internationalist Feminism: Women Writers of the Black Left, 1945–1995*. U of Illinois P, 2011.

Hobbs, Allyson. *A Chosen Exile: A History of Racial Passing in American Life*. Harvard UP, 2014.

Hopkins, Oz. "Black Family Looks Back," *Oregon Journal*, 1 Feb. 1977. Louise Thompson Patterson Papers, Stuart A. Rose Manuscript, Archives, and Rare Book Library, Emory University, box 4, folder 1.

Hughes, Langston. "Don't You Want to Be Free? A Poetry Play from Slavery Through the Blues to Now—and Then Some! With Singing, Music, and Dancing." 1938. *The Collected Works of Langston Hughes*, edited by Leslie Catherine Saunders, with Nancy Johnson, vol. 5, U of Missouri P, 2002, pp. 538–73.

———. *I Wonder as I Wander*. Hill & Wang, 1993.

———. *Not Without Laughter*. Simon & Schuster, 1996.

Hurston, Zora Neale. *Mules and Men*. HarperPerennial, 2008.

Lemke, Sieglinde. *Primitivist Modernism: Black Culture and the Origins of Transatlantic Modernism*. Oxford UP, 1998.

Makalani, Minkah. *In the Cause of Freedom: Radical Black Internationalism from Harlem to London, 1912–1939*. U of North Carolina P, 2011.

Maxwell, William J. *New Negro, Old Left: African American Writing and Communism Between the Wars*. Columbia UP, 1999.

McDuffie, Erik S. *Sojourning for Freedom: Black Women, American Communism, and the Making of Black Left Feminism*. Duke UP, 2011.

McKay, Nellie Y. "The Narrative Self: Race, Politics, and Culture in Black American Women's Autobiography." *Women, Autobiography, Theory: A Reader*, edited by Sidonie Smith and Julia Watson, U of Wisconsin P, 1998, pp. 96–107.

Naison, Mark. *Communists in Harlem during the Depression*. U of Illinois P, 1983.

Newlands, Francis G. "A Western View of the Race Question." *Annals of the American Academy of Political and Social Science*, vol. 34, no. 2, Sept. 1909, pp. 49–51.

Painter, Nell Irvin. *Exodusters: Black Migration to Kansas After Reconstruction*. W. W. Norton, 1986.

Patterson, Louise Thompson, Verdell Burdine, and Otto Rutherford. Interview by Margaret Wilkerson and Beverly John, part 1. Louise Thompson Patterson Papers, Stuart A. Rose Manuscript, Archives, and Rare Book Library, Emory University, box 27, folder 16. Typescript.

———. Interview by Margaret Wilkerson and Beverly John, part 2. Louise Thompson Patterson Papers, Stuart A. Rose Manuscript, Archives, and Rare Book Library, Emory University, box 28, folder 1. Typescript.

Rampersad, Arnold. *The Life of Langston Hughes*. Vol. 1, Oxford UP, 2002.

Rocha, Guy Louis. Letter to Margaret Wilkerson. 15 Sept. 1987. Louise Thompson Patterson Papers, Stuart A. Rose Manuscript, Archives, and Rare Book Library, Emory University, box 2, folder 23. Typescript.

Rutherford, Verdell Burdine. "History of the Boles and Burdine Families from 1904 to 1990." Louise Thompson Patterson Papers, Stuart A. Rose Manuscript, Archives, and Rare Book Library, Emory University, box 4, folder 1. Typescript.

Steiner, Michael C. "Varieties of Western American Regionalism." Introduction. *Regionalists on the Left: Radical Voices from the American West*, edited by Steiner, U of Oklahoma P, 2013, pp. 1–20.

Taylor, Quintard. *In Search of the Racial Frontier: African Americans in the American West, 1528–1990*. W. W. Norton, 1998.

Thompson [Patterson], Louise. "America's Mother." *New Order*, July 1973, p. 15.

———. "And So We Marched." *The Working Woman*, June 1933, p. 6.

———. "Chapter 1: Childhood/West." Draft A. Louise Thompson Patterson Papers, Stuart A. Rose Manuscript, Archives, and Rare Book Library, Emory University, box 19, folder 15. Typescript.

———. "Chapter 2: Pine Bluff/Hampton." Draft B. Louise Thompson Patterson Papers, Stuart A. Rose Manuscript, Archives, and Rare Book Library, Emory University, box 19, folder 18. Typescript.

———. "Chapter 3: Harlem in the 1920s." Louise Thompson Patterson Papers, Stuart A. Rose Manuscript, Archives, and Rare Book Library, Emory University, box 19, folder 20. Typescript.

———. "Goin' North." Louise Thompson Patterson Papers, Stuart A. Rose

Manuscript, Archives, and Rare Book Library, Emory University, box 19, folder 10. Typescript.

———. Interview. Louise Thompson Patterson Papers, Stuart A. Rose Manuscript, Archives, and Rare Book Library, Emory University, box 27, folder 1. Typescript.

———. Interview by Margaret Wilkerson. Louise Thompson Patterson Papers, Stuart A. Rose Manuscript, Archives, and Rare Book Library, Emory University, box 27, folder 5. Typescript.

———. Letter to Dolores Burdine. 18 Mar. 1917. Louise Thompson Patterson Papers, Stuart A. Rose Manuscript, Archives, and Rare Book Library, Emory University, box 4, folder 1. Manuscript.

———. Letter to Kathryn Bogle. 16 Sept. 1987. Louise Thompson Patterson Papers, Stuart A. Rose Manuscript, Archives, and Rare Book Library, Emory University, box 3, folder 4. Typescript.

———. Letter to Kathryn Bogle. 4 Nov. 1987. Louise Thompson Patterson Papers, Stuart A. Rose Manuscript, Archives, and Rare Book Library, Emory University, box 3, folder 4. Typescript.

———. Letter to Roosevelt Fitzgerald. 4 Nov. 1987. Louise Thompson Patterson Papers, Stuart A. Rose Manuscript, Archives, and Rare Book Library, Emory University, box 22, folder 23. Typescript.

———. Letter [signed "A Silent Onlooker"] to W. E. B. DuBois. 13 Oct. 1927. W. E. B. Du Bois Papers, Special Collections and University Archives, University of Massachusetts, Amherst, MS 312.

———. "Maggie the Courageous." Louise Thompson Patterson Papers, Stuart A. Rose Manuscript, Archives, and Rare Book Library, Emory University, box 19, folder 5. Manuscript.

———. "Negro Women in Our Party." *Party Organizer*, July 1937, pp. 25–27.

———. "The Promised Land." Louise Thompson Patterson Papers, Stuart A. Rose Manuscript, Archives, and Rare Book Library, Emory University, box 20, folder 13. Typescript.

———. "Southern Terror." *The Crisis*, vol. 41, no. 11, Nov. 1934, pp. 327–28.

———. "Toward a Brighter Dawn." *Woman Today*, Apr. 1936, pp. 14+.

Thompson, Lulu. Letter to Margaret [Maggie] Burdine. 27 June 1917. Louise Thompson Patterson Papers, Stuart A. Rose Manuscript, Archives, and Rare Book Library, Emory University, box 23, folder 3. Manuscript.

U.S. Bureau of the Census. *Thirteenth Census of the United States, 1910*. Population: Color or Race, Nativity, Parentage, and Sex. GPO, 1913.

———. *Thirteenth Census of the United States, 1910*. Oakland Ward 3, Alameda, CA. Roll T624_40. Records of the Bureau of the Census, Record Group 29, National Archives, Washington, D.C. Microfilm.

———. *Fourteenth Census of the United States Taken in the Year 1920*. Vol. 3, Composition and Characteristics of the Population by States. GPO, 1922.

Wilkerson, Margaret. Letter to Robert Nylen. 30 Aug. 1987. Louise Thompson Patterson Papers, Stuart A. Rose Manuscript, Archives, and Rare Book Library, Emory University, box 2, folder 23. Typescript.

14

Charlotte Perkins Gilman's *Herland*, Race, and the California Suffrage and Women's Club Movements, 1896–1911

DARCIE RIVES-EAST

While California is today frequently seen as a bastion of the American Left and liberal politics, its history in terms of race relations reveals contradictions in this image of tolerance and forward thinking. From Ku Klux Klan activities in the early twentieth century to the Rodney King verdict and subsequent riots of 1992, racism and racial tensions have and continue to shadow California politics and culture.[1] This essay will focus on one particular episode in this history of racial tension: the Progressive Era politics of the California suffrage and women's club movement from 1896 to 1911, and its relationship to writer and feminist Charlotte Perkins Gilman, who was a longtime resident of the state and active in the California suffrage and women's club cause. Both Gilman's writing and the suffrage/club effort occupy a complex position in the history of California and the political Left. On the one hand, both championed Progressive Era efforts to further women's rights and improve the general welfare of society. On the other, both reiterated a general Progressive Era opposition to racial equality that was anything but reformist.[2] We can see this tension if we examine Gilman's famous 1915 utopian novel *Herland* against the backdrop of the California suffrage and women's club movement. This essay argues that Gilman's participation in this movement influenced her erasure of women of color from her novel *Herland*, written four years after California's approval of the vote for women. If read in this way, we can understand the novel's interpretation of womanhood as more influenced by California politics and racial tensions than previously acknowledged.

Before critiquing Gilman's *Herland*, it is important to understand how and why she can be considered a writer of the early twentieth-century Left despite her racial views. Gilman was in step with the Progressive Era, a time of radical political and social reform that particularly targeted big business practices and poverty through improvements in workers' rights, public education, and civic enhancements.[3] Further, the Progressive Movement also focused on women's rights and women's suffrage. As a writer and political reformer, Gilman stood at the crossroads of Progressive class and gender causes by arguing that poverty and gender inequity went hand in hand; to eliminate the former, one had to first allow women to fully participate in the life of American society.[4] While she wrote numerous essays and gave frequent speeches on this topic,[5] nowhere did she illustrate her Progressive argument better than in her feminist utopia *Herland*. There, poverty is nonexistent because women are involved in all aspects of civic life. Their creativity and carefulness allow the Herland women to think of solutions to the problems of privation and penury that had not been resolved in America because women there were excluded from public life and decision making.[6] For Gilman, major social issues could not be tackled unless all citizens, men and women, could contribute their minds and efforts to the cause. And yet, by "all citizens" Gilman meant exclusively white men and women. No matter how radical or left-leaning Gilman could be—both professionally and personally[7]—she was nevertheless conservative in her attitudes about race in America. While the Progressive movement included African American activists such as Ida B. Wells and W. E. B. Du Bois, who fought Jim Crow and racial prejudice, white Progressive campaigners were at best indifferent to racial strife, or, like Gilman, opposed to racial equality.[8]

Although it is apparent to any reader of Gilman's *Herland* that her vision of an all-female society is racially exclusionist, what may not be so evident is the connection between the absence of women of color in the novel and Gilman's participation in the California women's suffrage and club movement during and after her residency in that state. In the years between 1896, when the first referendum on women's suffrage failed in California, and 1911, the year of its successful ratification, the state's suffrage and club movement reconstructed womanhood as entirely white. This interpretation appealed to white male voters, and to white women themselves, by reasserting that the allegiance of white women, both those of the working and upper classes, lay with the white male political establishment and not with women of the growing non-white populations, such as African Americans, in California. In other words, to gain the vote, the California suffrage movement spun it as less of a gender issue and more of a racial one. Gilman, a key participant in this suffrage and club movement, reflected this white-washed version of womanhood in her 1915 feminist utopia, only four years after ratification.

In the past decade of Gilman scholarship, critics have noted how Gilman's feminism focused solely on the welfare and status of white women (Ganobcsik-Williams, "Confronting" and "Intellectualism"; Fessenden; Lanser; Weinbaum; Knight; Seitler). These scholars have clearly demonstrated that based on her nonfiction and fiction writing, Gilman considered people of color and immigrants to be inferior and less developed than whites, and therefore not worthy of the civil rights she was demanding for white women like herself. Cynthia J. Davis points out that Gilman's racism became more virulent over time as she became more wedded to the Progressive Era desire for a "pure" society, free of disease and criminality, through the practice of racial eugenics (300–301). For example, in her 1908 essay "A Suggestion on the Negro Problem," Gilman argues that while slavery is morally wrong, black Americans are nonetheless less developed as a race than whites: "What can we do to promote the development of the backward race so that it may become an advantageous element in the community? This is not a question of 'equality' in any sense.... It is quite possible to have in a society members far inferior to other members, but yet essential to the life of the whole" (79–80).[9] She thus recommends that black Americans be kept separate from whites and forced into what amounts to another version of slavery (although Gilman denies this characterization, terming it "enlistment" instead) (81). She writes that black Americans should be formed into a "new army" of laborers for farms and factories that would be, in Gilman's own words, a "state organization of the negro, under conditions wholly to his advantage, and therefore to ours" (82), until African Americans are "self-supporting" (83).

This social Darwinian view of African Americans is also reflected in Gilman's fictional works, such as *Herland*, in which she details a paradisiacal society composed solely of white women, a society from which racial difference—and thus, in eugenics theory, disease, deformity, and criminality—has been eradicated. Such health and well-being had been created through what Van, the narrator, terms "negative eugenics," in which some women "had to forgo motherhood for their country" (69). Reading this novel alongside her essay on black Americans, we can see that for Gilman, the "appalling sacrifice" (69), as Van calls it, was in part the eradication of nonwhite elements from the gene pool of the Herland women. In Gilman's equation, white working-class women could be embraced in this definition of womanhood, given that Herland women labor in construction, farming, and manufacturing, as well as participate in intellectual and artistic endeavors. However, the word "woman" for Gilman certainly did not signify African American women or other women of color.

Such ideas of "pure" womanhood stem from Gilman's involvement in California gender and racial politics beginning in 1888, when Gilman moved to Pasadena from New England with her mother and her daughter, Katherine, after separating from her husband, Charles Walter Stetson.[10] There, she became involved in many Progressive Era reform movements and organizations aimed at improving social ills as well as expanding women's visibility and opportunities in the public sphere. Gilman traveled throughout California, speaking to various women's clubs about the vote and the place of women in society. She also became a representative of the Pacific Coast Woman's Congress Association and of the California Woman Suffrage Educational Association (CWSEA).[11] In these leadership positions, Gilman's notions of how to construct womanhood so that women could enter the political sphere without threatening the established power of white men made her one of many similar voices guiding how the California suffrage movement as a whole presented the 1896 referendum and, later, their second attempt at the vote in 1911.[12]

Gilman's vision of female citizenship was for her and other Progressive Era women both different and more civically minded than men's. For example, in 1891, she told Los Angeles clubwomen that women should become "municipal housekeepers," spearheading civic reforms and taking on responsibility for the health and welfare of not just the home, but of society (qtd. in Gullet, "Constructing" 579). As historian Gayle Gullet observes, "the audience responded most favorably to the calls to concern themselves with food poisoning, sewage systems, and city policing. Women would become a new kind of urban citizen, not a political man and not a private woman" (579). Gilman, who was also a member of the program committee for the 1895 Women's Congress in San Francisco, used this understanding of womanhood as the Congress's platform, which she entitled "Woman and the Home" (579). We see this ideal of the female public citizen as social caretaker embodied in the women of *Herland.* Motherhood there is the guiding principle in building an altruistic society that, according to narrator Van, "had no wars. They had had no kings, and no priests, and no aristocracies. They were sisters, and as they grew, they grew together—not by competition, but by united action" (61). This notion that female citizenship is necessary to overcome social ills was central to Gilman's and other club and suffrage leaders' efforts to gain women the vote in California.

Although Gilman does not explicitly address the issue of race in this understanding of woman as public citizen, it is nonetheless implied that this new female citizen was white. In Gilman's version of womanhood, she and other club and suffrage leaders "acknowledged that gaining the vote meant a dramatic change and promising that women citizens would establish a moral, and thus stable, social order" (Gullet, "Constructing" 580). Part of establishing this order meant reaffirming white supremacy in California, which was becoming increasingly racially and ethnically diverse from an influx of immigrants from abroad and nonwhite Americans from other states (e.g., African Americans fleeing the Jim Crow South). This diversity was often seen as the source of poverty, violence, and other social ills that concerned Progressives in California and nationwide (Davis 119). Indeed, Anna Howard Shaw, vice president of the National American Woman Suffrage Association (NAWSA), as well as a prominent representative of the Woman's Christian Temperance Union (WCTU), spoke throughout the state in 1895 before the vote on women's suffrage, reassuring male voters that suffrage leaders were white, Protestant, and, as such, loyal to white hegemony (Gullet, "Constructing" 580–81). Further, such campaigning foreshadowed what white women leaders in the state would do in 1911. Namely, when the suffrage leaders reached out to working-class women, they ignored black and Latina women and focused solely on those who were white, creating an alliance that was "class inclusive and racially exclusive" (580). However, despite such attempts to make women's suffrage palatable to male voters, California women did not gain the vote in 1896.

The 1896 referendum failed, particularly in the San Francisco and Oakland areas, because of the involvement of the Woman's Christian Temperance Union. The measure lost support particularly among the large immigrant population of San Francisco for whom beer and other alcohol sales was an important means of earning a living and for whom alcohol was a part of their cultural practices.[13] Indeed, in a report written by Ellen Clark Sargent (president of the California Woman Suffrage Association), and read by Mary G. Hay at the 1897 Convention of the National American Woman Suffrage Association, the author laments that those in favor of women's suffrage did not organize sufficiently in the working-class districts of San Francisco and Oakland; as a result, the 1896 amendment was defeated by liquor industry interests ("Proceedings of the 29th").[14] A different report from the same convention voices optimism, however. It claims that subsequent realization among working-class voters in San Francisco and Oakland of the extent of the liquor industry misinformation campaign had led many men to regret voting against the proposal and that they would support future efforts to give women the vote ("Proceedings of the 29th").

Despite such sanguinity, one of the problems facing California club and suffrage leaders in getting the vote back on the ballot was to reconstitute the nature of suffrage itself—to alter its image of both radicalism and prohibition. The beginnings of such a move can be seen in the 1897 NAWSA and CWSEA reports noted above. While the California NAWSA delegates acknowledge the input of the WCTU and Shaw in the cause, Sargent also emphasizes that the organization's focus on the vote and not on other issues, such as prohibition, gained the support of many men across the political spectrum ("Proceedings of the 29th"). Further, Ida H. Harper, the chairwoman of the California Press Committee, describes their efforts to win the approval of male voters during the 1896 campaign by using newspapers and other publications to persuade men that women should play a role in civic affairs ("Proceedings of the 29th").[15] These comments show how California clubwomen and the suffrage movement in general would begin to refashion their cause from one dominated by temperance to one based on uniting class but excluding race in defining a woman citizen whose ability to vote would appeal to the greatest number of men in California.[16]

As noted earlier, Gilman's *Herland* likewise deemphasizes radicalism in favor of altruistic motherhood, and it also does not stress the notion of prohibition. For example, in the novel, Terry, one of a male trio of explorers who are the first men to ever visit the all-female utopia, complains: "There's nothing to drink. These blessed women have no pleasant vices. I wish we could get out of here!" (98). Here, we can read Gilman as acknowledging the temperance cause among women who wanted the vote to instate prohibition, and yet the novel does not contain any impassioned discussion of temperance issues. We can view this silence on temperance through Gilman's own experience with the 1896 California suffrage cause, as it was the linking of temperance with the women's vote that in part led to the defeat of the referendum.

Interestingly, Gilman's relative silence on the temperance issue in *Herland* aligns her more with the women of color she would seek to erase in the same novel. An analysis of extant copies of the Los Angeles-based black newspaper *The California Eagle*, edited by Carlotta Bass, shows that the paper was staunchly Republican and AME (African Methodist Episcopal) in its stance. As such, it focused on racial uplift and combating Jim Crow discrimination and violence, rather than temperance and suffrage.[17] Though issues of the newspaper before 1914 are not available, what we see in editions published four years after women's suffrage was approved in California can help us understand how this paper, and how some in the African American community, would have responded to the temperance movement prior to 1914.

As befitting the paper's emphasis on religion, concern is expressed in editorial columns more generally about the conduct of African American men and women and its effect on gaining racial equality. For example, in her February 1914 editorial, "The Progress of the Negro," Mrs. Noah H. Thompson argues not for women's suffrage, but, rather, for black women's virtue: "The sweetest flower in the garden of morals is womanly modesty—that innate, intangible something that will not permit a true woman, not withstanding the degenerate fashions of the day, to disclose the sharp outlines of her figure and appear before the eyes of men in a manner conducive to the feeding of their worst appetites" (Thompson).

Such emphasis on the necessity of black women's modesty, rather than on suffrage or the desire for women to participate in politics, is understandable, given that African American women were struggling to be simply viewed as women like their white sisters. While white clubwomen and suffragists could afford to push against the "cult of domesticity" that still defined middle- and upper-class white women in the early twentieth century, black women could not. Indeed, African American women desired to be considered as virtuously feminine as white women to contest the licentious image forced on them by the white dominant culture since slavery.[18] For instance, Venetria K. Patton argues that because black women were framed during slavery as sexual, immodest, and not "true" women, postbellum African American women often sought and desired to enact the traditional forms of femininity expected of white women (Patton 94–95). These editorials in *The California Eagle* can therefore be understood as attempts to reinstate black women as a signified of the term "woman." Gilman and other white California leaders attempted to erase women of color from the definition of the word; in response, *The California Eagle*'s strategy to combat this erasure was to demand that black women first be allowed to inhabit the role of traditional femininity, to be recognized as women, rather than be removed altogether from the equation.

The focus on race rather than gender is evident throughout *The California Eagle*, which carefully and frequently reports how discriminatory practices against African Americans were rife throughout California. For example, one 1914 column denounces the Progressive administration of California governor Hiram Johnson for being Jim Crow in its segregation of the prison population: "It is hard for us [*The California Eagle*] to understand why a criminal's color gives him any preference, and we are constrained to say that this segregation is uncalled for and only in keeping with the present practices in vogue by the present party in power in this state" ("Progressives"). Of note here is how the newspaper characterizes the Progressive Party as not at all progressive in matters of race. Indeed, the editorial emphasizes its anti–Progressive Party stance by stating that while "they [the Johnson administration] have some Negro trimmers who will apologize and have the brazen effrontery to ask Negro voters to support the present administration," the majority of California's black male voters would not give their support ("Progressives").

The paper's anger at the Johnson administration is significant, given that it was under this regime that women won the right to vote in California in 1911. It highlights what would become a division between white women and women of color in terms of political allegiance and goals between 1896 and 1911. While Gilman and other club and suffrage leaders had certainly excluded women of color from their definition of womanhood in the lead-up to the 1896 referendum, those same women would stress this racial division even further to secure the vote in 1911. For example, Harper contends that during the 1896 campaign, the California Press Committee of the CSWA began to work with newspapers to publicize the cause ("Proceedings of the 29th"). While Harper's report does mention that publications by people of color did editorially support the vote ("Proceedings of the 29th"), this notation is in passing, and it is not at all clear which publications are being referred to. Instead, the report places more emphasis on the fact that Spanish, French, Italian, and Jewish publications favored women's suffrage ("Proceedings of the 29th"). Such focus indicates that "whiteness" was being used, to an extent, to appeal to some ethnic and racial groups as opposed to others (e.g., African Americans).

During the years between 1896 and 1911, more California white middle- and upper-class women became involved in Progressive Era notions of social improvement and uplift. One manifestation of this participation was the City Beautiful movement (Gullet, "Constructing" 584). Rather than focus on temperance or even suffrage, after 1896 white women like Gilman defined their citizenship in terms of social altruism by participating in women's clubs. These clubs worked to improve social welfare in urban areas and enhance the facilities and appearance of American cities, such as through the construction of parks and playgrounds in cities such as San Francisco.[19] The City Beautiful focus adopted by prominent white California clubwomen is reflected in the architecture and landscape of Gilman's *Herland* utopia. Van observes that there, "Everything was beauty, order, perfect cleanliness.... As we neared the center of town the houses stood thicker, ran together as it were, grew into rambling palaces grouped among parks and open squares, something as college buildings stand in their quiet greens" (20–21). Even Van's various descriptions of the Herland women's altruistic work ethic, in which all action is geared toward the benefit of their society, can be read as echoing the ideals of the white women's club movement.

Through Progressive causes such as the City Beautiful movement, white California clubwomen were constructing their citizenship along the lines that Gilman had drawn prior to 1896 and later in her 1915 novel. They combined the private and public sphere, thus marrying the concerns of traditional femininity (such as the health and welfare of mothers and children) with civic duty. In this way, even more so than in 1896, white middle- and upper-class women were able to create a nonthreatening version of womanhood in California politics, one that could inhabit the public arena without disrupting traditional expectations of gender. California clubwomen were, in other words, laying the groundwork for a second attempt at gaining the vote. By 1911, this foundation was evident. For instance, a pamphlet of the Political Equality

League of Los Angeles, addressed to "Mothers, Fathers, and All Good Citizens," urges ratification of the 1911 amendment. It describes women as mothers whose primary place is in the home but also as citizens who need the vote to maintain a quality public infrastructure that can support a good domestic environment ("Announcement"). This linkage of social welfare, mothers, and the vote is remarkably like Gilman's construction of womanhood nearly fifteen years earlier, during her involvement in California politics. It demonstrates how Gilman's understanding of womanhood, as she later develops it in *Herland*, mirrors that of other suffrage and club leaders in the state.

However, this connection of women and social welfare also drove a wedge more deeply between white and nonwhite women. The City Beautiful cause, in California as elsewhere, arose in response to the dominant white culture's fears about growing urban populations, especially Asian and black residents. For example, Van remarks in *Herland* that he "come[s] from California, and there's no country lovelier, but when it comes to towns—! I have often groaned at home to see the offensive mess man made in the fact of nature" (20). Improving cities became a means of dealing with poverty and urban blight but also encouraging the white working class to share a sense of values and civic pride with the white upper class (Gullet, "Constructing" 581). However, this alignment in terms of the women's movement was always volatile. White working-class women wanted the vote to ensure changes in labor practices. In this way, they were often at odds with the views of white middle- and upper-class women, who most often opposed labor strikes such as the 1907 San Francisco streetcar workers' walkout for better wages and working hours (Englander, "'We Want'" 218). Further, because many working-class white women were employed in industries that relied on liquor sales (e.g., restaurants or hotels), they were antiprohibitionist, unlike their upper-class sisters (218). In this context, white upper-class women courted white working-class women (and men) to form an admittedly uneasy and tenuous alliance to achieve the vote (218). For instance, the 1898 CWSEA report argues that if the suffrage movement in 1896 had clarified for white working-class men in San Francisco and Oakland that it was in the men's interest for their wives and daughters to gain the vote, then suffrage could have been ratified ("Proceedings of the 30th"). This "interest" was achieved in part by creating a common fear of the increasing racial diversity in California. Indeed, Gullet observes that Clara Burdette, "the first president of the [California] state federation of clubs," desired that the organization restrict membership to white women. In 1902, the General Federation of Women's Clubs (GFWC) followed through and voted to exclude African American women (Gullet, "Constructing" 583).

This strategy was used in California to redefine the word "woman" to mean exclusively white, to unite white women of different classes, and to demonstrate that white women were in alignment with the interests of white men. Certainly, the 1898 CWSEA report blames the 1896 referendum failure in part on immigrant voters and Chinese Americans, commenting derogatorily on their intelligence ("Proceedings of the 30th"). But more so, this strategy erased women of color, and they were rendered invisible in the California suffrage movement.

This invisibility is evident in Gilman's *Herland*. The absence of women of color in this novel is remarkable, considering that in her other writings Gilman is quite vocal about her thoughts on race, evolution, and social progress. Gilman even addresses racial miscegenation and its supposedly dire consequences in her 1911 novel, *The Crux;*[20] and yet, four years later, race is unseen in *Herland*. It is perhaps not a coincidence that Gilman removes race in a novel written after the successful efforts of white California clubwomen to gain the vote by likewise deleting women of color from the suffrage movement. In *Herland*, we learn that the all-female population descends from "Aryan stock, and were once in contact with the best civilization of the old world" (55). Further, the reader discovers that they were a "polygamous people, and a slave-holding people, like all of their time" (55). While the novel does not explicitly state that these slaves were nonwhite, given the historical connotation of the word "slaves" for American readers of the novel, racial difference would seem to be implied.

The novel then reveals that a cataclysm separated the men from the Herland women, leaving the female population subject to an uprising of male slaves, who attempted to rape and subdue them. Again, race is suggested here but is not made explicit. This uprising in the novel recalls the myth of rape committed by black men that justified lynchings and other terrorist acts against black Americans, as was reported frequently in the pages of *The California Eagle*. Gilman herself reinforced this myth in her 1912 essay "Should Women Use Violence?," stating that there would be fewer lynchings if white women carried revolvers (217).

In keeping with Gilman's reasoning that white women might need to use violence against nonwhite men, the white Herland women next slay the male slaves and, as time progresses, only a few female slaves remain to loyally serve their female masters. Again, the novel indicates the absent present—the there and not there—of the nonwhite woman—this loyalty mirroring the construction of the Mammy figure postbellum in advertising and other cultural texts as more devoted to the white family she serves than to her own.[21] Ultimately, after the death of these female slaves, the population that is left is entirely white and female, and these inhabitants continue to reproduce their white femininity via parthenogenesis.

If the novel is placed against the backdrop of California suffragist and club politics prior to 1911, it is remarkable how closely Gilman's novel reproduces and solidifies the white California women leaders' strategy of simultaneously using and then expunging race as a means of limiting the definition of "woman" to white women. In *Herland*, women of color are an absent present, both there and not there, as they were within the California suffrage movement. Ultimately, this tactic was successful in the second attempt at women's suffrage in 1911 and made it possible for California to approve the vote nine years before it became federal constitutional law.

Nevertheless, it is worth noting that though this strategy worked, it was not without its discontents within the California suffrage movement. The personal papers of one of California's most prominent club and suffrage leaders, Caroline Severance, bear out this point. Severance was a friend and colleague of Gilman's, and among her papers are several friendly letters between the two women (Gilman, letters). However, the two women did not see eye to eye on the question of equality between white women and women of color. Although this disagreement is not mentioned in their personal letters, in the drafts of speeches Severance wrote in the period from 1896 to 1914, she expresses disdain for white women's clubs, especially those in the American South, which would deny access to women of color. She argues that America cannot be considered free, Christian, or civilized if segregation and racial discrimination continue (Severance, "Color Line").

The fact that Severance's opinion was in the minority among Gilman and her fellow suffrage leaders and club members can be seen in the draft of her 1902 talk, "Color Question," given to members of the Los Angeles–based Friday Club. In it, she qualifies her support of women of color in response to the furor that her earlier opinion created. Severance's draft addresses the conflict raging among California clubwomen about admitting black women's clubs into the GFWC; as noted earlier, Clara Burdette, the president of the California women's clubs, along with most clubwomen, voted against their admittance, and this view carried the day. Severance writes that her views were misunderstood and that her only purpose was to recommend that the question of including black women's clubs be referred to the state, rather than national, level of the GFWC (Severance, "Color Question"). Here, Severance modulates her rhetoric, although she does maintain that the women's clubs should not include stipulations of race within their constitution (Severance, "Color Question"). This speech illustrates the prevalence of racism among white women suffrage and club leaders and the desire of Gilman and these leaders to exclude women of color from the construction of womanhood in the years preceding the 1911 suffrage ballot in California.

However, the goals and aims of California women of color, particularly African American women, also constituted a kind of absent presence. As noted earlier, black women's issues, as demonstrated by the African American press, were not foregrounded; instead, racial uplift and equality were most important, even in a newspaper edited by a woman of color. In the 1914 issues of *The California Eagle*, there is no commentary about the push for a federal constitutional amendment granting women's suffrage. Highlighted instead are discriminatory labor and housing practices in California, as well as extensive coverage of lynchings in the American South. It is not that black women leaders never addressed or desired gender parity, but, at the height of Jim Crow and racial terror in the United States, race outweighed gender in terms of most black women's political efforts. In her memoir, *Forty Years: Memoirs from the Pages of a Newspaper*, Carlotta Bass, editor in chief of *The Eagle*, illustrates this point with an anecdote about black clubwomen in Los Angeles in the spring of 1914. Bass recounts that an African American woman, Mary Johnson, had purchased a house in a majority white neighborhood in Los Angeles. One day, while she was absent, her infuriated white neighbors "entered her home, and when she returned, she found her furniture, bedding, kitchen utensils, and other belongings spread out on the front lawn. A crudely hand-painted sign across the nailed up door read: *Nigger if you value your hide don't let night catch you here.*" In response, Johnson turned to *The Eagle* and black clubwomen for help, and "that evening a brigade of a hundred women marched to the Johnson home." After repeated calls to the sheriff and a vigil at the house, the women were finally successful in forcing authorities to allow Johnson back into her home (Bass 95). Here, we see that while white clubwomen were focusing on suffrage, enlarging women's roles in the public sphere, and improving civic spaces, African American clubwomen were fighting for basic human dignity and civil rights.

Bass and *The Eagle*'s perspective on black women mirrors that of Booker T. Washington, one of the most prominent, though more conservative, African American leaders of the time.[22] For example, in a 1902 letter, in which he refuses Severance's request to speak on the issue of the integration of black women's clubs into the GFWC, Washington tersely writes that he is more concerned with larger issues of racism and racial uplift of African Americans. He argues that black women's focus should be on helping fellow African Americans in the South (Washington). Washington's comments underscore the pull women of color felt toward working first for the cause of racial equality and only secondly advocating for gender equity. Washington, *The Eagle*, and Bass's memoir together demonstrate that African American women's gender concerns were often of necessity subsumed within the larger fight against racial injustices and abuses. Whereas Gilman and fellow white California women club leaders erased race in favor of gender, *The California Eagle* and Bass viewed racial equality as the more pressing struggle.

Reading Gilman's novel *Herland* within the context of California suffragist, club, and racial politics from 1896 to 1911, we can see the novel and the political climate of the state as interconnected, with each illuminating the other in important ways. The absence of race in the novel becomes more than a statement of Gilman's own personal beliefs on ethnicity; it reflects a concerted effort by white California clubwomen to gain the vote by removing race from the cause. We can also understand this erasure as part of a larger racism that drove the black California press to foreground race rather than gender and to illustrate the violence and discrimination against black Americans in the state. Finally, an examination of the racial politics of *Herland* and the suffrage and club movements in California underscores that the state's politics have historically been more complicated than one might assume. Our contemporary image of California as a West Coast Left state can veil its history of discrimination and racial strife. Reading literature from the early twentieth century, such as Gilman's *Herland*, that was inspired by the state and its politics can rectify this obfuscation. The oft-quoted political truism, "as California goes, so goes the rest of the nation," would prove apt, as the nation would ratify the Nineteenth Amendment in 1920. However, this gain would come at a cost: a division between white women and women of color that still exists in feminist and gender politics to this day.

Notes

I would like to thank the following for the support and resources that enabled me to write this essay: the Augustana University ARAF (Augustana Research and Artist Fund) Grant; The Huntington Library Caroline M. Seymour (Caroline Maria Seymour) Severance Papers; and the USC (University of Southern California) Amy C. Ransome Collection on Women's Suffrage.

1. For a comprehensive history of race and racial tensions in California history and, in particular, the role of African Americans in the state, see Taylor; De Graaf, Mulroy, and Taylor; Katz; Allmendinger; and Gonzales-Day.

2. For an overview of racial issues in the Progressive Era, see Frankel and Dye, and Southern.
3. For a further discussion of the Progressive Era, see McGerr and Diner.
4. Gilman maintained that "[a] healthy social organism for both men and women ... requires the autonomy of women" (qtd. in Lane, introduction xi).
5. For a collection of Gilman's essays from her magazine *The Forerunner* and other publications, see *Charlotte Perkins Gilman: A Nonfiction Reader*, edited by Larry Ceplair (Columbia UP, 1991).
6. The narrator of *Herland*, Van, notes throughout chapter 6 ("Comparisons Are Odious") how the Herland women had managed to eradicate poverty through their collective work ethic (61–72).
7. Lane explains that Gilman was widely criticized in the California press because she had both amicably divorced her husband and allowed him custody of their daughter so that she could devote her time to the feminist Progressive cause. Gilman's actions were radical during a time when white, middle-class women were expected to be devoted wives and mothers (Lane, introduction viii).
8. See Southern for an extended discussion of the dissonance between white progressives' social reforms and their racist ideology.
9. In addition to characterizing African Americans as a "problem," Gilman also terms them a "menace" (80).
10. For a biography of Gilman's life and her California years, see Davis; see also Allen; Scharnhorst; Lane, *To Herland;* and Hill. Further, Gilman's diaries offer her own account of her time in California (Gilman, *Diaries*).
11. In the University of Southern California Amy C. Ransome Collection of Women's Suffrage, programs outlining the proceedings of these organizations list Gilman as Charlotte Perkins Stetson.
12. For a history of the suffrage cause in California, see Gullet, *Becoming Citizens;* Englander, *Class Conflict;* Cherny, Irwin, and Wilson; and Mead.
13. Englander, "'We Want'" 213–15; Paddison, "'Woman Is Everywhere'" 71; and Gullet, "Constructing" 581–83.
14. Sargent's decidedly elitist tone in her report reveals the deep divide between the middle- and upper-class white suffragists and the white working-class women with whom they sought common cause. See especially Englander, *Class Conflict and Class Coalition*, for an illuminating discussion of class politics in the California suffrage movement.
15. Meanwhile, following the 1896 defeat and despite the optimism of the CSWA reports at the 1897 national convention, California suffragists were "stunned by failure," and organizations like the CSWA "effectively went into hibernation for five years" (Englander, "'We Want'" 209).
16. The suffrage movement did not divorce itself completely from the WCTU or temperance, however. Englander observes, for instance, that as late as 1909, the WCTU

had publicly lent their support for the second attempt at suffrage in California (Englander, "'We Want'" 224).

17. See Gullet on how, after the failure of the 1896 amendment, it was clubwomen, interestingly more often of a Republican rather than a Progressive persuasion, who laid the groundwork for the eventual ratification of suffrage in 1911. Further, the California Republican party itself became more progressive after the election of Hiram Johnson as governor in 1910 (Gullet, "Constructing" 588).
18. See Carby for her famous analysis of black womanhood and its relationship to femininity at the turn into the twentieth century. See also Welter for perhaps the most definitive discussion of the idealization of domestic femininity that persisted into the early twentieth century.
19. For a further discussion of the importance of women's clubs in encouraging women to participate in American political and civic life, see Gullet, Englander, Flanagan, and Parker. See Tolson for a comprehensive analysis of racism within the white women's club movement. It should be noted that such racism produced an alternative club movement among black women, one that focused on racial issues rather than women's rights. For more on the African American women's club movement, see Hendricks, Lerner, and Scott.
20. For further reading on this topic, see Seitler and Tuttle.
21. See Deck for more on this point.
22. In opposition to other African American voices, notably W. E. B. Du Bois, Washington advocated a slow integration of African Americans into white-dominated society, a message that was obviously popular among many whites. Severance herself comments in her "Color Question" speech that Washington urges black Americans to turn to industry rather than politics for success. In return, in time, African Americans will be rewarded with civic equality. Severance proceeds to agree with Washington's approach ("Color Question"). It should be noted that while *The California Eagle* did not similarly advocate Washington's philosophy of measured integration, the paper did honor him as a great leader of African Americans.

Bibliography

Allen, Judith A. *The Feminism of Charlotte Perkins Gilman: Sexualities, Histories, Progressivism.* U of Chicago P, 2009.

Allmendinger, Blake. *Imagining the African American West.* U of Nebraska P, 2008.

"Announcement from the Political Equality League of Los Angeles Reminding Americans to Vote in 1911." Amy C. Ransome Collection on Women's Suffrage, Collection no. 0001, Regional History Collections, Special Collections, USC Libraries, U of Southern California, box 5, folder 26.

Bass, Carlotta. *Forty Years: Memoirs from the Pages of a Newspaper.* Los Angeles, Carlotta Bass [self-published], 1960.

Carby, Hazel V. *Reconstructing Womanhood: The Emergence of the Afro-American Woman Novelist.* Oxford UP, 1989.

Cherny, Robert W., Mary Ann Irwin, and Ann Marie Wilson, editors. *California Women and Politics: From the Gold Rush to the Great Depression.* U of Nebraska P, 2011.

Davis, Cynthia J. *Charlotte Perkins Gilman: A Biography.* Stanford UP, 2010.

Deck, Alice A. "'Now Then—Who Said Biscuits?': The Black Woman Cook as Fetish in Advertising, 1905–1953." *Kitchen Culture in America: Popular Representations of Food, Gender, and Race*, edited by Sherrie A. Inness, U of Pennsylvania P, 2001, pp. 69–93.

De Graaf, Lawrence B., Kevin Mulroy, and Quintard Taylor. *Seeking El Dorado: African Americans in California.* U of Washington P, 2001.

Englander, Susan. *Class Conflict and Class Coalition in the California Women's Suffrage Movement, 1907–1912.* Edwin Mellen, 1992.

———. "'We Want the Ballot for Very Different Reasons': Clubwomen, Union Women, and the Internal Politics of the Suffrage Movement, 1896–1911." *California Women and Politics: From the Gold Rush to the Great Depression*, edited by Robert W. Cherny, Mary Ann Irwin, and Ann Marie Wilson, U of Nebraska P, 2011, pp. 209–35.

Fessenden, Tracy. "Race, Religion, and the New Woman in America: The Case of Charlotte Perkins Gilman." *Furman Studies*, vol. 37, 1995, pp. 15–28.

Flanagan, Maureen A. "Gender and Urban Political Reform: The City Club and the Woman's City Club of Chicago in the Progressive Era." *American Historical Review*, vol. 95, no. 4, Oct. 1990, pp. 1032–50.

Frankel, Noralee, and Nancy S. Dye, editors. *Gender, Class, Race, and Reform in the Progressive Era.* U of Kentucky P, 1991.

Ganobcsik-Williams, Lisa. "Confronting Issues of Race, Class, and Ethnicity in *Herland*." *Approaches to Teaching Gilman's 'The Yellow Wall-Paper' and* Herland, edited by Denise D. Knight and Cynthia J. Davis, MLA, 2003, pp. 111–17.

———. "The Intellectualism of Charlotte Perkins Gilman: Evolutionary Perspectives on Race, Ethnicity, and Class." *Charlotte Perkins Gilman: Optimist Reformer*, edited by Jill Rudd and Val Gough, U of Iowa P, 1999, pp. 16–41.

Gilman, Charlotte Perkins. *The Diaries of Charlotte Perkins Gilman.* Edited by Denise D. Knight, UP of Virginia, 1994. 2 vols.

———. *Herland.* 1915. Kindle ed., Halcyon Press, 2010.

———. Letters to Caroline M. Seymour (Caroline Maria Seymour) Severance, 1820–1914. The Huntington Library, Caroline M. Seymour (Caroline Maria Seymour) Severance Papers, folder 20.

———. "Should Women Use Violence?" *Charlotte Perkins Gilman: A Nonfiction Reader*, edited by Larry Ceplair, Columbia UP, 1991, pp. 212–19.

———. "A Suggestion on the Negro Problem." *American Journal of Sociology*, vol. 14, no. 1, July 1908, pp. 78–85.

Gonzales-Day, Ken. *Lynching in the West: 1850–1935*. Duke UP, 2006.
Gullet, Gayle. *Becoming Citizens: The Emergence and Development of the California Women's Movement, 1880–1911*. U of Illinois P, 2000.
———. "Constructing the Woman Citizen and Struggling for the Vote in California, 1896–1911." *Pacific Historical Review*, vol. 69, no. 4, Nov. 2000, pp. 573–93.
Hendricks, Wanda A. *Gender, Race, and Politics in the Midwest: Black Club Women in Illinois*. Indiana UP, 2008.
Hill, Mary A. *Charlotte Perkins Gilman: The Making of a Radical Feminist*. Temple UP, 1980.
Katz, William Loren. *The Black West: A Documentary and Pictorial History of the African American Role in the Westward Expansion of the United States*. Touchstone, 1996.
Knight, Denise D. "Charlotte Perkins Gilman and the Shadow of Racism." *American Literary Realism*, vol. 32, no. 2, 2000, pp. 159–69.
Lane, Ann J. *To Herland and Beyond: The Life of Charlotte Perkins Gilman*. Pantheon, 1990.
———. Introduction. *Herland*, by Charlotte Perkins Gilman. 1915. Pantheon, 1979, pp. v–xxiii.
Lanser, Susan S. "Feminist Criticism, 'The Yellow Wall-Paper,' and the Politics of Color in America." *Feminist Studies*, vol. 15, no. 3, 1989, pp. 415–41.
Lerner, Gerda. "Early Community Work of Black Club Women." *Journal of Negro History*, vol. 59, no. 2, Apr. 1974, pp. 158–67.
Mead, Rebecca J. *How the Vote Was Won: Woman Suffrage in the Western United States, 1868–1914*. New York UP, 2004.
Paddison, Joshua. "'Woman Is Everywhere the Purifier': The Politics of Temperance, 1878–1900." *California Women and Politics: From the Gold Rush to the Great Depression*, edited by Robert W. Cherny, Mary Ann Irwin, and Ann Marie Wilson, U of Nebraska P, 2011, pp. 59–76.
Parker, Alison M. "Clubwomen, Reformers, Workers, and Feminists of the Gilded Age and Progressive Era." *Women's Rights: People and Perspectives*, edited by Crista DeLuzio, ABC-CLIO, 2010, pp. 57–78.
Patton, Venetria K. *Women in Chains: The Legacy of Slavery in Black Women's Fiction*. State U of New York P, 2000.
"Proceedings of the 29th Annual Convention of the National American Women Suffrage Association." 26–29 Jan. 1897. Amy C. Ransome Collection on Women's Suffrage, Collection no. 0001, Regional History Collections, Special Collections, USC Libraries, U of Southern California, box 6, folder 4.
"Proceedings of the 30th Annual Convention of the National American Women Suffrage Association." 15–19 Feb. 1898. Amy C. Ransome Collection on Women's Suffrage, Collection no. 0001, Regional History Collections, Special Collections, USC Libraries, U of Southern California, box 6, folder 5.

"The Progressives and Jim Crow." *California Eagle*, 21 Feb. 1914, n.p. *Internet Archive*. Accessed 11 June 2017.

Scharnhorst, Gary. *Charlotte Perkins Gilman*. Twayne, 1985.

Scott, Anne Firor. "Most Invisible of All: Black Women's Voluntary Associations." *Journal of Southern History*, vol. 56, no. 1, Feb. 1990, pp. 3–22.

Seitler, Dana. "Unnatural Selection: Mothers, Eugenic Feminism, and Charlotte Perkins Gilman's Regeneration Narratives." *American Quarterly*, vol. 55, no. 1, 2003, pp. 61–88.

Severance, Caroline M. Seymour. "Color Line [essay] before 1915." Caroline M. Seymour (Caroline Maria Seymour), 1820–1914. The Huntington Library, Caroline M. Seymour (Caroline Maria Seymour) Severance Papers, folder 65.

———. "Color Question [speech] 1902, Mar. 27." Caroline M. Seymour (Caroline Maria Seymour), 1820–1914. The Huntington Library, Caroline M. Seymour (Caroline Maria Seymour) Severance Papers, folder 66.

Southern, David W. *The Progressive Era and Race: Reaction and Reform, 1900–1917*. Harlan Davidson, 2005.

Taylor, Quintard. *In Search of the Racial Frontier: African Americans in the West, 1528–1900*. W. W. Norton, 1999.

Thompson, Mrs. Noah H. "The Progress of the Negro." *California Eagle*, 21 Feb. 1914, n.p. *Internet Archive*. Accessed 11 June 2017.

Tolson, Claudette L. *The Excluded and the Included: Chicago, White Supremacy and the Clubwomen's Movement, 1873–1915*. Dissertation, Loyola University of Chicago, 2008.

Tuttle, Jennifer S. "Gilman's *The Crux* and Owen Wister's *The Virginian*: Intertextuality and 'Woman's Manifest Destiny.'" *Charlotte Perkins Gilman and Her Contemporaries*, edited by Cynthia J. Davis and Denise D. Knight, U of Alabama P, 2004, pp. 127–38.

Washington, Booker T. "Letter to Severance, March 5, 1902." Caroline M. Seymour (Caroline Maria Seymour), 1820–1914. The Huntington Library, Caroline M. Seymour (Caroline Maria Seymour) Severance Papers, folder 66.

Weinbaum, Alys Eve. "Writing Feminist Genealogy: Charlotte Perkins Gilman, Racial Nationalism, and the Reproduction of Maternal Feminism." *Feminist Studies*, vol. 27, no. 2, 2001, pp. 271–302.

Welter, Barbara. "The Cult of True Womanhood: 1820–1860." *American Quarterly*, vol. 18, no. 2, pt. 1, Summer 1966, pp. 151–74.

Acknowledgments

The editor wishes to acknowledge the librarians and staff at the Bancroft Library of the University of California, Berkeley, for reliable and efficient assistance. The research for this book was undertaken with the support of a Northern Arizona University Faculty Grant, which allowed the editor to spend many happy and productive hours at the Bancroft Library. Thanks, too, to City Lights bookstore executive editor Elaine Katzenberger for answering so many questions over the years. To colleagues in the Western Literature Association, thanks for the critical context. And deep appreciation to colleagues and friends at Northern Arizona University for your steadfast commitment to academic freedom, which enables us to teach, research, and serve in a way that makes space for a just and sustainable society. Finally, in deep gratitude to *Left in the West* contributors, whose thoughtful engagement with the relationship between literature, culture, and progressive politics makes this volume possible.

Contributors

William M. Clements has published several books, chapters, articles, and reviews in literature, anthropology, folklore studies, and American Indian studies. He is a fellow of the American Folklore Society.

Audrey Goodman is a professor of English at Georgia State University and the author of two books on the history of southwestern literature and photography, *Translating Southwestern Landscapes* and *Lost Homelands*, as well as a contributor to *Postwestern Cultures*, Blackwell's *Companion to the Literature and Culture of the American West*, and Cambridge's *History of Western American Literature*. Her current research explores how contemporary women's photobooks imagine new relations between writers, communities, and lands in the U.S. West.

William V. Lombardi is associate professor of English at Feather River College. He has authored essays and reviews in *Western American Literature* and *ISLE*. His recent work appears in *Under the Western Sky: Essays on the Fiction and Music of Willy Vlautin*, published by University of Nevada Press.

Emily Lutenski is an associate professor in American Studies at Saint Louis University, and the author of *West of Harlem: African American Writers and the Borderlands*.

John S. McCormick is dean emeritus of the School of Humanities and Social Sciences at Salt Lake Community College. He has published books and articles in urban history, historic preservation, the built environment, and political history, including *A History of Utah Radicalism: Startling, Socialistic, and Decidedly Revolutionary* (co-authored with John R. Silvio).

José Navarro is an assistant professor of Ethnic Studies at Cal Poly, San Luis Obispo. His research and publications focus on Chicana/o gang narratives, Latinx film, and Latinx music.

Robert Yusef Rabiee is an assistant professor in the Intellectual Heritage Program at Temple University. His research and teaching focus on the long histories of U.S. political and cultural institutions, particularly in the nineteenth century.

DANIEL WAYNE RINN is a PhD candidate in the History Department at the University of Rochester. He studies the relationship between ideas and the environment in the United States. His recently published article "Liberty Hyde Bailey: Pragmatic Naturalism in the Garden" explores the intersection of Darwinism, pragmatism, and American environmental thought in the twentieth century.

DARCIE RIVES-EAST is an associate professor of English at Augustana University in Sioux Falls, South Dakota. Her publications include "Haunted by Violence: Edith Wharton's *The Decoration of Houses* and Her Gothic Fiction" in *The Edith Wharton Review;* "Watching the Detective: *Sherlock*, Surveillance, and British Fears Post-7/7" in *The Journal of Popular Culture;* and the forthcoming *Eyes Wide Open: Surveillance in British and American Television Post-9/11*, from Palgrave Macmillan.

JOHN D. SCHWETMAN is associate professor of English at the University of Minnesota, Duluth, and the author of such articles as "'Shadowy Objects in Test Tubes': Marking Grievance in Kazuo Ishiguro's *Never Let Me Go*" and "'I Was in Italy...and I Spoke Italian': Fighting Other People's Battles in Hemingway's *A Farewell to Arms.*" He is currently working on a book on twentieth-century U.S. travel narratives.

LISA J. UDEL is associate professor of English and Gender and Women's Studies at Illinois College. She is the author of such articles as "Revision and Resistance: The Politics of Native Women's Motherwork" and "Revising Strategies: The Intersection of Literature and Activism in Contemporary Native Women's Writing." Her current project examines contemporary Native women's life-writing.

BETTE S. WEIDMAN is associate professor emerita at Queens College, City University of New York, where she taught from 1968 to 2017. She is the author of *White on Red*, a study of nineteenth-century discussions of Native American Indians, two essays in the American Writers series, edited by Jay Parini, about Charles Frederick Briggs (1804–77) and Mari Sandoz, and numerous critical essays on Native American and antebellum American writers.

ALEX TRIMBLE YOUNG is an Honors Faculty Fellow in Barrett, the Honors College at Arizona State University. His recent work can be found in journals including *Western American Literature, a/b: Auto/Biography Studies*, and *Social Text.*

Index

M

About the Editor

Gioia Woods is a professor of Humanities and Comparative Cultural Studies at Northern Arizona University. She is the co-editor, along with Kathleen Boardman, of *Western Subjects: Autobiographical Writing in the North American West*, the author of the Western Writers Series monograph *Gary Paul Nabhan*, and a contributor to Blackwell's *Companion to the Literature and Culture of the American West*, Cambridge's *Companion to the Literature of the American West*, and Gale's *Dictionary of Literary Biography*. In addition to her research and publications on the literature and culture of the American West, she has published articles of biographical criticism and American and Italian ecological criticism. She is past president of the Western Literature Association and a longtime member of the Association for the Study of Literature and Environment. Her current research explores the literary and social history of San Francisco's City Lights bookstore and press.